Shiism

Heinz Halm

ISLAMIC SURVEYS
General Editor
CAROLE HILLENBRAND

EDINBURGH UNIVERSITY PRESS

Originally published in 1987
in German as *Die Schia* by
Wissenschaftliche Buchgesellschaft,
Darmstadt.

This edition translated from the
German by Janet Watson.

Edinburgh University Press
22 George Square, Edinburgh

Typeset in Linotron Trump Medieval
by Koinonia Ltd, Bury, and
printed in Great Britain by
Redwood Press Ltd,
Melksham, Wilts.

British Library Cataloguing
in Publication Data
Halm, Heinz
Shi'ism.– (Islamic surveys)
I. Title II. Series
297

ISBN 0 7486 0268 2 (cased)

Contents

Editor's note

One of the most frequent questions in the minds of students and the general public in the West who wish to understand more about Islam is the fundamental one: 'What is the difference between the Sunnis and the Shiites?' This book aims not only to answer this question but also to present the wide spectrum of beliefs within the different sub-groups which constitute the Shia.

Names which recur frequently in this book, such as Baghdad, Tehran, Qumm, Shia, Sunnis, Shiites, have not been transliterated. Quotations from the Quran have been taken from the English translation by Marmaduke Pickthall, *The Meaning of the Glorious Koran*, London, 1957.

One or two new passages have been added to the English version of Dr Halm's book. These take account of important events – such as the death of Āyatallāh Khumaynī, the unification of the two Yemens, and the recent disintegration of the USSR – which have taken place since the original German edition appeared in 1987.

Carole Hillenbrand

Foreword

Although some 10 per cent of the circa thousand million Muslims living today profess Shiism, hardly anyone apart from a few specialists had taken any notice of the Shiites before the Islamic Revolution in Iran in 1978-1979. Today the literature on Shiism has become almost unsurveyable, and a lot of chaff must be separated from the wheat. The suddenly awakened interest in the Shia results, of course, from the political events and, in particular, from the fears associated with them; after all, the heartlands of the Shia – Iraq, Iran and East Arabia – are the most important oil-producing countries of the Middle East. The political dynamism of Shiite Islam lies principally in its self-awareness as champion of the cause of the 'downtrodden' (Arabic *mustaḍʿafūn,* Pers. *mostaẓʿafīn)* against the 'powerful' (*mustakbirūn),* the oppressors, tyrants and exploiters of every kind throughout the world – a fight for which Shiite tradition provides not only an endless series of paradigms of suffering and rebellion, but also the utopia of the rightful government of the awaited Hidden Imam, the Mahdī who 'will fill the earth with justice and fairness just as it is at present full of injustice and tyranny'. A religious tradition over a millennium old offers an interpretation and a solution to the present social conflicts after externally-imposed recipes for solving the Islamic peoples' social and economic problems – capitalist and socialist – have failed and appear to have lost all their attractiveness.

I

The Beginnings of the Shia

NAME AND DEFINITION

'The religio-political opposition parties in early Islam' was the title given by Julius Wellhausen to his study of the beginnings of the Khārijites and the Shia, published in 1901.[1] In fact, the Arabic word *shīʿa* just means 'party'. *Shīʿat ʿAlī*, "ʿAlī's party', was the name given to those who sided with the Prophet's cousin and son-in-law, ʿAlī ibn Abī Ṭālib in the conflicts surrounding the succession of the murdered third Caliph ʿUthmān in 35/656.[2] The Shia emerged as a party in a political power struggle and they have never lost this original political character; now, as then, religion and politics are closely interrelated and neither belong to separate spheres in the Muslim consciousness. For the major part of their history the Shia were condemned to remain the political opposition, but they have never lost sight of their potential to hold power even in times of utmost weakness.[3]

If, on the other hand, an attempt is made to conceive of Shiism as a religious rather than a political phenomenon, it becomes apparent that it hardly lends itself to definition at all. This is partly because none of the categories familiar to us from Christianity fit it exactly, and partly also because it has had a long period of development during which its character has changed fundamentally several times.

For the beginnings of the separate development of Shiism the term 'schism' can certainly be used. The original Islamic community (*umma*) split during a dispute over true authority and the identity of their rightful religio-political leader (*imām*). However, when the losing group was forced into opposition, it soon developed special features which go beyond the original cause of the split: namely, a special relationship with their own authorities, the Imams, their own legal tradition which referred to the Imams, peculiarities of religious worship, their own particular festivals and places of pilgrimage, a special religious ethos characterised by a fervour to suffer for the cause, and finally something like a clergy peculiar to themselves. However, the differences between the Shiites and the majority of the Muslims – the Sunnis[4] – are not so large that the 'Twelver' or 'Sevener' Shia can be designated as separate religions; on the other hand, it is doubtful whether the groups the Shia itself has expelled as heretical – the Nuṣayrīs (ʿAlawīs), the Druze and the Bahā'īs – may be deemed to belong to Islam.

Theological and dogmatic differences play a subordinate role in differentiating between Sunna and Shia. The Shia is a creed only in so far as its adherents acknowledge one specific leader (*imām*), but it is not a separate dogma. The use of the dichotomy 'orthodoxy-heterodoxy' (or heresy) for the Sunna and the Shia provides a false picture, quite apart from the fact that it evaluates one-sidedly and is questionable as a religious category. For the same reason the term 'sect' is problematic since its counterpart 'church' does not exist in Islam. The characteristics of the sect as described by Max Weber[5] – a small number of adherents, lack of state recognition, spontaneous confession and freedom to join or not join, members' awareness that they belong to a religiously separate qualified élite – do not always apply to the Shia, while for certain other groups – such as the Druze – they are partially constituent and are permanent.[6]

Even less helpful are the terms used in the Arabic and Persian sources. In the terminology of Islamic authors – both Shiite and non-Shiite – the groups into which the original Islamic community split are denoted as *firaq* (sing. *firqa*), a noun from the Arabic verbal stem *faraqa* , split, divide, differentiate.[7] Shiite authors use the same term for the countless groups and trends within the Shia itself:[8] different opinions are denoted by *ra'y* (view), *ikhtilāf* (dissent) or *madhhab* (way, method).[9] Within the Twelver Shia the term *ṭā'ifa* (group, denomination) has prevailed as their own term for themselves alongside *shīʿa*. The Shiite scholar al-Ṭūsī (d. 460/1067) calls the Shia 'the group which is right' (*al-ṭā'ifa al-muḥaqqiqa*); and he in turn is given the honorific *shaykh al-ṭā'ifa* (the leading authority of the group) by the Shiites.

For Shiite authors the simple difference between 'the group which is right' and the 'breakaway groups' corresponds to an equally simple picture of their historical inception. 'The True (i.e. their own) View' existed from the beginning and never changed in essence, while the false teachings split off and went on dividing more and more from the original stem. This simple schema, as a plan and representation of the genesis of the Shia on which the Shiite heresy literature is based, does not of course do justice to its complicated genesis. In what follows, we shall therefore need to reformulate the essence of the respective Shiite groups in each case in the light of their historical development and changes from one era to another. The chapter divisions take this into account by being orientated to the important turning points in the development of each group.

SOURCES, LITERATURE AND REFERENCE WORKS

Academic research into the origins of the Shia starts with Julius Wellhausen's study mentioned at the beginning of this book, 'The religio-political opposition parties in early Islam' (1901), which is still the most authoritative work on the subject to date. Research into the Shia as a discipline in its own right has still not disentangled itself from general Islamic studies. Comparative religion is only just beginning to discover the Shia. Up to the present day there is still no overall comprehensive account, and most works deal with individual branches of the Shia and particular problems in their doctrine and history. In these the Imāmiyya or Twelver Shia has always stood out as the strongest branch, and it is not infrequently simply equated with 'the' Shia; in our everyday speech 'the Shiites' are without exception the Imāmīs of Iran and Lebanon. Because of their current political significance most space will also be given to the Imāmiyya in the present study.

Since the 19th century the boundless literature of the Twelver Shiites was disseminated in lithographs in the first instance, and then in an ever growing flood of printed works which appeared in the main centres of the Twelver Shia, such as Najaf in Iraq or Qumm and Tehran in Iran. Academically critical editions are rare. A large proportion of Imāmi literature has not yet been published. A modern bibliography only exists in Arabic: Āghā Buzurg al-Tihrānī, *al-Dharī'a ilā taṣānīf al-Shī'a* , 25 volumes, Tehran/Najaf 1936-78 (1355-98), an alphabetical catalogue of all known (Imāmī) book titles. Apart from that, sections of general literary histories dedicated to the Shia may be cited: Carl Brockelmann, *Geschichte der arabischen Litteratur*, Leiden ²1943-9; Supplements 1937-42; Fuat Sezgin, *Geschichte des arabischen Schrifttums*, Leiden, from 1963; for Persian: E. G. Browne, *A Literary History of Persia*, 4 volumes, London/Cambridge 1902-24; Charles A. Storey, *Persian Literature. A Bio-bibliographical Survey*, London, from 1927. Over the past few years the Muhammadi Trust based in London has been translating important works of Imāmī literature in order to promote its world-wide dissemination.[10]

Until lately, Dwight M. Donaldson, *The Shiite Religion*, London 1933 claimed first place among the academic accounts of the Shia; it has only recently been superseded by Moojan Momen, *An Introduction to Shi'i Islam. The History and Doctrine of Twelver Shi'ism*, Oxford 1985, a handbook full of names and dates with an extensive bibliography. Both accounts combine the early history of the Shia with the development of the Imāmī or Twelver Shia.

In accordance with the tradition of European Islamic studies academic works on the Shia are predominantly of a philological and historical nature. The present volume takes this into account by portraying the individual branches of the Shia in terms of their historical development. Comparative religion has only recently begun to take an interest in the Shia; this may well be principally due to the fact that primary sources in European languages were hardly accessible until now, and that the combination of oriental and religious studies is still a new phenomenon.

A series of important contributions to the study of the Shia has been produced by academics who themselves adhere to one of the Shiite creeds, for example, Seyyid Hossein Nasr, Husain F. Hamdani, Abbas Hamdani, Ismail K. Poonawala or Sami M. Makarem. The peculiarity of a standpoint and a perspective which owes as much to upbringing and religious allegiance as to the demands of academic methodology is discussed by the German orientalist Abdoljawad Falaturi in his essay 'Die Zwölfer-Schia aus der Sicht eines Schiiten: Probleme ihrer Untersuchung'.[11]

Apart from these there are representations of the Shia which are more like testimonies of belief than academic studies, for example, *Shiʿite Islam* by ʿAllāma Sayyid Muḥammad Ḥusayn Ṭabāṭabāʾī, a renowned Twelver Shia scholar with a traditional education (Albany 1975), or Husain M. Jafri, *Origins and Early Development of Shiʿa Islam*, London 1979. Works of this nature are authentic testimonies to modern Shiite self-understanding; according to Western terminology they should be reckoned more as primary sources than academic literature.

Even a rough attempt to catalogue available printed Shiite sources in Arabic or Persian would have gone beyond the scope of the present volume. Only the most important editions of main works have therefore been listed in the notes. I have also decided against a full bibliography. The breadth of the area treated here made it seem more appropriate to provide a general list of relevant literature at the end of each chapter, and the chronological order shows how the investigation has been conducted. (Cited works given in abbreviation in the notes are found in full in the list of works consulted at the end of the respective chapter.) In particular, I have listed primary sources translated into European languages which enable the non-orientalist to study the Shia using authentic material.

Finally, the two most important bibliographical aids which cover all publications dealing with the Shia are: *The Quarterly Index Islamicus* (earlier Pearson, *Index Islamicus*), London (Mansell), and the yearly *Abstracta Iranica*, Leiden, from 1978 onwards.

THE ISLAMIC COMMUNITY AFTER THE DEATH OF THE PROPHET

The cause of the early split in Islam, which has never been healed, lay in the social oppositions and tensions which already characterised the original community. At its inception, but principally during the course of its rapid and far-ranging expansion, the religio-political community (*umma*) established by the Prophet had to absorb a variety of social groups with very different traditions and interests. Their integration was never completely successful, and points of fracture were obvious from the beginning.

Under pressure from pagan patricians the Prophet was forced to flee his home town Mecca and relinquish the protection of his tribe, the Banū Hāshim; in September 622 he had to seek a new area of operation in the oasis settlement Yathrib (Medina[12]). A large number of his Meccan supporters joined his emigration (*hijra*) ; these 'emigrants' or 'exiles' (*muhājirūn*) – founder members of the Muslim faith – formed the original Islamic community together with the settled farming tribes in Medina who accepted the Prophet and followed his message – the 'helpers' (*anṣār*). In the next decade these two groups, which in a sense represented the original Islamic religious aristocracy, were joined by the sedentary or nomadic groups of the Arabian peninsula which set aside their eternal blood feuds in the *pax islamica* imposed by Muḥammad[13] and thus became able to channel their newly-harnessed energy outwards against the enemies of Islam.

The original Medinan community experienced a drastic change with the integration of the old pagan trading town of Mecca, and its mercantile aristocracy with its proud traditions, which had driven the Prophet and his first supporters out of Mecca and had then been embroiled with them in bloody conflicts which lasted for years. After capturing Mecca in 8/630 Muḥammad kept his Medinan residence; however, it was unavoidable that the old Meccan patrician families, who now became adherents of Islam for more or less opportunistic reasons, soon began to play an important role in the rapidly expanding community. Their business interests, which were principally directed towards Byzantine Syria, must have played a not inconsiderable role in the conquest policies of the early Islamic state.

The campaigns of the Islamic armies which advanced into Mesopotamia and Syria, and then into Iran and Egypt after the death of the Prophet in the year 11/632, within a short time greatly expanded the area conquered by the original community in Medina. Two further social elements were added as a result of the expansion. First, Arab tribal fighters from the campaigning armies who settled and were immediately assimilated in different regions of the Islamic empire (in particular in Iraq and in the Iranian East), and secondly, members of the subjugated peoples – Mesopotamians and Iranians, Syrians, Egyptians and Berbers – who were gradually converted to Islam. As clients (*mawālī* sing. *mawlā*) of particular prominent Companions of the Prophet, these new non-Arab converts were initially – despite the egalitarian claims of Islam – second-class Muslims; their struggle for social equality brought a new dynamic element into the history of early Islam.

When the Prophet Muḥammad died on 8th June 632 the problem of his succession could still be amicably solved by his closest companions (*ṣaḥāba*) even though Muḥammad did not leave a decree for the future guidance of the *umma*. The period of pure theocracy in which God had spoken directly to the believers through the mouth of the Prophet came to an end with the death of the Prophet; none of his companions claimed the charisma of an inspired prophet. It was only from those tribes of the Arabian peninsula, seeking to rid themselves of their bond with the *umma* of Medina, that new prophets with their own revelations emerged as champions of these struggles for independence. Nor had Muḥammad left behind a son and heir; and anyway the transfer of political authority from father to son had still not become a binding principle in the Arabian tribal society of the 7th century. The *umma* of Medina therefore put at its head as the Prophet's successor (*khalīfa*) one of the 'emigrants' (*muhājirūn*), Abū Bakr, who had fled from Mecca along with Muḥammad; the 'helpers' (*anṣār*) of Medina were unable to prevail with their own candidate against the Meccan emigrants. In spite of certain tensions the Medinan *umma* held together. During his two-year reign (11-13/632-634) Abū Bakr defeated those tribes which had rallied round their own prophets, and thus put an end to the principle of charismatic-prophetic succession once and for all.

The second Caliph, ʿUmar (13-23/634-644) was also one of the Meccan emigrants. The first phase of Islamic expansion beyond the bounds of the Arabian peninsula took place during his reign: in 16/637 after their victory at al-Qādisiyya by the Euphrates the Muslims conquered Persian-ruled Mesopotamia, and in 21/642 the defeat of the imperial Persian army at Nihāwand (south west of Hamadān) opened the way for the Arabs to conquer the Iranian highlands. At the same time Byzantine Syria was overrun; the occupation of Damascus in 14/635 was followed by the defeat of a Byzantine army in 15/636 on the Yarmuk, the capture of Jerusalem in 17/638 and the fall of Caesarea in 19/640. In the years 20-21/641-642 Byzantine Egypt was conquered and in 78/697 Carthage finally fell into the hands of the Arabs.

The election of the third Caliph, 'Uthmān, by an electing body (*shūrā*) of six leading Companions of the Prophet – including Muḥammad's cousin and son-in-law 'Alī – in the year 23/644 meant that the *umma* was headed for the first time by a representative of the Banū Umayya clan, the clan which had been predominant in Meccan aristocracy in pre-Islamic times and which had been among the most tenacious opponents of the new belief. As an early Muslim convert 'Uthmān was indeed no less qualified to succeed the Prophet than his two predecessors; however, his membership of the influential tribe may well have tipped the balance in his election. Through nepotism and patronage 'Uthmān favoured his relatives and supporters to such an extent that soon a large proportion of the provinces were in the hands of his clan; under him the old Meccan aristocracy which had once driven the Prophet out of the town now set about establishing power even within the Islamic community. The most powerful representative of the Umayyad clan was Mu'āwiya ibn Abī Sufyān, who had distinguished himself by the conquest of Caesarea in Palestine and after that lived in Damascus as the military governor (*amīr*) of Syria.

The rapid careers which many former opponents of Islam were making for themselves in the *umma* infuriated the pious old guard, and the fact that the Meccan hegemony was also set fair to have its way in the new order met with opposition from many tribes. With the murder of the Caliph 'Uthmān by discontented Muslims in 35/656 opposition within the *umma* burst out. The man who then became Caliph in Medina is the one whom the Shiites regard as the only rightful successor of the Prophet up to the present day: namely 'Alī ibn Abī Ṭālib, Muḥammad's then almost sixty-year-old cousin, the husband of Muḥammad's daughter Fāṭima and father of the Prophet's two grandsons al-Ḥasan and al-Ḥusayn. However, his election was disputed from the very beginning, and members and supporters of the Umayya clan left Medina and went to Syria. The result was the first difficult 'trial' (*fitna*) in the Islamic community – in which Muslim took up arms against Muslim.

Bibliography

W. M. Watt, *Muhammad at Mecca*, Oxford 1953; *Muhammad at Medina*, Oxford 1956. *The Cambridge History of Islam* I, Cambridge 1970. M. A. Shaban, *Islamic History. A New Interpretation, I, A.D. 600-750* (A.H. 132), Cambridge 1971. A. Noth, 'Früher Islam', in: U. Haarmann (ed.), *Geschichte der arabischen Welt*, Munich 1987, 11-100.

'ALI'S CALIPHATE (656-661)

'Alī's accession to the Caliphate in Medina in the year 35/656 is regarded by the Shiites as the long-overdue fulfilment of an arrangement which the Prophet himself was said to have made; according to Shiite tradition Muḥammad had, on several occasions, designated his cousin and son-in-law 'Alī ibn Abī Ṭālib as his successor and leader (*imām*) of the community (*umma*).

'Alī had been very close to the Prophet ever since the orphaned Muḥammad had been received into the house of his uncle Abū Ṭālib, 'Alī's father. The cousin was one of the first to follow the Prophet's message; according to Shiite tradition he was the second Muslim – after Muḥammad's wife Khadīja. (For the Sunnis he was the third – after Khadīja and Abū Bakr.) After the Hijra, 'Alī followed the Prophet to Medina where he became his son-in-law and confidant. He distinguished himself in battles against the pagan Meccans and played a prominent role in the subjugation of the Arabian peninsula to Islam.

On his return from his final 'farewell pilgrimage' to Mecca, on 18th Dhu'l-Ḥijja 10/16th March 632 at Ghadīr Khumm halfway between Mecca and Medina, the Prophet is said to have taken 'Alī by the hand in front of the resting pilgrims and said 'Everyone whose patron I am also has 'Alī as a patron' (*man kuntu mawlāhu fa-'Alī mawlāhu*).[14]

The Shiites interpret these words as 'Alī's designation (*naṣṣ*) as successor to the Prophet. According to their tradition those companions of the Prophet present – including the later Caliph 'Umar – congratulated 'Alī at the time and addressed him with the title 'Commander of the Faithful' (*amīr al-mu'minīn*). Muḥammad's utterance at Ghadīr Khumm is also handed down in Sunni tradition,[15] but it is interpreted differently by the Sunnis who claim that by saying this the Prophet wanted to back the weakened authority of 'Alī who was unpopular because of his severity. The Day of Ghadīr Khumm, 18th of the pilgrimage month Dhu'l-Ḥijja, was made into a festival day by later Shiite dynasties[16] and is still celebrated by the Shiites today.

Whatever Muḥammad may have meant by his utterance, it was probably not the designation of a successor. 'Alī was later a member of the council (*shūrā*) which elected the third Caliph 'Uthmān. After 'Uthmān's murder 'Alī was appointed as Caliph, not because of any designation, nor because of any hereditary principle – which did not, in any case, exist – rather, he was appointed as the candidate of those Muslims who wanted the original Islamic religious aristocracy to regain the upper hand against the growing influence of the Meccan aristocracy and its Syrian interests.

Apart from the 'Helpers' (*anṣār)* from Medina, ʿAlī's most loyal supporters were those Arab tribal fighters settled in the garrison town of Kūfa on the Euphrates who were pushing forward the Islamic conquest into the Iranian East. As in the case of Syria, Egypt and North Africa, the conquest of Mesopotamia and the Iranian highlands was the work of the Islamicised Arab tribes who fought in self-contained bands under the command of their own leaders. In order to secure the conquered lands they were settled into military camps (*amṣār* sing. *miṣr)* which remained purely Arab-Islamic islands amidst the subjugated foreign populace: Baṣra (14/635) and Kūfa (17/638) on the Euphrates, Fusṭāṭ Miṣr (Old Cairo, 20/641) on the Nile and al-Qayrawān (Kairouan, 34/654) in present-day Tunisia. In eastern Iran the oasis surrounding the old Persian border stronghold Merv (today Mary in the Turkmenia) served a similar purpose from 31/651. The Islamic fighters (*muqātila*) were settled in these camps and segregated according to tribe and clan in their own quarters around a central square with the mosque. Their commander (*amīr*) was also the governor of the province; he was in charge of collecting the tributes from the subjugated non-Muslims and dividing up between individual tribes and clans the stipends (*ʿaṭā'*) which were due to them according to the army roll. The Arab *muqātila* devoted themselves exclusively to conquest while trade and business lay in the hands of a steadily growing class of non-Arabs, partly non-Islamic indigenous people who were annexed to particular clans or leaders as clients (*mawālī,* sing. *mawlā).* The Islamic expansion was carried forward from these camps: from Baṣra and Kūfa to Iran, from eastern Iranian Merv to Central Asia, from Egyptian Fusṭāṭ to North Africa and from Kairouan to the Maghrib and into Spain. The Shia came into being and developed in the milieu of the garrison town of Kūfa on the Euphrates where the fighters were predominantly members of South Arabian tribes. It was here that ʿAlī found refuge and support during his fight for power.

The Shiites recognise ʿAlī as the only rightful Caliph and exclusively reserve for him the caliphal title 'Commander of the Faithful' (*amīr al-mu'minīn).* According to their tradition his short Caliphate (35-40/656-661) has been the only legitimate reign experienced by the Islamic community since the death of the Prophet. However, ʿAlī's Caliphate was disputed from the very beginning. As a beneficiary of the murder of his predecessor, ʿUthmān, he had to face the reproach of complicity in his murder, especially since he was forced to rely on the powers which had opposed ʿUthmān. His opponents were headed by the governor of Syria, the Umayyad Muʿāwiya who sought blood revenge for his cousin and declared ʿAlī's election invalid since he was only elected by a minority. In fact, after ʿUthmān's murder members of the Umayyad clan had fled from Medina and had taken no part in electing ʿAlī.

Muʿāwiya's refusal to pay homage and the defection of Syria made ʿAlī prepare for a campaign against the rebel. However, it never came to this because opposing forces were stirring elsewhere and appeared to be far more dangerous. In Mecca Muḥammad's widow ʿĀ'isha had declared herself against ʿAlī, and two influential Companions of the Prophet, Ṭalḥa and al-Zubayr, joined her, probably pursuing their own ambitions. With an armed following the three crossed the Arabian desert in order to incite the garrison towns on the Euphrates, Baṣra and Kūfa, against ʿAlī. The threatened loss of Iraq and the eastern Iranian provinces forced ʿAlī to act quickly; instead of Syria he turned first to Iraq where the rebels had brought Baṣra under their control. With the support of the tribal warriors from Kūfa ʿAlī advanced on Baṣra. Negotiations with the rebels failed and in a battle near Baṣra, during which ʿĀ'isha urged on the fighters from the back of a camel according to old Arabian custom, ʿAlī's troops gained victory. Ṭalḥa and al-Zubayr fell in the battle; ʿĀ'isha was taken prisoner and sent back to Medina under armed guard.

The 'Battle of the Camel' of 15th Jumādā II 36/9th December 656, in which two Muslim armies fought against each other for the first time, secured ʿAlī's control over the two Iraqi garrison towns. Using these as bases he was now able to take up the struggle against the Umayyad Muʿāwiya and the Syrians. After negotiations led to no result the Iraqi and Syrian armies clashed in the summer of 36-37/657 at Ṣiffīn on the mid-Euphrates (on the right bank, west of present-day al-Raqqa). After week-long skirmishes and isolated heavy fighting the two opponents finally agreed to let the conflict be settled by two neutral arbitrators with the Quran serving as the guiding principle. The object of arbitration was – so far as it can be reconstructed today – the question of whether the measures taken by ʿUthmān during his period of government were in keeping with divine revelation or whether they had been purely arbitrary acts. The decision would depend on whether complaints brought against ʿUthmān and his eventual forced removal had been justified or not, and whether Muʿāwiya was right to seek blood revenge and call to account the murderers protected by ʿAlī.

The fact that by agreeing to arbitration ʿAlī was indirectly offering up his Caliphate created violent protest within his own ranks. Many of his supporters considered it an offence against divine order that he should be willing to subject his proper rights to human verdict. When he then actually proceeded to nominate the Companion of the Prophet Abū Mūsā al-Ashʿarī as his arbitrator after returning to Kūfa from Ṣiffīn, the outraged dissidents left the garrison towns of Baṣra and Kūfa in droves and gathered on the Nahrawān canal east of the Tigris. The 'seceders' or Khārijites (*khawārij*, from *kharaja*, to go out, go off) demanded 'Alī's admission that by agreeing to arbitration he had committed an act of unbelief, and they demanded that he rescind his decision. The Caliph replied with weapons; in Ṣafar 38/July 658 the Khārijites were attacked at the Nahrawān canal and were decimated in a frightful onslaught.

The reports by Arab historians about the now assembled court of arbitration (*ḥukūma*) are contradictory and confused. Probably the two arbitrators – Abū Mūsā al-Ash'arī for 'Alī and 'Amr ibn al-'Āṣ, the conqueror of Egypt, for Mu'āwiya – met in Sha'bān 38/January 659 at the village of Adhruḥ (in southern Jordan between Petra and Ma'ān). What judgement the arbitrators pronounced and what conclusions those present in Adhruḥ drew from this cannot be conclusively ascertained from the contradictory reports, all of which date from a later time. The arbitrators appear to have agreed that 'Uthmān could not be incriminated for any actions which contravened divine law. From this it appears that 'Amr must, at least, have drawn the conclusion that being jointly responsible for the unjust killing of 'Uthmān, 'Alī had forfeited his right to rule. Homage as Caliph was then paid to the governor of Syria, the Umayyad Mu'āwiya, in Jerusalem in the summer of 40/660.

With that the *umma* was broken asunder. 'Alī, whose sphere of government had been reduced to Iraq, fell in Ramaḍān 40/January 661 by the door of a mosque in Kūfa at the hand of a certain 'Abd al-Raḥmān ibn Muljam, who was seeking revenge for the massacre of the Khārijites at al-Nahrawān. Two days after the attempted assassination 'Alī succumbed to his injuries.[17] The Caliphate of his opponent Mu'āwiya was then recognised almost everywhere (41-60/661-680).

It must be pointed out that there are no contemporary historical sources relating to the events of 'Alī's Caliphate. It was not until the 8th century that oral tradition was fixed in written form, and then only in monographs relating to individual events which were written down, particularly by 'Alī's Kufan partisans. In the case of these oldest collections of Shiite traditions in general, only the title and name of the author have survived. In a few instances, however, detailed citations have been transmitted in the writings of later chroniclers. One of the earliest collectors was the Kufan Jābir ibn Yazīd al-Ju'fī (d. 128/746) to whom the following titles have been ascribed: 'The Book of the (Battle of the) Camel' (*Kitāb al-Jamal*), the 'Book of Nahrawān', the 'Book of Ṣiffīn', 'The Murder of the Commander of the Faithful 'Alī' and a document about the martyrdom of 'Alī's son al-Ḥusayn. Abū Mikhnaf (d. 157/774), also from Kūfa, produced monographs about the

Battle of the Camel, Ṣiffīn, and other events relating to the early history of the Shia, which have been preserved for us in extracts by later historians. The oldest complete text of this kind is the 'Battle of Ṣiffīn' (*Waqʿat Ṣiffīn*) by the Kufan Shiite Naṣr ibn Muzāhim (d. 212/827) which exists in several editions.[18]

The fact that these Kufan monographs are all pro-Alid and anti-Umayyad will be no surprise; after the fall of the Umayyad dynasty this trend got its chance, and thus strongly influenced the earliest Islamic historical writing. Only modern historical research has begun to separate the different traditional trends and to elucidate the circumstances of their development. Erling Ladewig Petersen in his study *ʿAlī and Muʿāwiya in Early Arabic Tradition* (Copenhagen 1964) traced the different strands of tradition back to their sources and showed that they flowed together into a sort of compromise standard version around the end of the 3rd/9th century.

No less significant than the historical figure of ʿAlī ibn Abī Ṭālib, whose outlines modern research is attempting to trace, is the legendary transfigured image of ʿAlī traditionally handed down by the Shia. Details of his outer appearance are faithfully recorded. Even in Shiite texts he is the short-sighted, corpulent 'baldy' (*al-aṣlaʿ al-anzaʿ*). In the popular image his heroic characteristics are predominant: he is Ḥaydara (the lion), and Abū Turāb (the one covered in dust).[19] According to legend, at the time of Muḥammad's flight from Mecca he laid himself on Muḥammad's bed in order to confuse the pursuers. He not only conquered Fadak oasis and Yemen for Islam, but also protected the Prophet in the thick of battle. During the siege of the oasis town of Khaybar (north of Medina) he is said to have lifted the city gate from its hinges with superhuman strength, used it as a shield and then flung it into the ditch. In Shiite tradition ʿAlī is the embodiment of all young men's virtues (*futuwwa*). Popular illustrations normally portray him bearing the two-pronged sword Dhu 'l-Fiqār (or Dhu 'l-Fayqār)[20] inherited from the Prophet, fighting against the enemies of Islam or wild animals. His designation by the Prophet at Ghadīr Khumm is regarded as an indisputable fact among the Shiites. All those who opposed his rightful Caliphate – i.e. his three predecessors Abū Bakr, ʿUmar and ʿUthmān, his opponents Ṭalḥa and al-Zubayr and ʿĀ'isha, and also the two arbitrators at Adhruḥ, his murderer Ibn Muljam and, of course, his arch-enemy Muʿāwiya – are cursed by the Shiites. The loud vituperation of the forefathers (*sabb al-salaf*) at Shiite festivals and processions and the cursing of ʿAlī's opponents from the pulpit are fundamental characteristics of Shiite tradition and, even today, result in conflicts with the Sunnis who are provoked by vituperation directed against the first Caliphs and prominent Companions of the Prophet.

ʿAlī is also considered a model of eloquence by the Shiites; the speeches and sermons attributed to him – in fact exemplary instances of classical Arabic – have been handed down in a collection entitled 'The Path of Eloquence' (*Nahj al-balāgha)* which, however, did not appear until the 5th/11th century (see p. 53).

ʿAlī's grave near Kūfa, which was allegedly kept secret to begin with and only rediscovered by the sixth Imam (see below p. 30), has been the object of Shiite pilgrimages since the end of the 2nd/8th century. The pilgrimage place Najaf grew up around his shrine and remains one of the most important spiritual centres of the Shia up to the present day.

Bibliography

W. Sarasin, *Das Bild Alis bei den Historikern der Sunna*, Basel 1907. H. Lammens, *Etudes sur le règne du calife omaiyade Moʿâwiya Ier*, Paris 1908. G. Levi della Vida, 'Il califfato di ʿAlī secondo il Kitāb Ansāb al-A rāf di al-Balādhurī', *RSO* (1913), 127 507. L. Caetani, *Annali dell'Islam* IX and X, Milan 1926. L. Veccia Vaglieri, 'Il conflitto ʿAlī-Muʿāwiya e la secessione khārigita riesaminati alla luce di fonti ibāḍite', *AIUON* 4 (1952), 1-94; 'Traduzione di passi riguardanti il conflitto ʿAli-Muʿāwiya e la secessione khārigita', *AIUON* 5 (1953), 1-98; Art. ʿAlī ibn Abī Ṭālib, EI². R. Vesely, 'Die Anṣār im ersten Bürgerkriege (36 40)', *Archiv orientální* 26/1 (1958, 36-58. E. L. Petersen, "ʿAlī and Muʿāwiya; The rise of the Umayyad Caliphate, 656-661', *Acta Orientalia* 23 (1959), 157 ff.; ʿAlī and Muʿāwiya in Early Arabic Tradition, Copenhagen 1964. H. Laoust, 'Le rôle de ʿAlī dans la Sira chiite', *REI* 30 (1962), 7-26. J. Eliash, *ʿAlī b. Abī Ṭālib in Ithna-ʿAsharī Shīʿī Belief*, unpublished thesis, London 1966.

THE ABDICATION OF AL-ḤASAN (661)

ʿAlī left behind two sons from his marriage to Muḥammad's daughter Fāṭima, al-Ḥasan and al-Ḥusayn. The elder, al-Ḥasan, who was 36 or 37 years old at the time of the death of his father, is regarded as ʿAlī's rightful heir and successor by the Shiites. In Kūfa numerous supporters of his father rallied around him in order to defend Iraq against Muʿāwiya who was advancing from Syria. However, no battle ensued, either because al-Ḥasan saw his position to be hopeless, or – as maintained by Shiite tradition – because his love of peace made him withdraw to prevent renewed bloodshed among Muslims. In any case, his abdication was facilitated by a substantial sum of money and by the cession of the tax revenues of a Persian province; but apart from that, whether Muʿāwiya did in fact agree to make him his successor is questionable. Negotiations between the two armies at al-Madā'in (Ctesiphon) on the Tigris came to a successful conclusion, and after Muʿāwiya had occupied Kūfa, al-Ḥasan also appeared in the mosque there and publicly renounced his claim to the Caliphate in favour of the Umayyads. He left Iraq and, until his death (50/670 or 58/678), lived in Medina as a rich grand seigneur renowned above all for his numerous marriages, to which he owed the nickname *al-Miṭlāq*, 'the divorcer', and countless descendants.

Although the peace pact with Muʿāwiya is not concealed in Shiite tradition, it is not interpreted as a renunciation of the throne; for the sake of peace al-Ḥasan did indeed yield to force, but after his return to Medina he remained the rightful Imam and Caliph. Shiite sources consider that his Imamate ended only with his death.[21] The notion that al-Ḥasan paid tribute to Muʿāwiya as Caliph is denied by the Shiites. According to their tradition he would certainly have stepped forward with his claim after the death of Muʿāwiya, had the latter not had him poisoned beforehand.

Bibliography

L.Veccia Vaglieri, Art. (al-)Ḥasan b. ʿAlī b. ʿAbī Ṭālib, EI².

THE MARTYRDOM OF AL-ḤUSAYN AT KARBALĀʾ (680)

After al-Ḥasan's abdication the garrison towns of Baṣra and Kūfa were ruled by governors sent from Damascus. In Kūfa the Syrian governors met with open resistance because sympathies for ʿAlī and his sons and antipathy to the Umayyads remained very much alive amongst the tribal fighters. In the year 51/671 Muʿāwiya had to arrest a few spokesmen and bring them to Damascus where they were tried. Open revolt ensued when Muʿāwiya, before his death in 60/680, designated his son Yazīd to be his successor, thus for the first time attempting to establish a hereditary Caliphal dynasty. Old religiously motivated resentment against the until recently pagan Umayyad clan and its hunger for power united with the Iraqi tribal fighters to oppose the hegemony of the Syrians; ʿAlī's second son al-Ḥusayn was regarded as an appropriate pretender to be brought into play against the Umayyads.

ʿAlī's younger son by Fāṭima, al-Ḥusayn, was 54 years old when Muʿāwiya died, and lived in Medina. In order not to pay homage to Yazīd ibn Muʿāwiya he withdrew to Mecca, which had been regarded as an unassailable sanctuary even in pre-Islamic times. From here he established secret contacts with anti-Umayyad opposition in Kūfa, and in Dhu 'l-Ḥijja 60/September 680 he made his way to Iraq at their instigation. Accompanied by about fifty people – his wives and children as well as supporters – he marched from Mecca along the pilgrim road straight through the Arabian desert to Iraq. Because riders sent by the government blocked his road to Kūfa and also prevented his retreat to Medina he was forced to continue to march north along the Euphrates. Partisans from Kūfa reinforced his small group while government forces followed and shadowed him. When al-Ḥusayn did not comply with the summons of the governor of Kūfa and pay tribute to Yazīd, and government forces blocked his people's access to the river and to essential drinking water, battle ensued on 10th Muḥarram 61/10th October 680 on the plain of Karbalā'. Al-Ḥusayn's troops only amounted to about seventy combatants and were hopelessly outnumbered. The men were slaughtered, among them al-Ḥusayn's eldest son 'Alī al-Akbar. Al-Ḥusayn himself fell, struck down from all sides. The bodies were interred in al-Ghādiriyya near Karbalā'. The severed heads and the captured women and children were taken to Kūfa where the governor 'Ubaydallāh ibn Ziyād is said to have picked at al-Ḥusayn's teeth with his staff. Al-Ḥusayn's head was then sent to Damascus where it was again assaulted by the Caliph Yazīd. Al-Ḥusayn's dependants, including a younger son 'Alī, who had not taken part in the battle of Karbalā' because of an illness, were spared and allowed to go to Medina.

Julius Wellhausen emphasised the hopelessness of al-Ḥusayn's task and did not conceal his impression of 'the utter harmlessness of the hero'. However, he stressed the unforeseen effect of the Day of Karbalā': 'His martyrdom opened up a new era for the Shia; it was far more important for them than that of his father who was not the son of the Prophet's daughter. There are such things as events which have a tremendous effect, not so much through themselves and their inevitable consequences as through the memories they leave in the hearts and minds of men.'[22]

The Shiites, of course, see al-Ḥusayn's role quite differently. For them he is not the adventurer, blindly charging to his downfall, but rather the 'Prince of the Martyrs' (*sayyid al-shuhadā'*) whose passion is explicitly compared to that of Jesus. Aware of his certain death he goes his way unswervingly in order to give a sign to the world.[23]

The Day of Karbalā', the 'tenth' ('Āshūrā'), i.e. the 10th of the month of Muḥarram, became the most important festival day (see below p. 140); al-Ḥusayn's grave became the most visited Shiite place of pilgrimage. In the year 236/850 the Caliph al-Mutawakkil found himself compelled to destroy the shrine at Karbalā' in order to stop the Shiite pilgrimages.[24] Nevertheless, as early as 266/880 visitors were attested again – even from remote Yemen – as having travelled on to Karbalā' after the pilgrimage to Mecca and after visiting the Prophet's grave in Medina, to weep and lament at al-Ḥusayn's burial place.[25] Around the year 366/977 the traveller and geographer Ibn Ḥawqal reported a domed mausoleum over the grave.[26] After their destruction by plundering Bedouins, the Būyid 'Aḍud al-Dawla (see below p. 48) restored the shrines of 'Alī in Najaf and al-Ḥusayn in Karbalā' in the year 369/980.[27]

Al-Ḥusayn's head which had been taken to Damascus is said to have been returned to his dependants who buried it, although where it is interred is disputed. In Damascus itself the head of the martyr is honoured in a room on the east side of the Great Mosque; according to another tradition it was interred in Palestinian Ascalon where the Fāṭimid general al-Afḍal built a shrine for it in 491/1098. In order to protect it from the Crusaders the relic was transported in 548/1153 from there to Cairo, where it is still venerated today in al-Ḥusayn's martyr shrine (*al-mashhad al-Ḥusaynī*) near to the Azhar mosque.[28] According to other traditions the head is said to have been buried in Medina, Kūfa, Najaf, Karbalā', Raqqa on the Euphrates or even in remote Merv.

The earliest preserved source for the events of Karbalā' is the 'Book of the murder of al-Ḥusayn' (*Kitab maqtal al-Ḥusayn*) by the Kufan Abū Mikhnaf (d. 157/774) which is cited at length by the historian al-Ṭabarī (d. 310/923) in his annals.[30]

Primary sources in translation

Shaykh al-Mufīd, *Kitāb al-Irshād* (trans. Howard), 296 ff.

Secondary sources

J. Wellhausen, *Oppositionsparteien*, 61ff. M. Streck, 'Kerbela. 1. Name und Alter des Ortes. 2. Der Kopf des Ḥusain. 3. Zur Literatur', in: G. Weil (ed.), *Festschrift E. Sachau*, Berlin 1915, 393-405. L. Veccia Vaglieri, Art. (al-)Ḥusain b. 'Alī b. Abī Ṭālib, EI². E. Honigmann, Art. Karbalā', EI².

THE 'FOURER' SHIA OR KAYSĀNIYYA AND THE ORIGIN OF THE SHIITE EXPECTATION OF THE MAHDĪ

Under the Caliphate of the Umayyad Yazīd (60-64/680-683) 'Alī's party in Kūfa began to emerge more distinctly as a religious movement too. A circle of people was formed from among the notables of the Arab tribes of Kūfa who wanted to atone for their complicity in al-Ḥusayn's downfall by actively repenting sword in hand; the 'penitents' (tawwābūn) united with the slogan 'revenge for al-Ḥusayn' even though their aims were as yet unclear.

It must be borne in mind that the Shia originated in the Arabian milieu of Kūfa and may thus be understood neither as an expression of Iranian mentality – as has long been believed[31] – nor yet as the revenge of Aryan Iranianism on Islam and the Arabs;[32] 'the phenomenon of Shiism is as Arab in its roots as Islam itself'.[33]

Shiite aspirations – and we can speak of them in these terms from Karbalā' on – were advanced by the fact that the Umayyad Caliphate experienced a serious crisis after the death of Yazīd (64/683). In Mecca, Ibn al-Zubayr, son of ʿAlī's erstwhile opponent in the Battle of the Camel (see above p. 10), emerged as Caliph and was able to secure the support of Baṣra and Kūfa; at the same time, with the 'penitents' at their head, the Kufan Shiites called for the overthrow of the Umayyad Caliphate and prepared to march on Syria. There are said to have been around 4,000 men; Arabs from all tribes, predominantly from Kūfa but also from Baṣra and the old Persian metropolis Ctesiphon (Arab. al-Madā'in) on the Tigris.

They set off in 65/November 684, spent a day and a night weeping by the grave of al-Ḥusayn at Karbalā' and then moved up the Euphrates and the Khābūr. At Ra's al-ʿAyn, where they had set up camp, they were wiped out by Syrian troops at the beginning of January 685.

The spokesman for the Kufan Shiites, the Companion of the Prophet Sulaymān ibn Ṣurad from the Khuzāʿa tribe, perished with the 'penitents'. He was replaced by al-Mukhtār who had stayed behind in Kūfa. He was an Arab from the tribe of Thaqīf whose actual home was the town of Ṭa'if south east of Mecca. Al-Mukhtār was a typical representative of the Arab tribal nobility in the Iraqi camps: his father had fallen during the conquests fighting the Persians, he himself was related by marriage to a son of the Caliph ʿUmar, he had a house in Kūfa and an estate near the town, a large following of converted indigenous people rallied around him, and, of course, he received regular stipends from the incoming booty and tributes.

The Shiite revolt led by al-Mukhtār in Kūfa in the year 66/685 deserves close scrutiny. This was the catalyst for a succession of attitudes and concepts which would prove fundamental for the later Shia. The main source for these events is the monograph by the Kūfan Abū Mikhnaf (d. 157/774) on which al-Ṭabarī drew in his Chronicles.[34]

Since the time of Karbalā' the hopes of the Kufan Shiites were pinned on a third son of ʿAlī, Muḥammad, who was called the 'son of the Ḥanafite woman' (*ibn al-Ḥanafiyya)* because his mother was not the Prophet's daughter, Fāṭima, but one of ʿAlī's other wives from the Ḥanīfa tribe. Muḥammad ibn al-Ḥanafiyya lived in Medina; he played absolutely no part in what took place in Kūfa in his name, and had never acceded to the ruling position which people sought to prepare for him. Al-Mukhtār appeared as the self-appointed trustee of this third son of ʿAlī whom he declared to be the 'rightly-guided' (*al-Mahdī*) as opposed to the two 'wrongly-guided', the Umayyad in Damascus and the rival Caliph Ibn al-Zubayr in Mecca. The term *al-Mahdī* (passive participle of the verb *hadā*, 'to guide, to lead') which now appears for the first time amongst the Shia did not yet have the eschatological connotations which it would later assume. The 'rightly-guided' is simply the rightful Imam-Caliph appointed by God. It is also noteworthy that Muḥammad ibn al-Ḥanafiyya was not descended from the Prophet on either his father's or his mother's side; he was not the heir of the Prophet Muḥammad, but rather the heir of the Caliph ʿAlī.

In 66/October 685 al-Mukhtār rose up against the governor of Kūfa and brought both the town and the citadel under his authority. Alongside the Arab tribal fighters who formed the bulk of his following, non-Arab clients (*mawālī*) who had converted to Islam are mentioned in the ranks of the Shiites for the first time. Wellhausen saw the principal motive behind their participation in the Shiite intrigues as lying in the hope that a power-swing to the Shiites would bring them the recognition as socially equal Muslims for which they were striving – and thus also a share of the booty and tribute.[35] For over a year al-Mukhtār was able to hold his own against opposing tribal leaders, against the governors sent by Ibn al-Zubayr from Mecca and also against the troops of the Syrian Umayyads; after an unsuccessful revolt in Kūfa against his regime he had all those executed who were accused of complicity in the massacre at Karbalā'.

The pretender, Muḥammad ibn al-Ḥanafiyya, in whose name everything took place, refused to come to Kūfa and assume the heritage of his father ʿAlī, even though some of al-Mukhtār's supporters had already set up a throne decorated with silk and brocade. They danced around it in expectation of the imminent arrival of the Mahdī, and oracles were given from it.[36] The Shiite government of Kūfa, however, met with a hasty end when the governor of Baṣra – brother of the Meccan rival Caliph Ibn al-Zubayr – sent out an army which occupied unfortified Kūfa after two victories over the Shiites; al-Mukhtār met his death on 14th Ramaḍān 61/3rd April 687 during a sortie from the citadel. The conquerors took bloody revenge against the survivors – especially against the non-Arab *mawālī*.

After its failure, the 'Mahdī' Muḥammad ibn al-Ḥanafiyya denounced the revolt which had been led in his name; at the end of the Meccan rival Caliphate (73/692) he even sought out the victorious Umayyad ʿAbd al-Malik in Damascus in order to pay homage to him (78/697 or 79/698). Thereafter he lived peacefully in Medina and died in the year 81/700. This did not undermine the faith of his Kufan following. After the disappointment of political hopes which had been pinned on him, Shiite expectations began to adopt mythical characteristics. Under severe pressure from the Umayyad governor the Shia were only able to survive by going underground and all later Shiite religious books now name as spokesmen especially the humble people from the *mawālī* – handicraft workers, shopkeepers, money changers. At this time Shiism appears to be the Islam of the newly-converted non-Arab artisans and traders from Kūfa, while the proportion of Arab tribesmen diminished. A certain Kaysān, a former client of al-Mukhtār and chief of his bodyguard during the revolt, was named as the secret head. Within the circles of the 'Kaysanites' the Shia began to acquire a distinctive profile and formed ideas and concepts which were later to become a basic constituent of Shiite tradition, although the Kaysāniyya themselves soon disappeared and were absorbed by the continuing development of the Shia.

The Kaysāniyya can be termed the 'Fourer' Shia by analogy with the later 'Twelver' and 'Sevener' Shia since they recognised only four Imams in the Islamic *umma* after the Prophet. A line by the Kaysanite poet al-Sayyid al-Ḥimyarī says: 'There are four Imams: 'Alī and his three sons al-Ḥasan, al-Ḥusayn and Muḥammad' (ibn al-Ḥanafiyya).[37]

After the death of Muḥammad ibn al-Ḥanafiyya in the year 81/700 the hope was spread among the Shia that the Mahdī proclaimed by al-Mukhtār had not died, rather he was only hidden from the world. In fact he was said to be concealed in the gorges of Jabal Raḍwā north of Medina, guarded by lions and tigers and fed by mountain goats. In the imminent future he would emerge victorious from his hiding place, gather his followers around him, destroy the enemy, establish the authority of true Islam and 'fill the earth with justice and fairness'. The Mahdī's temporary banishment to Mount Raḍwā was interpreted as penance (*'uqūba)* for his mistake, i.e. for the tribute he had paid to the false Caliph 'Abd al-Malik in Damascus.[38]

It is in the mythically transfigured person of Muḥammad ibn al-Ḥanafiyya that Shiite expectations of the Mahdī first assume any sort of impressive form. The model, evolved by the Kaysanites at the beginning of the 8th century, of the 'occultation' or 'absence' (*ghayba*) and the expected return (*raj'a*) of the true Imam was later adopted by other branches of the Shia and further developed; the figure of the Mahdī finally even entered popular Sunni eschatology.[39] Just how far non-Muslim views – Jewish, Gnostic or Iranian – entered the Shia through the Kaysāniyya is debatable. The large proportion of non-Arab *mawālī* among the Shiite spokesmen from Kūfa in the 2nd/8th century is, however, noteworthy; and the fact that in some small groups and circles decidedly gnostic views abounded about the redemption of the world and the migration of the soul is not in question (on the teachings of these 'extremists' see below p. 156). Throughout the whole of the 2nd/8th century the Kaysāniyya had supporters in Iraq, particularly in Kūfa and al-Madā'in (Ctesiphon). The only direct evidence we have of this earliest form of the Shia are lines by the Arab poets Kuthayyir ʿAzza (d. 105/723) and al-Sayyid al-Ḥimyarī (d. between 170/787 and 179/795);[40] apart from this we only know of the Kaysāniyya from later Twelver Shia books on heresy such as that by Qummī (d. after 292/905).[41] In a few lines by the two above-mentioned poets the Kaysanites' hope and uncertainty are reflected in the long wait for the return of the Mahdī Muḥammad ibn al-Ḥanafiyya; Sayyid al-Himyarī says on one occasion: 'Even if he stays away from us for as long as Moses lived we will still be sure that he will return'.[42]

The same poet also speaks about opponents who mocked the Kaysanites because after seventy years they were still pinning their hopes on the return of a man who was long dead.[43] While some of the Kaysanites rallied in obscure groups around self-professed prophets of humble origin (see below p. 157), by the end of the 2nd/8th century the majority subscribed to the continued development of the Shia and turned to other Imams, as is expressly testified by the two poets. The constant oscillation between recognition of a real living Imam and hope of the return of a hidden Mahdī characterises the whole formative phase of the early Shia.

Primary sources in translation

M. J. Mashkur (trans.), 'An-Nawbahti. Les sectes îʿites', *RHR* 153 (1958), 200-10. H. Halm, *Die islamische Gnosis. Die extreme Schia und die Alawiten*, Zürich/Munich 1982, 49ff.

Secondary sources

J. Wellhausen, *Oppositionsparteien*, 74-95. S. Moscati, 'Per una storia dell'antica îʿa', *RSO* 30 (1955), 251-67. W. Al-Qāḍi, *Al-Kaysāniyya fi 'l-tā'rīkh wa 'l-adab*, Beirut 1974. W. Madelung, Art. al-Mahdī, EI².

THE REVOLT OF ZAYD IBN ʿALĪ (740) AND THE BEGINNINGS OF THE ZAYDIYYA

Neither al-Ḥusayn's younger son ʿAlī, who survived the massacre at Karbalā' (d. around 95/713) nor his son Muḥammad (d. around 115/733) played any political role; they lived in Medina and made no moves whatsoever to oppose Umayyad rule. The later Twelver Shia regard them – after ʿAlī, al-Ḥasan and al-Ḥusayn – as the fourth and fifth Imams (cf. the genealogical tree p. 22, nos. 20 and 25) and gives them honorific titles: ʿAlī ibn al-Ḥusayn is 'the embellishment of God's servants' (*Zayn al-ʿĀbidīn*) and – because of his frequent praying – 'the frequently prostrating one' (*al-Sajjād*) . A series of prayers ascribed to him have been put together by the Shiites in the 'Book of the Sajjād' (*al-Ṣaḥīfa al-sajjādiyya*).[44] His son Muḥammad has the honorific *Bāqir al-*

ʿilm, the 'render' or 'opener of knowledge', normally abbreviated as *al-Bāqir*.

Nevertheless, the political ambitions of the Ḥusaynid family were in no way relinquished. In the year 121/739 Zayd ibn ʿAlī, the half-brother of Bāqir (cf. genealogical tree no. 24) came to Kūfa and urged the Shiites to rebel against the Umayyads. However, his rebellion against the Caliph Hishām in 122/740 failed, and Zayd fell in Kūfa during a street battle against the governor's forces. His younger son Yaḥyā fled to Khurāsān (eastern Iran), but there fell into the hands of the Umayyads. He was released and attempted a second rebellion in the region of Herat (in western Afghanistan) but he too fell in battle against government forces (125/743).

One particular Shiite school of thought, the Zaydiyya, is linked to Zayd's short-lived Imamate. This school went its own way entirely, and for that reason should be considered separately (see below p. 206).

Bibliography

J. Wellhausen, *Oppositionsparteien*, 95-8. R. Strothmann, Art. Zayd b. ʿAlī, EI[2].

THE HĀSHIMIYYA AND THE REVOLT OF ʿABDALLĀH IBN MUʿĀWIYA (744)

Not least among the factors which contributed towards undermining and defeating the Umayyad Caliphate was Shiite opposition and agitation, and the perpetual hotbed of unrest, Kūfa, played a decisive role.

After Zayd's failed revolt (122/740) the Iraqi Shiites were once again without a leader. The Ḥasanid branch of the Alids had been discredited by al-Ḥasan's abdication, and al-Ḥusayn's descendants in Medina kept well away from politics. Around the middle of the 8th century the main body of Kufan Shiites appears to have shared Kaysanite hopes for the return of Muḥammad ibn al-Ḥanafiyya from Mount Raḍwā, and some rallied around spokesmen who set themselves up as plenipotentiaries for his son Abū Hāshim (cf. genealogical tree p. 22, no. 19). At this time the Shia had not yet committed themselves to any particular line of ʿAlī's descendants. The different groups and circles which we only know from later heresiographical literature cannot be clearly distinguished from each other, and their followings appear to have fluctuated. However, in Kūfa from about 102/720 the beginnings of an organisation and the first efforts towards systematic propaganda (*daʿwa*) are recognisable.

A certain Maysara is named as the leader initially. He was succeeded in 105/723-4 by Bukayr ibn Māhān, who acted for a good twenty years as the secret head of the Kufan Shia (d. 127/745). Bukayr appears to have been descended from the class of non-Arab *mawālī* and

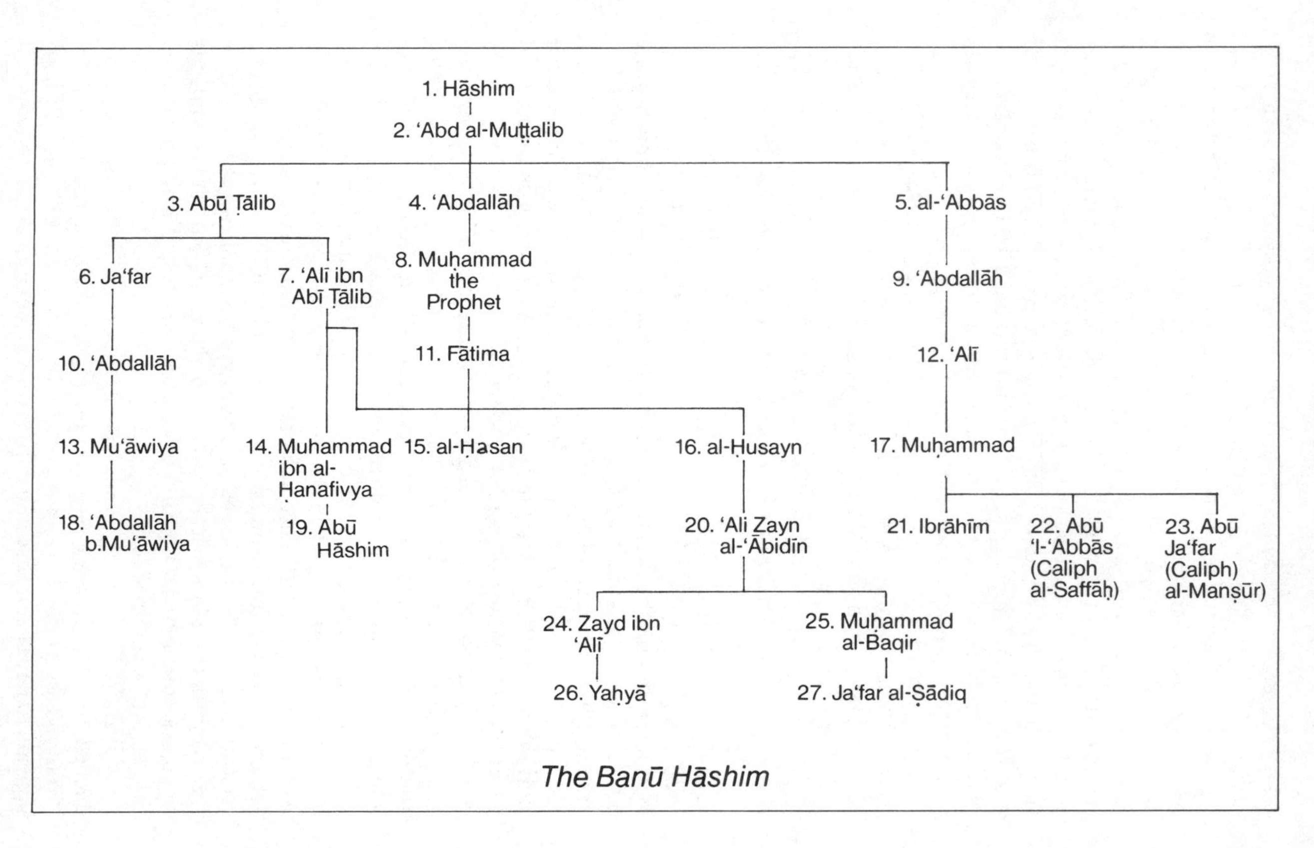

The Banū Hāshim

was perhaps of Iranian descent; the only thing reported about his past is his activity as an interpreter for the Islamic governor in North-West India.[45]

The secret agitation which Bukayr pursued for two decades is termed 'the propaganda of the Hāshimites' (*daʿwat Banī Hāshim)* in our sources and the whole group is called the *Hāshimiyya*.[46] Possibly the name 'Hāshimites' referred originally to *Abū* Hashim, son and heir of Muḥammad ibn al-Ḥanafiyya (genealogical tree no. 19); however it soon acquired a wider meaning: *Hāshim* is also the name of the clan of the Quraysh tribe to which the Prophet Muḥammad and his cousin ʿAlī belonged. Imperceptibly Shiite propaganda was now extended to the whole of the Banū Hāshim clan. In theory anyone from the holy tribe could be called to the head of the Islamic *umma* as Imam-Caliph, and at the same time by restricting the Caliphate to the Banū Hāshim the Banū Umayya were excluded from government.[47]

Under Maysara and Bukayr ibn Māhān 'Hāshimite' propaganda was directed from Kufa and transmitted by propagandists (*duʿat,* sing. *daʿī)* as far as the garrisons of eastern Iran, and under Kufan control a well organised cell of secret agitation was formed in Merv. Propaganda was not in fact made for any particular pretender, but rather for the claims to legitimacy of the Banū Hāshim in general. The identity of the future Imam-Caliph was not yet revealed and so the propaganda was made in the name of one as yet nameless, 'one from the House of Muḥammad who is acceptable' (*al-riḍā min āl Muḥammad)*. All anti-Umayyad forces were to gather under the banner of this as yet unnamed Imam.

Hāshimite propaganda did, in fact, succeed in bringing down the Umayyad Caliphate and in establishing a new régime, but the revolution took a completely different course from the one envisaged by its initiators. The Umayyad government had been shaken by internal disarray ever since the death of the Caliph Yazīd III (126/744), and in Iraq and Iran two revolts took place which resulted in the Umayyads' completely losing control over the east of the empire. The first of these revolts began in Kūfa. At the end of 127/744 the Kufan Shiites set up a certain ʿAbdallāh ibn Muʿāwiya as Imam. For the first time Hāshimite propaganda showed some effect: the pretender was not a descendant of ʿAlī at all, but rather of his brother, Jaʿfar ibn Abī Ṭālib (genealogical tree no. 18). He could therefore lay claim to the Caliphate on the grounds of his membership of the Banū Hāshim clan, and emerged as the *riḍā min āl Muḥammad* , 'the one from the House of Muḥammad who is acceptable'.[48] He was joined by the Shiites of al-Madā'in (Ctesiphon) which appears to have been the second largest Shiite stronghold in Iraq after Kūfa. However, he was unable to maintain his position in Kūfa and moved on, first to al-Madā'in, then back to the

Iranian highlands where he stayed first in Iṣfahān and then in the citadel of Iṣṭakhr by the ancient city of Persepolis; from there he ruled the whole of western Iran for two years. After being defeated by government troops in 129/746-7 he fled to Herat where he was eliminated by a rival (Abū Muslim). His supporters considered him to be in hiding, and believed he was living in the mountain of Iṣfahān whence he would return in triumph as the Mahdī. At this point the legend about the Mahdī Muḥammad ibn al-Ḥanafiyya hiding on Mount Raḍwā is transferred to another figure for the first time – a process which was to repeat itself several times in the history of the early Shia.

Primary sources in translation

M. J. Mashkur (trans.), 'An-Nawbahti. Les sectes î'ites', *RHR* 153 (1958), 213ff. H. Halm, *Die islamische Gnosis*, 64-9.

Secondary sources

J. Wellhausen, *The Arab Kingdom and its Fall*, Calcutta, 1927. T. Nagel, *Untersuchung zur Entstehung des abbasidischen Kalifates*, Bonn 1972. K. V. Zettersteen, Art. 'Abd Allāh b. Mu'āwiya, EI². D. M. Dunlop, Art. 'Abdallāh b. Mo'āvīa, Encycl. Iran.

THE ABBASID REVOLUTION (747-749)

Although 'Abdallāh ibn Mu'āwiya's revolt was only a single episode, it had suddenly uncovered the weakness of the Umayyad government. Hāshimite agitation in north-eastern Iran was more successful. Numerous Arab tribal fighters and their non-Arab clients had settled in the old border town of Merv (present-day Mary) as a base from which to drive the Islamic conquests forward into Central Asia. Since 128/745 a Persian freedman called Abū Muslim had been spreading propaganda as a Hāshimite agent among the Arabs and the mawālī of this large military town. He was an emissary of the Kufan Shiite leader Abū Salama al-Khallāl ('the pickle trader') who had succeeded the late Bukayr ibn Māhān the year before. Abū Muslim's mission was to sow propaganda for the unnamed Hāshimite pretender 'the one from the House of Muḥammad who is acceptable to all'. In fact Abū Muslim played a double game. He probably never had any intention of helping an Alid to power, but rather, without his Kufan employers' suspecting it, he pursued the political interests of the Banu 'l-'Abbās family to which he had been attached in his youth as a slave and to which he was still firmly tied by bonds of loyalty.[49]

Even the Banu 'l-'Abbās (Abbasids), descendants of Muḥammad's uncle al-'Abbās (genealogical tree p. 22 no. 5) were, as members of the

Hāshim clan, reckoned amongst the possible claimants for the Caliphate, but until now they had played no role in the anti-Umayyad opposition and clearly no one had counted on their political ambitions. They kept themselves warily in the background; and when the propagandist Abū Muslim appeared in Merv, his former owner and patron, the most senior of the Abbasids, Ibrāhīm (genealogical tree no. 21) busied himself with running his estates in al-Sharāt (in southern Jordan). Abu Muslim's propaganda in eastern Iran was, in fact, destined to help the Abbasids to the Caliphate, and thus the later arch-enemies of the Shia came to the throne with Shiite help – a fact which the Shiites have always remembered with considerable bitterness.

The course of the Abbasid revolution can only be outlined briefly here; for details, particularly for the complex motives behind the revolution, reference should be made to the specialist literature. The agitator Abū Muslim was able to rally enough malcontents around him – Arab fighters and Iranian *mawālī* – to risk open revolt against the weakened Umayyad régime, and on 1st Sha'ban 129/15th June 747 he unfurled the black banners of the unnamed Imam, the *riḍā*.[50] He was quickly able to establish his rule over eastern Iran. In the year 130/748 the rebel army began to march westwards, and after several victories it crossed the Tigris and the Euphrates and moved into Kūfa on 14th Muḥarram 132/2nd September 749.

After gaining military victory, the Imam for whom it had been fought, had to reveal his identity. Abū Salama, the Kufan Shiite leader, who had adopted the title 'wazīr of the House of the Prophet' (*wazīr āl Muḥammad*) still believed that he held the reins and that he could install a pretender of his choice as Caliph. He wrote to several Alids, including the Husaynid Ja'far al Ṣādiq (genealogical tree no. 27), offering them the Caliphate, but it appears that he only received refusals. In the meantime no less than fourteen members of the Abbasid family had gathered in Kūfa and brought forward their claims to the throne. With the support of the rebel army camped in front of the town their candidate Abu 'l-ʿAbbās (genealogical tree no. 22) was proclaimed Caliph (his brother Ibrāhīm was killed by the Umayyads at the last minute). Shortly afterwards Abū Salama, who only reluctantly resigned himself to this course of events, was eliminated. The short Caliphate of the first Abbasid (132-136/749-754) was followed by that of his brother, Abū Jaʿfar, who adopted the Mahdī title *al-Manṣūr* (the victorious) as a regnal title. In the year 145/762 he began to build a new residence, the 'city of peace' (*Madīnat al-Salām*) near the small village of Baghdad on the Tigris. By settling into the new capital the Caliph was able to get away from the influence of the Kufan Shiite milieu to which he owed his power.

The political goal of the Shia, the overthrow of the Umayyad 'usurpers', had finally been achieved; but no descendant of ʿAlī had ascended the throne, and in fact a new dynasty of usurpers had established itself, having outplayed the Shiites and once again condemned them to the role of powerless opposition. In their propaganda writings, in which they glorified their coup as an eschatological 'turning point' (*dawla*) and substantiated their claims to the Caliphate, the Abbasids drew upon Shiite tradition unscrupulously and used it as a propaganda legend. They maintained that Abū Hāshim, the son of Muḥammad ibn al-Ḥanafiyya (genealogical tree no. 19), had been poisoned by the Umayyad Caliph; the fatally ill Abū Hāshim was supposed to have found refuge on an Abbasid estate in al-Sharāt and on his death bed to have bequeathed to his host, Muḥammad ibn ʿAlī, father of the first two Abbasid Caliphs (genealogical tree no. 17) the heritage of his grandfather ʿAlī – that is to say rightful authority over the Islamic empire. This obscure story about the so-called will of Abū Hāshim is certainly a subsequent fabrication. The Abbasids themselves soon dissociated themselves from this version. Although they had gained power by clever manipulation of Shiite hopes they cut off all ties with the Kufan Shiites as soon as they were firmly in the saddle; ʿAlī's descendants, in particular those of the Ḥusaynid line, were seen as dangerous rivals whom they sought to keep under strict surveillance. The Shiites for their part, having come within reach of political power only to have it wrested away again at the last moment by unscrupulous usurpers, regarded the Abbasid Caliphate of Baghdad as their main enemy during the 500 years or so of its existence (until 656/1258) and longed for its downfall.

Bibliography

J. Wellhausen. *The Arab Kingdom and its Fall.* S. Moscati, 'Studi su Abū Muslim I-III', *Accademia Nazionale dei Lincei, Rendiconti morali* 1949, 323-35; 474-95; 1950, 89-105; 'Il testamento di Abū Hā im', *RSO* 27 (1952), 28-46. M. A. Shaban, *The Abbasid Revolution*, Cambridge 1970. T. Nagel, *Untersuchungen zur Entstehung des abbasidischen Kalifates*, Bonn 1972; 'Das Kalifat der Abbasiden', in U. Haarmann (ed.), *Geschichte der arabischen Welt*, Munich 1987, 101ff. M. Sharon, *Black Banners from the East. The Establishment of the Abbasid State – Incubation of a Revolt*, Jerusalem/Leiden 1983.

NOTES TO CHAPTER ONE

1 *Abh. der kgl. Ges. d. Wiss. zu Göttingen, phil.-hist. Kl., n.F.* vol. V, no. 2, Berlin 1901.
2 In this book the Islamic Hijra date is given before the Christian year.
3 'Einen Imamitenstaat im heilsgeschichtlich ökonomischen Sinn hat man aber stets erstrebt, d.h. ein Reich, dessen Geist und führende Geister imamitisch, wenn auch die Herrscher nicht Imame sind', R. Strothmann,

Die Zwölfer-Schīʿa, Leipzig 1926, 80.

4 From the Arabic *sunna*, 'habitual practice, norm, usage sanctioned by tradition'; what is meant by this is the exemplary and binding practice of the Prophet Muḥammad and his companions in all areas of life. Of course, the *sunna* of the Prophet is also obligatory for the Shiites; some of his companions and successors, however, being opponents of the Shia, are not recognised as authorities.

5 M. Weber, *'Kirchen' und 'Sekte' in Nordamerika. Eine kirchen- und sozialpolitische Skizze*, 1906.

6 However, it is not possible to join these groups voluntarily; Druzes and Nuṣayrīs/ʿAlawīs can only be born into the community.

7 Cf. (pseudo-) al-Nāshi' al-Akbar (Jaʿfar ibn Ḥarb), *Kitāb al-Uṣūl*, ed. J. van Ess, *Frühe muʿtazilitische Häresiographie*, Beirut 1971, §21; Nawbakhtī, *Firaq al-Shīʿa*, ed. H. Ritter, *Die Sekten der Schiʿa*, Istanbul 1931, 2.

8 Nawbakhtī, *Firaq al-Shīʿa*, in the title and *passim*.

9 For example Ibn al-Nadīm, *Fihrist*, ed. Tajaddod, 238; the *madhāhib* of the Ismāʿīliyya; 276, l. 2: *madhāhib al-Shīʿa*. cf. also the title of the book by al-Jāḥiẓ, *Risālat fī bayān madhāhib al-Shīʿa*.

10 The Muhammadi Trust of Great Britain and Northern Ireland, 9 Mt. Pleasant Road, London NW10 3EG.

11 In: *Festschrift Caskel* (ed. E. Gräf), Leiden 1968, 63-95.

12 It was not until after the Prophet's death that Yathrib acquired the name Madīnat al-Nabī, City of the Prophet.

13 W. M. Watt (1956).

14 Cf. Shaykh al-Mufīd, *Kitāb al-Irshād*. The Book of Guidance, English translation by I. K. A. Howard, London 1981, 123f. for just one of the numerous Shiite reports of ʿAlī's designation. There is an enormous number of such reports.

15 References in Wensinck, *Concordance de la tradition musulmane* VII, 334 a; L. Veccia-Vaglieri, Art. Ghadīr Khum, EI².

16 In the year 352/964 by the Būyid Muʿizz al-Dawla Aḥmad in Baghdad, in 362/973 by the Fāṭimid al-Muʿizz in Cairo.

17 Dates given for ʿAlī's death do not agree; he is said to have died on the 1st, 19th and 21st Ramaḍān 40 (8th, 26th, and 28th January 661).

18 For the earliest Shiite literature see F. Sezgin, *GAS* I, 525 ff. One of the later collections of traditions about the Battle of the Camel is in French translation: M. Rouhani, *La victoire de Bassora ou Al-Jamal par Cheikh al Moufid (948-1022)*, Paris 1974.

19 *Aṣlaʿ* means 'bald', *anzaʿ* 'bald over the temples'. For subsequent meanings of the no-longer clearly definable name *Abū Turāb* (Father of Dust) see E. Kohlberg, 'Abū Turāb', *BSOAS* 41 (1978), 347-52.

20 The sword relic was, as shown by a description from Fāṭimid times (Qāḍī al-Nuʿmān, *al-Majālis wa 'l-musāyarāt*, Tunis 1978, 114), not in fact double-tipped, but rather double-edged (*shafratānī*); this also explains the name *Dhu 'l-Faqār*, 'the one with the backbone': the blade was strengthened in the middle by a pole (*ʿamūd*). It was only popular iconography which came up with the - technically nonsensical - two tips.

21 Shaykh al-Mufīd, *Kitāb al-Irshād* (trans. Howard), 285 f.; cf. above note 14.

22 *Oppositionsparteien*, 70f.

23 S. H. M. Jafri, *Origins and Early Development of Shiʿa Islam*, London 1979, 200-4; M. Momen, *An Introduction to Shiʿi Islam*, Oxford 1985, 31f.

24 Al-Ṭabarī, *Annales* III, 1407.

25 *Sīrat Ibn Ḥawshab*, cited by Qāḍī al-Nuʿmān, *Iftitāh al-daʿwa*, ed. by A. al-Qāḍī, Beirut 1970, 39; ed. F. al-Dashrāwī, Tunis 1975, 9.
26 *Ṣūrat al-arḍ*, ed. J. H. Kramers, Leiden 1938-1939, 243, l. 13ff.
27 Ibn al-Athīr, *Kāmil*, s. a. 369.
28 Maqrīzī, *Khiṭaṭ* (Būlāq edition) I, 427. M van Berchem, 'La chaire de la Mosquée d'Hébron et le martyrion de la tête de Ḥusain à Ascalon, *Festschrift E. Sachau* (ed. G. Weil), Berlin 1915, 298-310. H. Müller, *Studien zum persischen Passionsspiel*, Freiburg i. Br. 1966, 28-31.
29 On Merv: Muqaddasī, *Aḥsan al-taqāsīm*, *BGA* III, 46 and 333.
30 *Annales* II, 288ff.
31 A. de Gobineau, *Les religions et philosophies dans l'Asie Centrale*, Paris 1865, 367; R. Dozy, *Essai sur l'histoire de l'islamisme*, Leiden/Paris 1879, 220f.; A. Müller, *Der Islam im Morgen- und Abendland* I, Berlin 1885, 327.
32 J. Kohler, 'Das Recht der orientalischen Völker', *Die Kultur der Gegenwart*, II, Part VII/1, Berlin/Leipzig 1914, 131.
33 I. Goldziher, *Vorlesungen über den Islam*, Heidelberg ^{2}1925, 233.
34 *Annales* II, 598ff.
35 *Oppositionsparteien*, 79f.
36 Al-Ṭabarī, *Annales* II, 703f.
37 *Kitāb al-Aghānī* VII, 9f. Cf. also Kuthayyir ʿAzza in *Aghānī* VIII, 32.
38 Qummī, *Kitāb al-Maqālāt wa 'l-firaq*, ed. M. G. Mashkūr, Tehran 1963, 27-32, §§66f.
39 Mahdī prophesies are already found in the canonical Ḥadīth collections of the Sunnis, such as, for example, *Kitāb al-Mahdī* in the *Sunan* by Abū Dā'wūd (d. 275/888).
40 *The Dīwān of Sayyid al-Ḥimyarī*, ed. Shākir Hādī Shakar, Beirut 1966.
41 Translated in H. Halm, *Die islamische Gnosis*, 49ff.
42 Nawbakhtī, *Firaq*, 26 = Qummī, *Maqālāt*, 36.
43 Qummi, *Maqālāt*, 31f.; *Aghānī* VIII, 32.
44 The translation of one of these prayers is found in W. C. Chittik, *A Shiʿite Anthology*, Albany 1980, 113ff.
45 Al-Ṭabarī, *Annales* II, 1467. Ṭabarī's source is al-Madā'inī (d. 228/843).
46 Al-Ṭabarī, *Annales* II, 1467, l. 8f.; 1589, l. 2; 1987, l. 18f.; 1989, l. 1.
47 For the extension of right of succession to the throne to all the Banū Hāshim see T. Nagel, *Untersuchungen zur Entstehung des abbasidischen Kalifats*, Bonn 1972, 70ff.
48 Abū Mikhnaf, cited by al-Ṭabarī, *Annales* II, 1879ff. On page 1880, l. 2f. it is expressly stated that: 'The Banū Hāshim have more claim to government (*awlā bi 'l-amr*) than the Banū Marwān' (i.e. the Umayyads).
49 Three versions are transmitted - two anonymously and one according to al-Madā'inī - by al-Ṭabarī, *Annales* II, 1726f. of how Abū Muslim was sold by the Abbasids to the Kufan Shiite leader Bukayr ibn Māhān.
50 Al-Ṭabarī, *Annales* II, 1968, l. 14: a preacher in Abū Muslim's camp praises the merits of the Banū Hāshim and reviles the Banū Umayya; 1989, l. 3: *al-riḍā min ahl bayt rasūl Allāh*; cf. 1988, l. 3.

II

The Imāmiyya or Twelver Shia

THE SIXTH IMAM JA'FAR AL ṢĀDIQ (702-765) AND THE BEGINNINGS OF THE IMĀMIYYA

One of the prominent Alids to whom Abū Salama offered the Caliphate after the victorious rebel army entered Kūfa was the then senior representative of the Ḥusaynid line, al-Ḥusayn's great-grandson Ja'far (cf. genealogical tree p. 22), whom the Shiites honour with the title 'the upright one' (*al-Ṣādiq*). Probably born in the year 83/702[1] he lived in Medina like his father and grandfather before him and did not become involved in political intrigues. He turned down the Caliphate offered by the Kufans, and in 148/765, sixteen years after the Abbasid revolution, he died in Medina and was interred there in the Baqī' cemetery.[2]

In spite of his political inactivity the Ḥusaynid line once more came to the fore with Ja'far al-Ṣādiq. The vainly awaited appearance of the 'hidden' Muḥammad ibn al-Ḥanafiyya from Mount Raḍwā, the failure of the Zaydī and Kaysanite revolts and finally the Abbasid coup appear to have caused a change in orientation among the Iraqi Shiite communities. Ja'far al-Ṣādiq now appeared to many to be 'Alī's real heir. The Kaysanite poet al-Sayyid al-Ḥimyarī confessed in one of his verses that he had switched allegiance out of disappointment over the non-appearance of the expected Mahdī and had 'ja'farised' (*taja'fartu*).[3] More and more Shiites now recognised the Ḥusaynids as the true Imams, and the Kaysanite or 'Fourer' Shia were now being absorbed into the Imāmi Shia. (Even the extreme gnostic groups of 'the Exaggerators', who attributed divine qualities to the Imam, swung over to the Ḥusaynid line during this period; Ja'far al-Ṣādiq had to distance himself from the fanatics; see below p. 157)

Imāmī tradition regards it as a matter of fact that there has been an unbroken community gathered around the descendants of al-Ḥusayn from the time of the catastrophe at Karbalā'. However, whether Ja'far's father and grandfather were in fact recognised as Imams in their lifetime is questionable at the very least, and it is possible that they were only counted as the fifth and sixth Imams at a later date. In any case, the Imāmī community only began to emerge at all clearly at the time of Ja'far who, to judge from the effect he had, appears to have had a charismatic personality. In later tradition he is held to be the founder of Shiite law, and even today the Shia are occasionally described as the 'Ja'far school' (*al-madhhab al-ja'farī*) by analogy with the four Sunni schools of law. In fact, a large proportion of Shiite law – the Twelver as much as the Sevener – is based upon numerous sayings, rules and decisions made by Jaʿfar, although we cannot substantiate their genuineness in any detail.

Jaʿfar had close contact with the Shiite communities in Iraq, and since he showed no political aspirations the new Abbasid rulers did not trouble him. He even went to visit the second Abbasid Caliph al-Manṣūr in Iraq, presumably to pay him tribute, though the Shiites dispute that; and he is said to have taken the opportunity to visit ʿAlī's grave in Najaf thus giving it new recognition.[4]

Jaʿfar's death in the year 148/765 flung the Shiite community into disarray and conflict; clearly the Shia had not yet found a watertight model which would regulate succession to the Imamate. Later Shiite heresies report half a dozen differing views regarding Jaʿfar's rightful successor.[5] This confusion probably stems from the fact that Jaʿfar's son Ismāʿīl, whom Jaʿfar had apparently designated himself, died before his father (at a later date the 'Ismāʿīli' or Sevener Shia were to trace their claims to him). Jaʿfar's eldest son ʿAbdallāh al-Afṭaḥ (the broad-headed) died just a few months after his father without leaving any sons himself (cf. genealogical tree p. 32).

According to the testimony of the Imāmī religious books a number of solutions were toyed with, which in fact, served more often as models for new schisms and groupings during the formative stage of the Shia. The notion of the 'absent' or 'hidden' (*ghā'ib*) Imam rivalled that of the present living Imam: some expected the return of the hidden Jaʿfar himself, others the return of his deceased son Ismāʿīl while yet others adhered to the living descendants of Ismāʿīl or to Jaʿfar's eldest son ʿAbdallāh al-Afṭaḥ. After the latter's death, the main body of the Shia appears to have rallied around his younger brother Mūsā. In fact two schools of thought survived for a long time side by side. The supporters of the one considered ʿAbdallāh al-Afṭaḥ to be the seventh Imam and his brother Mūsā to be the eighth (the *Afṭaḥiyya* or *Fuṭḥiyya*), while the others saw in Mūsā the direct successor of Jaʿfar al-Ṣādiq and excluded al-Afṭaḥ from the Imāmī line of succession. The latter group initially formulated the doctrine that with the single exception of al-Ḥasan and al-Ḥusayn the Imamate should only be passed from father to son, never from brother to brother: 'After the two Ḥasans two brothers will never hold the Imamate' (*inna 'l-imāmata lā takūnu fī akhawayni baʿda 'l-Ḥasanayn*).[6] This doctrine was to be embraced as the official teaching of the Twelver and Sevener Shia; the opposing view of the Afṭaḥiyya, however, enjoyed support for a long time and, after the death of the eighth and then again the eleventh Imam, gained a passing currency once more when in each case a brother of the deceased Imam was proclaimed successor by a group of supporters.

Primary sources in translation

M. J. Mashkur (trans.), 'An-Nawbahti. Les sectes î'ites', *RHR* 154 (1958), 93-5; 146 58. I. K. A. Howard (trans.), Shaykh al Mufīd, *Kitāb al-Irshād*, 393 ff. and 408 ff. W. C. Chittik, *A Shi'ite Anthology*, Albany 1980, 40 ff. (Extracts from *Biḥār al-anwār* by Majlisī about the fifth and sixth Imams).

Secondary sources

W. M. Watt, 'Sidelights on Early Imamate Doctrine. 2. The Fuṭ'ḥiyya or Aftahiyya', *SI* 31 (1970), 293 ff. T. Fahd, 'Ğa'far as-sadiq et la tradition scientifique arabe', in: *Le Shī'isme imâmate. Colloque de Strasbourg* (6-9 May 1968), Paris 1970, 131-41. M. G. S. Hodgson, Art. Dja'far al-Ṣādiḳ, EI².

THE SEVENTH IMAM MŪSĀ AL-KĀẒIM (745-799) AND THE WĀQIFITES

Ja'far al-Ṣādiq was the last Imam to die in Medina and to be buried there in the Baqī' cemetery. All subsequent Imams died in Iraq in Abbasid custody, and Imāmī tradition assumes that all were poisoned at the Caliph's bidding. The growing community which in Iraq mainly rallied around the Ḥusaynid line appears to have disturbed the Abbasids to such an extent that they brought all potential pretenders to the throne to court as a precautionary measure, and kept them there under prison-like surveillance.

The first to meet this fate was Ja'far's son Mūsā (b. 128/745).[7] The Caliph Hārūn al-Rashīd took him with him to Iraq in the year 177/793 after his pilgrimage, and held him in custody in Baṣra and then in Baghdad. Even in the new capital, which soon surpassed the old Iraqi metropolises al-Madā'in (Ctesiphon) and Kūfa in size and significance, there was a Shiite community from very early on, which presumably continued to expand with the enforced arrest of the seventh Imam. Even in court circles there were Shiites who occasionally managed to attain influential positions. A certain 'Alī ibn Yaqṭīn, the son of an earlier Abbasid propagandist from Kūfa, held high offices under the Caliphs al-Mahdī, al-Hādī and Hārūn al-Rashīd, even though he was a devoted follower of the sixth and seventh Imams; and the Imam Mūsā himself is said to have encouraged him to use his influential position to protect the Shiites: 'God has friends with the ruler through whom he protects his friends.'[8]

The Imam Mūsā, also named *al-Kāẓim* ('the reserved one', 'the one who is shrouded in silence', 'the self-controlled one'), died in 183/799, supposedly poisoned at Hārūn al-Rashīd's behest. He was buried in the cemetery for Arab aristocracy in north Baghdad, and his grave and that

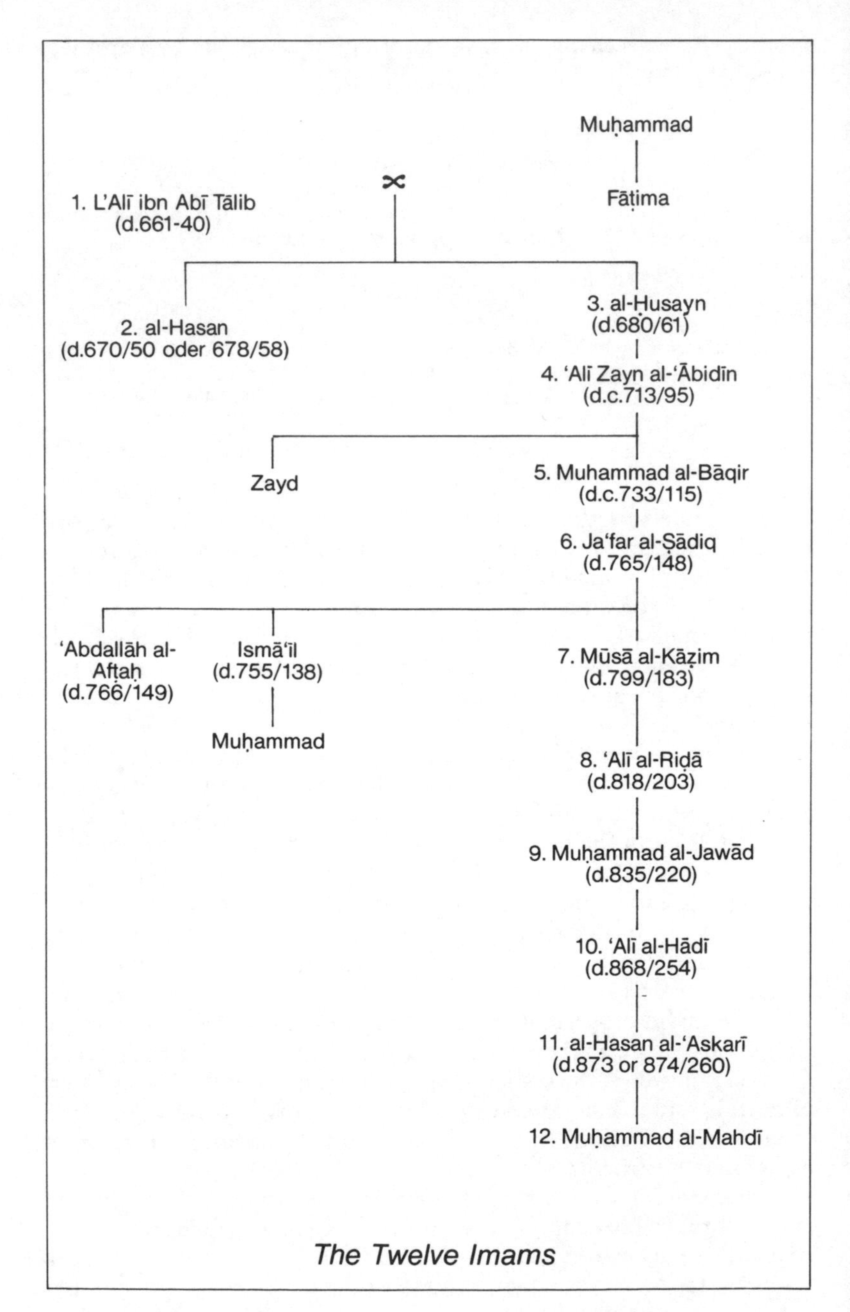

The Twelve Imams

of his grandson continue to be visited by the Shiites up to the present day. The shrine of 'the two Kāẓims' (*al-Kāẓimayn*, today al-Kāẓimiyya) is one of the largest Shiite centres of pilgrimage in Iraq.

The death of the seventh Imam led to the emergence of a separate branch of the Shia, in whose teachings certain essential characteristics of the later Twelver Shia were developed. Those Shiites who believed that Mūsā al-Kāẓim had not died but was only hidden, and awaited his return as Mahdī, were called *al-wāqifa* ('the ones who remain still') by their opponents because they let the succession of Imams end with him and contested any transfer of the Imamate to his son. Several Wāqifites, mainly Kufans, defended the 'occultation' (*ghayba*) of the seventh Imam in special documents of which only the titles are still extant.[9] The youngest of these authors, al-Ḥasan ibn Muḥammad ibn Samā'a al-Kūfī, died in 263/876-7. Towards the end of the 3rd/9th century the Wāqifiyya, the earliest instance of a 'Sevener' Shia, appears to have merged with the Twelver Shia which was now firmly establishing itself and which adopted the notion of the occultation (*ghayba*) of the last Imam from them.

Primary sources in translation

M. J. Mashkur (trans.), 'An-Nawbahti. Les sectes ī'ites', *RHR* 154 (1958), 158-63. I. K. A. Howard (trans.), Shaykh al-Mufīd, *Kitāb al-Irshād*, 436 ff.

Secondary source

W. M. Watt, 'Sidelights on Early Imamate Doctrine. 3. The Wāqifa, *SI* 31 (1970), 295 ff.

THE IMAMS UNDER THE GUARDIANSHIP OF THE ABBASIDS

The son of Mūsā al Kāẓim, the eighth Imam 'Alī al-Riḍā (the agreeable one, Pers. *Reżā*), lived in Medina after the deportation of his father until 201/816 when Caliph Ma'mūn, son of Hārūn al-Rashīd, had him taken to his residence in eastern Iranian Merv. There, 'Alī – who was in his early fifties – was surprisingly proclaimed successor to the throne and married to one of the Caliph's daughters; the black banners of the Abbasids were replaced by green – the colour of the House of the Prophet. There has been much speculation about al-Ma'mūn's motives, but the problem can be disregarded here because the episode had no real significance for the development of the Shia themselves. When the princes who had been excluded from the succession revolted in Baghdad, the Caliph prepared to march west; 'Alī al-Riḍā, who accompanied him, died on the way at Ṭūs, at the age of fifty-five (203/818). That the Caliph may have killed him is not only claimed by the

Shia but is also believed by a number of historians; it is, of course, not provable. The Caliph buried ʿAlī al-Riḍā beside the grave of his own father, Hārūn al-Rashīd, near Ṭūs. Like all Imams' graves the 'martyr's shrine' (*mashhad*) of ʿAlī al-Riḍā soon became a place of pilgrimage for the Shiites, and Mashhad, the town which arose around the sanctuary, was soon to surpass the older Ṭūs.

Al-Ma'mūn also attempted to develop close ties between al-Riḍā's seven-year-old son, Muḥammad *al-Jawād* (the liberal one) or *al-Taqī* (the God-fearer) and the ruling dynasty, giving him one of his daughters in marriage and keeping him at court in Baghdad. Eight years later al-Jawād was allowed to return with his family to Medina, but in 200/835 the Caliph al-Muʿtaṣim, the brother and successor of al-Ma'mūn, fetched him (now aged twenty-four) back to Baghdad. He died there in the same year and was interred beside his grandfather Mūsā al-Kāẓim (*al-Kāẓimayn* = the two Kāẓims).

Al-Jawād left a small son called ʿAlī (b. 212/827 or 214/829) who was brought from Medina to the new Caliphal residence Sāmarrā on the Tigris (between Baghdad and Takrīt) by the Caliph al-Mutawakkil in 233/848.[10] The tenth Imam died there in 254/868 and was buried beside his house. He is usually called *al-Hādī* (the guide to what is right) by the Shiites and also *al-Naqī* (the excellent one). His oppressor, the Caliph al-Mutawakkil, is particularly hated by the Shiites because he destroyed al-Ḥusayn's tomb at Karbalā' in 236/850 in order to stop the Shiite pilgrimages.

The eleventh Imam, al-Hādī's son al-Ḥasan (b. circa 231/845) was nicknamed *al-ʿAskarī* because he had been forced to lived in the Caliph's army camp (*ʿaskār*) in Sāmarrā; like the graves of the other Imams the shrine of 'the two ʿAskarīs' (*al- ʿAskariyyayn*) in Sāmarrā is an object of Shiite pilgrimages to the present day.

Primary sources in translation

M. J. Mashkur (trans.), 'An-Nawbahti. Les sectes îʿites', *RHR* 154 (1958), 163-72; 146-58. I. K. A. Howard (trans.), Shaykh al-Mufīd, *Kitāb al-Irshād*, 461-523. W. C. Chittik, *A Shiʿite Anthology*, Albany 1980, 43-51 (from *Biḥār al-anwār* by Majlisī).

Secondary sources

F. Gabrieli, *Al-Ma'mūn e gli ʿAlidi*, Leipzig 1929 (with the text of the proclamation document for al-Riḍā, 38-45). D. Sourdel, 'La politique religieuse du caliphe ʿabbaside al-Ma'mūn', *REI* 30 (1962), 27-48. B. Lewis, Art. ʿAlī ar-Riḍā, EI². H. Halm, Art. ʿAskarī, Encycl. Iran.

THE 'LESSER OCCULTATION' OF THE TWELFTH IMAM AND THE PERIOD OF THE FOUR 'AMBASSADORS' (874-941)

When the eleventh Imam al-Ḥasan al-ʿAskarī died in Sāmarrā on 1st or 8th Rabiʿ I 260[11] (25th December 873 or 1st January 874) at the age of twenty-eight he left no son. This interruption in the line of Imams plunged the Imāmī Shia into a serious crisis. Just as with the death of the sixth Imam, Jaʿfar al-Ṣadiq, this resulted in a series of differing opinions regarding succession in the Imamate. Shiite religious books list a dozen or so rival groups, and coin a concept of their own for this phase in Shiite history: *al-ḥayra,* the confusion. As in similar previous situations the deceased Imam was considered by some supporters to be simply in 'occultation' and they awaited his return as Mahdī; others tranferred the Imamate to al-ʿAskarī's surviving brother Jaʿfar, who had appropriated the late Imam's estate. What finally prevailed, however, was the supposition that the eleventh Imam had in fact left behind a son, a child called Muḥammad who had been hidden from the Caliph's grasp by his father out of caution (*taqiyya*) and had been seen by none except a few trusted acquaintances.[12] Shiite tradition gives the year of his birth as 255/869, so he would have been five years old at the time of his father's death. Several witnesses are cited who claimed to have seen the twelfth Imam at his birth, as a small child or as a youthful pilgrim in Mecca or Medina.[13]

After the death of his father the twelfth Imam was 'absent' (*ghā'ib*) and concealed somewhere. On the other hand he had not been removed from the earth altogether, since according to Imāmī interpretation the world could not survive for one moment without the presence of an Imam. The legend that he disappeared into the ice-house (Pers. *sirdāb*) of his father's house does not yet appear in the earliest Imāmī sources; it was not until the beginning of the 13th century (606/1209) that the cave beneath the mosque at the shrine of the *ʿAskariyyayn* in Sāmarrā became a place of pilgrimage. The pilgrim enters the room (*ḥujrat al-ghayba*) through the 'gate of disappearance' (*bāb al-ghayba*); in the corner of the room the well (*bi'r al-ghayba*) is shown into which the Imam is said to have disappeared.[14]

At first it seems to have been accepted that the Imam would head his community in the immediate future, and that further Imams would succeed him. It was certainly not yet settled that the twelfth Imam would also be the last, and that his occultation (*ghayba*) would last longer than a natural human lifetime. However, during the course of the 4th/10th century it became more urgently necessary that the ever longer period of absence should be plausibly explained to doubting and opposing fellow believers, and for this purpose the earliest *ghayba* books (see below p. 41) list as precedents a number of mythical 'long livers' (*muʿammarūn*) who were supposed to demonstrate that a longer than average lifespan was certainly nothing out of the ordinary.

The occultation of the twelfth Imam presented the Shia with a difficult question: namely, who should lead the community until the return of the Imam-Mahdī? It appears at first that associates of the deceased eleventh Imam continued to collect and administer fixed taxes from the believers. One of them, Abū ʿAmr al-ʿAmrī, was called the 'butter dealer' (*al-Sammān*) because he carried the money collected from Iraqi communities to Sāmarrā hidden in a butter sack. Written petitions from the believers would be answered by the Imam's confidants in the form of written decrees (*tawqīʿ*) which would be interpreted or passed off as the answers of the Hidden Imam. Those who mediated between the believers and the Imam were called 'ambassadors' or 'mediators' (*sufarā'*, sing. *safīr*) or even 'plenipotentiaries' or 'trustees' (*wukalā'*, sing. *wakīl*) in the oldest Imāmī sources. Originally it appears that several such contact people were known;[15] only later was a list of four successive *safīrs* canonised.

The community organisation of the 'Twelvers' does not develop reasonably clear contours until 900, at a time when the capital of the empire, Baghdad, was superseding Kūfa which became less and less significant even as the centre of Shiism. In the year 279/892 the Caliph al-Muʿtaḍid finally abandoned the palace town of Sāmarrā, where the last Imams had spent their final days and the Caliph's court returned to Baghdad after almost sixty years. Meanwhile there were Shiites in a few highly placed official families, and thus the Shia were able to count on influential patrons even at court and in the administration. A significant role was played in particular by the extended Persian Nawbakhtī family whose forefather Nawbakht had been the court astrologer of the second Abbasid Caliph al-Manṣūr. In the 4th/10th century several Nawbakhtīs served as state secretaries (*kuttāb*, sing. *kātib*) in the offices (*dīwāns*) of the empire's central administration in Baghdad. Under al-Muqtadir, the last independent Caliph in Baghdad (295-320/903-932), the Shiite secretary ʿAlī ibn Muḥammad ibn al-Furāt held the office of vizier three times; in 325/937 under the Caliph al-Raḍī, a Nawbakhtī, al-Ḥusayn ibn ʿAlī, was appointed vizier.

In the circles of the Baghdadī Nawbakhtīs the doctrine regarding the representation of the Hidden Imam by an 'ambassador' (*safīr*) appears to have taken the form which is still valid today. According to Shiite tradition the believers communicated with the Imam through four *safīrs* who succeeded one another without a break from the time of the Imam's disappearance. The Shiites considered the first of these *safīrs* to be the above mentioned 'butter dealer', Abū 'Amr 'Uthmān ibn Sa'īd al-'Amrī, an old associate of the tenth and eleventh Imams who was succeeded by his son Abū Ja'far Muḥammad al-'Amrī (d. 305/917). The third *safīr* was a Nawbakhtī, Abu 'l-Qāsim al-Ḥusayn ibn Rawḥ al-Qummī, who, before his death in 326/938, designated a certain Abu 'l-Ḥusayn 'Alī ibn Muḥammad al-Sāmarrī (probably more correctly al-Simmarī[16]) as his successor. Shiite tradition about the activities of these four *safīrs* has generally been accepted up to the present time without further examination, but it is probably unhistorical. A more recent study has shown that Ibn Rawḥ al-Nawbakhtī, the 'third' *safīr*, was the first actually to claim to be the sole authorised agent of the Hidden Imam, and thus to be the head of the Shia until his return.[17] It can be demonstrated that the notion that the Imam is represented by a single *safīr* was propagated by Nawbakhtī's Baghdadī circle and it was presumably also invented there; the two supposed predecessors of Ibn Rawḥ al-Nawbakhtī, the two 'Amrīs, were probably promoted to the rank of *safīr* posthumously in order to substantiate continuity of the office from the time of the *ghayba* of the Imam.

From time to time Ibn Rawḥ al-Nawbakhtī had to operate underground, and after the downfall and execution of his patron and protector, the vizier Ibn al-Furāt (312/924), he spent a considerable time in prison. During his detention his acquaintance 'Alī ibn Muḥammad al-Shalmaghānī attempted to usurp leadership of the Shiite community. Al-Shalmaghānī, who had very self-willed doctrines, was the last of the great heretics of the early Shia.[18] On his deathbed in 326/938 al-Nawbakhtī designated 'Alī ibn Muḥammad al-Sāmarrī/Simmarī as his successor; this 'fourth' *safīr*, who only held office for three years – he died in 329/941 – is regarded by the Shiites as the last person to have corresponded with the Hidden Imam.

Primary sources in translation

M. J. Mashkur (trans.), 'An-Nawbahti. Les sectes ī'ites', *RHR* 155 (1959), 63-78.
I. K. A. Howard (trans.), Shaykh al-Mufīd, *Kitāb al-Irshād*, 534 ff.

Secondary sources

A. Iqbāl, *Khāndān-e Nawbakhtī*, Tehran 1311/1933. L. Massignon, 'Les origines shī'ites de la famille vizirale des Banu'l-Furat', *Mélanges Gaudefroy-Demombynes*, Cairo 1935-1945, 25-9 (reprinted in Massignon, *Opera Minora*, Beirut 1963, I, 484 ff.). J. Ali, 'Die beiden ersten Safīre des Zwölften Imams', *Der Islam* 25 (1939), 197-227. E. Kohlberg, 'From Imāmiyya to Ithnā-'Ashariyya', *BSOAS* 39 (1976), 521-43. J. M. Hussain, *The Occultation of the Twelfth Imam. A Historical Background*, London 1982. (This book published by the

Muhammadi Trust can be regarded as an official portrayal of today's Twelver Shia doctrine.) V. Klemm, 'Die vier *sufarā'* des Zwölften Imam. Zur formativen Periode der Zwölfer īa', *WdO* 15 (1984), 126-43.

THE 'GREATER OCCULTATION' (941) AND THE AWAITED RETURN OF THE MAHDĪ-QĀ'IM

The claim of Ibn Rawḥ al-Nawbakhtī and his Baghdadi circle to represent the twelfth Imam during his absence was apparently not generally recognised and could not be enforced, and soon after the death of the 'fourth' *safīr* ʿAlī ibn Muḥammad al-Sāmarrī/Simmarī in the year 329/941 the conception of an 'ambassadorial' office (*sifāra*) was waived. Although the Twelver Shia canonised the line of the four *safīrs* it was not continued, and that heralded the end of the first attempt to institutionalise regular representation of the Hidden Imam and to give the Shia a leader.

According to Shiite tradition it was the Hidden Imam himself who, in view of increasing tyranny and oppression in the world, cut off the last link with his community in order to retreat into 'total occultation' (*al-ghayba al-tāmma)*. In a letter delivered to the fourth *safīr*, the text of which has been handed down orally, he instructed him six days before his death to designate no successor; anyone who claimed in the future to have met the Hidden Imam was a fraud.[19]

From the year 329/941 the twelfth Imam has therefore been living in the 'greater' occultation (*al-ghayba al-kubrā)*. At his future reappearance he will help the Shiites defeat all their adversaries, for God promised Moses: 'My righteous slaves will inherit the earth.' (Quran 21, 105). The Shiites supplement this promise, which they relate to themselves, with a saying of the Prophet Muḥammad: 'Day and night will not end before God has sent a man forth from my house who bears the same name as I. He will fill the world with justice and equity just as it was filled with oppression and tyranny before.'[20] According to this tradition the twelfth Imam and the future Mahdī was called Muḥammad like the Prophet. He is described as a 'young man of medium stature with an attractive face and beautiful hair which falls to his shoulders; a light radiates from his face; his hair and beard are black.'[21] According to usual terminology he is the 'awaited one' (*al-muntaẓar)*, the 'rightly-guided one' (*al-mahdī)*, the 'one who cares about justice' (*al-qā'im bi 'l-ḥaqq)*, or abbreviated to *al-Qā'im*, which then also means 'the one who arises, the ariser'. For reasons of caution (*taqiyya)* in times of persecution code names such as 'the creditor' (*al-gharīm)* are used because the Mahdī would one day demand back the loan – leadership of the Islamic *umma*. In contrast to earlier Imams who were passive and peaceful he would be 'the one with the sword' (*sāḥib al-sayf*). The appearance (*qiyām*) of the Mahdī-Qā'im will be preceded by terrible signs which are certified by countless sayings attributed to the earlier Imams: eclipses of the sun and moon, earthquakes and plagues of locusts will plunge the world into chaos; the sun will stay still or rise in the West, the Euphrates and Tigris will overflow their banks, fire will drop from the sky and devour Kūfa and Baghdad, the power of the non-believers will spread, false *mahdīs* will spring up at the ends of the earth and wage bloody battles against one another. But in the end storms will sweep the earth clean and remove all diseases from the true believers. Then the Mahdī will appear in the sanctuary of Mecca between the corner (*rukn*) of the Ka'ba and the 'place where Abraham stood' (*maqām Ibrāhīm*), one of the places known by every Meccan pilgrim, from where Abraham had once overlooked the sanctuary he had built. It is not known when that will happen; nevertheless Shiite tradition knows that it will be on the 10th Muḥarram, the day of al-Ḥusayn's martyrdom at Karbalā', and in a year with an even number. The Mahdī will set out from Mecca to Kūfa accompanied by angels. In Kūfa he will destroy the false mosques, slay the refractory unbelievers and preach to the remainder in a new mosque. He will connect the shrines of 'Alī and al-Ḥusayn in Najaf and Karbalā' with a canal, by the banks of which paradisaical life will burgeon.

Under the Mahdī's rule there will be paradise on earth; no one will have to give state-prescribed alms (*zakāt*) any more because there will no longer be people in need. The whole earth will be under the rightful rule of the Mahdī which will last for seven or nineteen years – each one of which will be as long as ten normal years. What will happen after that no one knows, but Shiite authors speculate that the resurrection of the dead and the Last Judgement will follow directly.[22]

Primary sources in translation

I. K. A. Howard (trans.), Shaykh al-Mufīd, *Kitāb al-Irshād*, 524 ff.

Secondary sources

J. M. Hussain, *The Occultation of the Twelfth Imam*, London 1982. A. A. Sachedina, *Islamic Messianism. The Idea of the Mahdi in Twelver Shī'ism*, Albany 1981.

THE BEGINNINGS OF IMĀMĪ LITERATURE AND THE FORMULATION OF THE 'TWELVER' DOCTRINE

The belief that the twelfth Imam went into 'occultation' in the year 260/873-4 gradually prevailed in the 4th/10th century against other Shiite Imāmī teachings, and it was not until then that the 'Imāmīs' became 'Twelvers' (*Ithnā'ashariyya).* The Wāqifites, the 'ones who stay still', had yet to be subdued and won over, because they were still awaiting the return of the seventh Imam Mūsā al-Kāẓim, just as the supporters of Ja'far were awaiting the brother of the eleventh Imam. In addition, the extremists and fanatics, the 'exaggerators' (*ghulāt),* had to be opposed as much as ever before, with their teachings of the divinity of the Imam and the transmigration of the soul. And then, too, a far more dangerous new rival was added to the old ones: after the death of the eleventh Imam in southern Iraq Ismā'īlī or Sevener Shia propaganda appeared which (probably looking back to an older conception of the Imamate) offered a new and arbitrary solution to the crisis in the Imamate and, now, began to run a successful mission, especially among the disappointed Imāmīs (see below p. 166). The earliest Twelver Shia literature has therefore a polemical and apologetic character; its typical genre developed out of conflict with other Shiite groups and to a lesser extent with the Sunnis.

The earliest Shiite writings were (as mentioned above, p. 11) monographs concerning the main events of the earliest history of the Shia whose orally reported details needed to be substantiated: the Battle of the Camel, the massacres at Nahrawān and Ṣiffīn, the drama at Karbalā', the revolt of al-Mukhtār. Authors and titles are generally known only from the bibliographical indices (*fihrist)* of the 10th and 11th centuries,[23] and only very few of the writings are extant – for example extensive citations from the works of the Kufan Abū Mikhnaf (d. 157/774) to which the historian al-Ṭabarī referred in his Universal History, or the monograph of the Kufan Naṣr ibn Muzāhim (d. 212/827) about the Battle of Ṣiffīn.[24] It was not until the second half of the 3rd/9th century that all the historical material was put together in universal histories. The oldest work of this type which Shiite tradition preserves in an unfalsified form is the Chronicle (*ta'rīkh)* of Ibn Wāḍiḥ al-Ya'qūbī, written in 279/891–2, which goes up to the year 258/872.[25] (It is disputed whether or not the historian al-Mas'ūdī (d. 346/957) whom the Shiites claim as one of their own and to whom a book about 'Alī's rightful successors is attributed can in fact be regarded as a Shiite author.[26])

After the founding of Baghdad in 145/762 we find a succession of authors in the circle of the Abbasid Caliph's court who made no secret of their Shiite convictions, and who made their views known even in the religio-political disputations arranged, for example, by the vizier Yaḥyā al-Barmakī (d. 190/805) under Hārūn al-Rashīd to discuss the principal theological problems raised by the rigorous monotheistic nature of Islam: for example, the question of the nature of God and the problem of human free will in view of divine predestination. One of the participants in the courtly debates was Hishām ibn al-Ḥakam (d. 199/814) who had moved to Baghdad from Kūfa and quite openly advocated Shiite positions, such as the primacy of ʿAlī over the first two Caliphs Abū Bakr and ʿUmar, or the damning of ʿAlī's opponents in the Battle of the Camel. However, neither Hishām ibn al-Ḥakam nor the other Baghdadi Shiites of his time – such as Muḥammad ibn ʿAlī ibn al-Nuʿmān, called the 'Devil of the Archway' (*shayṭān al-ṭāq)* by his opponents – can be assigned definitely to any one particular Shiite group. Their opponents describe them vaguely as 'Rafiḍites' (*rawāfiḍ*, sing. *rāfiḍ)*, i.e. 'Rejectors' or 'Abandoners', ostensibly because they had deserted Abū Bakr and ʿUmar or, according to another explanation, because they considered the revolt of Zayd ibn ʿAlī in Kufa in the year 122/740 to be unrighteous. Their partisanship for ʿAlī does not, however, appear to have kept the Rāfiḍites from seeking the favour of the Abbasid Caliphs.

The abusive term 'Rāfiḍites' for all Shiites (with the exception of the Zaydīs) seems to have continued throughout the whole of the 3rd/9th century, and was still occasionally being used later; but gradually the term *Imāmiyya* prevailed for non-Zaydī Shiites who followed the Husaynid Imams. The earliest works of Imāmī literature are the *ghayba* books of the Wāqifites, mentioned earlier, in which the occultation of the seventh Imam Mūsā al-Kāẓim (d. 183/799) is claimed and substantiated. This genre, of which we have several titles and authors but no original texts, provided a model for later Twelver Shia *ghayba* literature.

The doctrine of the *ghayba* of the twelfth Imam Muḥammad al-Mahdī had first of all to prevail against earlier Imāmī doctrines, in particular against the Wāqifites, the supporters of Jaʿfar and the newly emerging Ismāʿīlīs; at the same time the teachings of the Ḥusaynid Imamate had to be traced back to the events at Karbalāʾ while all other Imāmī teachings fell under condemnation as heretical deviations. This apologetic need was filled by systematic representations of 'splits' and 'schisms' (*firaq*, sing. *firqa)* which interpreted different groupings of the early Shia quite unhistorically as being each the result of defection from the line of the true Imams. A prototypical example of the genre appears to have been a book by the above-mentioned Rāfiḍite, Hishām ibn al-Hakam, about 'People's differences of opinion with regard to the Imamate' (*ikhtilāf al-nās fī 'l-imāma)* which, of course, could not yet have had any Twelver Shia trend; it served nevertheless as a model and source for the 'Schisms of the Shia' (*Firaq al-shīʿa)* by the Twelver al-Ḥasan ibn Mūsā al-Nawbakhtī (d. between 300 and 310/912 and 922), a nephew of the Shiite state secretary (*kātib)* Abū Sahl Ismāʿīl al-Nawbakhtī. The *Firaq* by al-Nawbakhtī is extant; so too the subsequent 'Book of Treatises and Schisms' (*Kitāb al-maqālāt wa 'l-firaq)* by Saʿd ibn ʿAbdallāh al-Qummī, which must have been written before 292/905. These two texts (the first of which has been translated into French) are our most important sources for the development of the Shia in its formative stage.[27]

This propagation of the correct Imāmī doctrine went hand in hand with the fight against the heretical deification of the Imams which the so-called 'exaggerators' (*ghulāt)* associated with gnostic ideas of the migration of the soul and redemption. The *ghulāt* not only taught this in their own circles but attributed it to the Imams themselves in their apocalyptic writings (see below p. 156 ff). Several authors of treatises with titles like 'Refutation of the Exaggerators' (*al-Radd ʿala 'l-ghulāt)* are known by name, including the above-mentioned al-Ḥasan ibn Mūsā al-Nawbakhtī and his uncle, the state secretary Abū Sahl Ismāʿīl, but no work of this genre has been preserved.[28]

The collection of orally transmitted sayings of the Imams – of course only those which confirmed orthodox doctrine – formed the essential prerequisite for the work of the apologists. Just as from the 3rd/9th century the Sunnis had felt the need to collect the countless sayings of the Prophet in circulation, to sift through them and to separate those which were presumably true from those which were false (e.g. the collection of Bukharī, d. 256/870), so the Shiites were now putting together the sayings of the Imams and arranging them in compendia according to subject. The earliest of these collections still being used is *al-Kāfi fī ʿilm al-dīn* 'The One who is Competent in Religious Science', by Muḥammad ibn Yaʿqūb al-Kulaynī (or al-Kulīnī). The author came from the Persian village Kulayn (Arabic variant Kulīn) between Rayy (near present-day Tehran) and Qumm, and it was in Qumm that he heard most of the Shiite transmitters whom he cited. Later he moved to Baghdad where he probably died in 329/940–1. Kulaynī's *Kāfī* – eight volumes in its modern edition[29] – arranges the sayings of the Imams by subject, and classification is made according to the requirements of religious practice and law. Volume I deals with creeds and the Imamate, volume II with belief and unbelief, volume III with ritual purity, burial, ritual prayer (*ṣalāt*) and alms tax (*zakāt*), volume IV with fasting and pilgrimage, volume V with Holy War, legal earnings and marriage, volume VI with slavery, divorce and so on. Apart from this collection, and a few no longer extant polemical pamphlets against the Ismāʿīlīs Kulaynī wrote a work – also lost – about those who transmit the sayings of the Imams. Just as in the Sunni study of traditions, so too in the Shiite critical interest was concerned far less with the content of individual traditions than with the reliability of informants and those who handed them down. The so-called 'men' (*rijāl*) books deal with the critique of traditions, or more precisely of transmitters, listing those who heard the individual Imams and their contemporaries and giving them critical ratings – 'reliable', 'weak', 'exaggerator'. The compiler of the earliest extant work of this type is Muḥammad ibn ʿUmar al-Kashshī (or Kishshī) from eastern Iranian Kish (Arab. Kash or Kish)[30] who died about 340/951.

All these works are written in Arabic, the language of Islamic scholarship – as indeed is the bulk of Shiite literature up to the present day – even though an increasing number of authors are Iranian. The origin of the authors can be seen from their names, as the Shia began to gain a foothold in the towns of the Iranian highlands; beside the Kufans and Baghdadis an increasing number of people appear from the west of Iran (Nihāwand, Hamadān, Qazvīn, Rayy) and from the east (Nīshāpūr, Ṭūs, Kish, Samarqand). The earliest Shia stronghold in Iran is Qumm (in deference to Persian pronunciation it is occasionally spelled Ghom in western publications) south of Rayy/Tehran. According to local tradition the town, which had probably been destroyed during the Islamic conquest, was resettled in the year 94/712–3 by Arabs of the Ashʿarī tribe who had had to leave Kūfa on account of their Shiite beliefs. Qumm is thus a branch of the original Shiite community of Kūfa, and it maintained its character as an Arab colony for a long time. At the end of the 4th/10th century the traveller and geographer Ibn Ḥawqal described the majority of the population as – though now indeed Persian speaking – Arabs of Shiite creed,[31] and yet another author of the 6th/12th century speaks of the 'Arabs from Qumm'.[32] When Fāṭima al-Maʿṣūma (the sinless one), the sister of the eighth Imam, travelled to Iran in the year 201/816–7 to search for her brother who was now successor to the throne, and then fell dangerously ill in Sāva she was taken to Qumm to die among her fellow-believers; with its golden dome the shrine over her grave dominates the townscape to the present day.

The name *al-Qummī* is given to a whole series of early Shiite traditionalists and authors, including a few prominent 'exaggerators' (*ghulāt*) ; but in about 255/869 the heretics were driven out of Qumm by the head of the dominant Ashʿarī tribe, Aḥmad ibn Muḥammad, and after that the town became a sanctuary of orthodox Imāmī tradition. The author of the heresiological book *al-Maqālāt wa'l-firaq*, Sa'd ibn 'Abdallāh (before 292/905) was a Qummī, and likewise the third *safīr* Ibn Rawḥ al-Nawbakhtī. Kulaynī, who came from near Qumm, collected most of the traditions for his *Kāfī* there. The most eminent Imāmī author of the 4th/10th century also came from Qumm: Muḥammad ibn 'Alī ibn Bābūya (Arabised: *Bābawayhī)* al-Qummī, also called *al-Ṣadūq* (the lover of truth), one of the fathers of the Imāmī Shia. He was born about 306/918 in Qumm, the son of a prominent Shiite scholar, and to collect traditions he travelled through the whole of Iran to Samarqand, made the pilgrimage to Mecca and spent time on several occasions in Baghdad. He died in Rayy in 381/991. Only a dozen works remain from the 300 or so ascribed to him, and these include his collection of traditions *man lā yaḥḍuruhu 'l-faqīh*, 'He who has no scholar in his proximity' (i.e. he can teach himself from this book). After Kulaynī's *Kāfī* this repeatedly published work[33] is the second of the 'four books' (*al-kutub al-arba'a)* of the canonised Imāmī collections of traditions. His 'Treatise on the articles of faith' (*risālat al-i'tiqādāt)* puts the doctrines of the Twelver Shia together for the first time[34] (the text is translated into English; see the list of works cited at the end of this chapter).

Ibn Bābūya's most important contribution towards the formulation of the doctrines of the Twelver Shia lies in his arguments and substantiations for the existence of the Hidden Imam. Twelver Shia *ghayba* treatises modelled on the Wāqifite example have been attested since the disappearance of the twelfth Imam,[35] but, for a long time ideas bound up with the *ghayba* remained vague or were doubted altogether. Muḥammad ibn Ibrāhīm ibn Abī Zaynab al-Nu'mānī complains in the introduction to his *Kitāb al-ghayba* (completed in 342/953), the oldest extant work of its type,[36] that most of his fellow-believers did not know who the Hidden Imam was, or even disputed his existence.[37] Ibn Bābūya made similar observations when he stopped in Nīshāpūr on his way back from a pilgrimage to the shrine of the Imam 'Alī al-Riḍā in Mash-had; there he was bombarded with questions about the Hidden Imam. That induced him to write a paper in defence of the teachings of *ghayba*, the full title of which was 'The perfection of religion and consummation of grace – confirmation of occultation and removal of confusion' (*Ikmāl al-dīn wa-itmām al-ni'ma fī ithbāt al-ghayba wa-kashf al-ḥayra)*.[38] It was in this treatise that the representation of the Hidden Imam by four successive *safīrs* was given its canonical form; nevertheless, throughout the whole of the 5th/11th century Imāmī authors still had to defend and substantiate the *ghayba* in special treatises.

As with the *ghayba* and the *sifāra*, the Twelver Shia conception of the organisation of the Imamate (*imāma*) was only finally formalised by the authors of the 4th/10th century. Under the Umayyad Caliphate the Iraqi Shiites had constantly attempted to bring an Alid or at least a Hāshimite to power by means of armed force. The Abbasid Revolution in fact did then lead to a Hāshimite Caliph, but Shiite hopes were none the less disappointed. Attempts to set up an Alid Imam at the head of the revived *umma* by means of a second revolution were continued mainly by the Zaydīs and the Ismāʿīlīs; the Imāmīs, on the other hand, soon relinquished all political aspirations and became a purely religious community. Certainly the attitude of the sixth Caliph Jaʿfar al-Ṣādiq, who had turned down the Caliphate, decisively influenced the quietist attitude of the Imāmiyya, and the Imāmīs soon became accustomed to the political impotence of their martyr Imams. After the death of the eleventh Imam hopes for a Shiite Caliphate were once and for all postponed until the ever more distant future, and took on increasingly eschatological characteristics. The figure of the Imam was endowed with superhuman attributes: his authority does not depend on political might but rather on a particular learned lore (*ʿilm)* through which God had distinguished him from other mortals, he does not owe his official authority to appointment by a group of men but rather to divine investiture, only he can transfer his charisma to his official successor by means of designation (*naṣṣ*). He is infallible in his decisions because by divine grace he is immune (*maʿṣūm)* from sinful wrong (*khaṭaʾ)* and from plain error (*ḍalāl)*. He is not only the head of the community but also the visible 'proof' (*ḥujja)* of the truth of divine revelation; without his presence the world would not exist for a single moment – and incidentally this is also an argument in favour of the necessary existence of the Hidden Imam. Just as the Twelfth Imam evaded his adversaries out of 'caution' (*taqiyya)* so the simple believer may conceal his loyalty to the True Imam and deny his affiliation to the Shia in times of threat or persecution; this dissimulation, which the Shiites are allowed under certain circumstances, is explained in the Quranic verse 16,106 where those who desert the true faith are threatened with God's anger 'save him who is forced thereto and whose heart is still content with the Faith.'

The Imamate theory of the Twelvers is principally based on transmitted sayings of the sixth Imam Jaʿfar al-Ṣādiq, but it is questionable whether it did in fact find its final form at his time and through him as is frequently assumed.[39] The Twelver collection of traditions did not appear until the 4th/10th century and it is difficult to judge the authenticity of the individual sayings of the Imams. It is more likely that the Imāmī conception of the nature of the Imamate only began to be shaped in the 3rd/9th century, and probably was not finally established until after the death of the eleventh Imam. The development has hardly been researched in detail. The Shiites may already have had the possibility of practising dissimilation (*taqiyya*) declared unobjectionable by their Imams, but *taqiyya* only became obligatory in Ibn Bābūya's works.[40] The idea of the Imam being God's 'proof' for mankind (*ḥujja ʿalā ʿabīdih*) already appears in the *Firaq* books at the end of the 3rd/9th century;[41] the belief that the *ḥujja* guarantees the continuity of the world simply through its presence is first substantiated by traditions in Kulaynī's *Kāfī* (d. 329/941).[42] Even the concept of *ʿiṣma* is only developed gradually at first. Ibn Bābūya (d. 381/991) still considered the Imam to be immune (*maʿṣūm*) only from sinful offences and not from mistakes (*sahw*) which anyone can make; his pupil, Shaykh al-Mufīd (d.413/1022), however, considered the Imam to be absolutely infallible.[43]

Primary sources in translation

Al-Nawbakhtī, *Firaq al-Shīʿa,* trans. M. J. Mashkur, 'Les sectes îʿites', *RHR* 153–5, 1958–1959. Al-Kulaynī, *Kāfī,* trans. M. H. Rizvi, I, Tehran 1978. Ibn Bābōye al-Qummī: *Kamāl al-dīn,* trans. E. Möller, *Beiträge zur Mahdi-Lehre des Islams. I. Ibn Babuje el Kummis Kitābu kamālid-dīni wa tamāmin-niʿmati fi ithbātil-raibati wa kaschfil-hairati. Erstes Stück,* Heidelberg 1901. *Risālat al-iʿtiqādāt,* trans. A. A. A. Fyzee, *A Shīʿite Creed. A Translation of Risālatu'l Iʿtiqādāt of Muḥammad b. ʿAlī Ibn Bābawayhi al-Qummī known as Shaykh Ṣadūq,* Oxford 1942 (Islamic Research Association Series, no. 9).

Secondary sources

A. A. A. Fyzee, 'The Creed of Ibn Bābawayhi', *Journal of the Bombay University,* 12 (1943), 70-86. W. M. Watt, 'The Rāfiḍites: A Preliminary Study', *Oriens* 16 (1963), 110–21; 'Sidelights on Early Imamate Doctrine. 1. The Early Imāmates and the Muʿtazilites', *SI* 31 (1970), 288–93. W. Madelung, 'Bemerkungen zur imamitischen Firaq-Literatur', *Der Islam* 43 (1967), 37–52; 'The Shiite and Kharijite Contribution to Pre-Ashʿarite Kalām', in: P. Moreweje (ed.), *Islamic Philosophical Theology,* Albany 1979, 120–39; Art. Imāma, ʿIṣma, EI[2]. G. Vajda, 'Le problème de la vision de Dieu (*ru'ya*) d'après quelques auteurs īʿites duodécimains', in: *Le shīʿisme imāmite, Colloque de Strasbourg,* Paris 1970, 31-54 (about Kulaynī and Ibn Bābūya). E. Kohlberg, 'From Imāmiyya to Ithnā-ʿAshariyya', *BSOAS* 39 (1979), 677 ff. M. Serdani, *Der verborgene Imam. Eine Untersuchung der chiliastischen Gedanken im schiitischen Islam nach Ibn Bābōye (d. 991): Kamāl ad-dīn wa-tamām al-niʿma,* Diss. Bochum 1979. F. Sezgin, *GAS* I, 525–52. T. Nagel, *Staat und Glaubensgemeinschaft im Islam,* Zurich/Munich 1981, I, 184–222.

THE SHIA UNDER THE PROTECTION OF THE BŪYIDS (945–1055)

From the beginning of the 4th/10th century the political power of the Baghdad Caliph had been increasingly eroded. Large sections of the empire were being ruled by dynasties of governors whose power was now only nominally granted by the Caliph. Thus the Iranian Sāmānids in Bukhara ruled over eastern Iran and Central Asia; a family of Arab chieftains, the Ḥamdānids, had been governing northern Mesopotamia (Mosul) since 293/905 with the support of Bedouin tribes and would soon also rule northern Syria (Aleppo); the whole of western Iran fell under the government of an Iranian condottiere by the name of Mardāwīj (315-323/927-935), and since 323/935 the Ikhshīd (E. Iran. *khshid* = Shah) Muḥammad ibn Ṭujj had been ruling over Egypt and southern Syria. However, while all these *de facto* independent regional dynasties continued to name the Baghdad Caliph as their nominal leader on their coins and in their benediction at the end of the Friday sermon (*khuṭba)*, in the Maghrib in the year 297/909 the Ismāʿīlī Fāṭimids had established a threateningly expanding rival Caliphate (see below p. 172 ff). In Spain, of course, the Abbasid Caliphate had not been recognised from the very beginning.

The political power of the Abbasid Caliphs was thus confined to Iraq, but even here it was by no means uncontested as was demonstrated by local governments in Baṣra and Khūzistān. Then there was the internal weakness of the Caliphate: second-generation princes had been disputing succession to the throne since 320/932. From 324/936 actual power in Baghdad lay with the commander-in-chief (*amīr al-umarā')* who for the first time now combined the highest military command with the highest civil authority. This office was disputed in unrelenting bloody fights by influential courtiers, army leaders, officials and provincial governors who attempted to play off the rival princes one against the other.

Under these circumstances the Būyid family came to power. Their forefather Būya (Pers. actually Boë; Arabised also as Buwayh) was a mercenary leader from Daylam, the mountain area to the south of the Caspian Sea which includes the valleys of Safīd Rūd and its river sources Shāh Rūd and Qizil Uzan. In the 4th/10th century Daylam played a rather similar role in the Islamic world to that of Switzerland since the 16th century in the West. The mountain valleys proved to be an inexhaustible source of soldiers, and companies of Daylamite mercenaries with their own leaders and officers served in Shīrāz and Iṣfahān as well as in Baghdad and Cairo. Islam had only established itself gradually at first in Daylam, and the Daylamites generally came to know about it through Shiite propagandists and missionaries. For a long time Daylam remained a stronghold for Zaydī and Ismāʿīlī Shiism.

The Būyids were also Shiites, and after their rise to power in western Iran and Baghdad the Shia found them to be powerful patrons and protectors. Būya and his sons ʿAlī, al-Ḥasan and Aḥmad grew up as mercenaries and officers in the service of the Daylamite condottiere Mardāwīj, who in 315/927 organised a semi-independent principality for himself in north-west Iran. So, too, from 320/932 the Būya sons had been seizing the towns of western Iran; since then the eldest, ʿAlī, controlled Fārs (the ancient Persis) from Shīrāz, from Iṣfahān his brother al-Ḥasan governed the north with Hamadān and Rayy, while the youngest, Aḥmad, meddled in the battles for power in Iraq. At the end of 334/945 the Caliph distinguished him with the title Commander-in-Chief and the honorific title *Muʿizz al-dawla* – 'he who helps the dynasty achieve honour'. Under Muʿizz al-Dawla (334–356/945–967) and his nephew Fanā-Khusraw *ʿAḍud al-Dawla* (Arm of the Dynasty), who combined ruling their western Iranian home heartlands with the office of commander-in-chief in Baghdad from 367/978, the family's power reached its apex. The role of the Caliph was confined to that of nominal state leader and representative of the unity of Islam. The reality of power was expressed in the fact that ʿAḍud al-Dawla, as the leading Islamic ruler, adopted the old Persian title of a 'king of kings' (*shāhānshāh*) from about 359/970 and even claimed to be descended from the pre-Islamic royal dynasty of the Sasanians.

The Būyids made no secret of their Shiite beliefs, but they never attempted to replace the Sunni Caliphate with an Alid Imam, and the great majority of their subjects in Iraq and Iran remained Sunni. Nevertheless, they did protect and encourage the Shiites and led the way towards the inner and outer consolidation of the Twelver Shia.

Like the majority of their Daylamite compatriots the Būyids were also originally Zaydīs, and in 347/958 Muʿizz al-Dawla set up one of Zayd's descendants as doyen or 'head' (*naqīb*) of the Alids.[44] Then, under the influence of his Imāmī vizier al-Muhallabī, he took the Twelvers under his special protection. They were very strongly represented in a few quarters in Baghdad – such as al-Karkh on the western bank south of the 'Round City' of al-Manṣūr and also in the quarter Bāb al-Ṭāq on the eastern bank – and street fights often took place between them and the Sunnis. The vizier sent his Daylamite mercenaries to suppress the unrest and exiled anti-Shiite ring-leaders and agitators. On the 10th Muḥarram 352/8th February 963 the Shiites were, for the first time, officially able to celebrate the remembrance of al-Ḥusayn's martyrdom at Karbalāʾ: 'On the 10th Muḥarram the *sūqs* were closed in Baghdad and business was suspended; the butchers did not slaughter and the cooks did not cook. People kept asking for a sip of water.[45] In the *sūqs* tents (*qibāb*) were erected and draped with felt covers; women went round with loose hair to strike their faces in the *sūqs*, and lamentations for the death of al-Ḥusayn sprang up.'[46] At the end of the same Hijrī year, on the 18th Dhu 'l-Ḥijja 352/7th January

964 the second main Shiite festival was openly celebrated in remembrance of the Prophet's designation of ʿAlī: 'On Wednesday night, 18th Dhu 'l-Ḥijja, on the day of Ghadīr Khumm, fires were lit, drums rolled and trumpets were blown; early in the morning people went to visit the graves of the Qurashites.'[47]

In particular the Būyids paid attention to protecting and adorning the graves of the Imams. Muʿizz al-Dawla was buried beside the graves of the seventh and ninth Imams, 'the two Kāẓims', to the north of Baghdad. An inscription which he set up in Persepolis in 363/974 showed ʿAḍud al-Dawla to be an admirer of the twelve Imams; in the year 369/979 after Bedouins from the Syrian desert had plundered the shrines of ʿAlī in Najaf and of al-Ḥusayn in Karbalā' he placed the sanctuaries under his personal protection and extended them.[48] ʿAlī's grave had only recently been definitively located in Najaf; however, as late as 332/944 al-Masʿūdī reproduced several contradictory versions, according to which ʿAlī had been buried in the mosque or the citadel at Kūfa, next to Fāṭima's grave in Medina or – since the camel with the coffin had gone astray in the desert – in the tribal area of the Ṭayyi'.[49] The grave which was supposedly in Najaf west of Kūfa was decorated for the first time with a domed pavillion (*chahār ṭāq*) by the Shiite Ḥamdānid of Mosul, Abu 'l-Hayjā' (d. 317/929);[50] from now on it was usual for distinguished Shiites to be interred in the vicinity of ʿAlī's shrine (*mashhad ʿAlī*). In 410/1011 the grave, which had been restored thanks to ʿAḍud al-Dawla after its devastation by the Bedouins in 369/979, was protected from further assault by a surrounding wall similar to al-Ḥusayn's grave at Karbalā'. Pilgrimages made by the Būyid rulers or high dignitaries to the Imams' graves were no rarity and the great vied with each other to endow the shrines with rich donations.

The descendants of ʿAlī and Fāṭima, who could lay claim to the title *sayyid* (lord), enjoyed special rights; they were supported by pensions (*rizq*) the allocation of which was the responsibility of their doyen or spokesman (*naqīb*). The latter had also to control the management and supervision of the Alid family trees (*shajara, silsila-nāma, ansāb al-ashrāf*) and to ensure that no unauthorised person obtained their privileges surreptitiously. The Alids (or Ṭālibids, after ʿAlī's father Abū Ṭālib) who were also recognisable by two braids of hair, originally received one gold dinar per year from the state treasury but since the Caliphate of Muʿtaḍid (279–289/892–902) they received a quarter of a dinar. Under the Būyids the social prestige of the Alids or *Sharīfs* (Arab. *sharīf* : nobleman, aristocrat) grew, their extended families had now become a sort of religious aristocracy, and they settled by the holy shrines in considerable numbers, above all in Mashhad, where they received the income arising from religious endowments (*awqāf*).[51] In the large towns and particularly in Baghdad, the office of the *naqīb*, who exercised his own jurisdiction over his peers, became a socially and politically influential position.[52]

Under the Būyids, however, there was as yet no question of Iraq or Iran becoming Shiite, the Sunni Caliph continued to be the offical head of Islam and a large majority of the population confessed Sunnism. Tensions and frictions between the two creeds were the order of the day. The invectives uttered by the Shiites against those Companions of the Prophet traditionally regarded as ʿAlī's opponents and betrayers during their processions on the Day of ʿĀshūrā' regularly led to bloody incidents and street fights; after unrest and a large fire in the Shiite quarter of al-Karkh in the year 362/973 there were said to be several thousand dead, and the government was forced to prohibit Shiite processions from time to time (for example in 382/992, in 392/1002 and again in 406/1015). In the year 443/1051 angry Sunnis even destroyed the shrines of the two Imams in al-Kāẓimayn and desecrated the graves of the Būyids buried there; it was only with difficulty that *the naqīb* of the Alids was able to restrain them from actually taking the bodies of the Imams out of the graves.[53]

Like the Būyids in Baghdad and western Iran, the Arab Ḥamdānids in Mosul and Aleppo also encouraged the Shiites. There was already talk of the Mosul Ḥamdānid Abu 'l-Hayjā' building a dome over ʿAlī's grave; in Aleppo, which was destined to remain a Shiite stronghold until the 6th/12th century, the Ḥamdānid Ṣayf al-Dawla patronised the Iṣfahānī Abu 'l-Faraj, a descendant of the last Umayyad Caliph Marwān, who not only made a significant contribution to Shiite martyrology (and genealogy) with his 'Murder of the Ṭālibis' (*Maqātil al-Ṭālibiyyīn*),[54] but also produced the most comprehensive collection of ancient Arabic poetry with his 'Book of Songs' (*Kitāb al-Aghānī*). He died in Aleppo in 365/967.

Bibliography

A. Mez, *Die Renaissance des Islams*, Heidelberg 1922 (Reprint Hildesheim 1968), Ch. 5: Die Schîʿah, 55-68. A. K. S. Lambton, 'An Account of the Tārīkhi Qumm,' *BSOAS* 12 (1948), 586–96 (Qumm in the 10th century). H. Busse, *Chalif und Grosskönig. Die Buyiden im Iraq (945-1055)*, Beirut 1969; esp. 405 ff.: Die islamischen Konfessionen. C. E. Bosworth, *The Ghaznavids. Their Empire in Afghanistan and Eastern Iran 994: 1040*, Beirut ²1973; esp. 194 f.: The Shīʿa: Sayyids and Ismāʿīlīs. – *The Cambridge History of Iran IV, The Period from the Arab Invasion to the Saljuqs*, Cambridge 1975.

THE BAGHDAD SCHOOL: RATIONALISTIC THEOLOGY (KALĀM) AND THE PRINCIPLES OF JURISPRUDENCE (UṢŪL AL-FIQH)

The century of the Būyids is the era of the Twelver Shia "church fathers". A number of authors in the 10th and 11th centuries produced the authoritative canonical literature which differentiated Imāmī doctrines from those of other Shiite creeds and defended them from attack by non-Shiites. In this process the western Iranian towns of Qumm and Rayy (which lay in the original sphere of Buyid influence and sufficiently far away from Baghdad) played the leading role at first. In Qumm, together with the collections of traditions by Kulaynī (d. 329/941) and Ibn Bābūya al-Qummī, traditional material was codified which has served up to the present day as thc basis for Shiitc law. In Rayy Ibn Babuya spent his last years as a guest and protégé of the Būyid Rukn al-Dawla.

Ibn Bābūya had, however, spent time in Baghdad on several occasions, and in the Caliphal capital he left behind a whole generation of scholars who received his works with critical acclaim and expanded on them. Fundamental impulses emanated from this Baghdadi school which steered the Imāmī Shia in a particular direction. It was the Baghdadis who produced the principles of jurisprudence (*uṣūl al-fiqh*) henceforth used by the Imāmīs, and assigned reason (*ʿaql*) a fundamental role. Their adoption of reasoned argumentation (*kalām*) in jurisprudence and theology paved the way for the future development of the Shia up to the time of the Islamic Republic of Āyatallāh Khumaynī.

The first exponent of the 'rationalist' Baghdad School was Muḥammad ibn Muḥammad ibn al-Nuʿmān al-Ḥārithī, also known as al-Shaykh al-Mufīd (the learned shaykh), a member of the Ḥārith clan from the Meccan Quraysh tribe. He worked in Baghdad in a small mosque to the west of the city,[55] and as a pupil of Ibn Bābūya he endeavoured to collect and sift through the transmitted sayings of the Imams which he put together in his book 'Book of Guidance' (*Kitāb al-irshād*).[56] He devoted a critical commentary to the Articles of Faith (*iʿtiqādāt*) by Ibn Bābūya.[57] In this work he mainly criticised overemphasis on the transmitted word and Ibn Bābūya's rejection of reasoning and drawing conclusions in all those instances where tradition had no precedent. Al-Mufīd declared himself emphatically in favour of the method of dialectic (*kalām:* literally speech), that is to say thinking, reasoned argument, presenting a case and making a judgement, even in matters of belief; and for this he accepted traditions based on a single transmitter only in a few exceptional cases, and had therefore to reject much traditional material. The method of *kalām* was developed by the Muʿtazilite theological and philosophical schools in 2nd/8th century Baṣra and Baghdad. From 218/833 until 232/847 the doctrines of the Muʿtazilites more or less constituted the state dogma of the Abbasid Caliphs, but they were then proscribed. The method of *kalām* together with its dogmas – in particular regarding human free-will and the temporal creation of the Quranic word – was also rejected by the Sunni legal schools which were now consolidating themselves. The Shiites, and in particular the Zaydīs and the Imāmīs, were later to inherit the Muʿtazilite *kalām*, and this inheritance was to give the Twelver Shia its own essential character; the successes of the Iranian Shia today cannot be understood without taking this into account.

Together with the method of *kalām* Shaykh al-Mufīd also adopted individual dogmas from the Muʿtazilites. He decidedly rejected, for example, Ibn Bābūya's view that God creates men's deeds – and therefore also their sins – through his omniscient prescience. Muʿtazilite denial of predestination and acceptance of free will, essential prerequisites for God's justice on the Last Day, were thus accepted and maintained by the Shia, in contrast to the Sunna.

In the discipline of the principles of jurisprudence (*uṣūl al-fiqh*) Shaykh al-Mufīd formulated essential positions of the Imāmiyya, but his main work in this field is no longer extant and is known only from later quotations.[58] Shiite jurisprudence developed later than that of the Sunnis, and it could therefore make use of the concepts defined, in particular, by al-Shāfiʿī (d. 204/819 in Cairo) and discuss them in critical detail. For example, the Sunni term for consensus (*ijmāʿ*) of the Islamic community as an obligatory norm was adopted by al-Mufīd in typical Shiite manner and redefined: the consensus of the community is only right when it corresponds to the opinion of the Imam, and thus the opinion of the Imam is always decisive and for all practical purposes replaces the consensus which can only ever be established with great difficulty. Deduction by analogy (*qiyās*), together with independent legal judgement based on individual deliberation (*ijtihād*), on the other hand, were rejected. This is a remarkable position to adopt in view of the fact that the principle of *ijtihād* was later to become the main instrument of the Shiite mullahs. The use of rational (*ʿaql*) methods was certainly permitted by al-Mufīd, but only as an aid to handle partially contradictory traditions which remained the sole means of gaining certain knowledge (*ʿilm*). The search for an obligatory text (*naṣṣ*) remains absolutely necessary and cannot be replaced by rational considerations.

In numerous writings – in particular in his 'Main Treatises' (*Awāʾil al-maqālāt*) [59] – Shaykh al-Mufīd discussed and analysed all possible non-Shiite authorities and authors: the Muʿtazilites whose points of view he frequently shared, the Zaydīs, the Sunni and Shiite traditionalists, the mystic al-Ḥallāj, the writer al-Jāḥiẓ and others. At the same time he corresponded by letter with Shiite communities in the east and the west, from Central Asian Khwārazm to Egypt. When he died in Baghdad in 413/1022 he was buried by the shrines of al-Kāẓimayn.

The two Mūsawīs, the brothers al-Sharīf al-Raḍī (the agreeable nobleman) and al-Sharīf al-Murtaḍā (the nobleman with whom one agrees), direct descendants of the seventh Imam Mūsā al-Kāẓim, are especially typical of the prominent position of the Shiites in Būyid Baghdad. Their father al-Ṭāhir al-Mūsawī had held the post of Alid spokesman (*naqīb).* During their father's lifetime the younger son al-Raḍī (Muḥammad ibn Ṭāhir) deputised for him. After his father's death the son inherited the office, which was then transferred to his brother al-Murtaḍā in 406/1015. As official spokesmen for the Baghdadi descendants of the Prophet the two Sharīfs were also highly regarded at the court of the Abbasid Caliph and were not without influence. When the Caliph al-Qādir and the Būyid Bahā' al-Dawla openly disputed the Alid descent of the Fāṭimid rival Caliph in Cairo in a manifesto in the year 402/1011, the two Sharīfs were among the signatories.[60]

The social position and political influence of Sharīf al-Raḍī are indicative of the trust that leading Shiites enjoyed in Baghdadi court circles. Al-Raḍī was several times distinguished by being appointed commander of the pilgrim caravan (*amīr al-ḥajj*), and control of the *maẓālim* – complaints against encroachments by the authorities – was entrusted to him as deputy to the Caliph, with whom he was linked by personal friendship. Although his Shiite commitment was not in doubt he did not hesitate to appear in the official black robe of the Abbasids. Al-Raḍī's interests lay more in literature than in theology or law. He compiled an anthology of transmitted sayings, speeches and letters attributed to ʿAlī which, from a philological and rhetorical point of view, he regarded as worthy to serve as a model of classical Arabic. His 'Way of Rhetoric' (*Nahj al-balāgha)* is still today considered by the Sunnis to be a standard for classical Arabic.[61] The authenticity of the pieces is, however, disputed; we know that at the time of the Caliph al-Ma'mūn (198-218/813-833) approximately 200 speeches and sermons attributed to ʿAlī were in circulation, and that this number soon doubled.

When Sharīf al-Raḍī died in 406/1015 his elder brother al-Murtaḍā ʿAlī ibn Ṭāhir (436/1044) succeeded him in the office of *naqīb* . Sharīf al-Murtaḍā had studied with his Shiite mentor al-Mufīd and also with several Muʿtazilite authorities, including the Qāḍī ʿAbd al-Jabbār of Rayy, and he was even more of a committed supporter of *kalām* than al-Mufīd. In him reason (*ʿaql*) certainly gained the upper hand over tradition (*naql*). Every transmitted saying of the Prophet or one of the Imams had to be subjected to the yardstick of reason; and if it contradicted reason this was seen as proof of its lack of authenticity. Renunciation of the use of proper reason by simply relying on the authority of others (*taqlīd*) would inevitably lead to unbelief. However, even reason had to move within boundaries set by tradition, and traditions which did not run counter to reason – with the exception of the *āḥād* (see above p. 51) – set the obligatory standard. Independent judgement (*ijtihād*) – in later times the main weapon of the Imāmī legal scholars – still played a secondary role in al-Murtaḍā's 'Access to the Principles of Law' (*al-Dharīʿa ilā uṣūl al-sharīʿa*),[62] as for example in cases where it is a question of fixing the direction of prayer (*qibla*), or even in juristic questions of detail such as property law for which (as, for example, inheritance law) there are no special rules embodied in the Quran.[63] Use of *ijtihād* was therefore limited to questions which were left open by revelation and tradition, and in accordance with the ideas of the time these were regarded as unimportant questions and side-issues. Shaykh al-Mufīd certainly cannot have suspected the far-reaching implications the (admittedly limited) adoption and use of this principle of independent legal judgement would have for the Shia in modern times.

Muḥammad ibn al-Ḥasan al-Ṭūsī (385-460/995-1067), one of the most significant authors not only of the Būyid era but also of the Twelver Shia in general, was a contemporary of the two Mūsawī Sharīfs. In the year 408/1017 he went to Baghdad from his home town, eastern Iranian Ṭūs (near present-day Mashhad), and became a pupil of Shaykh al-Mufīd (d. 1022) and Sharīf al-Murtaḍā (d. 1044). When his house was set on fire during one of the many anti-Shiite pogroms in the year 448/1056 he moved to the shrine at Najaf where he died in 460/1067 (according to others in 458/1065). His two main works, the 'Consideration of the Disputed Traditions' (*al-istibṣār fīmā ukhtulifa fīhi min al-akhbār*)[64] and the 'Appeal of Decisions' (*Tahdhīb al-aḥkām*),[65] together with *Kāfī* by Kulaynī and *Man lā yaḥḍuruhu 'l-faqīh* by Ibn Bābūya, constitute the 'Four Books' of the Shiites.

The output of Shaykh al-Ṭūsī and his teachers shows the main concern of the Shiites of the Būyid period. In the first place, it was necessary to separate genuine traditions from false; it was not only al-Ṭūsī's 'Disputed Traditions' which dealt with this task, but also the 'men' (*rijāl*) books in general, which distinguished reliable handers-down of the Imams' sayings from dubious ones.[66] This became all the more necessary once al-Ṭūsī – in contrast to his teacher al-Murtaḍā – took up the case of traditions transmitted by only one informant (*āḥād*), provided that the latter could definitely be classified as a member of the 'group which is right' (*al-ṭā'ifa al-muḥiqqa*) i.e. the Imāmiyya. On the secure basis of sanctified tradition now being established – and after considerable delay compared to similarly directed efforts by the Sunnis – systemisation of Shiite law and definition of its principles could be settled; Ṭūsī's 'Tool of the Principles' (*'Uddat al-uṣūl*)[67] laid the keystone. Although the 'Authority of the Community' (*Shaykh al-ṭā'ifa*), as al-Ṭūsī was called by the Shiites, emphasised the importance of tradition even more strongly than Sharīf al-Murtaḍā, and played down the role of reason, he did not reject the admissibility of reasoned argument and at least did not block the way for its later development. A century or so after his death the 'Book of Refutation' (*Kitāb al-naqd* see below p. 60) which appeared around 565/1170 acknowledged that the Shiite school of those who knew the 'fundamental principles' (*madhhab-i shī'a-yi uṣūliyya*) had prevailed against the purely traditionalist school.

One must not, however, lose sight of the purely theoretical character of Shiite law. It had been developed by private scholars and was used only, if at all, in the ritual of Imāmī communities. As long as the twelfth Imam remained in occultation tyranny and injustice would govern the world; only after his return as Mahdī would rightful order be established. Until that time it would be necessary to cope with the prevailing conditions; and the longer the *ghayba* lasted, the more important it would be to define the Shiites' relationship with unjust secular authority.

Even the Imāmī authors of the 5th/11th century found that they were still having to defend the doctrine of the *ghayba* of the twelfth Imam in special treatises, especially against internal Shiite opponents. Shaykh al-Mufīd was the first to seek logical rational arguments to explain the necessity of the Imam's disappearance,[68] his pupil al-Murtaḍā took the same approach.[69] Al-Murtaḍā, however, declares that groups with deviant doctrines on the Imamate – the Kaysānites and supporters of the *ghayba* of the sixth Imam Ja'far al-Ṣādiq (Nāwūsites)[70] or of the seventh Imam Mūsā (Wāqifites) – either disappeared during his time or were only to be found in very small numbers, which proved that their teaching was false.

The arguments with which Shaykh al-Mufīd, Sharīf al-Murtaḍā and even Shaykh al-Ṭūsī[71] sought to substantiate the *ghayba* of the twelfth Imam by rational argument (*dalīl 'aqlī*) stem from the old Mu'tazilite principles that God is just and that man is responsible for his own actions. Since man is fallible and consequently in need of guidance, divine grace (*luṭf*) cannot but grant mankind the benefit of rightful guidance at all times by an Imam who is immune (*maʿṣūm*) from sin and error.[72] Since the ruling Caliphs are notoriously sinful and fallible and act tyrannically, there must be a Hidden Imam; without the latter's existence mankind would be forsaken by God, man would indubitably go astray and could not be called to account by a just God. Sharīf al-Murtaḍā explains the continuation of the *ghayba* in terms of the perpetual tyranny of those who had forced the Imam into occultation. So long as usurpers reign and true believers continue to be persecuted the True Imam is prevented from exercising his rights and is threatened in life and limb; he not only may but must therefore remove himself from the clutches of the tyrannical false Imam. This is a remarkable argument from an author who went in and out of the Abbasid court.

The somewhat ambiguous position adopted by the two Sharīfs al-Raḍī and al-Murtaḍā at the Baghdad court forced the Shiites to theoretical consideration of the question how they should relate to the actual authorities during the *ghayba*. Were obedience and taxes owed to the Abbasid Caliph who was both an usurper and tyrant (*jā'ir*) ? Was it permissible to serve either him or his Būyid steward without being guilty of treason? In the 4th/10th century two Shiite writers raised the problem of the exercise of government (*ʿamal al-sulṭān*) in treatises which are no longer extant.[73] Later on Sharīf al-Murtaḍā addressed the problem in his own reasoning manner in a short work entitled 'The problems of working in the government'.[74] According to his interpretation, acceptance of office to serve a false (*mubṭil*) ruler, although in principle inadmissible, may be allowed under certain circumstances – for example under duress – and indeed is obligatory when the office enables the person to see that justice is done. The Biblical Joseph himself asked the tyrant Pharaoh to put him in charge of the granaries of the land (Quran 12,55). ʿAlī too was forced to take part in the electoral body which selected ʿUthmān as Caliph, even though such a body was illegal. Later ʿAlī caused himself to be elected although through his designation by the Prophet – and only through this – he had long been the intended successor anyway. Whoever, therefore, holds office under an illegitimate régime and holds it silently in the name and by order of the True (*muḥiqq*) Imam, as long as he acts in a recognisably just fashion he can also claim obedience. A saying by the sixth Imam Jaʿfar al-Ṣādiq considered the service of an illegitimate ruler to be just under one condition: 'Fulfilment of the needs of fellow-believers atones for collaboration with government.'[75]

Al-Murtaḍā's pupil Shaykh al-Ṭūsī is much more guarded on this question. Under certain conditions the service of an illegitimate ruler may be desirable, but it is never obligatory. On the other hand, the service of a ruler who recognises the true Imam and rules in his name according to the principles of Imāmī law is not only unobjectionable but necessary; such a provisional leader – the Būyids were in mind, of course – and the representative of the Hidden Imām-Mahdī is entitled to obedience from the Shiite brotherhood. It is thus by no means the case that – as is occasionally claimed – the Twelvers recognise no legitimate state authority whatsoever during the absence of the Imam. ʿAlī's instructions to his governor in Egypt, Mālik al-Ashtar, reported in *Nahj al-balāgha*, show how the Shiites imagined the just rule of a pious governor of the absent Imam, indicating a programme of ideal government and administration modelled on the Iranian 'mirrors for princes'.[76]

Legitimate government is, therefore, permissible in the Imam's absence, but it does require his explicit authorisation. But who can consider himself authorised, and which of the Hidden Imam's prerogatives may the authorised representative exercise? This question has concerned the Imamis again and again from the time of the *ghayba*; the history of the Twelver Shia could be written from the answers which have been given to this question up to the present day. In principle, the prerogatives of the Imam – applying corporal punishment (*ḥudūd*, sing. *ḥadd*) as laid down in the Quran, leading the Friday prayers, raising legal taxes, commanding Holy War (*jihād*) – are considered to be in abeyance (*sāqiṭ*, literally: invalid)[77] during the Imam's absence because they can only be exercised appropriately by an infallible (*maʿṣūm*) Imam. In fact, Shiite scholars (*ʿulamāʾ*) or legal experts (*fuqahāʾ*) have, in the course of time, appropriated these prerogatives one after another – a process which dragged on for centuries and only comes to an end in our own day. The beginnings of this development can be observed with the 'church fathers' of the Būyid period. Al-Kulaynī was already encouraging the Shiites not to subject themselves when in dispute to the judgement of the secular ruler – the Ṭāghūt, named after a idol mentioned in the Quran – or to the arbitration of the 'Judges of tyranny' (*quḍāt al-jawr*), but rather to call upon arbitrators from their own ranks.[78] Ibn Bābūya cites a saying by the twelfth Imam: 'Whenever new cases arise, turn to the transmitters of our (i.e. the Imams') words because they are my proof (*ḥujja*) for you and I am God's proof for them.'[79] Shaykh al-Mufīd conceded to the *ʿulamāʾ* the right to impose and carry out Quranic corporal punishment (*ḥudūd*).[80] The vicarious role of the *ʿulamāʾ* is already widely defined in theoretical terms by al-Ṭūsī, who allows the prerogatives of the Hidden Imam to be exercised by scholars in cases of necessity: 'The only one who is entitled to judge among the people and between disputing parties is he to whom the true rulers (the Imams) have given authority in this regard, and they (the Imams) have conferred this upon the jurists of their party (*shīʿa*) for the time when they are not in the position to exercise it.'[81] Here the future role of the learned class as the collective representative (*nā'ib al-ʿāmm)* of the Hidden Imam is already anticipated. Nevertheless, the scholars' exercise of the Imams' prerogatives continued to be in dispute for centuries, even in the 7th/13th century Muḥaqqiq al-Ḥillī (see below p. 67) regarded it as more correct that the Quranic *ḥadd* punishments were considered to be annulled during the Imam's absence.[82] It was not until the end of the 18th century that Shiite mullahs did in fact enforce the *ḥudūd* (see below p. 107). Whether the Friday prayers were valid during the *ghayba* and who could legitimately collect taxes during the Imam's absence were points of issue into the 16th century,[83] and the interpretation that scholars could declare Holy War vicariously for the Imam was not enforced until the 19th century (see below p. 107).

The writings of Shaykh al-Mufīd, Sharīf al-Murtaḍā and Shaykh al-Ṭūsī were a decisive influence on the Twelver Shia and pointed the way to their future development. How comprehensive the Imāmī literature was under the Būyids (and how much of it is now missing) is demonstrated by three large bibliographical works which appeared in the Būyid period, all three written by Shiites. In the year 377/987-8 the Baghdadi bookseller Ibn al-Nadīm – a Shiite, as shown by the terminology he uses – completed his famous index of authors and books (*fihrist*).[84] The work by Aḥmad ibn ʿAlī al-Najāshī (d. 450/1058) about Shiite traditionalists and writers is one of our most important sources for the bibliographies of prominent Shiites;[85] and the 'Index of Books of the Shia' (*fihrist kutub al-shīʿa*) by al-Ṭūsī (d. 460/1067) lists no fewer than 1,000 Shiite authors and their works.

Primary sources in translation

1. *Shaykh al-Mufīd:*
Kitāb al-Jamal, trans. M. Rouhani, *La victoire de Bassora ou Al-Jamal, par Cheikh al Moufid (948-102),* Paris 1974. *Awā'il al-maqālāt,* trans. (with detailed commentary) D. Sourdel, 'L'imamisme vu par le Cheikh al Mufīd', *REI* 40 (1972), 217-96. *Kitāb al-Irshād,* trans. I. K. A. Howard, *Kitāb al-Irshād. The Book of Guidance into the Lives of the Twelve Imams,* London 1981.
2. *Al-Sharīf al-Murtaḍā:*
Risālat al-ghayba, trans. A. A. Sachedina, 'A Treatise on the Occultation of the Twelfth Imamite Imam', *SI* 48 (1978), 109-24. *Mas'ala fī 'l-ʿamal maʿa 'l-ṣulṭān,* trans. W. Madelung, 'A Treatise of the Sharīf al-Murtaḍā on the Legality of Working for the Government', *BSOAS* 43 (1980), 18-31.
3. *Al-Sharīf al-Raḍī:*
Nahj al-balāgha, trans. Mufti Jafar Husain, *Nahjul Balagha. Sermons, Letters and Sayings of Imam ʿAli,* Qum 1395/1975 (Centre of Islamic Studies). ʿAlī's letter to Mālik al-Ashtar from *Nahj al-balāgha* is translated by W. C. Chittik, 'The Ruler and Society', in: Chittik, *A Shiʿite Anthology,* Albany 1980, 68-82.

Secondary sources

L. Veccia Vaglieri, 'Sul Nahġ al-balag'ah e sul su compilatore a -„arīf ar-Raḍī', *AION* 8 (1958), 1-46. J. Schacht, *The Origins of Muhammadan Jurisprudence*, Oxford 1950; *An Introduction to Islamic Law*, Oxford 1964. H. J. Kornrumpf, 'Untersuchungen zum Bild 'Alīs und des frühen Islams bei den Shiiten (according to Nahj al-Balāgha by Sharīf al-Raḍī)', *Der Islam* 45 (1969), 1-63 and 261-98. W. Madelung, 'Imamism and Mu'tazilite Theology', in: *Le Shī'isme imâmite, Colloque de Strasbourg*, Paris 1970, 13-30; 'Authority in Twelver Shiism in the Absence of the Imam', in: *La notion d'autorité au Moyen Age. Islam, Byzance, Occident, Colloques internationaux de la Napoule*, Paris 1982, 163-73. F. Gabrieli, 'Imamisme et littérature sous les Buyides', in: *Le Shī'isme imamite, Colloque de Strasbourg*, Paris 1970, 105-13. R. Brunschvig, 'Les *uṣûl al-fiqh* imamites à leur stade ancien (X[e] et XIe siècles) ibid, 201-13. H. Löschner, *Die dogmatischen Grundlagen des šī'itischen Rechts*, Cologne 1971. D. Sourdel, 'Les conceptions imamites au début du XIe siècle' d' après le Shaykh al-Mufīd, in: D. S. Richards (ed.), *Islamic Civilisation 950-1150*, Oxford 1973, 187-200. M. J. McDermott, *The Theology of al-Shaikh al-Mufīd (d. 413/1022)*, Diss. Chicago 1971, Beirut 1978. S. A. Arjomand, *The Shadow of God and the Hidden Imam. Religion, Political Order and Societal Change in Shi'ite Iran from the Beginnings to 1890*, Chicago/London 1984, 32-65: 'Sectarian Shi'ism within the Islamic Body Politic – Eighth/Second to the Thirteenth/Seventh Century'.

THE SULTANATE OF THE SELJUQS (1040-1194) AND THE SUNNI REACTION

The campaigns of the Arab conquerors across the Oxus (Amū Daryā) from around 50/670, the conquest of Bukhara (90/709) and Samarqand (92/711) and Arab advances towards Chāch (Tashkent) and Farghāna from 94/713 brought Islam into Central Asia and introduced Islam to the Turkic peoples. The only Turks to be found in the large towns of the Islamic heartlands in the subsequent three centuries were those imported as slaves, but from the beginning of the 5th/11th century Turkic nomadic tribes in north-east Iran began to put stronger pressure on the urbanised territories of Khurāsān. In the year 426/1035 the dam broke. Led by chiefs of the Seljuq tribe 10,000 horsemen of the Turkic Oghuz people (Arab: *al-Ghuzz*) crossed the Oxus in search of grazing areas south of the river. In 429/1037-1038 Seljuq's grandson Ṭughril seized the large eastern Iranian towns of Merv, Herat and Nīshāpūr, and in 431/1040 in order to legitimise his rule over the captured lands he sent a message of victory to the Caliph in Baghdad who honoured and acknowledged him with the title *al-sulṭān al-mu'aẓẓam* (the mighty ruler). After taking possession of western Iran in 447/December 1055 Sultan Ṭughril appeared at the head of his troops before the gates of Baghdad, and the Caliph al-Qā'im had no choice but to give way to superior force. Installed by the Caliph as 'King of the East and West' (*malik al-mashriq wa 'l-maghrib*) (449/1058) the Seljuq

Sultan now took the place of the Būyid King of Kings (*shāhānshāh*) and assumed the role of champion of Sunni orthodoxy, especially against the rival Fāṭimid Caliphate in Cairo. Under the first three Seljuq sultans, Ṭughril (d. 455/1063), Alp Arslān (455-465/1063-1072) and Malikshāh (465-485/1072-1092) a new Islamic empire emerged which stretched from Central Asia to northern Syria (conquest of Aleppo in 463/1071); and after Alp Arslān's victory over the Byzantine Emperor Romanus IV Diogenes at Manzikert (north of Lake Van) in August 1071 expanded it into central Anatolia.

Like all Central Asian Turks the Seljuqs were zealous Sunnis (of the Ḥanafite persuasion) and they owed their power mainly to the role assigned to them by the Caliph as champions against the superior and threatening Shia of the 4th/10th century. As early as 445/1053 – and therefore even before the capture of Baghdad – Ṭughril's vizier al-Kundurī had had the Shiites cursed from every pulpit in his Iranian realm. After the establishment of the empire, however, the Seljuq sultans and their viziers did at least manage to form a policy of tolerance towards the moderate Twelver Shiites (the Ismāʿīlīs, on the other hand, were regarded as partisans of the Egyptian Fāṭimids and thus as deadly enemies of the Baghdad Caliph; they could thus only operate conspiratorially in the realm of the Seljuqs). Malikshāh's vizier, Niẓām al-Mulk, himself a zealous (*Shāfiʿī*) Sunni, is even praised by Shiite writers for his advancement of the *sayyids* and the Imāmī scholars; yet in his 'Book of Politics' (*Siyāsetnāma*) he emphatically demanded the expulsion of supporters of the 'evil Iraqi doctrine' i.e. the Shiites, from all public offices.[87]

For the situation of the Shia under the rule of the Seljuqs we have an excellent source in the Persian 'Book of Refutation' (*Kitāb al-naqḍ*) which the Shiite ʿAbd al-Jalīl Qazvīnī Rāzī wrote sometime between 555/1160 and 565/1170 in order to repel the attacks of a fellow-believer who had recently apostasised to the Sunni faith.[88] Reflecting the origins of the author, the *Kitāb al-naqḍ* supplies particularly detailed information about north-west Iran where, besides the old Iraqi centres of Kūfa and Baghdad, the strongholds of the Twelver Shia now lay: Rayy, Varāmīn, Qazvīn, Āva (Āba), Qumm and Kāshān.[89] The Shiites were also represented very strongly in the areas south east of the Caspian Sea: Māzandarān with the towns of Sārī and Iram, Astarābād, Gurgān and Dihistān. There were, too, significant Shiite communities in the large eastern Iranian towns of Sabzavār, Nīshāpūr and Ṭūs. The shrine (*mashhad*) near Ṭūs of the eighth Imam ʿAlī al-Riḍā (Pers. *Reżā*) attracted numerous pilgrims even during the time of the Seljuqs, and according to an apocryphal saying of the Prophet transmitted by the Shiites a single visit (*ziyāra*) to the grave was equivalent to seventy pilgrimages to Mecca.[90] Every town of any size now had its own Alid spokesman (*naqīb*) who controlled the genealogical trees and distributed the pensions (*idrārāt:* disbursements) bequeathed by pious donors. The graves of the *sayyids* or descendants of the Imam even became increasingly popular among the Sunni population as local places of pilgrimage;[91] in Hamadān, for example, the great mausoleum of an anonymous Alid, Gunbad-i ʿAlawiyyin, has been preserved from the time of the Seljuqs. In Rayy near Tehran the mausoleum of Sayyid ʿAbd al-ʿAẓīm still dominates the town today, as does the dome of the tomb of Fāṭima al-Maʿṣūma, a daughter of the Imam Mūsā al-Kāẓim in Qumm.

The Shiites soon made themselves felt again after being dislodged from the political scene at the beginning of Seljuq rule. Under Sultan Malikshāh, who visited the shrines in Najaf and Karbalā' after his visit to Baghdad in 479/1086, a Shiite from Qumm became Finance Minister (*mustawfī*), and from then on Shiite viziers – in particular from Qumm, Āva and Kāshān – were no longer a rarity. Two out of the six viziers of Sultan Sanjar (511-552/1118-1157) were Shiites. The renegade cited in *Kitāb al-naqḍ* complains that: 'At this time (c. 555/1160) there is no Turk's palace in which ten or fifteen Shiites might not be found; they are even state secretaries in the government.'[92]

These officials and courtiers appeared as benefactors and patrons of the Shiite minority. Not only did they support the *sayyid* families but they also endowed the shrines of the Imams with rich donations. One particularly zealous promoter of the Shiite places of pilgrimage was Majd al-Mulk, Finance Minister (*mustawfī*) under the Sultans Malikshāh and Berk Yārūq (487-498/1094-1105): 'His donations to the graves of the Imams and of the Sayyids descended from Fāṭima in the form of endowments (*waqf*), contributions for provisions and expenditure for lighting (of the shrines) are still being paid out today' reports ʿAbd al Jalīl Qazvīnī in *Kitāb al-naqḍ*. [93] The minister also constructed a dome over the graves of the four Imams, al-Ḥasan, ʿAlī Zayn al-ʿAbidīn, Muḥammad al-Bāqir and Jaʿfar al-Ṣādiq in the Baqīʿ cemetery in Medina, undertook new construction work at the Kāẓimayn shrine near Baghdad and built numerous *imāmzādas* in Rayy and elsewhere.

In particular, following the Sunni example, high-ranking Shiites promoted their *ṭā'ifa* by founding colleges for their own denomination. The institution of the religio-juristic school (*madrasa*) first appeared in north-east Iran in the 4th/10th century and was spread by the Seljuqs over the whole of Iran to Iraq, Syria and Asia Minor.[94] Originally endowed by private scholars who then taught their own circle of students in the building they had founded, by the time of the Seljuqs madrasas had become favourite objects of religious endowment for the rulers and great men who were no scholars themselves. Usually the donor would appoint a well-known jurist of his own denomination as professor (*mudarris*) and the teaching office would frequently remain within the family. The schools of the vizier Niẓām al-Mulk were epoch-making; in order to promote his own denomination – he was a Shāfiʿī Sunni – he established these schools in Merv, Herat, Balkh, Nīshāpūr, Iṣfahān, Āmul in Ṭabaristān, Baṣra, Baghdad and Mosul.[95] The Seljuqs themselves, similarly, founded Ḥanafite schools.

Again in *Kitāb al-naqḍ* we are well informed about the Shiite madrasas of the Seljuq period in the north-west Iranian province of Jibāl. The author Qazvīnī lists nine Shiite schools in Rayy where he himself taught, the same number in Qumm, including one associated with the shrine of Fāṭima al-Maʿṣūm, four in Kāshān and two each in Āva and Varāmīn.[96] We possess only odd pieces of information about the towns of the Iranian north east; among them Bayhaq/Sabzavār where the Shiites had a madrasa.[97]

We also learn from *Kitāb al-naqḍ* that the graves of the *Imāmzādas*, local sanctuaries which were now beginning to cover Iran with their green domes, attracted more than just the Shiites; on the Day of ʿĀshūrā' in Baghdad, Rayy, Hamadān and Iṣfahān, the Sunnis, too, put on a public display of weeping for al-Ḥusayn and were even permitted to curse the Umayyad Caliphs. It would appear that the borderline between this kind of support for the Prophet's family which was permissible for the Sunnis too (*tashayyuʿ ḥasan*) and firm Shiite belief (*tashayyuʿ*) was fluid. While the Shia was initially only the tolerated creed of a minority under the Seljuq sultans, their significance grew steadily, particularly in the 6th/12th century. The future national Iranian religion developed from the time of the Seljuqs within the framework of the Iranian-Turkic community – and was later strengthened by the Turkic-Mongol contribution – at least in the area of popular devotional practices. The Iranisation of immigrant Turks went hand in hand with their becoming Shiites.[98] Moreover, in the eyes of Shiite writers, the Turkic steppe fighters had an eschatological role as the troops of the awaited Mahdī: 'With God's help his warriors will be those Turkish border fighters (*ghāzī*) who are today indubitably the masters of the world.' A poet from the time of (Jaʿfar) al-Ṣādiq announced the appearance of the Mahdī with the victory of the Turks... 'The Prophet has urged the Turkish Ghāzīs to ensure the victory of the Mahdī at the end of time. With the help of the Turks the Mahdī will break the strongholds of the Persian Ismāʿīlīs (see below p. 188) and bring an end to the rival Fāṭimid Caliphate in

Egypt, but the Abbasids in Baghdad he will treat with politeness and respect as his cousins on his father's side.'[99]

The Seljuq period certainly gave Shiite literature a number of important works which are still in use today, but no decisive innovations. The elder Ṭabrisī (Tafrishī), al-Faḍl ibn al-Ḥasan (d. 548/1153) wrote several Shiite commentaries on the Quran;[100] the younger Ṭabrisī, Aḥmad ibn ʿAlī (d. 599/1202) once again defended the doctrine of the twelve Imams;[101] Ibn Shahrāshūb al-Mazandarani (Muḥammad ibn ʿAlī – d. 588/1192) wrote a bibliographical lexicon of Shiite scholars and writers.[102] Outside the Seljuq realm the Sharīf Abu 'l-Maʿālī Muḥammad ibn ʿUbaydallāh, a descendant of the fourth Imam ʿAlī Zayn al-ʿĀbidīn, was working in the east; in the year 485/1092 he wrote his 'Account of the Religions (*bayān al-adyān*) in Persian for Sultan Masʿūd III of Ghazna (south west from Kabul) of which parts III and IV deal with the Islamic denominations, especially those of the Shiites.[103]

Bibliography

The Cambridge History of Iran V, The Saljuq and Mongol Periods, Cambridge 1968, Chapter 3: Religion in the Saljuq Period; esp. 290 ff.: Shiʿism (A. Bausani).

J. Calmard, 'Le chiisme imamite en Iran à l'époque seldjoukide d'après le Kitāb al-naqḍ', *Le Monde iranien et l'Islam* IV (1971), 43-67.

THE SHIA UNDER MONGOL RULE

The Mongol invasion of Iran in the middle of the 7th/13th century was greeted by Shiite writers with anticipations and hopes similar to those aroused when the Turkish Seljuqs invaded 200 years earlier. Apocalyptic predictions attributed to ʿAlī circulated widely; according to these, riders from the steppes would put an end to the sinful city of Baghdad and the Abbasid dynasty of usurpers: 'People with small pupils and with faces like encrusted shields attired in iron, bald-headed and beardless.'[104] As with the Turks the Shiites now applied these prophecies to the Mongols and pinned great hopes on them.

The Mongols did in fact liberate the Shia from their two most powerful rivals: the Sevener Shiite Ismāʿīlīs (Assassins) of Iran and the Abbasid Caliphs of Baghdad. An Imāmī scholar played no insignificant role in this. Born in 597/1201 in Ṭūs and educated there as an Imāmī, Naṣīr al-Dīn Ṭūsī (Abū Jaʿfar Muḥammad ibn Muḥammad) was portrayed as an typical exponent of the political aspirations of the Shia at that time by Rudolph Strothmann (1926) in his sketch of the Twelver Shia in the Mongol period. Naṣīr al-Dīn Ṭūsī, one of the most important mathematicians and astronomers to emerge from the Islamic world, began his career as a young man serving the local

Ismā'īlī prince from Sartakht in east Iranian Quhistān; but when he tried to commend himself to the Baghdad court with a panegyric poem to the Caliph he fell into disgrace with his patron and was taken to Daylam where he was allowed to continue his scientific work in semi-imprisonment in the Ismā'īlī citadels of Alamūt and Maymūndiz (see below p. 185 ff). When the Mongol Khan Hülegü, a grandson of Genghiz Khan and brother of the Great Khans Möngke and Kubilai, was preparing to conquer Iran, Ṭūsī was sent by the Ismā'īlīs as a negotiator to the Mongol camp, but having no loyalty to those who had commissioned him he delivered the Assassin citadels, which had for so long been a thorn in the flesh of the Abbasid-Seljuq empire, into the hands of the Mongols. With the occupation and destruction of Alamūt in 654/1256 Hülegü broke the back of the Ismā'īlī cause in Iran.

Naṣīr al-Dīn Ṭūsī accompanied the Mongol Khan on his western campaigns of conquest. One anecdote shows him in the camp – with one foot already in the stirrup – answering a pupil's philosophical questions, while the vanguard of the Mongols was already at grips with the enemy. He urged Hülegü on to conquer Baghdad and was present when the Caliphal capital fell on 4th Ṣafar 656/10th February 1058. He also talked his master out of his scruples when the latter hesitated to execute the last Abbasid Caliph al-Musta'ṣim, pointing out that even the decapitation of John the Baptist and the murder of 'Alī and al-Ḥusayn had not been avenged by terrible divine judgement. And so the last Caliph met his end by throttling (the Mongol having balked at spilling his blood). Shiite writers extol Naṣīr al Dīn's participation in the overthrow of the hated Abbasids, and the historian Khwānsārī judged that Ṭūsī attended the Mongol Khan to Baghdad 'in order to lead the (true) servants (of God) on the right path, to bring wellbeing to the land, to cut the last link in the chain of violence and outrage, to extinguish the fire of tyranny and confusion by scattering the circle of the Abbasid kingdom and generally murdering supporters of these depraved people until their filthy blood ran in rivers and thus caused it to flow into the waters of the Tigris and from there into Hell fire, home of perdition, place of the wretched and the villainous.'[105]

According to the judgement of Strothmann, Naṣīr al-Dīn was the 'driving, one is tempted to say, evil spirit behind Hülegü'[106]. But, of course, it was not the Shiites who brought the Mongols across Iran; the overthrow of the Abbasid Caliphate had been decided in the court of the Great Khan and would have succeeded even without Shiite support. But Ṭūsī may have attempted to channel the flood overtaking the Islamic lands into courses pleasing to God; he 'enlisted ... these blind forces in the service of the Shia.'[107] Besides, the vizier of the last Abbasid Caliph, the Shiite Ibn al-'Alqamī, also appears to have participated in the overthrow of the dynasty.[108] Although neither he nor Ṭūsī was able to protect the Baghdad Shiite suburb al-Karkh from plunder, or the shrine at al-Kāẓimayn from destruction,[109] the two sanctuaries on the Euphrates, Najaf and Karbalā', managed to escape devastation. This was because the small town of al-Ḥilla on the Euphrates, whose Shiite notables willingly submitted to the Mongols, received them in friendly fashion and built them a bridge over the Euphrates; a force of one hundred Mongols was then detached to protect 'Alī's grave in Najaf.[110]

The first Iranian Mongol Khans (Il-Khāns) cultivated the sympathies of the Shiites for the new government, although they were not Muslims themselves and were religiously neutral. Under the second Il-Khān Abāqā, the renowned historian 'Aṭā Malik-i Juvaynī, governor of Iraq, rebuilt the shrine of Kāẓimayn and established a student hostel at Najaf in 666/1267; and Najaf, where leading Shiites now wanted to be buried, emerged even more strongly as a centre of Imāmī learning. The world traveller Ibn Baṭṭūṭa visited the sanctuary at Karbalā' in the year 727/1326 and described it as: 'a small town, surrounded by palm gardens and watered by the Euphrates. The holy district lies in the middle of the town; it has a madrasa and a venerable zāwiya;[111] there the visitor is given a meal. There are door keepers and attendants at the entrance to the holy area without whose permission no one can enter. One kisses the noble threshold made of silver. Lamps of gold and silver hang over the holy grave and silk curtains hang at the doors.'[112]

Naṣīr al-Din Ṭūsī's scientific work as a mathematician and head of the observatory in Marāgha in Āzarbayjān[113] and as a doctor – he operated on the Khan Abāqā for an abscess – need not detain us here. Far more significant for the Shia is his role as confidant and vizier of the first two Il-Khāns Hülegü and Abāqā, as administrator and overseer of the religious endowments (*awqāf*) and also as an Imāmī writer. Through his open declaration for the Imāmī Shia – he wrote two works on the principles of the Imāmī faith and a treatise on the Imamate[114] – the powerful minister substantially promoted the Shiite cause; Strothmann even declares that 'in a sense the dreadful days of the Mongols came to be outwardly the Golden Age of Shiism.'[115]

The empire of the Mongol Il-Khāns did not, however, become a Shiite state. Iran was still predominantly Sunni at that time; and when the Khan Ghāzān adopted Islam under the name Maḥmūd in the year 694/1295 and thousands of Mongols followed his example, this all took place under the influence of a Sunni-Ḥanafite scholar. The Khan nevertheless exempted the sayyids from all taxes and had special hostels built for them at the places of pilgrimage – Karbalā', for example, had one such 'nobles' house' (*dār al-siyāda*); and he visited Karbalā' and Ṭūs and furnished the shrines with rich endowments.[116] After much vacillation his brother Öljeitü (ruled 703-716/1304-1316) converted to the Imāmiyya around 710/1310 under the influence of the most important Twelver Shiite of the time, Ibn al-Muṭahhar al-Ḥillī. The names of the Twelve Imams were stamped on his coins and preachers were ordered to name only ʿAlī and his descendants in the benediction at the end of the Friday sermon (*khuṭba*). The Khan is even said to have considered going to Medina to destroy the graves of Abū Bakr and ʿUmar. Öljeitü's pro-Shiite policies, however, met with embittered resistance from the Sunnis, especially in Baghdad, Iṣfahān and Shīrāz where a threatening crowd prevented any alteration of the *khuṭba;* and in Iṣfahān serious arguments took place between the Shiites and the Sunnis, during which parts of the town were destroyed.[117] After Öljeitü's death in 716/1316 the Il-Khāns returned to the Sunna.

Besides the Shiite ministers and trusted advisors of the Mongol Khans there were also 'spokesmen' of the Alids who now represented the Shiites vis-à-vis the state. As head of his denomination the highest spokesman (*naqīb al-nuqabā'*) in the Mongol period held a position similar to that of the Catholicos of the Nestorians or the Maphrian of the Jacobites. Important men held the office of the chief *naqīb* in the Mongol period, for example Sayyid Tāj al-Dīn Abu 'l-Faḍl Muḥammad, and later ʿAlī ibn Mūsā al-Ṭā'ūsī (d. 664/1266), a native of al-Ḥilla and as a scholar 'one of the quiet of the land' whose portrait Strothmann contrasts with that of the brilliant courtier Naṣīr al-Dīn Ṭūsī.[118]

Primary sources in translation

B. Scarcia Amoretti, 'La Risālat al-imāma di Naṣīr al-Dīn Ṭūsī, *RSO* 47 (1972), 247-76.

Secondary sources

R. Strothmann, *Die Zwölfer-Shiʿa. Zwei religionsgeschichtliche Charakterbilder aus der Mongolenzeit*, Leipzig 1926; Art. al-Ṭūsī, Naṣīr al-Dīn, EI[1]. B. Spuler, *Die Mongolen in Iran*, Berlin ²1955; esp. 178 ff.: Die religiösen Verhältnisse unter den Ilchanen, and 198 ff.: Das Verhältnis der Mongolen zu den Religionen. (Including a map in the appendix showing the spread of religious denominations, by Ḥamdullāh Mustawfī.) – *The Cambridge History of Iran V, The Saljuq and Mongol Periods*, Cambridge 1968, Ch. 7, 538 ff.: Religion under the Mongols (A. Bausani). M. M. Mazzaoui, *The Origins of the Safavids*, Wiesbaden 1972, Ch. III, 22-40: Shīʿism under the Mongols. D. Krawulsky, *Iran – Das Reich der Ilḥāne. Eine topographisch-historische Studie*, Wiesbaden 1978 (with numerous details about Shiite communities in individual towns and villages). W. Madelung, 'Naṣīr ad-Dīn Ṭūsī's Ethics between Philosophy, Shiʿism, and Sufism', in: R. G. Hovannisian (ed.), *Ethics in Islam*, Malibu 1985, 85-101.

THE SCHOOL OF ḤILLA AND THE FOUNDATIONS OF SHIITE LAW: IJTIHĀD AND TAQLĪD

The town of Ḥilla on the Euphrates became the most significant centre of Imāmī learning during the Mongol period; Qumm had already been devastated and depopulated by the first Mongol invasion in 621/1224 and lay in ruins for the whole of the 14th century.[119] Ḥilla owed its existence to a small local dynasty of Bedouin amirs from the tribe of the Asad, the Banū Mazyad whose rule over southern Iraq had been recognised by the Būyids as early as the 4th/10th century; their mobile encampment (*ḥilla*) which had been set up permanently from 397/1006 at al-Jāmiʿayn on the Babylon arm of the Euphrates was surrounded with a wall by the Amir Ṣadaqa and made into a permanent residence.[120] The Mazyad amirs declared themselves for the Twelver Shia as their Būyid masters had done, and promoted scholars of the Imāmī creed. The jurists from Ḥilla sought to support the rationalistic endeavours of Sharīf al-Murtaḍā against the traditionalism of Shaykh al-Ṭūsī (see above p. 54), and Muḥammad ibn Idrīs al-ʿIjlī al-Ḥillī (d. 598/1202) firmly established the intellect (*ʿaql*) as the principle of legal judgement.[121] This tendency became stronger when Ḥilla superseded Qumm and Baghdad as the stronghold of learned Shiism after the Mongol conquest; we have already discussed the role played by the notables of Ḥilla during the occupation of Iraq by the Mongols and the protection received by the town in recognition from the Il-Khāns.

Two scholars from Ḥilla, in particular, steered the development of Imāmī law in the direction which was later to prevail universally. The elder, Abu 'l-Qāsim Jaʿfar ibn al-Ḥasan al-Ḥillī, called *al-Muḥaqqiq* (approx: the one who checks what is true) was born in 602/1205 and, therefore, fifty-three years old at the time of the Mongol invasion, and died in 676/1277 in Baghdad.[122] He wrote a manual of Imāmī law still in use today entitled 'Laws in Islam – Problems of the Permitted and the Prohibited' (*sharāʾiʿ al-islām fī masāʾil al-ḥalāl wa 'l-ḥarām*) which has been commentated on several times and of which he himself wrote a practical summary (*mukhtaṣar*).[123]

While the work by al-Muḥaqqiq al-Ḥillī served and still continues to serve practical needs it was al-Ḥasan ibn Yūsuf ibn ʿAlī ibn al-Muṭahhar al-Ḥillī, called *al-ʿAllāma* (the most learned one) and two generations younger, who completed work on the theoretical foundations of Twelver Shiite law. His father played a leading role in the surrender of Ḥilla to the Mongols and even joined Hülegü's military camp at Baghdad; the son – born in 648/1250 and only seven years old at the time of the Mongol invasion – was at first a pupil of his father and uncle in Ḥilla and then studied with Naṣīr al-Dīn Ṭūsī on whose 'Abstract of the Doctrines' (*Tajrīd al-iʿtiqād*) he later wrote a commentary.[124] Around 705/1305 he went to Tabrīz to the court of the Il-Khān Öljeitü who, after some vacillation, declared allegiance to the Imāmī Shia under his influence and stamped the names of the twelve Imams on his coins (see above p. 66). At the court of the Khan the ʿAllāma al-Ḥillī held a position of trust similar to that of his teacher Naṣīr al-Dīn Ṭūsī before him in Hülegü's army camp; when he died in 726/1325 he was interred by the shrine in Mashhad where his grave is still visited by Shiite pilgrims today.

The ʿAllāma al-Ḥillī, the first Shiite scholar to bear the name *Āyatallāh* (Arab: *āyatallāh:* God's sign), provided a theoretical corroboration for the until then disputed principle of legal ruling based on individual intellectual 'effort' (*ijtihād*). With the enforcement of this principle, which held the reasoning intellect (*ʿaql*) of the jurist to be capable of giving valid judgement even in religious matters, he paved the way for the later – also political – role of the Shiite scholars, the mullahs and the *āyatallāhs*. The Arabic verb *ijtahada* (with the verbal noun *ijtihād*) means 'to exert oneself, to struggle', the active participle *mujtahid* therefore literally means 'he who exerts himself, struggles'. Even in the juristic terminology of the Sunnis it denotes someone who, on the basis of his knowledge of the foundations of jurisprudence (*uṣūl al-fiqh*), is both capable of and justified in reaching binding decisions on questions of law and ritual through the exertion of his own intellect – *ijtihād*.

The principle of *ijtihād*, legal ruling by means of rational consideration, is closely connected with the old discipline of *kalām*, reasoned argument in matters of revelation, as promulgated from the 2nd/8th century in Iraq by the theological school of the Muʿtazilites. In Sunni Islam after the proscribing of the Muʿtazilites in 235/849, the rationalism of *kalām* was superseded by the traditionalism of the Sunni legal schools which emphasised the revealed and transmitted word; to the Sunnis the 'door of *ijtihād*'' has since then been regarded as closed.[125] The Twelver Shia, on the other hand, preserved the rationalistic principle of *kalām* which had been embodied in the legal thinking of the Shia by Shaykh al-Mufīd (d. 413/1022) and his pupil Sharīf al-Murtaḍā (d. 436/1044) in particular, even though it had not yet been generally enforced (see above p. 52).

The ʿAllāma al-Ḥillī completed this development.[126] His fundamental work bears the title 'The points of departure from which knowledge of the principles is attained' (*mabādi' al-wuṣūl ilā 'ilm al-uṣūl*).[127] In the final chapter of this book the 'Allāma outlines precisely the principles of *ijtihād*.[128] He defines *ijtihād* as 'the utmost exertion of the faculties to speculate (*naẓar*) on those questions of the law which are subject to conjecture (*ẓannīya*)'. The essential characteristic of *ijtihād* is its fallibility: 'because sometimes it is wrong, sometimes right'.[129] The prophets and messengers of God were therefore denied *ijtihād*, since their message would otherwise be unreliable; on occasions the Prophet had to wait until a revelation came to him and could not seek recourse to *ijtihād*. Neither could the Imams use *ijtihād*: 'since they are infallible'. Their decisions depend either on instruction (*ta'līm*) from the Prophet or on divine inspiration (*ilhām*).

It was therefore exclusively the scholars (*'ulamā'*) to whom *ijtihād* applied, i.e. 'the discovery (*istinbāṭ*) of decisions on the basis of general precepts (*'umūmāt*) in the Quran and Sunna and by weighing up (*tarjīḥ*) contradictory arguments'. A precondition for this is that the scholar is in a position to draw binding conclusions on newly raised questions on the basis of what is unequivocally set forth as revealed law (*dalā'il shar'iyya*). However, the *mujtahid* requires special knowledge and skills: first, he must know the laws and rules of language in order to know the meanings of words and their possible connotations in any given context; then he must have command of the possibilities of weighing up arguments when they contradict each other. He must, of course, know the Revelation, but it is not necessary for him to know the Quran by heart. It is sufficient to know the 500 relevant verses; but it is particularly important that he can distinguish the abrogated Quranic verses from those which abrogate.[130] He must be sufficiently familiar with the tradition of the sayings of the Prophet and the Imams to know where to find the required references in large collections and, obviously, he must be trained in the discipline of the opinion of the 'men' (*rijāl*), i.e. the handers-down of tradition, and in the evaluation of repeatedly (*mutawātir*) and singly (*āḥād*) transmitted traditions. In addition he must be aware of the prevailing consensus (*ijmā'*) of the scholars so that his decision does not conflict with it. In any case, he can only have recourse to the method of *ijtihād* when the divine law gives no unequivocal definitive instruction (*dalīl qaṭ'ī*).

The characteristic of the scholars' *ijtihād* is its fallibility as opposed to the infallibility of the Prophets and the Imams. 'Whoever goes astray with *ijtihād* commits no sin',[131] since if two mujtahids each assume their own arguments to be correct, one of these assumptions must be wrong, even when both have judged to the best of their knowledge. The mujtahid can therefore revise his decisions, and the one seeking advice (*mustaftī*) must then abide by the later decision. Of course, someone who follows the incorrect recommendation of a scholar does not sin either; the layman is dependent on the competence of the expert and is even obliged to subject himself to the expert's authority. The term *ijtihād* corresponds to the term *taqlīd*. The verbal noun of the verb *qallada* can be translated as 'authorisation': whoever is not qualified to use *ijtihād* – and this includes the great majority of unlearned people – 'authorises' the scholars to do so and assigns them the task of reaching a decision and also the reponsibility of bowing to their judgement. The *mujtahid* faces the *muqallid*, the 'authoriser', who then subjects himself to the authority of the 'authorised' (*muqallad*). The mass of people are therefore spared the effort of *ijtihād* so they are not kept from their daily tasks by incessant speculation; 'if the vast majority were burdened with *ijtihād* in (legal) questions the world order would consequently be disturbed and everyone would be more concerned with discussing (juristic) problems than with his livelihood'.[132] The individual believer who is neither required to exercise *ijtihād* nor capable of doing so, must therefore look for an authority to whom he can subject himself; 'if two are of equal worth in seeking expert opinion (*istiftā'*) he should choose the one he wants; if one of the two is superior in every respect this is the one he must follow; if either of them excels the other in a particular point it is best to keep to the word of the more knowledgeable (in each case).'[133]

A principle of Shiite law, formulated later, is already implicit in these statements by the 'Allāma al-Ḥillī: certainly no mujtahid is infallible, but nevertheless 'every mujtahid is right (*kull mujtahid muṣīb*)';[134] the contradictoriness of two pieces of legal advice does not prevent them from being obligatory because, in the absence of the solely infallible Imam, all decisions by the scholars are only provisional. Meanwhile the decisions of a mujtahid are only binding as long as he is alive: 'if a non-mujtahid delivers an affidavit citing a mujtahid, what he says is not acceptable if he cites a deceased mujtahid, for dead men have no authority (*lā qawla li 'l-mayyit*)';[135] consensus on a doctrine can in fact only be determined in the lifetime of the teacher, in live discussion and debate; if the dissenter dies then the consensus is upheld.

The many angles from which the 'Allāma al-Ḥillī explained the principle of *ijtihād* and *taqlīd* already contain in a nutshell the entire later development of the Imāmī 'clergy', the mullahs and āyatallāhs. The two fundamental characteristics – the fallibility and revisability of *ijtihād* and its restriction to a living authority – give this instrument of legal ruling its flexibility and dynamic. A scholarly class of infallible mujtahids would soon have discredited itself by its unavoidable contradictions; appeal to long-deceased authorities would have stifled any development and frozen Shiite law in traditionalist immobility. Infallible authority was reserved for the Hidden Imam and thus removed into a distant future; the company of his fallible representatives, the scholars, could now devote themselves to the practical task of handling current questions without being too tied to the authority of the written word. In fact, the Shiite mujtahids – the āyatallahs of today – are anything but fundamentalist; they are rather – in the original sense of the word – the exact opposite.

However, it was centuries before the Shiite clergy in Iran began to play a political role based on the principles of *ijtihād* and *taqlīd* developed theoretically by the 'Allāma al-Ḥillī; the development which led to today's situation in Iran certainly had its theoretical basis in the writings of the 'Allāma al-Ḥillī but it was not until the 17th century that it actually got under way.

Primary sources in translation

Al-Muḥaqqiq al-Ḥillī: *Sharā'i' al-islām*, trans. A. Querry, *Droit Musulman. Recueil de lois concernant les musulmans schyites*, 2 volumes, Paris 1871/72. Al-'Allāma Ibn al-Muṭahhar al-Ḥillī: *Al-Bâbu 'l-Ḥâdî 'Ashar. A Treatise on the Principles of Shiite Theology, by Ḥasan b. Yûsuf b. 'Alî Ibnu'l-Muṭahhar al-Ḥillī, with commentary by Miqdad-i-Faḍil al-Ḥillī*; Engl. by W. McElwee Miller, London 1928 (reprint London 1958).

Secondary sources

H. Laoust, 'Les fondements de l'imamat dans le Minhāǧ d'al-Ḥillī', REI 46 (1978), 3-55; 'Les fondements de l'autorité dans le "Minhāǧ d'al-Ḥillī"', in: *La notion d'autorité au Moyen Age. Islam, Byzance, Occident. Colloques internationaux de la Napoule*, Paris 1982, 175-87. W. Madelung, 'Authority in Twelver Shiism in the Absence of the Imam', *ibid*, 163-71.

THE SHIA AND THE DERVISH ORDERS IN THE 14TH CENTURY

After the death of the last Il-Khān Abū Sa'īd in 736/1335 the Iranian Mongol empire disintegrated. It was initially replaced by regional Mongol dynasties such as the Jalāyirids in Mesopotamia and Āzarbayjān; then two large tribal confederations were formed in northern Syria and eastern Anatolia from the Turcoman or Oghuz tribes which had infiltrated since the 11th century, the Āq Qoyūnlū (White Sheep) with their centre at Āmid on the upper Tigris (modern Diyarbakr) and the Qarā Qoyūnlū (Black Sheep) around Arjīsh (Erciş on the northern shore of Lake Van. The two tribal federations survived the disastrous western campaigns of Tīmūr (from 788/1386), the Samarqand-based descendant of Genghiz Khan – the Āq Qoyūnlū as his allies, the Qarā Qoyūnlū as his opponents – and after Tīmūr's death in 807/1405 they contested for power in western Iran. In 813/1410 the prince of the Qarā Qoyūnlū, Qarā Yūsuf, finally seized the old Mongol capital Tabrīz; one year later he conquered Iraq and soon the Turcomans advanced in the south as far as Iṣfahān and Fars. The tribal confederation of the Black Sheep entered on the inheritance of the Mongol rulers and reached the peak of their power under Jahānshāh (841-872/1438-1467) while the Tīmūrids' rule over north-east Iran (with Afghanistan and Central Asia) was curbed.

The religious tendencies of these Mongol or Turcoman princes – if they had any at all – were not very marked and can only be determined with difficulty. Sporadic Shiite tendencies must not be overrated; thus the founder of the Jalāyirid principality, Ḥasan-i Buzurg (d. 757/1356), chose Najaf as his residence in his last years; the Qarā Qoyūnlū Jahānshāh praised ʿAlī in his poems;[136] his brother Aspand, as governor of Iraq, even attempted to enforce the Twelver Shia as the official creed. But that does not say very much; Jahānshāh's coins have Shiite formulae on the front, and the names of the first three Caliphs on the back;[137] Jawhar-Shād, wife of the Tīmūrid Shāh Rukh (807-850/1405-1447) – irrespective of her Sunni faith – endowed the shrine of the eighth Imam in Mashhad with a magnificent mosque.

From the time of the Mongols, veneration of ʿAlī and the Imams spread far and wide even in Sunni circles and especially through the popularisation of Islamic mysticism, Sufism.[138] Precisely in the period of which we are speaking even the Shia were so affected by this mystical trend that quite a few observers were led to the conclusion that Shiism and Sufism were identical in essence, two sides of one coin, and that indeed Shiism was only the outer exoteric form of Islamic mysticism. This interpretation, disseminated by the French orientalist Henry Corbin (1903-1978) in numerous lectures and publications,[139] and which was taken up by Sayyid Hossein Naṣr[140] (and ultimately goes back to the Iranian mystic Ḥaydar-i Āmulī; see below p. 74) has been repeatedly criticised as unhistorical,[141] in particular by Hamid Algar who points out emphatically that veneration of the twelve Imams in the mystical orders of the Mongol and Tīmūrid era 'was neither borrowed from the Shia nor was it a proto-Shiite element', rather it was a general characteristic of the orders.[142]

Islamic mysticism, which sought its religious goal less in the detailed fulfilment of the cultic and legal duties of Islam than in a personal divine experience, the climax of which came after gradual effacement of one's own ego in the contemplation of God or even in becoming one with God, had its first great exponents on Iraqi-Iranian soil in Bāyazīd Bisṭāmī (d. 261/874 or 264/877) and Ḥallāj (executed

309/922); the Persian mystic 'Aṭṭār is said to have lost his life during the Mongol invasion in 618/1221. The mystics' activities, in particular their often dubious ecstasy-promoting practices, aroused the suspicions of Sunni and Shiite scholars equally; moreover, for the Shia the absolute authority exercised by the Sufi master (Arab. *shaykh* or *murshid,* Pers. *pīr*) over the novice (*murīd*) is hardly compatible with the exclusive authority of the Imams. In the Sunna, however, Sufism in its moderate and refined form was reconciled with the canonical law of *sharī'a* in the 11th century by the work of the jurist, theologian and mystic al-Ghazālī (d. 505/1111).

The following of the mystical path (*ṭarīqa*) was not fundamentally bound to any single confession. Most Sufis considered dogmatic, ritual and legal differences, and occasionally even differences between different religions, as secondary or even completely meaningless. Thus the mystical tendency, even though it was certainly not of specifically Shiite origin, would affect the Shia no less than the Sunna. The fact that an adherent of the Twelver Shia could follow the mystical path at the same time is shown by the example of the vizier Naṣīr al-Dīn Ṭūsī who, as well as his work in natural science, his philosophical writings following the metaphysician Avicenna and his treatises on Imāmī dogmatics, was also occupied with mysticism and corresponded with the Anatolian mystic Jalal al-Dīn Rūmī (d. 672/1273 in Konya). Ṭūsī composed a treatise on the mystical path in which he leads the reader through thirty steps – from belief, by way of atonement, asceticism, solitude and love of God, to final obliteration of the self (*fanā'*) and absorption in God.[143] The document is dedicated to the Sunni historian and vizier 'Aṭā Malik-i Juvaynī who certainly had as little actual tendency towards asceticism, flight from this world and self-obliteration as the author himself. The later Shia, however, did not take offence and held the work in high esteem; the fact that Ṭūsī allowed himself to be dragged into the worldy concerns of a pagan ruler has even been extolled by later commentators as the ultimate sacrifice, indeed as the martyrdom of a great and pious man who could only work for the good of his fellow-believers in this way.[144]

In the 12th and 13th centuries when the personal relationship between the Sufi master and his adepts began to be firmly established and institutionalised into congregations which resembled orders (Arab. *ṭarīqa,* Pers. *ṭarīqat*), they attempted to trace their own respective tradition back in an uninterrupted teacher-student chain (*silsila*) to the Prophet, and even to the Archangel Gabriel. 'Alī, the closest acquaintance of the Prophet, was generally integrated into these chains as the second human teacher of the mystical path, and in several ṭarīqas he is followed by the Imams, generally up to the eighth,

ʿAlī al-Riḍā. Membership of such a ṭarīqa did not necessarily indicate a specific Shiite allegiance, but it is clear that the expansion of the ṭarīqas from Central Asia to Anatolia did promote veneration of ʿAlī and his sons and grandsons, which Shiite propaganda and mission could then turn to account in the 16th century. An example of the moderate Shiism (*tashayyuʿ ḥasan*) of the dervishes is found in the remarks made by Najm al-Dīn Kubrā, a mystical teacher in Central Asian Khwārazm (on the lower Amū Daryā), who was killed in 618/1221 at the time of the Mongol invasion. Although a Sunni himself he showed great reverence for ʿAlī and the Imams; after his death Shiite tendencies in the Kubrawīyya ṭarīqa increased further, and the order to which several ṭarīqas in Iran could later be traced back slid over imperceptibly into the Shiite camp. Even the Sunni mystic Yaḥyā al-Bākharzī, who worked in Bukhara, put together prayers in a document written in 723/1323 which were said to be attributed to the twelve Imams.

The most significant Twelver Shiite mystic of the 14th century was the Ḥusaynid Sayyid Ḥaydar-i Āmulī (d. after 787/1385) who served at first as vizier at the small court of the Bāwandids in his home town of Āmul in Māzandarān beside the Caspian Sea, but settled in Iraq after a religious crisis and a pilgrimage, during which he studied in Baghdad under the son of the ʿAllāma al-Ḥillī. Ḥaydar-i Āmulī 'acclimatised' the work of the mystic Ibn ʿArabī (d. 638/1240 in Damascus) in Iraq and combined the latter's ideas with his own Shiite views into a highly original synthesis. As with Ibn ʿArabī's treatment of Jesus, so the twelve Imams in Ḥaydar-i Āmulī's 'Collection of secrets' (*Jāmiʿ al-asrār*) become bearers and mediators of the divine light working in the Prophet Muhammad (*nūr muḥammadī*) and thus channels of mystical enlightenment. So mysticism and Shiism unite and become the esoteric side of Islam, the 'divine wisdom' (*ḥikmat-i ilāhī*).[145]

One characteristic of this period which is very important for the future history of Iran is the development of isolated ṭarīqas into militant Shiite fighting federations which gained political significance in the 14th century – if only in local settings initially – for the first time since the disintegration of the Mongol Il-Khānid empire. The earliest example is the ṭarīqa of the Shaykhiyya-Jūriyya which goes back to the 'Pole of the gnostics' (*Quṭb al-ʿĀrifīn*) Shaykh-i Khalīfa (d. 736/1335) and his successor Shaykh Ḥasan-i Jūrī (d. 743/1342). The wandering dervish Shaykh-i Khalīfa from Māzandarān on the Caspian Sea set himself up as a mystical teacher in the mosque of Bayhaq/Sabzavār (east of Tehran) where he preached the imminent appearance (*ẓuhūr*) of the Mahdī and urged the Shiites to prepare themselves for Holy War. He attracted supporters who were mainly recruited from amongst the urban craftsmen and small tradesmen, but his activities aroused the suspicion and hatred of the Sunnis to whom he finally fell victim in 736/1335. His pupil Shaykh Ḥasan-i Jūrī disseminated the teachings of his master in the large Iranian towns of Nīshāpūr, Ṭūs and Abīvard; and at the same time through propaganda he supported the *amīrs* of the local dynasty of the Sarbadārs from Bayhaq/Sabzavār, who emerged as Iranian and Shiite champions against foreign Mongol rule after the death of the last Il-Khān Abū Sa'īd in 1335. The small principality of Sarbadār was able to hold on to its independence until its overthrow by Tīmūr in 783/1381 and anticipates the later founding of the Shiite-Iranian state of the Ṣafavids. The Sarbadārs stamped the names of the twelve Imams on their coins and twice a day a saddled and magnificently caparisoned horse would be led out in front of the town gates of Sabzavār for the Mahdī, when he appeared, to mount immediately[146] – a custom witnessed in several Iranian towns by the geographer Yāqūt[147] and testified to at Ḥilla in Iraq by the traveller Ibn Baṭṭūṭa.[148] When the last Sarbadār 'Alī Mu'ayyad had to submit to the conqueror Tīmūr in 788/1386, and was asked by the latter which faith he confessed, he is said to have cleverly concealed his Shiism and to have answered cunningly: 'People have the religion of their rulers'. He practised 'dissimulation' (*taqiyya*) as the sixth Imam had required of his followers.[149]

It was this same 'Alī Mu'ayyad who attempted to fetch probably the most important Imāmī scholar of his time to the court at Sabzavār, the Lebanese Muḥammad ibn Makkī al-'Āmilī al-Jizzīnī (from Jizzīn east of Sidon). The latter had studied in Ḥilla under the son of the 'Allāma al-Ḥillī and had then returned to his home in the southern Lebanese Jabal 'Āmil (in the hinterland of Sidon and Tyre) where he promoted the teachings of the Twelver Shia in the mountain villages. As a result of his work Jabal 'Āmil became a stronghold of the Imāmiyya (and in recent times was the starting point for Shiite expansion in Lebanon).[150] Ibn Makkī al-'Āmilī could not respond to his summons to the court of the Sarbadārs because the Egyptian Sultan Barqūq had imprisoned him in Damascus; in prison he wrote the missive 'The Shimmer from Damascus' (*al-lum'a al-dimashqiyya*), an abridged study of Imāmī faith and law intended for the Sarbadārs.[151] In the year 786/1384 Sultan Barqūq had him executed, and he is still venerated by the Shiites today as the 'first martyr' (*al-shahīd al-awwal*).

As at Sabzavār, a minor Iranian-Shiite state appeared at the same time at Āmul in Māzandarān. Its founder was the Ḥusaynid Sayyid and Shiite dervish Mīr Qiwām al-Dīn Mar'ashī, a descendant of the fourth Imam 'Alī Zayn al-'Ābidīn, whose father was a pupil of Jūrī in Sabzavār. The Shiite dervish dynasty founded by Sayyid Mar'ashī was able to maintain its position in Āmul and Sārī on the Caspian Sea from 762/1361 until the conquest of Māzandarān by Tīmūr in 794/1392.[152]

The typically close connection between mystical aspiration and pro-Alid – if not decidedly Shiite – conviction in the dervish orders of the Mongol and post-Mongol eras is found also in Iran, Iraq, Syria and Asia Minor among the young men's leagues, the *futuwwa*. These were brotherhoods with a paramilitary character which were recruited mainly from the artisan class and, under the slogan of youthful prowess (*futuwwa* from the Arabic *fatā* ; young man), cultivated a guild-like solidarity and fellowship as a municipal society. ʿAlī was both patron and model for members of the *futuwwa* leagues; their motto read *lā fatā illā ʿAlī* (ʿAlī is the proficient youth *par excellence*). This did not necessarily make the *futuwwa* leagues Shiite institutions, for the Abbasid Caliph al-Nāṣir (575-622/1180-1225) had sought to set himself up as the head of the *futuwwa* movement. Like the ṭarīqas of the Sufis they too disseminated pro-Alid sentiments very widely among the urban population, which responded readily to Shiite propaganda. This was particularly true in Asia Minor where several Turcoman amirates had been established after the collapse of Mongol rule around 1300. At the court of Jandar-oğlu at Qasṭamūnī (Kastamonu) in northern Anatolia the oldest Turkish version known to us of the passion story at Karbalāʾ (*maqtal-i Ḥusayn*) originated; but at the same time – and probably even by the same writer – came a novel about Abū Muslim, champion of the Abbasid cause.[153] Convinced Imāmīs were not yet to be found among the Turks of Asia Minor at this time; no Shiite document as such was disseminated, let alone originated, there, but popular sympathies for ʿAlī and al-Ḥusayn spread by Sufism and the *futuwwa* led to 'a kind of inner "Shiitisation" of Sunnism'[154] and prepared the way for the Shia in particular in eastern Anatolia.

Bibliography

M. Molé, Les Kubrawiya entre Sunnisme et Shiisme aux huitième et neuvième siècles de l'Hégire', *REI* 29 (1961), 61-142. R. Gramlich, *Die schiitischen Derwischorden Persiens* I, Wiesbaden 1965. C. Cahen, 'Le problème du shîʿisme dans l'Asie mineure turque préottomane', in: *Le shîʿisme imamite, Colloque de Strasbourg*, Paris 1970, 115-29. J. M. Smith, *The History of the Sarbadār Dynasty 1336-1381 A.D. and its Sources*, Paris 1970 (esp. 55-60: Religion and the Sarbadārs). P. Antes, *Zur Theologie der Schiʿa. Eine Untersuchung des Gāmiʿ al-asrār wa-manbaʿ al-anwār von Sayyid Ḥaidar Āmolī*, Freiburg i. Br. 1971 (Islamkundl. Untersuchungen 16). H. R. Roemer, 'Das turkmenische Intermezzo – Persiche Geschichte zwischen Mongolen und Safaviden', *Archäolog. Mitteilungen aus Iran*, N.F.9, 1976, 263-97. J. Aubin, 'Aux origines d'un mouvement populaire médiéval, le cheykhisme du Bayhaq et du Nichâpour', *Studia Iranica* 5 (1976), 213-24. F. Taeschner, *Zünfte und*

Bruderschaften im Islam, Zurich/Munich 1979, Ch. V: Die Einmündung der futuwwa in das Derwischtum im Iran der Mongolenzeit, 227 ff. D. Krawulsky, 'Untersuchungen zur ī'itischen Tradition von Beyhaq. Ein Beitrag zur Frage der Verbreitung der „ī'a in Persien', *Studia Arabica et Islamica, Festschrift I. Abbas*, Beirut 1981, 293-311. S. A. Arjomand, *The Shadow of God and the Hidden Imam*, Chicago 1984, 69-71: 'Militant Messianism in the Shi'ite "Republic" of the Sardabārs, 1338-81'. – *The Cambridge History of Iran VI, The Timurid and Safavid Periods*, Ch. 1: The Jalayirids, Muzaffarids and Sardabārs; Ch. 4: The Türkmen Dynasties (H. R. Roemer). A. Hourani, 'From Jabal 'Āmil to Persia', *BSOAS* 49 (1986), 133-40.

THE EXTREME SHIITE MAHDĪ MOVEMENTS OF THE 15TH CENTURY

The post-Mongol era in Iran, Iraq and eastern Anatolia was characterised by political instability and incessant wars between rival rulers; and a large proportion of the Iranian towns were destroyed during Tīmūr's campaigns of conquest. A superior religious authority could not establish itself under such conditions, any more than a stable political power; on the other hand, chaos and misery gave rise to millenarianism and hopes for the imminent appearance of the saviour figure who would restore order to the fragmented Islamic world. Uncontrolled by any religious authority, chiliastic movements had free rein. The promise of the imminent return of the Mahdī had earlier drawn crowds of militant supporters to the Shaykhiyya-Jūriyya orders and legitimised the rule of the Sarbadārs. It was not long before pretenders appeared, claiming to be the returned Twelfth Imam or his reincarnation; and it was not unusual for them to claim to participate in the divinity of the Imams themselves, which made them appear as extremists or exaggerators (*ghulāt*) in the eyes of the Imāmīs.

The first of these Mahdis was a wandering dervish from Astarābād on the south-east corner of the Caspian Sea, Fażlallāh Astarābādī, the son of the town's judge and a supposed descendant of the seventh Imam Mūsā al-Kāẓim. After a long period of seclusion in Iṣfahān and Tabrīz he felt that he had been summoned by an inner voice to be 'ruler of the age' (*ṣāḥib al-zamān*) i.e. the present Imam; and in about 788/1386 he explained his appearance as the 'manifestation of the (divine) majesty' (*ẓuhūr-i kibriyā'*)'. He based his claim to be the True Imam on the knowledge revealed to him of the secret meaning of the letters of the alphabet, of the Quranic verses and of the ritual actions prescribed for Muslims. Fażlallāh was imprisoned in Bākū in 796/1394 at the bidding of Tīmūr's son Mīrānshāh, and was executed shortly after that at Alanjaq near Nakhchevān on the Araxes. His supporters, called the *Ḥurūfiyya* (from Arabic *ḥurūf;* letters) because of their interpretation of the alphabet, venerated their master as the incarnation of God; and the prayer at his shrine at Alanjaq began with the formula 'there is no God but Fāh' (shortened from Fażlallāh). His early return (*raj'a*) as the 'Master of the Sword' (*ṣāḥib-i sayf*), i.e. as the victorious Imām-Mahdī, was expected to take place imminently. Fażlallāh's successor (*khalīfa*) 'Alī al-A'lā even appears to have seen the returned master in the Qarā-Qoyūnlū Sultan Qarā Yūsuf, who defeated the murderer Mīrānshāh, and to have placed great hopes on him (in vain, as things turned out). 'Alī al-A'lā was executed in 822/1419 for heresy. The Ḥurūfiyya sects which had spread to the towns of Iran, eastern Anatolia and Syria had to endure severe persecution; their remnants later appear to have merged with the dervish orders of the Bektashis.

Muḥammad ibn Muḥammad ibn 'Abdallāh, called *Nūrbakhsh* (gift of light) was a generation younger. The son of one of the Arabs who had migrated to Iran from the coast of the Gulf, he was born in 795/1392 in east Iranian Qāyin and in his early years attached himself to a Sufi master in Khuttalān on the upper Amū Daryā (in present-day Tājikistān), the Kubrawī dervish Khwāja Isḥāq al-Khuttalānī. It was he who presented the young adept in the circle of his supporters as the descendant of the seventh Imam Mūsā al-Kāẓim and as the awaited Mahdī. He now appeared as the 'Imam and Caliph of all Muslims'. Sultan Shāhrukh, the son and successor of Tīmūr, intervened and in the year 828/1425 he had the master al-Khuttalānī and about eighty of his disciples executed; but he spared the Mahdī, supposedly on account of his youth, but perhaps also out of awe at the charisma of the Prophet's descendant, and simply had him interned in Herat and later in Shīrāz. After his release Nūrbakhsh went to Iraq where he visited the shrines of the Imams and studied in Ḥilla with the Imāmī scholar Aḥmad ibn Fahd al-Ḥillī (d. 841/1437). When he rallied supporters around him in Kurdistān for a second time and renewed his claim to the Imamate and Caliphate he was arrested once again; Shāhrukh brought him to Herat and forced him to abjure publicly from the pulpit. Finally he settled in the vicinity of Rayy where he died in 869/1464. In his 'Treatise on right guidance' (*Risālat al-hudā* c. 856/1451) he argued his claim at length that the light of the 'rightly-guided' (*al-Mahdī*) had inhabited his body; moreover, besides the visions vouchsafed to him he also produced rational 'proofs' for his claim – following the example of the Ḥilla school. In Ṣafavid Iran (see below p. 84 ff) the Nūrbakhshiyya sect were unable to establish themselves; they found refuge in Kashmir where a pupil of Nūrbakhsh's son had emigrated, and they survive up to the present day in the deep valleys of Baltistān in the Hindu Kush.

At about the same time as Nūrbakhsh a third Mahdī appeared in southern Iraq: Muḥammad ibn Falāḥ, founder of the Musha'sha' sects.[155] Like Nūrbakhsh he too was a pupil of the Imāmī scholar Muḥammad ibn Fahd in Ḥilla and became his son-in-law. Muḥammad ibn Falāḥ first appeared as the 'legal guardian' (*walī*) of the awaited Mahdī, but in 840/1436 he disclosed his identity as the 'veil' (*ḥājib*) of the twelfth Imam. He set himself up in Ḥuwayza (Pers. Ḥoveyze) in Khūzistān and gained supporters from among the Arabs of the region. In his 'Word of the Mahdi' (*kalām al-Mahdī*) he revealed the identity of all the prophets, Imams and holy men and presented himself as the last in the series of their reincarnations. When he was disavowed by his erstwhile teacher al-Ḥillī he declared the latter to be an unbeliever and urged his supporters to wage Holy War. In 857/1453 he plundered and burnt not only Ḥilla but also ʿAlī's shrine at Najaf and even threatened Baghdad. The Qarā-Qoyūnlū Turcomans were able to defeat his troops in the field but they could not capture the Mahdī; they contented themselves with a formal recognition of their supremacy over Khūzistān. After Ibn Falāḥ's death in 866/1461 or 870/1465 his son ʿAlī took his place and consistently developed his father's doctrines. The traditional interpretation by the Twelver Shia of the *ghayba* of the twelfth Imam had already become meaningless in ʿAlī's father's teaching; instead of an Imam who was indeed hidden but corporeal and living on earth, there was the eternal substance of 'the' Imam which made use of ever new worldy veils which themselves had no actual identity. Since this substance was in essence divine, not only did Ibn Falāḥ's son appear as the reincarnation of all earlier prophets and Imams but he also claimed divine status; at their mystical seances the Mushaʿshaʿ used the sentence ''Alī is God' (*ʿAlī Allāh*) as their recitation formula (*dhikr*). The Mushaʿshaʿ dynasty held its ground in Khūzistān until the 17th century; their residence at Ḥuwayza remained a centre for the sect even after its conquest by the Ṣafavids in 914/1508. It was left to the Mushaʿshaʿ prince Mubārak (998-1025/1589-1616), now a loyal vassal of the Ṣafavid Shāh, to abjure the doctrines of his fathers; and he called an Imāmī jurist, ʿAbd al-Laṭīf Jāmiʿ, to his court to instruct his subjects in proper Twelver faith. In certain details – for example in their picture of Christ – the doctrine of the Mushaʿshaʿ sect shows surprising correspondences with the faith of the gnostic baptist sects of the Mandaeans,[156] who lived in the southern Iraqi marshlands; and the Mushaʿshaʿ doctrines again appear to have had a strong influence on the organisation of the syncretist sect of the ʿAlī-Ilāhī (the deifiers of ʿAlī) or Ahl-i Ḥaqq (Supporters of the Truth) in Lūristān and the region of Kirmānshāh.[157]

The most successful Mahdī, however, was to be the one who came forward at the end of the century in north-west Iran – the Ṣafavid Ismāʿīl whose propaganda shows all the characteristics of the Shia of the period: a close affinity to Sufism, a tendency towards a military state of the dervish type, a chiliastic expectation of the Mahdī, and the deification of the Imam-Mahdī.

The eponymous forefather of the later Ṣafavid dynasty, Shaykh Ṣafī al-Dīn Isḥāq, was a dervish probably of Kurdish origin who enjoyed high religious prestige in his home town of Ardabīl in Āzarbayjān. He was not a Shiite, or at least no more so than other Sufis who traditionally cultivated veneration of ʿAlī and the Imams. The hermitage cell (*zāwiya*) of Shaykh Ṣafī al-Dīn in Ardabīl continued to enjoy great prestige after his death in 735/1334 under the protection of his descendants; but the Ṣafaviyya order only obtained more than local significance when Ṣafī's great-grandson was forced to leave Ardabīl in 852/1448 and began to lead a vagrant nomadic life in eastern Anatolia, northern Syria and Mesopotamia. In 861/1456 Junayd found refuge in Āmid (Diyarbakr) on the upper Tigris at the court of the Turcoman prince of the White Sheep (Āq Qoyūnlū), Uzun Ḥasan, who married the young dervish shaykh to his daughter Khadīja. Junayd began to recruit supporters among the nomadic Turcoman tribes whom he commanded as border fighters (*ghāzī*) in the Holy War against the Christian Georgians and the Circassians of the Caucasus. After he fell in battle in 804/1460 his son Shaykh Ḥaydar succeeded him and managed to return to Ardabīl and take over leadership of the order. It was Ḥaydar who – supposedly after ʿAlī appeared to him in a dream – prescribed red caps (*tāj-i Ḥaydarī*) put together out of twelve triangular gussets, and from then on they were called *Qizilbāsh* (redheads) in Turkish.

Like his father before him, Ḥaydar too sent his 'representatives' (*khalīfa*) to the Turcoman tribes which had linked up with the Ṣafaviyya order and urged them to wage Holy War against the unbelievers. It is hardly surprising that the character of the order changed substantially under these conditions. Ḥaydar was no longer the traditional Sufi Shaykh who operated in a circle of a dozen adepts; rather he was the leader of a large and powerful force of religious fighters. The word *ṣūfī* increasingly acquired the meaning of 'active Muslim'.[158] Ḥaydar then led his predominantly Turcoman following with the consent of the Āq Qoyūnlū Sultan Yaʿqūb into *jihād* against the Georgians and the Circassians; the growing might of the dervishes, however, soon appeared as a sinister threat to the Islamic rulers and the Shaykh finally fell foul of their alliance. He was killed in battle at the foot of the Elburz mountains near to Ṭabarsarān against the prince of the White Sheep (Āq Qoyūnlū) and the Shah of Shirvān (in the present-day Soviet republic of Āzarbayjān) in 893/1488.

We know hardly anything about the religious ideas of Junayd and Ḥaydar. Their veneration of ʿAlī and the Imams appears to have been restricted to what was usual among the dervishes. The court historian of the Āq Qoyūnlū, Khunjī, reports that the Qizilbāsh had quite openly called Shaykh Junayd God (*ilāh*) and his son the Son of God (*ibn Allāh*); 'to honour him they say: "He is the living one and there is no God but he"'[159] Although this report came from a notorious opponent of the Ṣafavids it need not necessarily be false; but perhaps it says more about the supporters of the Shaykhs of Ardabīl than it does about the Shaykhs themselves.

Extreme Shiite characteristics of this nature are first definitely attested for Ḥaydar's son Ismā'īl. They possibly stem from his teacher, Shams al-Dīn Lāhījī, who had brought up the young Ismā'īl during his exile at the small Shiite court of Gīlān on the Caspian Sea.[160] In the year 905/1499 the twelve-year-old Ismā'īl became the charismatic leader at the head of his father's Qizilbāsh supporters, who enthusiastically thronged to him in his first campaign against eastern Anatolian Arzinjān (Erzincan) the following year. The main body of the Qizilbāsh troops to whom Ismā'īl owed his rise to power in Iran were still drawn from the nomadic Turcoman tribes of eastern Anatolia, Āzarbayjān and northern Mesopotamia who barely concealed the pagan shamanistic traditions of their native steppeland under a superficial allegiance to Islam. In contrast to W. Hinz who sees the original impulse of Iranian national consciousness in the rise of the Ṣafavids which then led on to the foundation of the Iranian state, V. Minorsky and J. Aubin show that the Ṣafavid movement in its infancy owed practically nothing to sedentary urban or rural Iran and the canonised Twelver Shia. The rule of the Qizilbāsh did not differ in type from that of the Turcoman confederations of the Qarā Qoyūnlū and Āq Qoyūnlū, upon whose heritage they entered. When the fanatical troops of the Qizilbāsh broke out from Āzarbayjān and overran Iran this in no way signified for Iran a national spontaneous rebirth; rather it was a revived foreign invasion by nomadic tribes, this time from the west, comparable in its disastrous effects to the invasions of the Mongols and Tīmūr's campaigns. Cases of ritual cannibalism (*zandi-khvārī*) – the consumption of slain enemies – were described in the chronicles, as is also the fact that Shāh Ismā'īl, following one of the ancient customs of the steppe peoples, had a drinking vessel made from the skull of the Özbek Khan Shaybānī after defeating him. The Shiism of Ismā'īl and his Qizilbāsh following in any case had very unorthodox, indeed extreme characteristics. I. Mélikoff even speaks of an independent Qizilbāsh religion which was certainly no Shiite Islam, but was rather, strictly speaking, a Turcoman paganism which Ṣafavid propaganda merely provided with a thin Islamic varnish and 'rendered Ṣūfī and Shiite'.[161]

The poems of the *dīwān* in the Azeri-Turkic language which Shāh Ismā'īl wrote under the pen-name Khaṭā'ī demonstrate an ambitious sense of mission on the part of the young Shaykh, whose utterances can hardly be measured in terms of Imāmī orthodoxy. He makes it quite clear that he regards himself as the awaited Mahdī:

The rightly-guided Mahdī has arrived!...
The Mahdī's epoch has begun[162]

According to a popular account Ismā'īl is said to have emerged from the wood in front of his supporters wearing the sword of the Hidden Imam (*ṣāḥib-i zamān*). However, he is not only the Mahdī, but also a reincarnation of 'Alī and the twelve Imams:

I am Ismā'īl, I came into the world;
I walk on earth as in heaven;
The unknowing shall know me:
I am 'Alī, 'Alī is me!

I am the divine truth; I come from God.
I am one of the twelve Imams.
The four corners (of the earth) I occupy.
I am the same as the omnipotence of 'Alī.[163]

Muḥammad Muṣṭafā, Seal of the Prophets, has arrived...
My Imams Ja'far-i Ṣādiq and 'Alī Mūsā Riḍā have come.[164]

Muḥammad, 'Alī, the Imams and Shāh Ismā'īl are themselves no more than the veils in which the divine light (*nūr-i ilāhī*) has presented itself ever since the creation of the world in ever new disguises:

The elected one has slipped into a thousand and one garments
and wandered the earth.[165]

Throw thyself down!...
Adam has put on new clothes;
God has come! God has come![166]

I am identical to God...
Come, look now at the divine truth , thou erring blind man:
I am the Absolute Primal Moving Cause of whom men speak![167]

These unequivocal utterances which run throughout the whole of Shāh Ismā'īl's *dīwān* can hardly be played down as pure poetic licence, as has occasionally been attempted. The fanatical sacrificial courage of the disciples (*murīdān*) corresponded to the sense of mission of the mystical leader (*murshid*), as their battle cry testifies: 'My master and spiritual leader for whom I sacrifice myself!'[168] European travellers testify that these were no empty words; an anonymous Venetian observed: 'This Sophy (Sufi) is loved and venerated as God by his people, especially by his soldiers, some of whom go into battle without armour in the expectation that their lord Ismael will protect them. The name of God has been forgotten in the whole of Persia, now only the name of Ismael is known. When someone falls – whether from horseback or as a foot-soldier – he calls upon no other God than the Shiac (Shaykh) using the name in two ways: either as God Shiac, or as Prophet; as the Musulmans say: "laylla yllala Mahamet resuralla", the Persians say "Laylla yllala Ismael velialla."[169] Apart from that they all consider him to be immortal – especially his soldiers.'[170]

Bibliography

1. *On the general religious situation:*
A. Schimmel, 'The Ornament of the Saints. The Religious Situation in Pre-Safavid Times', *Iranian Studies* 7 (1974), 88-111. A. Falaturi, *Die Vorbereitung des iranischen Volkes für die Annahme der Schia zu Beginn der Safawiden-Zeit,* in: U. Haarmann/P. Bachmann (eds), *Die islamische Welt zwischen Mittelalter und Neuzeit, Festschrift für H. R. Roemer,* Beirut 1979, 132-45. E. Glassen, 'Krisenbewusstsein und Heilserwartung in der islamischen Welt zu Beginn der Neuzeit', ibid, 167-97. S. A. Arjomand, *The Shadow of God and the Hidden Imam,* Chicago 1984, Ch. II: Millenarian Religio-Political Movements in the Fourteenth/Eighth and Fifteenth/Ninth Centuries, 66-84. – *The Cambridge History of Iran VI, The Timurid and Safavid Periods,* Cambridge 1986, Ch. 12, 610 ff.: Religion in the Timurid and Safavid Period (B. Scarcia Amoretti).
2. *The Ḥurūfiyya:*
E. G. Browne, 'Some Notes on the Literature and Doctrines of the Ḥurūfī Sect', JRAS (1898), 61-94; 'Further Notes on the Literature of the Ḥurūfīs and Their Connection with the Bektāshī Order of Dervishes', *JRAS* (1907), 533-81. C. Huart, *Textes persans relatifs à la secte des Ḥourufis,* Leiden 1909. H. Ritter, 'Die Anfänge der Hurūfī-Sekte', *Oriens* 7 (1954), 1-54. A. Bausani, Art. Ḥurūfiyya, EI². H. Algar, Art. Astarābādī, Fażollāh, Encycl. Iran.
3. *The Nūrbakhshiyya:*
D. S. Margoliouth, Art. Nūrbakhshiya, EI¹. G. Ṣadaqiyānlū, *Taḥqīq dar aḥval va-āṣār-e Sayyid Moḥammad Nūrbakhsh Ovaysī Qohestānī,* Tehran 1351/1972.
4. *The Musha'sha':*
W. Caskel, 'Ein Mahdī des 15. Jahrhunderts. Saijid Muḥammad ibn Falāḥ und seine Nachkommen', *Islamica* 4 (1931), 48-93. A. Kasravī, *Musha'sha'iyyān, Aḥmad Tabrīzī ya bakhṣī az tārīkh-e Khūzistān,* Tehran ²1330/1951. V. Minorsky, Art. Musha'sha', EI² Suppl., 1937.
5. *Early Ṣafavids and Qizilbāsh:*
E. D. Ross, 'The early Years of Shāh Ismā'īl, Founder of the Ṣafavī Dynasty', *JRAS* 28 (1896), 249-340. W. Hinz, *Irans Aufstieg zum Nationalstaat im fünfzehnten Jahrhundert,* Berlin/Leipzig 1936. Gh. Sarwar, *History of Shāh Ismā'īl Ṣafawī,* Aligarh 1939. V. Minorsky, 'The Poetry of Shāh Ismā'īl' I, *BSOAS* 10 (1940-1942), 1006-53. T. Gandjeï, *Il canzoniere di Šāh Ismā'īl Ḫaṭā'ī,* Naples 1959. E. Glassen, *Die frühen Ṣafawiden nach Qāżī Aḥmad Qumī,* Freiburg i. Br. 1970; 'Schah Ismā'īl, ein Mahdī der anatolischen Turkmenen?' *ZDMG* 121 (1971), 61-9. M. M. Mazzaoui, The Origins of the

Ṣafawids. „Ī'ism, Ṣūfism, and the Gulāt, Wiesbaden 1972. O. Efendiev, 'Le rôle des tribus de la langue turque dans la création de l'État Safavide', *Turcica* 6 (1975), 24-33. I. Mélikoff, 'Le problème Ḳizilbaş', *Turcica* 6 (1975), 49-67. S.A. Arjomand, *The Shadow of God and the Hidden Imam*, Chicago 1984, 77 ff.: The Rise of the Safavids: Theophanic Domination and Militant Chiliasm. H. R. Roemer, 'Die turkmenischen Qïzïlba – Gründer und Opfer der safawidischen Theokratie', *ZDMG* 135 (1985), 227-40. – *The Cambridge History of Iran* VI, 190 ff.: The Background of the Safavids; 209 ff.: Ismā'īl I (H. R. Roemer); 629 ff.: The Qizilbāsh; 634 ff.: Shah Ismā'īl (B. Scarcia Amoretti). M. Haneda, *Le Châh et les Qizilbāš. Le système militaire safavide*, Berlin 1987.

THE ṢAFAVID PERIOD: THE SHĀH AS THE REPRESENTATIVE OF THE HIDDEN IMAM

The Ṣafavid Ismā'īl's rise to become ruler of Iran was effected within only two years. In 905/1499 the twelve-year-old Shaykh left his exile on the Caspian Sea and headed the Qizilbāsh; at the end of 906/1500 he defeated the Shāh of Shirvān and conquered his towns of Shamākhā and Bākū; in the summer of 907/1501 at Sharūr near Nakhchivān on the Araxes he put the Āq-Qoyūnlū Sultan Alvand to flight and immediately afterwards – in July or August 1501 – he was able to make his triumphal entry into Alvand's capital Tabrīz. Here he assumed the ancient Iranian title of King of Kings (*shāhānshāh*) and set up the Shia as the ruling faith.

'On Friday he caused the *khaṭīb* (preacher) of that town to read the *khuṭba* (Friday sermon) for the Twelve Imams and to add to the call for prayer the beautiful formula 'I testify that 'Alī is the friend of God!' and the sentence 'Hasten to the best of deeds'. After the *khuṭba*, they said from the pulpits: ' A curse upon Abū Bakr, 'Umar, 'Uthmān and the other accursed of the Umayyads and Abbasids!' The fateful order was issued which required everyone in the whole of the empire to proceed in the following way: revile and curse in the market places the three accursed ones and kill anyone who refuses to do so!'[171]

During this first Shiite Friday sermon the Qizilbāsh kept watch in order to suppress any displeasure on the part of the predominantly Sunni population. Crowds of Qizilbāsh swept through the town cursing the first three Caliphs, and anyone who did not reply 'May the cursing increase and not decrease' came off badly. The cleansing of the sinful town began with the public execution of 300 prostitutes.

The fanatical sense of self-sacrifice on the part of the Qizilbāsh gave the young Shāh one victory after another in the following decade. In 908/1503 Hamadān, Iṣfahān and Shīrāz – all Sunni strongholds – were conquered, and the following year, Yazd and Kirmān; in 914/1508, after defeating the Özbek Khan Shaybānī at Merv, eastern Iran was also conquered with Mashhad, Herat and Balkh. However, the charismatic murshid suffered a serious setback when the champion of the Sunna in the west, the Ottoman Sultan Selim, bloodily persecuted the Turcoman Qizilbāsh in eastern Anatolia and in August 920/1514 inflicted a heavy defeat on the Ṣafavid army at Chaldirān (between Tabrīz and Lake Urmia) – principally because of his superior artillery which the Ṣafavids were unable to match. The catastrophe was not only a heavy blow to the religious prestige of the 'reincarnated 'Alī', but also resulted in the loss of eastern Anatolia, the main recruiting ground of the Qizilbash. At that time, however, Shāh Ismā'īl was able to recover from both setbacks; the régime's departure from the extreme ideas of the Qizilbāsh and a turn towards the orthodox legalistic Twelver Shia had already taken place. None the less, the spread of the new faith in Iran did not proceed smoothly. The population of Iran – like that of Afghanistan and Central Asia – was still predominantly Sunni;[172] by the beginning of the 16th century there was not yet any Twelver Shiite theologico-juristic tradition worth mentioning.[173] The only Imāmī book they had been able to find at Shāh Ismā'īl's enthronment in Tabrīz was the 'Dogmas of Islam' (*Qawā'id al-Islām*) written in Arabic by the Iraqi scholar 'Allāma al-Ḥillī (d. 726/1325)[174] which thus enjoyed rather unanticipated respect. Ismā'īl's son and successor Ṭahmāsp later had the text translated into Persian in order to make it accessible to the ordinary people.

The caste of Imāmī legal scholars (*'ulamā'*) re-emerged as a result of the support they received from the Ṣafavids and, at the same time, the character of the Ṣafavid government itself began to change under the influence of these same *'ulamā'*. The extreme ideas of the Qizilbāsh were refined and brought within bounds, and the 'transition from popular Shiism to high Shiism'[175] begins to be evident. The dīwān of Ismā'īl 'Khaṭā'ī' was cleansed of its over-blasphemous lines and even the biography of the forefather of the dynasty, the *Ṣafwat al-Ṣafā'*, was revised. The Alid genealogical tree, by which what was in fact a Kurdish family established its specious descent from the seventh Imam Mūsā al-Kāẓim, was also now officially proclaimed. The defeat of Chaldirān, which destroyed the Mahdī aura of Shāh Ismā'īl appears to have made the new orientation and the creation of a 'new form of authority'[176] necessary. Alleged descent from the Prophet, the Sayyid line (*siyāda*), which the Shaykhs of the Ṣafavid order had no doubt claimed for themselves back in Ardabīl,[177] now allowed the Shāh to appear, if no longer as the Mahdī himself, at any rate as his sole legitimate representative and agent during the *ghayba*, and thus as the spiritual head of the Shia and indeed of the whole Islamic *umma*. The Ṣafavids thus recreated a ruler's office with universal claims for the first time since the end of the Baghdad Caliphate, combining both the highest secular and supreme spiritual power. The champion of the

Sunna, the Ottoman Sultan of Istanbul, responded by bearing the title of Caliph as well as that of Sultan after the conquest of Syria and Egypt in 922/1517.

As a relative and the sole legitimate representative of the Hidden Imam the Ṣafavid Shāh was now the highest religious authority of the Shia. Nevertheless he delegated the administration of religious affairs to a deputy appointed by him, paid by him, and who could be dismissed by him: the Ṣadr. The office of Ṣadr (Arab: head, chief) was not created by the Ṣafavids and can already be traced in the 15th century under the Sunni Tīmūrids.[178] The task of the Ṣadr was to supervise the legal system and the religious endowments; under a Shiite regime there was a commitment to spread the Twelver Shia faith and to enforce it generally, to guarantee its purity and to proceed against any opposition, deviation or innovation. The first holder of the office (907/1501) was the Qāḍī Shams al-Dīn from Lāhījān in Gīlān, tutor of the young Ismāʿīl during his period of exile. His successor, the Qāḍī Muḥammad Kāshānī (909-915/1503-1510) distinguished himself by his persecution of the Sunnis, and several prominent scholars fell victim to his legal proceedings. He was succeeded by the Sayyid Sharīf al-Dīn ʿAlī Shīrāzī who was not only a spiritual dignitary, but also – as can quite often be observed in the militant state of the Ṣafavid order – held high military rank (Arab: *amīr*, Pers. *mīr*). He, and the fourth Ṣadr, Amir ʿAbd al-Bāqī Yazdī, fell in 1514 at the battle of Chaldirān. This dual nature of the Ṣadr office, which was greatly coveted and disputed, naturally dragged its holder into political arguments and court intrigue. In the year 917/1511 it is reported for the first time that the Ṣadr Sayyid ʿAlī Shīrāzī left court because of his differences with the deputy (*vakīl*) of the Shāh and, under the pretext of a pilgrim visit (*ziyāra*) to the shrines of Najaf and Karbalāʾ, managed to escape from the Shāh's influence and clutches – a model for the future for all Shiite clerics in Iran who came into conflict with secular power.

The first holders of the Ṣadr office under Shāh Ismāʿīl were certainly zealous in their Shiite convictions, but on the whole they had not yet had the later normal education in Imāmī law, conditions for which were generally lacking in Iran at the time. Their religious passion was initially concentrated on quite elementary and external matters. Thus the Ṣadr Amīr Jalāl al-Dīn Sīranjī Astarābādī (920-931/1514-1525) was renowned for the fact that no one since Shaykh Ṭūsī had done so much to spread the Twelver Shia: punishment of villains (that is to say, those of a different faith), rejection of heretical innovations, prohibition of what was unlawful, care for muezzins and prayer leaders, the enjoining of duties such as the Friday prayer or Ramaḍān fast. The Ṣadr Amīr Muʿizz al-Dīn Muḥammad Iṣfahānī (935-943/1529-1536) dealt severely with opium caves, wine cellars and gambling dens.[179]

Measures taken by the Ṣadr were meanwhile not only directed against miscreants, lukewarm Shiites and believers of other faiths, but also against the unorthodox Shiism of the Qizilbāsh whose unbridled fanaticism could be reconciled with the requirements of an orderly state system less and less as time went on. Ismā'īl's son and successor Ṭahmāsp (930-984/1524-1576) was still venerated by the Qizilbāsh as the incarnation of God. In the year 962/1555 a few of his supporters publicly proclaimed him as the awaited Mahdī, but he took action against this and had the spokesmen executed for heresy. Under the influence of the Imāmī legal scholars the dynasty gradually emancipated itself from the radical wing which had helped it to power. The most important theoretical juristic literature of the Twelver Shia which – because it was written in Arabic – was inaccessible to the main body of the Iranian population was now translated into Persian on Ṭahmāsp's orders, and the first step was thus taken towards the gradual conversion of the Iranians to Shiism. Arab scholars brought to court by Ṭahmāsp contributed not a little to this conversion. They came mainly from the two most significant centres of Shiite learning in the 15th century: from the Gulf coast (Baḥrayn, al-Qaṭīf and al-Aḥsa', today's Hufuf) and from Jabal 'Āmil in south Lebanon. South Lebanon – Shiite from the time of early Islam – had followed the rationalist school of Ḥilla (see above p. 67) since the impact of the 'first martyr' Ibn Makkī al-'Āmilī (d. 786/1384). Out of this tradition came the scholar 'Alī ibn 'Abd al-'Ālī al-Karakī al-'Āmilī from Karak Nūḥ in the Biqā' plain. From about 909/1504 he lived beside 'Alī's shrine in Najaf; in 916/1510, like other Shiite scholars living in Iraq, he followed Shāh Ismā'īl's call to the newly-conquered eastern Iran (Mashhad, Herat) but then returned again to Najaf. Under Shāh Ṭahmāsp he paid lengthy visits to Iran on several occasions, had great honours heaped upon him by the ruler and was endowed with far-reaching powers to spread Twelver Shiism. The honorific titles conferred on him by the Shāh in his deeds testify to this – 'Seal of the Mujtahids' (*khātam al-mujtahidīn*) and even 'Deputy of the Imam' (*nā'ib al-imām*) – as do the profitable endowments in Najaf of which al-Karakī became administrator and beneficiary. He received authority to install Shiite leaders of the Friday prayer (*pīsh-namāz*) everywhere, and the foreign scholar thereby came into conflict with the Ṣadr whose responsibility was thus diminished. The Shāh, however, sided with his special plenipotentiary and replaced the refractory Ṣadr Ghiyāth al-Dīn Manṣūr Dashtakī in the year 938/1531 by a Persian pupil of Karakī, Mu'izz al-Dīn Muḥammad Iṣfahānī. In the following year the Shāh confirmed in an official deed to al-Karakī the right to install and remove at will all religious functionaries in the empire. Through al-Karakī's action the Ḥilla school received official recognition and emphatic support from a ruler for the first time, thus mapping out the future path for the development of the Shiite clergy in Iran.

Not only were the principles of the Ḥilla school – the methods of *kalām, ijtihād* and *taqlīd* – transplanted to Iran under the influence of al-Karakī but also now for the first time individual prerogatives of the Hidden Imam were vicariously transferred to qualified Shiite scholars. The question as to whether anyone had the right to hold the Friday prayer in the absence of the Imam had been disputed until then; al-Karakī now answered emphatically in the affirmative. The Friday prayer was not only permissible but in fact obligatory if a qualified scholar was available to lead it.[180] Similarly disputed was the question of raising taxes (*kharāj*) from conquered land which, according to old juristic theory, was the common property of all Muslims. Al-Karakī took a position on this matter too: raising of taxes by the secular ruler in place of the Hidden Imam was not only permissible but it was also necessary in the interests of Muslims, and a Shiite scholar who was qualified to be a representative of the Hidden Imam – al-Karakī was doubtless thinking of himself – committed no sin when he raised such taxes on the order of the 'tyrant' (*jā'ir*) or was endowed with them by him.[181] Concerning his support of a secular – and therefore fundamentally unjust – government, al-Karakī called upon the example of prominent Shiite scholars of earlier times, for example the Sharīfs al-Murtaḍā and al-Raḍī under the Būyids and Naṣīr al-Dīn Ṭūsī and 'Allāma al-Ḥillī under the Mongols.[182]

Al-Karakī's opinion on these questions, which was strongly attacked by some of his fellow-believers, played no small part in supporting the legitimisation of the Ṣafavid dynasty and also in strengthening his own position as the representative (*nā'ib*) of the Hidden Imam. Nevertheless his uncontested position as 'the mujtahid of his time' (*mujtahid al-zamān*) was not institutionalised and was not continued after his death (in 940/1534) even though this honorific was passed on to his son. Decades later there was still no question of Iran's becoming completely Shiite. In the years 983/1575-6 shortly before Ṭahmāsp's death, there was even a Sunni reaction at the court which was officially supported by his son Ismā'īl II (984-985/1576-1578). But this was only a short interlude. Ṭahmāsp's grandson Shāh 'Abbās I (996-1038/1588-1629) not only conclusively put an end to the influence of the radical Qizilbāsh but even attempted to restrict that of the Sufis and the Imāmī legal scholars in order to replace them as the sole leading authority during the absence of the Hidden Imam. Under him Ṣafavid absolutism attained its zenith. Supported by an army which was centrally led, with up-to-date equipment and loyal to him personally, and which was no longer recruited from the Turcoman tribes but rather from Armenian, Georgian and Circassian renegades, Shāh ʿAbbās (who moreover chose Iṣfahān as the new capital), was able to deprive the Qizilbāsh of their influence altogether. The dervish orders were persecuted and disappeared almost completely from Iran; a few dwindled to merely local significance; others, such as the Niʿmatallāhiyya, sought refuge in India and did not return to Iran until the 19th century.[183] The word *ṣūfī*, simply synonymous with 'pious Muslim' at the beginning of the dynasty, now almost acquired the meaning of 'heretic'.

On the other hand, the orthodox Twelver Shia enjoyed the Shāh's favour and help. After the reconquest of Khurāsān in 1006/1598 ʿAbbās restored the Mashhad shrine which had been plundered and destroyed by the Özbeks and, fulfilling a vow, in 1010/1601 made the pilgrimage by foot from Iṣfahān to Mashhad. The march took twenty-eight days and was joined by countless pious men. On a later pilgrimage (1021/1610) the Shāh undertook repairs to the buildings and improved the town's water supply by installing qanāts and reservoirs.[184] After a successful campaign against Georgia and Shirvān, including the occupation of Tiflīs, Darband, Bākū and Shamākhā, he converted the whole of his private real estate (*amlāk*) into a religious endowment (*waqf*) in favour of the 'fourteen sinless ones' (*chahārdah maʿṣūm*) i.e. Muḥammad, Fāṭima and the twelve Imāms. This included the rows of shops on the four sides of the Shāh square in Iṣfahān (*chahār bāzār*), two caravanserais and numerous bath houses in Iṣfahān, Qazvīn and elsewhere. The legitimate administrators of the endowment, the yearly income of which came to around 7,000 tumans, were the Shāh himself and his successors on the throne; control of the use of the money came under the jurisdiction of the Ṣadr. The income was set aside for the poor, legal scholars, students of Shiite law and for all expenditure made 'on the path of religion and the state' (*dar rāh-i dīn va dawlat*). At the same time the Shāh also bequeathed his moveable assets to the big religious institutions: jewels and trinkets, thoroughbred horses, camels, herds of sheep. His books on jurisprudence went to the shrine at Mashhad; his Persian books on history and poetry and his porcelain went to the original sanctuary of the dynasty in Ardabīl (where the 'porcelain house' – *chīnī-khāna* – can be still seen today).

Apart from Mashhad, Qumm in particular received a new impetus. The town, destroyed by the Mongols in 1224 had revived under the Tīmūrids in the 15th century and the Turcoman Sultans of the 'White Sheep' had frequently used it as their winter quarters – a use continued by Shāhs Ismāʿīl and Ṭahmāsp. When Iraq, together with the shrines at

Najaf and Karbalā', was finally lost to the Ottomans, the prestige of the Iranian sanctuaries rose sharply. Shāh 'Abbas founded a madrasa and a pilgrim hostel in Qumm, scholars and pilgrims flocked there in ever greater numbers, sayyids settled and were buried there so that soon hundreds of graves of the Imams' descendants (*imām-zāda*) were to be found in Qumm.

In the year 1010/1601 al-Baḥrayn – i.e. the eastern Gulf coast – a predominantly Shiite stretch of land, came under the Shāh's rule, and in 1033/1624 he reconquered Iraq which had been occupied by the Ottomans. In Baghdad Sunni notables suffered severe persecution, and the mausolea of the great Sunni legal teacher Abū Ḥanīfa (d. 150/767) and that of the mystic and founder of the order 'Abd al-Qādir al-Jīlānī (d. 561/1166) were plundered and destroyed. The shrine at Kāẓimayn, on the other hand, was endowed richly by Shāh 'Abbās. The Shāh even kept winter camps (*qishlāq*) at the shrines on the Euphrates; in Najaf he had the canals cleaned which had been constructed by his ancestor Shāh Ismā'īl, and he paid the obligatory visit to al-Ḥusayn's grave in Karbalā'. However, as early as 1048/1638 the Ottomans conquered Baghdad for the second time and thus the Shāh's sovereignty over the Shiite sanctuaries of Iraq was finally ended.

Primary sources in translation

E. Glassen, *Die frühen Safawiden nach Qāżī Aḥmad Qumī*, Freiburg i. Br. 1970. H. Müller, *Die Chronik Ḫulāṣat at-tawārīḫ des Qāżī Aḥmad Qumī. Der Abschnitt über Schah 'Abbās I.* Wiesbaden 1964.

Secondary sources

L.-L. Bellan, *Chah 'Abbās I. Sa vie, son histoire*, Paris 1932. A. K. S. Lambton, 'Quis custodiet custodes? Some Reflections on the Persian Theory of Government', *SI* 5 (1956), 125-48; 6 (1957), 125-46. J. Aubin, 'Etudes safavides, I. „āh Ismā'īl et les notables de l'Iraq persan', *JESHO* 2 (1959), 37-81; 'La politique religieuse des Ṣafavides', in: *Le shī'isme imâmite, Colloque de Strasbourg*, Paris 1970, 235-44. R. M. Savory, 'The Principal Offices of the Ṣafavid State During the Reign of Isma'il I. (907-30/1501-24)', *BSOAS* 232 (1960), 91-105; 'The Consolidation of Ṣafawid Power in Persia', *Der Islam* 41 (1965), 71-94; 'Some Reflections on Totalitarian Tendencies in the Ṣafavid State', *Der Islam* 53 (1976), 226-41; *Iran under the Ṣafavids*, London 1980. H. Sohrweide, 'Der Sieg der Ṣafaviden in Persien und seine Rückwirkung auf die Schiiten Anatoliens im 16. Jh.', *Der Islam* 41 (1965), 117-37. E. Glassen, 'Schah Ismā'īl und die Theologen seiner Zeit', *Der Islam* 48 (1972), 254-68. S. H. Nasr, 'Religion in Safavid Persia', *Iranian Studies* 7 (1974), 287-93. W. Madelung, 'Shiite Discussions on the Legality of the *kharāj*', *Proceedings of the Ninth Congress of the Union Européenne des Arabisants et Islamisants*, Leiden 1981, 193-202; Art. al-Karakī, EI². S. A. Arjomand, *The Shadow of God and the Hidden Imam*, Chicago 1984, Part II: Shi'ism as the Religion of the State under the Safavids, 1501-1722, 103 ff. A. Hourani, 'From Jabal 'Āmil to Persia', *BSOAS* 49 (1986), 133-40. – *The Cambridge History of Iran VI, The Timurid and Safavid Periods*, Ch. 5: The Safavid Period, 189 ff. (H. R. Roemer); Ch. 6: The Safavid Administrative System, 351 ff. (R. M. Savory); Ch. 12: Religion in the Timurid and Safavid Periods, 610 ff. (B. Scarcia Amoretti).

REVELATION, METAPHYSICS AND GNOSIS: THE THEOSOPHICAL SCHOOL OF IṢFAHĀN (17TH CENTURY)

During the reign of Shāh 'Abbās I (996-1038/1588-1629) the extreme Shia of the Qizilbāsh type was finally subdued and the mystical dervish orders were persecuted and banished. Imāmī legal scholars (*'ulamā'*) from the Ḥilla school, procured by Karakī, held the field. Their steadily growing influence depended on the fact that they gradually brought two particular religious functions under their control: in the small towns and villages that of the prayer leaders (*pīsh-namāz*) and in the capital of the empire and the provinces – Iṣfahān, Tabrīz, Qazvīn, Mashhad and so on – that of the 'Elder of Islam' (*Shaykh al-islām*), which now evolved into the highest regional religious authority. All the same, at the beginning of the 17th century, Shiism was not the sole faith to be found, nor had all the divergent trends within the Shia disappeared. Opposition to rationalism and the pedantic learning of the Imāmī jurists and to their principles of *ijtihād* and *taqlīd* had in no way died down; various forms of dissent stirred against the scholars' claim to represent the Hidden Imam solely by virtue of their learning. It came in the first place from the traditionalist scholars (*akhbārī*) who attributed authority only to the word of the Quran, the Prophet and the Imāms, and rejected point-blank the *ijtihād* of the scholars; their spokesman was the Persian Mullah Muḥammad Amīr Astarābādī (d. 1036/1626) who lived in Mecca and Medina.[185] At the same time, even though the dervish orders had been shattered, the mystical tradition continued with its promise of a direct individual experience of God. Moreover, in aristocratic circles the old Iranian educational ideal lived on, combining the Islamic – now Shiite – faith with the study of natural science and Neoplatonic philosophy in the tradition of al-Fārābī or Ibn Sīnā (Avicenna). In the 13th century Naṣīr al-Dīn Ṭūsī had personified this ideal magnificently (see above p. 63). One of the last great universal scholars of this type was Bahā' al-Dīn al-'Āmilī, popular in Iran up to the present day, known as Shaykh-i Bahā'ī (not to be mistaken with the later founder of the Bahā'ī religion; see below p. 110). He originated from Lebanese Baalbak and came to Persia at the age of thirteen with his father, a Shiite scholar; after studying in Qazvīn and Herat he eventually settled in Iṣfahān. He was a mathematician and logician, astronomer and alchemist, irrigation engineer, horticulturalist and architect – he cooperated in planning the Shāh mosque at Iṣfahān – and he was also a poet and a jurist. His Shiite legal compendium *Jāmiʿ-i ʿAbbāsī* in Persian dedicated to Shāh ʿAbbās is still in use today; and in addition he composed mystical epic poems (*masnavī*) such as the 'Book of the Parrot' (*Ṭūṭī-nāma*). The fact that under Shāh ʿAbbās such a man could become *Shaykh al-islām* of the capital Iṣfahān is characteristic of the then still open Shiism at least of the court, which was attempting to escape not only the power of the Qizilbāsh but also the growing influence of the *ʿulamā'*.

Favoured by the successors of ʿAbbās I, Shāh Ṣafī (1038-1052/1629-1642) and ʿAbbās II (1052-1077/1642-1666) the 'anti-clerical' philosophical, mystical and gnostic trends within the Shia in the 17th century experienced one final upsurge. In particular it was ʿAbbās II who incurred censure from the legal scholars because he founded hermitages for individual dervishes, and in 1055/1645 together with Sayyid Ḥusayn Sulṭān al-ʿUlamā' he promoted a man to the position of grand vizier who was closely connected with the mystic-gnostic theosophical school at Iṣfahān and patronised its supporters.

The founder of the school at Iṣfahān was the Ḥusaynid Sayyid Mīr Muḥammad Bāqir Astarābādī, called *Dāmād*, 'the son-in-law', after his father who was Karakī's son-in-law. After studying in Mashhad he worked mainly in Iṣfahān; in his old age he accompanied Shāh Ṣafī to the shrines in Iraq where he died in 1040/1630 and was buried at the sanctuary in Najaf. Mīr Dāmād's comprehensive work – the scholarly prose being in Arabic as usual, the poetry in Persian – is a remarkable synthesis of three quite different spiritual traditions: in the first place the Twelver Shia doctrines (as *Shaykh al-islām* of Iṣfahān, Mīr Dāmād had led the coronation celebrations for Shāh Ṣafī), then the Aristotelian-Neoplatonic metaphysics which had been amalgamated with Islamic belief by Fārābī and Ibn Sīnā (Avicenna) in the 10th and 11th centuries, and finally illuminative wisdom (*ishrāq*) in the tradition of Suhrawardī (executed in Aleppo in 587/1191)[186] and Ibn ʿArabī (d. 638/1240 in Damascus). For the school founded in Iṣfahān by Mīr Dāmād, divine revelation (*sharʿ*), human intellect (*ʿaql*) and mystical enlightenment (*kashf*) in visions are equally paths to recognition of the sole truth. Rational speculation corroborates the revealed truths of faith, and the results of metaphysical speculation can again be seen directly in mystical vision. Mīr Dāmād describes how such a vision had been vouchsafed to him after mystical exercises (*dhikr*) on 15th Shaʿbān in the year 1023 (20th September 1614) – the night of the birth of the twelfth Imam – in Iṣfahān.[187] When illuminative wisdom (*ishrāq*) is bestowed upon the visionary it reveals to him the origin of his selfhood and, at the same time, shows his soul the way home; 'source' (*mabda'*) and 'target' (*ma'ād*) are therefore key concepts in Iṣfahānī theosophy (Arab. *ḥikma ilāhiyya:* divine wisdom, Pers. *ḥikmat-i ilāhī*). The mystical component is unmistakable, but after the persecution of the dervish orders it was not advisable to confess Sufism too publicly; the mystical experience was therefore camouflaged by a term which had been unusual until then, *'irfān* (recognition, gnosis).

The most important representative of the Iṣfahān school was Ṣadr al-Dīn Shīrāzī, known as Mullā Ṣadrā, pupil and closest confidant of Mīr Dāmād. Son of an aristocrat from Shīrāz, he was educated in Iṣfahān with Shaykh-i Bahā'ī and Mīr Dāmād, and after several years of seclusion in Kahak near Qumm he was invited to teach in Shīrāz by Shah 'Abbas II and worked there until his death (in 1050/1640) at a school founded by the governor of Fārs, Allāhverdi Khān. From Mullā Ṣadrā's numerous Arabic writings the 'Four Intellectual Excursions' deserves particular mention and is considered to be the *chef d'oeuvre* of the whole school.[188]

The theosophy of Iṣfahān was transplanted by Mullā Ṣadrā to Qumm and Shīrāz; above all in Qumm it had prominent advocates in Mullā Ṣadrā's pupil and son-in-law 'Abd al-Razzaq Lāhījī (d. 1072/1661) and his pupil Qazi Sa'id Qummī (d. 1103/1691) who was a doctor as well as being the town judge. Another of Mullā Ṣadrā's sons-in-law, Mullā Muḥsin Fayż Kāshānī (d. 1091/1680) worked in his home town of Kāshān where his miraculous grave is still venerated today.

Favoured and promoted by the Shāhs Ṣafī and 'Abbās II the school enjoyed an undisturbed period of flowering; and it was only a reaction on the part of the *'ulamā'*, which set in in a more acute form at the end of the 17th century and was taken up at court as well as elsewhere, that brought about its violent end. Attacked by the legal scholars of the Ḥilla school in numerous writings, and demonised as 'followers of an unbelieving Greek' (Aristotle) and as advocates of heretical innovations (*bid'a*) the theosophers were banned by the orthodox jurists. Under Shāh Sulaymān (1077-1105/1666-1694) Qāżī Sa'īd Qummī was imprisoned in the Alamūt citadel. Shāh Sulṭān Ḥusayn I (1105-1135/1694-1722) was under the influence of the *'ulamā'* right from the beginning of his reign, and at his bidding the Sufi seminary (khānqāh) of Mullā Muḥsin Fayż in Kāshān was destroyed and its inhabitants killed; renowned advocates of the school went into exile.

As editors, translators and interpreters the French orientalist Henry Corbin and the two Persian Sayyids Jalāl al-Dīn Āshtiyānī[189] and Hossein Naṣr deserve particular mention as leading scholars bound by personal commitment to the school as well as by scholarly interest; nevertheless, their inclination to consider the theosophy of Iṣfahān as the proper inner essence of the Shia and, indeed, of Islam generally, has not remained undisputed.[190]

Primary sources in translation

Mollâ Ṣadra Shirazi, Le Livre des Pénétrations métaphysiques (Kitâb al-Mashâ'ir), ed./trans. H. Corbin, Tehran/Paris 1964 (Bibliothèque iranienne 10).
J. W. Morris, *The Wisdom of the Throne. An Introduction to the Philosophy of Mulla Sadra*, Princeton 1981 (Eng. trans. of Mullā Ṣadrā's *al-Ḥikma al-'arshiyya*).

Secondary sources

M. Horten, *Das philosophische System des Schirazi*, Straşburg 1913. H. Corbin, 'Confessions extatiques de Mīr Dāmād, maître de théologie à Isfahan', *Mélanges Massignon*, Damascus 1956, 331-78; 'Une grande figure du shî'isme iranien, Mīr Dāmād', *Orientalia Romana* 1 (1958), 23-49; 'La place de Mollâ Sadrâ Shîrâzî dans la philosophie iranienne', *SI* 18 (1963), 81-113; 'Imâmologie et philosophie', in: *Le Shî'isme imâmite, Colloques de Strasbourg*, Paris 1970, 143-74. S. H. Nasr, 'The School of Ispahan', in: M. M. Sharif (ed.), *A History of Muslim Philosophy* II, Wiesbaden 1966, 904-32; *Ṣadr al-Dīn Shīrāzī and His Transcendent Theosophy. Background, Life and Works*, Tehran 1978; 'The Metaphysics of Sadr al-Dîn Shîrâzî and Islamic Philosophy in Qajar Iran', in: C. E. Bosworth/C. Hillenbrand (eds), *Qajar Iran*, Edinburgh 1983, 177-98; 'Spiritual Movements, Philosophy and Theology in the Safavid Period, in *CHI* VI, Ch. 13, 656 ff. A. Newman, 'Towards a Reconsideration of the "Iṣfahān School of Philosophy": Shaykh Bahā'ī and the Role of the Safawid 'ulamā'', *Studia Iranica* 15 (1986), 165-99.

THE INFALLIBLE MUJTAHID – AN ABANDONED CONCEPTION OF THE 17TH CENTURY

The violent imposition of Shiism in Iran ordered from the top was an act of Ṣafavid absolutism to which some commentators attribute 'caesaro-papist' characteristics.[191] It enabled the Shiite religious and legal scholars (*'ulamā'*) , the mullahs as they were usually called (Arab: mawlā: lord, master) to acquire social and soon also political influence such as they had never enjoyed before: as prayer leaders (*pīsh-namāz*) and directors of the Friday divine service (imām jum'a) in the great mosques, as legal experts (*muftī*) and judges (*qāḍī Per. qāżī*), as regional spiritual authorities (*shaykh al-islām*) in the provincial capitals, as administrators of the assets of the now enormously increased religious endowments (*waqf*) and as provisional beneficiaries of the share actually due to the Imam (*sahm-i imām*) taken from the believers' taxes as prescribed by the Quran (see below p. 106). Shāh 'Abbās I had certainly subordinated their influence to his central power, placing it under the control of the Ṣadr; but under his weaker successors not only did the power of the Ṣadr dwindle, eventually involving only superintendence of the endowments, but also the absolutism of the Shāh himself increasingly diminished. As against the central power, the position of the ʿulamāʾ gained in importance and self-awareness so that by the 17th century they were able to contest the claim of the royal house to represent the Hidden Imam through its sanctified lineage.

Mullah Aḥmad Ardabīlī (d. 993/1585), who lived in Najaf, decidedly opposed the raising of taxes by any 'tyrannical' power, and declined the invitation of Ṭahmāsp and ʿAbbās I to court, had already in a letter to him described the rule of ʿAbbās I as a 'loaned kingdom' (*mulk-i ʿāriyat*).[192] The French traveller Jean Chardin who stayed at the Iṣfahān court between 1666-7 and 1672-7, described with what for a European at that time was an extraordinarily intimate awareness the background of the opposition between king and 'clergy'.[193] 'The ruling house bases its claim to power solely on its descent from ʿAlī without considering any additional qualifications such as learning or the leading of a pious life to be necessary; however, it is exactly that which was expected by 'the pious (*gens d'église*) including all devotees and all those who confess themselves as people who precisely fulfil the religious duties'.[194] Chardin put together the 'devotees'' arguments against the dynasty in a whole catalogue of rhetorical questions: 'How can it be possible that these infamous kings who drink wine and are driven by passion are God's representatives, and that they communicate with Heaven to obtain the necessary light to guide the believers? How can they solve matters of conscience and doubts concerning the faith as a representative of God must do – they, who can sometimes barely read? Since our kings are unjust people their rule is a tyranny to which God has subjected us in order to punish us after withdrawing His Prophet's legitimate successor from the world. The highest throne of the universe is only fit for a *mouchtehed* (*mujtahid*), someone who possesses more holiness and knowledge than common people. Since the *mouchtehed* is holy, and consequently a peaceable person, a king is needed who can wield the sword to exercise justice, but he can only be his (the mujtahid's) minister and must be dependent on him.'[195] We hear that a certain Mullah Qāsim preached these ideas from his hermitage in a suburb of Iṣfahān and was in great demand until the Shāh had him seized and put away. Chardin also reports which alternatives he and his like-minded contemporaries contemplated: The power of the Shāh must be controlled by a 'mouchtehed massoum' (*mujtahid maʿṣūm*) i.e. an infallible mujtahid, a scholar who – like the Prophet and the Imāms – is immune from sin and error.'[196] A name was also brought into play: the twenty-year-old son of the *shaykh al-islām* from Iṣfahān and of a daughter of Shāh ʿAbbās fulfilled all the qualifications: besides his descent from ʿAlī (through the Ṣafavid princess) he possessed learning and piety which the ruler lacked; this 'pure branch of the Imāms' should supersede the accursed shoot of the House of the Prophet.[197]

The fact that the tensions observed by Chardin in 1666 between the Shāh and the *ʿulamāʾ* were not unique is testified by Engelbert Kaempfer from Lemgo who stayed at the Iṣfahān court between 1684 and 1685 as a doctor and secretary to a Swedish legation. He recorded his observations and experiences in 'Amoenitates exoticae' published in 1712:

> It is believed that the perspicacity of the modschtehed enables him to reach the infallible (!) decision in every moral dilemma, the solution of all doubts of belief and the correct interpretation of the Quran (the Muhammadan bible) and the oral traditions of the Prophet and the twelve Holy Imams. Surprisingly enough, the religious scholars and secretaries also hold the view which lies behind the simple conviction of the people: that in fact according to divine law the modschtahed, as the highest spiritual leader, is entitled to rule the Moslems while the Shah is only required to observe and implement reports of the supreme pastor. According to this, the modschtehed properly speaking decides for war and peace; without his advice no matters of importance can be undertaken in governing the believers. They substantiate this interpretation, which places unreasonable demands on the Shah, by putting forward the following considerations. If the Moslems are to be guided by divine decree then Allah must make His will known to a mortal. But to whom? Surely not to a secular leader who is bound to the earth and the body? That would be an unworthy abode for Allah! His spririt only manifests itself to the soul of a totally spiritualised person who, having renounced all worldly desires, devotes himself entirely to the contemplation of God, feels his earthly being to be a painful prison and strives on the path of eternal salvation. For that reason Allah's will is only made known to the Holy Imams, i.e. to the successors of Muḥammad in the office of prophet, and in these days exclusively to their successors, the modschtaheds. The Shah, however, to whom God has entrusted his people and the guidance of his state, should draw his decisions from the words of the modschtaheds of his time.'[198]

The notion of the 'infallible mujtahid' (*mujtahid-i maʿṣūm*) that the *ʿulamāʾ* play off against the sinful Shāh in Chardin's report could not survive in this form. The mujtahid of later times is fallible while the special gift of the grace of protection (*'iṣma*) from sin and error is reserved for the Imams (see below p. 101). Just how far the concept of *mujtahid-i ma'ṣūm* is reflected in the contemporary scholarly literature of the *'ulamā'* has not yet been investigated. Kaempfer's 'modschtahed of the age' *mujtahid-i zamān* – al-Karakī had already borne this title (see above p. 88) – is, by contrast, the model for the future. As the highest spiritual authority and representative of the Hidden Imam, but without the latter's charisma of infallibility, the mujtahid now becomes the controller and where necessary the opponent of every merely secular power.

THE VICTORY OF THE UṢŪLĪ SCHOOL (18TH CENTURY)

In Ṣafavid Iran of the 16th and 17th centuries there were a great number of schools of thought in the Imāmī Shia which by no means co-existed harmoniously. The canonical jurists (who for their part were split into the schools of the Akhbārīs and the Uṣūlīs) opposed the extremism of the Qizilbāsh, the Sufism of the dervish orders and the gnostic theosophy of the Iṣfahān school. In the 18th century this great variety dwindled. The scholars of the Uṣūlī school, who were brought into the country by the dynasty and were provided with special privileges, survived at the cost of the other groups and finally freed themselves from the power of the Shāh. The position of the legal scholars now increasingly acquired the characteristics of a regular clergy who opposed the secular rulers in public ever more frequently in order finally to seize power in the state. While the Ṣafavid Shāh was able to maintain his position as head of the Shiite community until the end of the dynasty, the influence of the 'ulamā' increased noticeably as Safavid absolutism weakened under the last rulers. The last Shāh from the house of Ṣafī, Sulṭān Ḥusayn I (1105-1135/1694-1722), was under the influence of the spiritual leaders to such an extent that he was derided as 'Mullah Ḥusayn'. The influence of the mullahs not only grew with the steadily increasing endowment land they administered, but also as a result of their close family relationships with the local landowner class and the artisan middle classes of the towns, the bāzārīs, whose interests they represented against the remote central authority and its tax officials – a constellation which was to be of great significance for the modern history of Iran.

Juristic thinking among the Twelver Shia came down in the form of the rationalistic method of drawing conclusions and presenting arguments (*kalām*) propagated in Iran by the Lebanese al-Karakī under Shah Ṭahmāsp together with the principles of *ijtihād* and *taqlīd* as developed and systematised by the Ḥilla school in the 13th century (see above p. 67). Of course the Uṣūlīs, supporters of the 'principles' (Arabic *uṣūl,* sing. *aṣl*), did not succeed without a fight; particularly outside the Ṣafavid area of influence, around the shrines of Iraq or in remote Mecca and Medina the Akhbārīs, supporters of the 'traditions' (Arabic *akhbār,* sing. *khabar*) put up stubborn resistance. Supported by the collection of traditions by Kulaynī (d. 329/940) and Ibn Bābūya (d. 381/991) which had not yet been contaminated by the poison of *kalām,* in numerous treatises the Akhbārīs disputed the jurists' ability to reach independent legal decisions and their claim to represent the Hidden Imām, and they awarded sole authority to the transmitted word of the Prophet and the Imams. Generally this position went hand in hand with condemning collaboration with the 'tyrannical' (*jā'ir* or *ẓālim*) rule of the Shāh. The principle of *ijtihād* prevailed to a large extent in 17th century Iran at least and, as we have seen, could already be brought into play against the absolutism of the Shāh in the second half of the century.

Under the last Ṣafavids, in particular the bigoted Shāh Ḥusayn, the *'ulamā'* or mullahs in Iran completed the process of the enforced imposition of Shiism, as defined by the jurists. An outstanding role was played in this by Muḥammad Bāqir Majlisī (1038-1111/1627-1700)[199], a mullah who sharply rejected the views of his father, a well-known mystic and theosopher. Shāh Sulṭān Ḥusayn was under the influence of Majlisī even before he ascended to the throne. As *shaykh al-islām* of Iṣfahān (before 1687) the latter led the coronation ceremonies in 1694 and was rewarded by the Shāh with far-reaching authority to enforce vigorous measures against all offenders and deviators. As a kind of grand inquisitor he led an operation to cleanse the Shia in Iran of all trace of Sufism, philosophy and gnosis; we have already referred to the persecutions which the Iṣfahān school had to endure. Majlisī adroitly introduced into the new orthodoxy the widespread traditionalist position, veneration of the Imams, the graves of the Imams and the descendants of the Imams and a high respect for the sayings attributed to the Imams. He compiled the most comprehensive corpus of Shiite traditions, the 'Seas of Lights' (*Biḥār al-anwār*), putting together all the Imam traditions which were accessible to him. The printed edition of the enormous work (Tehran 1376-1392/1956-1972) comprises no less than 110 volumes; and this ocean of Shiite learning can only be navigated with the help of the 'Ship of the Seas' (*Safīnat al-biḥār*), a very important, two-volume work by 'Abbās al-Qummī (Najaf 1355/1936). This superabundant traditional material is not, however, claimed by the Akhbārī school as the sole legal authority and source, but serves rather as an aid for the independent reasoning of the mujtahids upon whom the role of collective representation of the Hidden Imam devolves.

The development of the Shiite lawyer caste into a clergy appeared to have a logical conclusion when Shāh Sulṭān Ḥusayn entrusted Mullah Muḥammad Bāqir Khātūnābādī with the newly created office of the 'Highest Mullah' (*mullah-bāshī)* in the year 1124/1712:

> On the last Sunday of the month of Rabīʿ II of the year 1124 (15th June 1712) the Illustrious Vicariate (!) and Exalted Majesty ordered that his Excellence, the Mujtahid of the Age, Amīr Muḥammad Bāqir – may God protect him from harm – be the head (*ra'īs*) of all scholars (*'ulamā'*), spiritual notables and dignatories; and that in the audience of his Majesty no one have priority – whether sitting or standing – over the Mujtahid of the Age.[200]

This newly created role of supreme spiritual leader found obvious expression in the building of the Madrasa-mosque complex on the Chāharbāgh boulevard in Iṣfahān (1706-1714) whose first professor was the *mullah-bāshī* and which matches the Shāh mosque in magnificence. The Chāharbāgh madrasa did not, however, become the Vatican of the Shia; the Shia's artificially created head of the hierarchy was unable to succeed against the collective force of the mujtahids and after the downfall of the dynasty it soon lost its significance.

In 1135/1722 the internally weakened Ṣafavid empire fell victim to an invasion of Sunni Afghans who occupied and destroyed Iṣfahan and maintained their position there until 1729. The restoration of Iran's independence was the work of Nadir Khan, an officer from the Turcoman tribe of the Afshār whose grazing areas were the western and northern edges of the Dasht-i Kavīr desert. With the support of the warriors of this erstwhile Qizilbāsh tribe, Nādir drove off the Afghans and extended his campaigns into Afghanistan, the Caucasus and Iraq, and later even into north-west India (Kabul and Peshawar 1738; Lahore and Delhi 1739). Nādir, who had initially emerged as the agent of the Ṣafavid dynasty, had himself crowned Shāh in 1736. In his dealings with the feudal lords of the Turcoman tribes which supported him he had already made known his intention to destroy Shiite predominance in Iran. As he envisaged it, the Shia should take its place alongside the four Sunni legal schools as a fifth 'Jaʿfarī' school, so named after the sixth Imam Jaʿfar al-Ṣādiq whose importance was thus lowered to the same rank as that of the founders of the other schools of law – Abū Ḥanīfa, al-Shāfiʿī, etc. The Shiite *'ulamā'* themselves, with their legal formalisation of the Shia, had contributed quite substantially to this development.[201] On 10th October 1743 Sunni *'ulamā'* from Balkh, Qandahār and other towns of the Iranian East deposited a document in the treasury of ʿAlī's shrine in Najaf which certified that the Iranian population had abjured the Shia and had informed the Ottoman sultan as champion of the Sunna.[202] Nādir Shah then proceeded not only to attempt to restrain the influence of the mullahs by abolishing the office of Ṣadr and the spiritual (*sharīʿī*) law courts but he also withdrew their economic basis by confiscating their – legally inviolable – religious endowments. The *shaykh al-islām* from Iṣfahān was executed because of his resistance and the *mullah-bāshī*, Mīrzā ʿAbd al-Ḥusayn paid the penalty of death for supporting the Ṣafavid dynasty. Nādir Shah's rule appeared to the Shiite clergy as religious persecution; many *ʿulamā'* went into exile to the holy 'thresholds' (*ʿatabāt*) in Iraq, Ottoman since 1638, where they settled beside the shrines of Kāẓimayn, Najaf and Karbalā'. It was only then that Karbalā' emerged on a par with Najaf as a significant centre of Shiite learning.

Nādir Shah's centralist and absolutist policies not only turned the Shiite clergy against him, but also the Turcoman feudal lords of northern Iran who had emerged from the erstwhile military aristocracy of the Qizilbāsh, especially those from the tribes of the Afshār and the Qājār. Nādir's murder in 1747 heralded a time of troubles and rivalry between his own descendants, the Afshār and the Qājār, the Ṣafavid princes and the Afghans. The urban *ʿulamā'* played no particular part in these battles for power which were mainly fought out by the large nomad confederations. The Afshār plundered the shrine at Mashhad and even melted down the golden railings which surrounded the grave of the Imam ʿAlī al-Riḍā. Only the Iranian family of the Zand, which was able to assert itself in 1750 as the local dynasty in Shīrāz with the help of the Zagros tribes, demonstrated decidedly Shiite tendencies: the twelve districts of the town were each consecrated to one of the twelve Imams, and the *shaykh al-islām* of Shīrāz, installed by the ruler, controlled the reopened spiritual courts. Karīm Khān Zand built madrasas and mosques in Shīrāz including the famous Vakīl mosque. The Zand, however, claimed absolutely no religious authority for themselves and as joint rulers even renounced the Iranian title of great king (*shāhānshāh*); they were satisfied with the modest rank of a trustee (*vakīl*) for a future re-established Ṣafavid Shāh.

The interregnum between the fall of the Ṣafavids in 1722 and the establishment of the Qājār government in 1796 is the period in which the Shiite clergy in Iran acquired the form in which they have since been known. An important prerequisite for this was the disappearance of the only dynasty with the charisma of descent from the Prophet and the seventh Imam, and thus the only serious rival in the struggle for the leadership of the Shia; neither the Afshār or Qājārī Turcomans nor the Zand, and certainly not the anti-Shiite Nādir Shāh, were real competitors for the increasingly self-confident mujtahids.

A second prerequisite for the growing independence of the Iranian clergy was the possibility of exile to the holy 'thresholds' (*ʿatabāt*). The Shiite shrines in Iraq – Najaf, Karbalā', al-Kāẓimayn near Baghdad and al-ʿAskariyyayn in Sāmarrā – were under Ottoman domination from 1638 and were thus beyond the reach of the Shāh. Since the Ottoman Sultans generally left the Shiite sanctuaries unharmed and, moreover, sometimes supported opponents of the Shāh for political reasons, the *ʿatabāt* increasingly served as an asylum for the Iranian *ʿulamā'* who had, for one reason or another, come into conflict with their own authorities. For the first time during the period of Nādir Shāh's anti-Shiite policies, Iranian *ʿulamā'* made their way to Iraq in great numbers in order to stir up opposition against the Shāh from a secure place of exile – a pattern of behaviour which was to set a precedent and to prove its efficacy right up to the days of the Āyatallāh Khumaynī.

The third and decisive prerequisite for the rise of the *ʿulamā'* to political power, was the conclusive victory of the Uṣūlī school over the Akhbārīs, even at the Iraqi shrines where every opposition to the principles of *ijtihād* and *taqlīd* was now being silenced. The victorious Uṣūlīs condemned the Akhbārīs' principle of regarding only the word of the Quran and the sayings of the Imams as the guiding principle for believers, as a heretical innovation for which they held Mullah Muḥammad Amīn Astarābādī (d. 1033/1624) responsible. This perspective is not historically correct since in fact the doctrine of the Uṣūlīs was itself the innovation which can be traced back to the introduction of *kalām* into Shiite legal scholarship by Shaykh al-Mufīd and his school.

The Uṣūlīs' appeal to reason (*ʿaql*) as opposed to the simple observance of tradition (*naql*) had a number of momentous implications. While the Akhbārīs recognised tradition as the only authority and thus left full authority to the Hidden Imam, the Uṣūlīs replaced this authority by that of living men. The Imam 'is divested of his functions as the future real head of state' and displaced by a collective representative; his role is reduced to that of a venerated saint who is appealed to as a advocate in matters of daily concern.[203] While for the Akhbārīs the believer can obtain absolute certainty (*yaqīn*) from tradition in all questions of faith, the *ijtihād* of the Uṣūlīs can only lead to an uncertain assumption or opinion (*ẓann*). The conception of the infallible mujtahid which had occasionally been brought into play in the 17th century against the absolutism of the Ṣafavids was not enforced; as ʿAllāma al-Ḥillī had already postulated, the mujtahid is not *maʿṣūm*, immune from error and sin, but rather by using reason he is necessarily fallible. The mujtahid is therefore also responsible for what he says and does. In this emphasis on human free will and responsibility the Twelver Shia is also the inheritor of earlier Muʿtazilite rationalism. Differences of opinion and opposing standpoints among the mujtahids are not only allowed for by the system, but the whole system is actually based on the fact that binding authority must itself necessarily be fallible. However, in order to keep confusion to a minimum, authority is restricted to a few – and certainly only living – persons, and any appeal to dead mujtahids is considered taboo. At the same time the individual unlearned believer is permitted to shift his own responsibility onto one of the learned experts (*taqlīd*).

The enforcement of these principles of the Ḥilla school actually created the Shiite clergy as we know it. Reason as a source of obligatory but revisable decisions, and the believer's duty to use the authority of living, fallible people gave Twelver Shiite legal scholarship a flexibility, and a capability to react to unforeseen developments possessed neither by their opponents, the traditionalist Akhbārīs, nor even the Sunni legal schools. M. Momen renders the term *ijtihād* as 'innovative interpretation by independent judgement' and stress is laid on the word 'innovative'.[204] From the 19th century this flexibility of *ijtihād* has allowed the mujtahids to figure ever more frequently as an opposition to the political power. As has already been explained above on p. 71 it is therefore inaccurate to describe the mujtahids – or Āyatallāhs, as the most renowned of them are known today – as fundamentalists. Rigidly sticking to the literal sense of the transmitted word, which is typical of fundamentalism, is indeed precisely the characteristic of the conquered Akhbārī school.

The Uṣūlīs' decisive victory over the Akhbārīs took place at the Iraqi shrines. The conqueror of the traditionalism cultivated there was Āghā Muḥammad Bāqir Wāḥid Bihbihānī, an Iṣfahānī who remained in Karbalāʾ after completing his studies and for a long lifetime (1117-1208/1705-93) led the fight against the Akhbārīs who were branded as heretics for being innovators, and broke their dominance at the 'thresholds'. He is thus considered to be the reviver (*mujaddid*) of the true faith, and indeed the founder (*muʾassis*) of Shiite orthodoxy. With no hesitation Bihbihānī disputed his opponents' adherence to Islam, declaring them to be unbelieving (*takfīr*) – a fatal precedent as the 19th century was to demonstrate. He did not even shrink from physical violence; surrounded by his guards armed with cudgels, the 'masters of anger' (*mīr-ghaḍab*), he controlled the streets of Karbalāʾ and had corporal punishment carried out on his own verdict. After the Akhbārīs his favourite victims were the dervishes.

The Akhbārīs were not conclusively defeated, however, until after the establishment of the Qājār dynasty (1796). The Uṣūlī Shaykh Jaʿfar al-Najafī succeeded in driving his opponent Mīrzā Muḥammad Akhbārī from the holy shrines. Akhbārī fled to Tehran where he was once more able to gain short-term favour at court by means of the 'miracle of the head': he wagered with the Qājār ruler Fatḥ ʿAlī Shāh that with supernatural help he could procure the head of Zizianov, the Russian commander besieging Bākū, and in return the Shāh was to make the Akhbārī doctrine the official creed. When the head of the Russian general did in fact arrive in Tehran within forty days the Shāh did not keep his promise, and Akhbārī was once again exiled to Baghdad.[205] The Uṣūlīs now had the upper hand at the Tehran court; the Akhbārīs lost their old strongholds of Kirmān and Hamadān and from then on no longer played any fundamental role in Iran. Mīrzā Muḥammad Akhbārī, who had moved back to the shrine of Kāẓimayn, was killed there in 1816 by an angry mob of Uṣūlī followers. His descendants continue up to the present day to live in Baṣra which together with its surrounding area has remained (after the island of Baḥrayn) the last refuge of the Akhbārī school. At the 'thresholds', as in Iran, the mujtahids now ruled the roost.

Bibliography

L. Lockhart, *Nadir Shah*, London 1938; *The Fall of the Safavi Dynasty and the Afghan Occupation of Persia*, Cambridge 1958. G. Scarcia, 'Intorno alle controversie tra Aḫbārī e Uṣūlī presso gli Imāmiti di Persia', *RSO* 33 (1958), 211-50. L. Binder, 'The Proofs of Islam: Religion and Politics in Iran', in: G. Makdisi (ed.), *Arabic and Islamic Studies in Honor of H.A.R. Gibb*, Cambridge/Mass. 1965, 118-40. N.R. Keddie, 'The Roots of the Ulama's Power in Modern Iran', *SI* 29 (1969), 31-53. H. Algar, *Religion and State in Iran 1785-1906. The Role of the Ulama in the Qajar Period*, Berkeley/Los Angeles 1969; 'Shiʿism and Iran in the Eighteenth Century', in: Th. Naff/R. Owen (eds), *Studies in Eighteenth Century Islamic History*, Carbondale/Edwardsville, Ill. 1977, 288-302. K.H. Pampus, *Die theologische Enzyklopädie Biḥār al-Anwār des Muḥammad Bāqir al-Mağlisī (1073-1110 A.H. = 1627-1699 A.D.). Ein Beitrag zur Literaturgeschichte des Šīʿa in der Ṣafawidenzeit*, thesis Bonn 1970. J.R. Perry, *Karim Khan Zand. A History of Iran*, 1747-1779, Chicago/London 1973. S.A. Arjomand, 'The Office of Mullā-bāshī in Shiʿite Iran', *SI* 57 (1983), 135-46; *The Shadow of God and the Hidden Imam. Religion, Political Order, and Societal Change in Shiʿite Iran from the Beginning to 1890*, Chicago/London 1984. J. Cole, 'Shiʿi Clerics in Iraq and Iran, 1722-1780: The Akhbari-Usuli Conflict Reconsidered', *Iranian Studies* 18 (1985), 3-34.

SHIITE ORTHODOXY UNDER THE QĀJĀRS

The re-unification of Iran was the work of the princes of the Turcoman Qājār tribe whose grazing areas lay in the north, south of the Caspian Sea. Āghā Muḥammad Khān Qājār made the hitherto insignificant town of Tehran near Rayy his residence; and from there he brought about the destruction of Zand power in Shīrāz and Kirmān (1794) and conquered north-east Iran (Khurāsān), Āzarbayjān, Armenia and Georgia (1795). In 1796 in Tehran he assumed the title of King of Kings(*shāhānshāh*).

The fact that the new dynasty saw itself as the champion of the Shia had already been demonstrated by Āghā Muḥammad Khān at his coronation in 1200/1785 when he wore a sword consecrated at the Ṣafavid shrine at Ardabīl. He had the bones of his ancestors taken to Najaf from Astarābād (south-east of the Caspian Sea) and gilded the dome over the shrine at Karbalā'. His successor Fatḥ 'Alī Shāh (1797-1834) emulated him in this respect; he made pilgrimages every year to Qumm and exempted its inhabitants from all taxes. He endowed the shrine at Qumm with rich donations and founded the madrasa Fayżiyya there. After wresting Mashhad from the Afshārs he undertook repairs to the shrine there too. Nevertheless, Karbalā' suffered a heavy blow under his government: the strict Sunni Wahhābīs, for whom every form of grave worship was considered a heretical innovation (*bid'a*) set upon the shrines on the Euphrates from the Arabian desert. In April 1217/1802 Karbalā' was devastated and plundered and the assault claimed about 2,000 victims from among the town's inhabitants.

For all the pious passion that the Qājār rulers evinced, the fact that they were unable to play the role which the Ṣafavids had played successfully cannot be overlooked. The Turcoman ancestry of the dynasty was too obvious for them to be able to claim descent from the Imams or to base their claim to religious leadership on the charisma of their origins. The Qājār Shāh could not appear as the representative of the Hidden Imam. This role now devolved upon the legal scholars almost of its own accord. The concept of 'collective vicariate' (Arabic *al-niyāba al-'āmma,* Pers. *niyābet-i 'āmmah*) of the mujtahids which had already been under discussion in the late Ṣafavid period[206] now came to be widely accepted. The pious Fatḥ 'Alī Shāh sought to draw prominent scholars to his court in Tehran, but most of them still hesitated to have dealings with the 'usurped' secular power.

Under the rule of the Qājārs (1796-1925) the development of the legal class into a clergy, and of the victorious Uṣūlī school into the norm of Shiite orthodoxy was completed. Tendencies towards a hierarchy of religious classes now became discernible. The majority of simple mullahs only had jurisdiction over the application of already unambiguously laid-down rules and regulations in Islamic law, the *furū'* (literally: branches), while a group of highly qualified scholars selected on the basis of their knowledge of the principles of legal ruling, the *uṣūl* (literally: roots), was qualified to reach independent and binding decisions (*ijtihād*). Even the concept of the partial competence (*ijtihād mutajazzī*) of individual scholars in certain specialised areas of religious law, repeatedly advocated in former days, was now given up. Authority was possessed only by one who had 'absolute' all-embracing competence (*ijtihād muṭlaq*).[207] During the course of the 19th century the number of such qualified mujtahids rose sharply. While there could hardly have been more than a dozen scholars of this rank in the first half of the century, under Nāṣir al-Dīn Shāh (1848-1896) already more than 175 mujtahids can be identified.[208] Now not only the simple believer, who increasingly became a 'layman', was obliged to use *taqlīd* and subject himself to the authority of a mujtahid but also the ordinary mullah; the highly qualified mujtahid became the 'reference point for imitation' (*marja' al-taqlīd*).[209] The *marja' al-taqlīd* is that mujtahid to whom the individual believer shifts his responsibility in matters of faith, subjecting himself to his expert judgement and blindly following his decisions. In principle every mujtahid is a *marja' al-taqlīd*. However, since the 19th century, there has been a recognisable tendency towards developing a hierarchical head in the person of a single *marja' al-taqlīd* who is generally acknowledged as the highest authority. Even earlier, individual *'ulamā'* were recognised as 'mujtahid of the age' (*mujtahid al-zamān*), for example, Karakī at the beginning of the 16th century and Majlisī at the end of the 17th century; but it was not until the 19th century that this trend became stronger. In the first half of the century Shaykh Muḥammad Ḥasan (d. 1266/1850), writer of the most important work on Shiite jurisprudence in post-Ṣafavid Iran, was dominant.[210] Shortly before his death he formally designated his pupil, the Shaykh al-Ṭā'ifa from Khūzistān Murtażā Shūshtarī (or Dizfulī) Anṣārī (d. 1281/1864), who after a fairly long stay in Iran lived in Najaf from 1249/1833; and after the death of his teacher was for the first time generally recognised as the highest *marja' al-taqlīd* , not only at the shrines of Iraq but also in Iran and by the Shiites of Arabia, Turkey and India.[211]

Only the most knowledgeable and learned (Arabic *al-a'lam*) could be considered for the position of the highest *marja' al-taqlīd*; but until today it continues to be disputed whether and how qualification for the *a'lamiyya* can be determined. Opponents of a hierarchical head doubt that it can be possible at all, especially since, as they see it, no one person can be uniformly the most knowledgeable in all areas of religious learning. The rank of the sole highest *marja' al-taqlīd* can therefore only be based on general spontaneous recognition and cannot be institutionalised; times when a single uncontested *marja'* has dominated are always followed by phases of rivalry between contending mujtahids. After the death of Murtażā Anṣārī in 1864 no successor was able to set himself up until Mīrzā Muḥammad Ḥasan Shīrāzī was established as the sole *marjaʿ* by general recognition of his *aʿlamiyya.* For the first time he made the Sāmarrā shrine, the place where the twelfth Imam disappeared and where he himself settled, a centre for Shiite learning. After his death in 1312/1895 disputes over his succession once more split the community.[212]

The tendency towards establishing a hierarchy with the highest authority at its head was only one of the characteristics of that process during the course of which the class of Shiite legal scholars evolved into a clergy. Another feature was the gradual appropriation of the prerogatives of the Hidden Imam by the *ʿulamāʾ*. According to widespread opinion the functions, which only the rightful head of the Islamic community, the Imam, could exercise , were suspended (*sāqiṭ:* literally: invalid) for the duration of his absence (*ghayba*) , and no one had the right to assume them. However, sheer necessity soon led to some of these functions being exercised by representatives. The schools of Baghdad (al-Mufīd and al-Murtażā) and al-Ḥilla (al-ʿAllāma al-Ḥillī) had already thought over these problems in detail, though they only became acute when the Ṣafavids set about establishing a Shiite state and a Shiite clergy.

Of central significance was the question of the use of taxes which the believers had to pay to the Prophet and later to the Imams. The Quranic verse 8,41 'Whatever ye take as spoils of war, lo! a fifth thereof is for Allah, and for the messenger and for the kinsman (who hath need) and orphans and the needy and the wayfarers' does not apply solely to spoils of war for the Shiite scholars as it does for the Sunnis, but rather to every kind of acquisition and gain; hence in Shiite law, the fifth (*khums*) is a form of income tax. How this was to be raised and distributed during the absence of the Hidden Imam had repeatedly concerned the Shiite *ʿulamāʾ* from the time of al-Kulaynī (d. 329/940).[213] It was suggested that the taxpayer should bury the *khums* until the Hidden Imam returned, or that he should keep it and hand it over to a trustee before he died; according to another interpretation, it was not at all obligatory to pay the *khums* during the *ghayba*. From the time of al-Ṭūsī (d. 460/1067) the notion which prevailed was that which declared payment of the *khums* to be obligatory and the following procedure was to be observed in its distribution: the *khums* was to be divided equally between the six groups entitled to it as mentioned in the Quran; moreover, God's portion, that of the Prophet and his relatives – thus three-sixths of the *khums* – formed the 'Imam's share' (*sahm-i Imām*) while the remaining three-sixths was intended for the orphans, the needy and travellers from the Prophet's family – i.e. for needy sayyids (*sahm-i sādāt*). These last three-sixths could be collected by the *'ulamā'* accordingly, but had to be passed on to those entitled to them. It was different with the Hidden Imam's share, because it would not only be impracticable to hoard it until his return but to do so would hardly be beneficial for Islam. In the Ḥilla school the opinion was becoming generally accepted that the legal scholars, as the collective representative of the Imam, should raise this income tax from the believers and use it for the general good of the Shiite community.[214] This principle only attained practical significance, however, from the time of the Ṣafavids with the formation of the Iranian clergy; in the 19th century it was the *marja' al-taqlīd* who had his assistants collect the *khums* from those believers who willingly subjected themselves to his authority. Besides the income from religious endowments (*waqf*) – either as the direct benefactor or as the trustee – and the fees for notarial functions (certification and registration of contracts, wills, marriages, etc.) in *sahm-i imām* the *'ulamā'* thus had a third important source of income which ensured them a status which was largely independent of the state.

A second prerogative of the Hidden Imam which the *'ulamā'* had already appropriated during the Ṣafavid era was leading the Friday prayer and the Friday sermon (*khuṭba*). Al-Karakī had declared assumption of both functions by qualified legal scholars to be both permissible and necessary and, with the support of the Shāh, he installed learned jurists as *pīsh-namāz* and *imām-jum'a* throughout Iran.

Another of the exclusive prerogatives of the Imam was the imposing and execution of corporal punishment (*ḥudūd*, sing. *ḥadd*) as laid down in the Quran – i.e. by divine revelation – such as cutting off the right hand for theft (Quran 5,38). Although al-Mufīd, al-Murtaḍā and 'Allāma al-Ḥillī had already declared the carrying out of *ḥudūd* to be permissible in the Imam's absence, the matter was still in dispute.[215] However, from the end of the 18th century the divine instruction to the Imam 'to order good and to forbid evil' (*al-amr bi 'l-ma'rūf wa 'l-nahy 'an al-munkar*) was considered by the mujtahids to be an obvious function of their own position. In Karbalā' we saw Muḥammad Bāqir Bihbihānī impose death sentences which were carried out by his henchmen (see above p. 102); his pupil, Sayyid Muḥammad Bāqir Shaftī Rashtī (from Shaft near Rasht on the Caspian Sea; 1180-1260/1766-1844) behaved similarly as the *shaykh al-islām* of Iṣfahān and defended the application of the *ḥudūd* by the mujtahids in a special treatise.[216]

For the time being the last of the Hidden Imam's prerogatives which the mujtahids appropriated in the 19th century was the right to declare and to conduct the Holy War (*jihād*) against unbelievers. For earlier writers from the quietist school of thought it had been quite obvious that only the Imam or a representative directly nominated by him could proclaim *jihād.* This was the opinion of the Muḥaqqiq al-Ḥillī, and out of caution he had also recommended refraining from execution of the *ḥudūd.* There was no change in this view up until the Ṣafavid period.[217] It was not until the Russians advanced into the Transcaucasus (1804-1813) at the beginning of the Qājār period that the *'ulamā'* put forward the claim to represent the Hidden Imam in this function as well. Shaykh Ja'far (d. 1227/1812) explained in his *Kashf al-ghiṭā'* [218] (1809) that where the Imam was absent the mujtahids – or, to be more exact, the best (*afḍal*) of them – had the right to declare the *jihād.* He empowered the Shāh to lead *jihād* against the Russians and to use the Imam's share of the spoils for the good of the Muslims: 'Since I am a mujtahid and one of those who can claim to be the agent of the Lord of the Age (i.e. of the Imam) I permit the Sultan . . . Fatḥ 'Alī Shāh to take what is needful for the equipping of soldiers and armies and to use it in order to drive out the unbelievers, rebels and apostates.'[219] After the Peace of Gulistān (1813) which acknowledged Russia's authority over the Transcaucasus, the claim of the *'ulamā'* remained purely theoretical at first. The Russians' aggressive treatment, however, especially of the Muslim Circassians and Chechens, soon gave rise to constant complaints and in Iran pressure built on Fatḥ 'Alī Shāh once more to declare *jihād* against the unbelievers. Behind this was the next in line to the throne,'Abbās Mīrzā, who, as governor of Tabrīz, wanted to create a reformed army (*niẓām-i jadīd*) on the European model to win back the territories lost to the Tsars. The crown prince made clever use of religious propaganda: from Karbalā' a grandson of Muḥammad Bāqir Bihbihānī, the mujtahid Āghā Sayyid Muḥammad Iṣfahānī, exhorted the Shāh to do his duty at last. In June he appeared in Tehran, pressurised the Shāh, and called the *'ulamā'* to come to the court. Numerous mullahs and mujtahids therefore followed the Shāh to the summer camp at Sulṭāniyya. He finally gave way to their pressure and on 1st July he dismissed the Russian envoy. The Holy War was, however, a catastrophe; in the second Russian war the Shāh lost the whole of the Transcaucasus which he finally had to cede to the Tsar during peace negotiations at Turkumānchāy in 1828.[220]

The clerical characteristics which the *'ulamā'* acquired in the 19th century also included the use of excommunication to maintain the purity of orthodoxy – defined solely by the *'ulamā'*; a function which the *'ulamā'* had not had until then either in the Sunna or in the Shia. The 'charge of unbelief' (*takfīr*) [221] which deprives a person branded as such of his Muslim status and puts him on a level with Christians,

Jews and Zoroastrians was neither formalised nor generally obligatory, but in its effect it was comparable to Catholic excommunication. Any mujtahid could pronounce the *takfīr*; whether it was enforced or not depended on his social standing and his political influence. Often enough militant mujtahids directed excommunication against one another.

The Akhbārīs had been the first victims of this new weapon, struck down by Bihbihānī's *takfīr* (see above p. 102); the second victims were the Sufis. The return from India of the highest pīr of the Niʿmatallahi dervish order, Maʿṣūm ʿAlī Shāh, had led to a revival of Sufism in Iran. Thereafter the mujtahids successfully turned to the bigoted Fatḥ ʿAlī Shāh who readily agreed to their demands. Bihbihānī's son Āghā Muḥammad ʿAlī Bihbihānī pronounced the *takfīr* against the dervishes and distinguished himself by persecuting them to such an extent that the name *Ṣūfī-Kush* (Sufi killer) was attached to him. He was responsible for the murder of the Niʿmatallāhī-Pīr. Fatḥ ʿAlī Shah's successor, however, Muḥammad Shāh (1834-1848) had mystical tendencies himself and brought a temporary end to the destructive fury of the orthodox mujtahids.

The next victims were the Shiite gnostics and theosophists, successors of the Iṣfahān school, who boasted of direct personal enlightenment and laid claim to a charismatic privilege conceded by the *ʿulamā'* only to the Prophet and the Imams. Their most important representative was Shaykh Aḥmad Aḥsā'ī (from al-Aḥsā/Hufūf in eastern Arabia), who after a long stay at the 'thresholds' in Iraq in 1221/1806 came on pilgrimage to Mashhad and then settled in Yazd. He appealed to intuitive revelation (*kashf:* disclosure) which was vouchsafed to him in dreams by the Prophet and the Imams. The *ʿulamā'* took particular offence at his spiritual interpretation of the Prophet's journey to heaven and the resurrection of the dead, both of which he explained as symbols of the mystical journey of the soul to its origin. While Shaykh Aḥmad Aḥsā'ī was very highly esteemed among the people and in courtly circles, the *takfīr* which Mullah Ḥājj Taqī Burghānī of Qazvīn pronounced against him in 1822 was not without its effect. The 'Shaykhiyya' was marginalised as a sect; but after the death of Shaykh Aḥmad (1241/1826) it was able to grow in organisational strength under his successor Sayyid Kāẓim Rashtī (d. 1259/1843 or 1260/1844) in Karbalā' by institutionalising transfer of the charisma of direct responsibility from one head of the sect to the next.

The last form of heterodox Shiism which fell victim to the orthodoxy of the *ʿulamā'* was the extreme Mahdism which, in the year 1260/1844, exactly 1,000 (lunar) years after the disappearance of the twelfth Imām, was revived in a chiliastic movement. In the year 1259/1843 a young sayyid ʿAlī Muḥammad from Shīrāz (b. 1819) predicted the reappearance (*ẓuhūr*) of the Hidden Imām in Karbalā' at the beginning of the Hijra year 1261 (1th January 1845) and declared himself to be his 'gate' (*bāb*) in Būshīrah on the Gulf coast. The governor of Fārs gave in to pressure from the *ʿulamā'* and fetched the Bāb to Shīrāz; there and again later in Iṣfahān he was confronted by a group of orthodox *ʿulamā'* and, after a disputation, was forced to recant. The vizier Ḥājjī Mīrzā Āghāsī then had him imprisoned in Āzarbayjān. When the Bāb declared himself to be the Hidden Imam at the end of 1847, and as Mahdī and Qā'im announced Islamic law to be annulled because the end of time had now begun, he was taken to Tabrīz and after a second disputation was once again forced to recant and flogged. The *shaykh al-islām* from Tabrīz brandished the whip with his own hand. At first, in spite of several *takfīr* judgements by leading mujtahids, he remained unharmed, but when his supporters in Māzandarān on the Caspian Sea and in Zanjān proceeded to public armed rebellion the Bāb was executed on 8th July 1850 (1266) A.H. in Tabrīz. Militarily crushed and hit by the excommunication of *takfīr* Bābism soon petered out in Iran. Nevertheless, the founder of the Bahā'ī religion emerged from its ranks, Mīrzā Ḥusayn ʿAlī Nūrī Bahā'allāh (d. 1309/1892) who – quite in keeping with the tradition of Shah Ismāʿīl and the Qizilbāsh of the 15th century – identified himself as the 'divine manifestation' (*maẓhar ilāhī*) and claimed to continue the line of the Prophets sent from God. In the 20th century Baha'ism has developed into an independent religion with a universal claim and a world-wide mission so that it can no longer be described as a Shiite sect today.

Primary sources in translation

C. Frank, 'Über den schiitischen Mudschtahid,' *Islamica* 2 (1926-7), 171-92 (Persian text and translation of a description of the function of the mujtahid, produced in 1920 in Berlin by Mīrzā Faḍl-ʿAlī Mujtahid-i Tabrīzī for C. Frank). H. Busse, *History of Persia under Qajar Rule. Translated from the Persian of Hasan-e Fasā'īs Fārsnāma-ye Nāṣerī*, New York/London 1972. H. Taherzade, *Selections from the Writings of the Bab*, Baha'i World Center 1976, [2]1978.

Secondary sources

Hermann Roemer, *Die Bābī-Behā'ī. Eine Studie zur Religionsgeschichte des Islams*, Potsdam 1911. E.G. Browne, *Materials for the Study of the Babi Religion*, Cambridge 1918. G. Scarcia, 'A proposito del problema della sovranità presso gli Imāmiti', *AIUON* 7 (1957), 95-126; Kerman 1905: La 'guerra tra „eiḫī e Bālāsārī', AIUON 13 (1963), 186-203. H. Algar, *Religion and State in Iran, 1758-1906. The Role of the Ulama in the Qajar Period*, Berkeley/Los Angeles 1969. A.K.S. Lambton, 'A Nineteenth Century View of *jihād*,' *SI* 32 (1970), 181-

92. E. Kohlberg, 'The Development of the Imami Shi'i Doctrine of *jihād*, *ZDMG* 126 (1976), 64-86. V. Rafati, *The Development of Shaykhi Thought in Shī'ī Islam*, unpublished thesis, University of California, Los Angeles, 1979. D.M. MacEoin, *From Shaykhism to Babism: A Study in Charismatic Renewal in Shī'ī Islam*, unpublished thesis, Cambridge 1979; 'Early Shaikhī reactions to the Bāb and his Claims', in: M. Momen (ed.), *Studies in Bābī and Bahā'ī History* I, Los Angeles 1982, 1-47. D.M. MacEoin, 'Changes in Charismatic Authority in Qajar Shi'ism' in C. E. Bosworth/C. Hillenbrand (eds), *Qajar Iran. Political, Social and Cultural Change 1800-1925*, Edinburgh 1983, 148-76. A. Amanat, *The Early Years of the Babi Movement*, unpublished thesis Oxford 1981. M. Momen, *The Bābī and Bahā'ī Religions, 1844-1944: Some Contemporary Western Accounts*, Oxford 1981; 'The Trial of Mullā 'Alī Basṭāmī: A Combined Sunni-Shi'i fatwā Against the Bāb', in: *Iran* 20 (1982), 113-43. A. Sachedina, '*Al-Khums:* The Fifth in the Imāmī Shī'ī Legal System', *JNES* 39 (1980), 275-89. N. Calder, '*Zakāt* in Imāmī Shī'ī Jurisprudence', *BSOAS* 44 (1981), 468-80; 'Khums in Imāmī Shī'ī Jurisprudence, From the Tenth to the Sixteenth Century A.D.', *BSOAS* 45 (1982), 39-47. W. Madelung, 'Authority in Twelver Shiism in the Absence of the Imam,' in: *La notion d'autorité au Moyen Age. Islam, Byzance, Occident, Colloques internationaux de la Napoule*, Paris 1982, 163-73. J.R. Cole, 'Imami Jurisprudence and the Role of the Ulama: Mortaza Ansari on Emulating the Supreme Exemplar', in: N. R. Keddie (ed.), *Religion and Politics in Iran. Shi'ism from Quietism to Revolution*, New Haven/London 1983, 33-46. S.A. Arjomand, *The Shadow of God and the Hidden Imam*, Chicago/London 1984, Part III, The Shi'ite Hierocracy and the State, 1785-1890, 213 ff. A. Kazemi Moussavi, 'The Establishment of the Position of Marja'iyyat-i Taqlid in the Twelver-Shi'i Community', *Iranian Studies* 18 (1985), 35-51. P. Smith, *The Babi and Baha'i Religion. From Messianic Shi'ism to a World Religion*, Cambridge 1987.

THE CLERGY AS OPPONENTS OF SECULAR POWER: TOBACCO CONCESSION AND CONSTITUTIONAL CONFLICT

The first Qājār rulers' renunciation of religious charisma and spiritual authority and their eagerly demonstrated Shiite tendencies made it easy for the '*ulamā*' to recognise the Shāh as the legitimate holder of secular power. Under Fatḥ 'Alī Shāh (1797-1834) it came to a balance of interests between the throne and the clergy, indeed to a sort of 'unspoken concordat';[222] Arjomand stresses that no treatises were composed on the illegitimacy of secular power during the Qājār period. The Sayyid Ja'far Kashtī (d. 1267/1850) even developed a doctrine of dual – spiritual and secular – representation of the Hidden Imam which the Shāh and the '*ulamā*' could exercise jointly: only the Imam combined secular and spiritual power in his person; from the time of the *ghayba* the two powers had been divided between two representatives (*nā'ib*); the Shāh dealt with law and order and thus produced the external conditions for the application of the *sharī'a* over which the '*ulamā*' for their part had jurisdiction.[223] In this way

Kashtī gave the dynasty a welcome legitimacy, but at the same time reserved the exclusive authority of the scholars to oversee the application of religious law and to maintain its purity. Cooperation between the throne and the clergy was therefore only able to function for as long as the Shāh behaved as a pious Shiite. The first friction was already apparent under Fatḥ ʿAlī Shāh; and his successor Muḥammad Shāh (1834-1848), who gave the Sufis donations and let many of them attain influential positions, soon rekindled the old deep-seated mistrust of the *ʿulamā'* against any kind of secular authority. The French diplomat Gobineau tells of a mullah who, when summoned before Muḥammad Shāh, lifted the carpet in front of the throne with his stick and sat on the bare floor to prevent himself being defiled by kingship.[224] The *shaykh al-islām* from Iṣfahān, Sayyid Muḥammad Bāqir Shaftī Rashtī (d. 1260/1844) was even able to risk publicly supporting a rebel pretender to the throne against the Shāh.

The continued worsening of relations between the *ʿulamā'* and the Qājār dynasty in the second half of the 19th century resulted principally from the efforts of the rulers and their chief ministers to reform the Iranian state on the European model. Not only did European advisors and European ideas come into the country, displeasing the *ʿulamā'*, but in addition the Qājār reform projects aimed at a rigid centralisation which, even if it failed to remove all the particularist authorities – tribal princes, big feudal landowners, provincial governors and clergy – would at least subject them to the Shāh's control.

As in the Ottoman empire the reforms in Iran were instituted first in the military sector. Two lost wars against Russia and growing pressure from Great Britain in the east necessitated modernisation of the army in terms of structure, equipment and training. Compulsory and voluntary reforms, however, disturbed old privileges and sacred customs. In the Turkumānchāy peace treaty (see above p. 108) the Russians had insisted that quarrels between Muslims and non-Muslim foreigners were to be handled by newly established special mixed courts – the first serious intervention into the privileges of the legal scholars and an open violation of the *sharīʿa*.

Conflicts between the crown and the clergy intensified during the long reign of Nāṣir al-Dīn Shāh (1848-1896) whose first grand vizier Mīrzā Taqī Khān Amīr Kabīr (1848-1851), an initiator of important steps to reform and centralisation drew the disapproval of the *ʿulamā'* on himself and his master. Like Nādir Shāh a century earlier he also sought to subject spiritual (*sharīʿī*) jurisdiction to state control and to restrict it by establishing secular (*ʿurfī*) law courts.Moreover the Shāh and his minister obstinately attempted to curtail the right of asylum (*bast*) which had spread from the sanctuaries of the shrines to the great mosques and eventually even to the houses of prominent mujtahids. The absolutist régime could not countenance such free areas, which removed political opponents as well as criminals from the intervention of the state. The state even sought to control the administration of religious endowments (*waqf*) by the sayyids and the mullahs. In the first European-style cabinet (1858) there was not only a minister of justice but also a minister of endowments. Apart from that, the opening of the first high school, the 'House of Knowledge' (*dār al-funūn*) in Iṣfahān in the year 1850 was a heavy blow to the 'educational privilege of the *'ulamā'*. Nāṣir al-Dīn Shāh, who travelled to Europe on three occasions, not only brought foreign advisers and instructors to the country but by concessions and privileges even enticed foreign entrepreneurs to invest in Iran. Thus in 1872 the British-born Julius de Reuter received large concessions to build railways and roads, to exploit woods and mines and to set up a national bank. While it was mainly Russian pressure which forced the Shāh to buy back the Reuter concession in 1873, the *'ulamā'* also increasingly opposed the growing influence of European entrepreneurs. Ever more frequently they posed as the defenders of the interests of the Iranian people against foreign exploitation and against an irresponsible régime ready to sell out Iran. Even before this, the *'ulamā'* had frequently acted as the champions of local and regional interests against the state and its governors and tax collectors, authorities perceived as remote and tyrannical: 'the continuity of the power of the *'ulamā'* was conducive to their close ties with the community to whom the state – especially in the provinces – by contrast appeared foreign and superficial, something which periodically pounced to extort taxes and enlist soldiers.'[225] More and more, respected local mujtahids forced tyrannical and brutal representatives of the state into retreat. This dual role of the *'ulamā'* as representatives of the Iranian people's interests against foreign influence and against the absolutism of the Shāh had been developing continuously ever since the lost wars against Russia,[226] and one and a half centuries later it would eventually lead to the downfall of the monarchy.

The extensive concessions to the Russians (in 1879 fishing rights in the whole of the Caspian Sea) and the British (establishment of the Imperial Bank of Persia in 1889) were grist to the mill for the opposition. It came to a first big trial of strength when on 8th March 1890 Nāsir al-Dīn Shāh granted a monopoly over control of the tobacco industry and over the sale and export of Iranian tobacco for fifty years to the Briton Gerald Talbot who in return would be liable to pay the Iranian state an annual fixed sum of £15,000 and 25% of his profits. The foreign tobacco monopoly did not affect the producers, who even profited from the regular sale of their commodity for cash, but rather the bazaar dealers and money lenders whose income was threatened by it; but it was precisely with this urban middle class that the mullahs were closely connected by origin, marital ties and common interests. Agitation emanating from Shīrāz and Tabrīz against the foreign tobacco monopoly soon spread to Iṣfahān, Mashhad and Tehran; support came from the holy 'thresholds' in Iraq, especially from Sāmarrā from where Mīrzā Ḥasan Shīrāzī, who was generally acknowledged as the highest *marja' al-taqlīd*, addressed the Shāh through letters and telegrams demanding that he take back the concession. At the beginning of December 1891 a formal legal opinion (*fatwā*) was disseminated which declared the use of tobacco to be unlawful and be tantamount to war against the Hidden Imam. The *fatwā* was generally attributed to Shīrāzī, and it was immediately obeyed. The tobacco shops in the bazaars closed down, the hookahs disappeared, and the general boycott on all tobacco products made the concession worthless. The Shāh attempted in vain to persuade the Tehran mujtahid Mīrzā Ḥasan Āshtiyānī to declare the *fatwā* invalid; it was only when the government gave way and repealed the concession on 28th December that the mujtahids also came round. On 6th January 1892 Āshtiyānī summoned the population of Iran to attend to their daily business and on 26th January a telegram from the *marja' al-taqlīd* Shīrāzī in Sāmarrā declared the use of tobacco to be permissible and the boycott to be over.[227]

The mujtahids' fight against the tobacco monopoly was a dress rehearsal for the constitutional conflict of 1905-1906. Plans for constructing a road from Julfa on the Russian border to Tabrīz raised fears of a Russian invasion; resistance to growing Russian influence blazed up in the destruction of a half-completed main building of the Russian Bank in Tehran, which, moreover, was to be erected on the site of an earlier religious foundation (November 1905). When two Tehran bazaar merchants were punished with the bastinado on 12th December 1905 because they were supposedly responsible for higher sugar prices a protesting crowd gathered in the Shāh mosque of the capital. When government agents caused panic among the gathered people and the crowd dispersed, the *'ulamā'* switched to open resistance. They left Tehran, seat of the God-forsaken government, in droves and took asylum in the *Imāmzāda* shrine of 'Abd al-'Aẓīm (near old Rayy, south of Tehran) from where they conveyed their demands to the Shāh: the removal of the governor of Tehran, dismissal of the Belgian customs minister Naus, application of the *sharī'a*, and appointment of a group to safeguard justice (*'adālat-khāna*).

There was no generally recognised *marja' al-taqlīd* after the death of Mīrzā Sayyid Ḥasan Shīrāzī in Sāmarrā (1895). At the head of the Iranian *'ulamā'* were the two Tehran mujtahids Sayyid 'Abdallāh Bihbihānī and Sayyid Muḥammad Ṭabāṭabā'ī. When they left the asylum of the shrine on 14th January 1906 and went to negotiate in Tehran they were welcomed enthusiastically by the people of the capital. The mujtahids' negotiations were accompanied by bloody unrest in Shīrāz, Tehran, and Mashhad where government troops carried out a bloodbath in the courtyard of the shrine of the Imam 'Alī al-Riḍā. When the soldiers fired on the crowd in Tehran which was mourning a young sayyid shot by an officer, about 2,000 *'ulamā'* left the capital once again and went into asylum (*bast*) in Qumm (15th July 1906). More than 14,000 people, mainly Tehran bāzārīs, sought asylum in the grounds of the summer residence of the British Embassy in Qulhak, near Tehran, and the Shāh was now publicly compared with the Umayyad Caliph Yazīd who was responsible for al-Ḥusayn's martyrdom at Karbalā'. The government gave way and dismissed the minister 'Ayn al-Dawla, who became the scapegoat. The *'ulamā'* returned to Tehran in triumph (18th August 1906).

At first the opposition's main demand had been the establishment of a 'place of justice' (*'adalat-khāna*), a control mechanism which would ensure that the government applied Islamic law. Only gradually the call was heard for a parliamentary assembly (*majlis*) to draw up a constitution (*mashrūṭa*). The *'ulamā'* thus adopted one of the demands of the numerically small European-orientated progressive liberal intelligentsia with whom they had entered into a remarkable alliance. Of course, the *'ulamā'* were not guided by liberal or democratic ideas. For them constitution and parliament were only the means by which to shake the autocratic and centralistic régime of the Shāh and to bring their own political influence to bear. On 7th October 1906 the first 'Assembly of the National Council' (*majlis-i shūrā-yi millī*) consisting of 156 deputies met. The majority of the delegates were made up of bāzārīs and members of artisan guilds. One fifth were *'ulamā'*. The two leading mujtahids, Ṭabāṭabā'ī and Bihbihānī, were not members of the parliament but did occasionally participate in debates. A committee worked out a 'basic law' (*qānūn-i asāsī*) which Shāh Muẓaffar al-Dīn delayed signing until 30th December 1906. After his death on 8th January 1907 the constitution received an important appendix (*mutammim*) on 7th October 1907 which the new Shāh Muḥammad 'Alī signed after some resistance.

Iran's first constitution was modelled largely on Belgium's liberal constitution of 1831, but also bore obvious signs of the cooperation of the *'ulamā'* especially in the extensive appendix. According to article 1 of the rider the Twelver Shiite faith (*madhhab-i Ja'farī*) became Iran's state religion on which the Shāh was to swear (article 39). With whom actual sovereignty lay remained undecided. According to article 35 of the appendix it was assigned to the Shāh by the nation, but – as a concession to the clergy – only as a 'divine gift'.[288] The *'ulamā* safeguarded their claim to sole representation of the Hidden Imam in article 2 of the appendix by having parliamentary decisions controlled by a group of five mujtahids who had to ratify the compatibility of all laws with the *sharī'a;* these five were to be coopted by parliament from twenty of the mujtahids put forward by the country's *'ulamā'* .

The different interests of the *'ulamā'* and the liberal-democratic delegates (who mainly came from the commercially developed northern province of Āzarbayjān) soon came to the fore in the majlis and led to tensions which the Shāh sought to exploit. In June 1908, Shāh Muḥammad 'Alī attempted a coup d'état. He fired on the parliamentary building and dissolved the majlis, but on 16th July 1909 he had to abdicate and flee to Russia after revolutionary troops marched on Tehran from Gīlān on the Caspian Sea, and from Iṣfahān. The second majlis (1909-1911) attempted to solve the country's financial problems with the help of the American expert Shuster, but came to grief as a result of the resistance of the Russians and Britons who had divided Iran up into spheres of influence on 31st August 1907. The Regent Nāṣir al-Mulk (for the minor Shāh Aḥmad) gave way to pressure from the Great Powers, dissolved the majlis, which tried in vain to offer resistance, and dismissed Shuster. That spelt the end of the short-lived alliance between the *'ulamā'* and the liberal-democratic forces.

Primary sources in translation

The text of the 1906 constitution and the 1907 appendix have been translated into English by E.G. Browne, *Persian Revolution*, 362 ff. (the complete Persian text is in *Lughat-nāma* Vol. 28, *Qānūn-i asasī*).

Secondary sources

E.G. Browne, *The Persian Revolution of 1905-1909*, Cambridge 1910, ²1966. A. Kasravi, *Tārīkh-i Mashrūṭi-yi Īrān*, Tehran 1961/1340. A.K.S. Lambton, 'Secret Societies and the Persian Revolution of 1905-1906', '*St. Anthony's Papers* 4 (1958), 43-60;' 'The Tobacco Regie: Prelude to Revolution', *SI* 22 (1965), 119-57 and 23 (1965), 71-90; 'The Persian 'ulamā' and Constitutional Reform', in: *Le shī'isme imâmite, Colloque de Strasbourg*, Paris 1970, 245-69. P. Avery, *Modern Iran*, London 1965. N.R. Keddie, 'The Origins of the Religious-Radical Alliance in Iran', in: *Past and Present* 34 (1966), 70-80; newly published in Keddie, *Iran. Religion, Politics and Society*, London 1980, 53-65; 'Popular Participation in the Persian Revolution of 1905-1911', *ibid*, 66-79. H. Algar, *Religion and State in Iran, 1758-1906. The Role of the Ulama in the Qajar*

Period, Berkeley/Los Angeles 1969. J. Calmard, 'L'Iran sous Nâseroddin Chāh et les derniers Qadjar', *Le Monde iranien et l'Islam* IV, Geneva/Paris 1976-7, 165-94. A. Hairi, *Shī'ism and Constitutionalism in Iran. A Study of the Role Played by the Persian Residents of Iraq in Iranian Politics*, Leiden 1977. E. Abrahamian, 'The Crowd in the Persian Revolution', *Iranian Studies* 2 (1969), 128-50; 'The Causes of the Constitutional Revolution in Iran', *IJMES* 10(1979), 381-414. A. Fathi, 'The Role of the 'Rebels' in the Constitutional Movement in Iran', *IJMES* 10 (1979), 55-66. S.A. Arjomand, 'The Ulama's Traditionalist Opposition to Parliamentarianism: 1907-1909', *MES* 17 (1981), 174-90. T. Nagel, *Staat und Glaubensgemeinschaft im Islam II*, Zurich/Munich 1981, 266-306.

THE SHIITE CLERGY AND THE PAHLAVĪ DYNASTY (1925-1979)

Constitutional revolution and civil war, together with the growing influence of Russia and Great Britain during the First World War, weakened the Qājār régime and strengthened centrifugal powers in Iran. In Rasht on the Caspian Sea the Soviet republic of Gīlān was proclaimed after a Soviet intervention in May 1920, while in the economically strong northern province of Āzarbayjān separatist tendencies made themselves felt, and in Khūzistān on the Persian Gulf the British supported the independence movement of the Arabian tribal leader Shaykh Khaz'al in order to gain access to the oil deposits discovered there in 1908. The imminent disintegration of Iran, however, caused nationalist forces to enter the fray; on 20th February 1921 the journalist Żiya' al-Dīn Ṭabāṭabā'ī mounted a coup with the support of the Cossack brigades of Colonel Riżā Khān which marched from Qazvīn to Tehran and occupied the capital.[229] Riżā Khān became war minister and head of the army (*sardār-i sipāh*) in Ṭabāṭabā'ī's cabinet, but in October 1923 he took over the government himself. Inspired by the example of Kemal Atatürk's new Turkey, he appears to have tried initially to establish a lay republic for Iran modelled on Kemal's example, but he changed his plans when *'ulamā'* resistance became apparent.

When several mujtahids who had had to leave Najaf and Karbalā' in 1922 because of their anti-British agitation found refuge in Qumm, Riżā Khān sought them out there in March 1924 in order to convince them that he was not trying to set up a republic based on the Turkish model. In order to demonstrate his good Shiite intentions he even took part in the 'Āshūrā' procession in Tehran in August 1924. Thereupon the *'ulamā'*, who had meanwhile returned to Iraq, sent the premier an icon of 'Alī and a sword which al-Ḥusayn's half-brother 'Abbās is said to have wielded at Karbalā'.[230] Riżā reciprocated by making a pilgrimage to Najaf where he promised the leading mujtahids – Mīrzā

Muḥammad Ḥusayn Nā'īnī and Ḥājjī Sayyid Abu 'l-Ḥasan Mūsavī Iṣfahānī – that he would at last apply article 2 of the appendix to the 1907 constitution which provided for control of parliamentary legislation by a committee of five mujtahids.

On 31st October 1925 the Tehran Parliament declared the deposition of the last Qājār Shāh Aḥmad, who was living abroad, and on 12th December they set up Riżā Khān as Shāh. The majority of the *'ulamā'* had no objections to the change of régime; the preservation of a monarchy in traditional form seemed most likely to offer them a guarantee that there would be no lay experiments such as those in Turkey. The fact that this hope was illusory was soon to be demonstrated. Throughout his reign (1925-1941) Riżā (Reza) Shāh obstinately and persistently pursued his aim of reforming the Iranian state on the European model, strengthening the absolutism of the crown and repressing the influence of the clergy.

The series of laws which cut back the old privileges of the *'ulamā'* had already begun during Reza's period in office as premier. The military service statute of 28th May 1925 had certainly exempted from compulsory service those religious students (*ṭullāb*) who could be shown to be capable of *ijtihād (ijāza-yi ijtihād)* by the testimony of a recognised mujtahid, but the law required them to sit an additional exam before the state examining board.[231] The repression of the religious (*sharī'ī*) courts in favour of secular (*'urfī*) courts and the introduction of a code of civil law on the French model in the year 1926 restricted even further the *'ulama'*'s monopoly over jurisdiction; the heaviest blow was dealt by the statute of 17th March 1932 which removed the religious judges' notarial function at the certification and registration of legal affairs and contracts. With that the *'ulamā'* not only lost a large part of their social influence, but with the loss of notarial fees also one of their most important sources of income.

At the same time Reza Shāh continued to press on with the secularisation of the educational system. In 1930 the Ministry of Education issued a timetable for religious education which was followed in 1934 by similar regulations for higher religious studies.[232] In 1935 a theological faculty was set up at the newly founded University of Tehran, and from December 1936 only those who had acquired an academic degree in law could act as a judge. In addition to this there were clothing laws modelled on Kemal's example: in 1929 European clothing was prescribed for men. The *'ulamā'* were exempted from this, but state commissions decided who was a cleric and who was not. In 1936 it was forbidden to wear the veil (*chadur*), and the Shāh sought to stop public processions of mourning and flagellation and the passion plays and recitations during Muḥarram (see below p. 139 ff).

Reza Shāh's policies did not encounter any energetic united resistance from the clergy. There were isolated acts of resistance, and Sayyid Ḥasan Mudarris, an opponent of Reza Shāh, was killed in prison in 1938. The protests of individual *'ulamā'* against the spread of European bad habits remained as isolated episodes, for example the angry sermon by Ayatallah Bafqi against the ladies at court who visited the shrine of Fāṭima al-Ma'ṣuma in Qumm without wearing the veil. After Bāfqī's sermon General Tīmūrtāsh is said to have surrounded the shrine with artillery, penetrated the shrine wearing boots and spurs, and dragged the Āyatallāh out of the holy area by his beard. The cleric died in exile in 1944 in the asylum of the shrine of Shāh 'Abd al-'Aẓīm in Rayy.[233]

With the help of his modernised army Reza Shāh was able not only to defeat separatist forces in the north and west of the country but also to suppress any resistance to his internal policies. In the 1930s the Shiite clergy did not oppose the Shāh's military dictatorship, since a large proportion of the religious students had modern and liberal views. The journal *Humāyūn* issued in Qumm from 1934 by the anti-clerical liberal journalist and historian Aḥmad Kasravī exercised great influence along the same lines. Even amongst the opposition the constitutionalists and the liberals, the laicists and the modernists set the tone. Against that the traditional religious forces had firstly to reorganise and reform, and Qumm now began to play a leading role again for the first time in centuries. In the 1920s the town not only outstripped Mashhad, the old Iranian centre of Shiite studies, but even the *'atabāt* of Iraq where the activities of the *'ulamā'* had been severely curtailed by British mandatory power (from 1920).

The most significant character among the *'ulamā'* of Qumm was the Āyatallāh 'Abd al-Karīm Yazdī Hā'irī (b. 1859), the only Iranian mujtahid who was acknowledged as *marja'-i taqlīd* in the 1920s beside the two authorities of Najaf, Abu 'l-Ḥasan Iṣfahānī and Muḥammad Ḥusayn Nā'īnī. Hā'irī, who had lived for a time in Najaf and Karbalā', taught in western Iranian Arāk (south east of Hamadān) from 1913 until 1922. There a large group of pupils, including the young Khumaynī (b. 1902 in Khumayn, 60 km to the south east), rallied around him. In 1922 Hā'irī moved to Qumm where he taught until his death in 1937. It is due to his work that the town became the most important 'place of learning' (*ḥawza-yi 'ilmiyya*) of the Iranian Twelver Shia, and as a result of his indefatigable activity Qumm acquired several new madrasas, a library, hospital, casual accommodation and cemeteries.[234] Hā'irī did not become involved in politics; like his pupil and successor Burūjirdī he personified the traditional type of conservative Imāmī scholar for whom all secular matters were an abomination which should be avoided as far as possible. This political abstinence of the leading *'ulamā'* certainly made it easier for the Shāh to pursue his policies of centralisation and secularisation of the state.

Reza Shāh's marked leanings towards the German Reich led to his downfall during the Second World War. Because of his refusal to deport German advisors staying in Iran, British and Soviet troops marched into Iran in August 1941 and forced the Shāh to abdicate in favour of his son Muḥammad Riżā. The Soviet occupying force encouraged Āzarbayjānī and Kurdish struggles for autonomy in their area of influence while the British controlled the oilfields in the south and provided their Soviet allies on Iranian territory with supplies. In view of the young Shāh's weakness the *'ulamā'* were now able to win back a number of the positions they had lost under Reza Shāh. In 1948 fifteen mujtahids issued a formal legal opinion (*fatwā*) which forbade women to show themselves in public without wearing the veil; even the Muḥarram processions soon returned to the streets. Most of the *'ulamā'*, however, kept themselves at a distance from the activities of the post-1943 political parties, all of which had to a greater or lesser extent absorbed western ideas. Āyatallāh Ḥusayn ibn 'Alī Ṭabāṭabā'ī Burūjirdī (1875-1962), who was teaching in Qumm and from 1949 had been generally recognised as the supreme *marja'-i taqlīd,* invited around 2,000 *'ulamā'* to the Fayżiyya madrasa in Qumm in February 1949 and placed them under obligation to join no party and not to meddle in political affairs.[235] He himself, a pious literary scholar like his predecessor Hā'irī, only rarely gave any public response to everyday political questions. Even during the struggle over nationalisation of the Anglo-Iranian Oil Company (AIOC) the clergy conspicuously held themselves back. The leader of the National Front, Dr Muḥammad Muṣaddiq, who was called upon by the majlis on 30th April 1951 to be Prime Minister and who put through nationalisation of the AIOC the following day, could not unreservedly depend on the clergy's support. The National Front was suspect to the *'ulamā'* on account of its liberal ideas and its cooperation with the left, and when Muṣaddiq prepared a law introducing womens' voting rights at the end of 1952 the objection of leading mujtahids, including Burūjirdī, defeated the plan. The *'ulamā'* were not displeased to witness Muṣaddiq's downfall at the hands of a CIA-instigated military coup on 19th August 1953 and the subsequent battering of the National Front. After the downfall of their rivals, the laicist-liberal leftist opposition, the clergy were prepared to work closely with the crown, and the as yet not firmly established Shāh found himself forced to make a number of concessions. He promised a statute which would forbid the production and sale of alcohol, extended religious instruction in the schools once more, and in 1955 he allowed the *'ulamā'* a free hand against the hated Bahā'ī sect whose dome in Tehran was pulled down with the Shāh's consent and the army's cooperation; calls to the people to oppose the Baha'is by Mullah Muḥammad Taqī Falsafi had previously been transmitted by national radio. The Shāh did however successfully resist the *'ulamā'*'s demands to outlaw all Bahā'īs and seize their property.[236]

Freed from national opposition and supported by the USA the Shāh soon found an opportunity to resume his father's policies of modernisation of the country and strict centralisation, and the clergy found themselves back in their old role as the people's sole representatives against tyrannical rule and non-Islamic influences. In February 1960 the highest *marja'-i taqlīd* Burūjirdī opposed in a letter the outline of a land-reform bill which the government had put before parliament. The clergy's opposition to the Shāh's land reform only partially stemmed from self-interest. While it was not unusual for the large scholarly families to have considerable landholdings, the vast majority of the mullahs were more at home in urban surroundings or even represented the interests of rural smallholders who were intended to benefit from the reform.[237] Probably of greater consequence were fears that the clergy might lose control over the endowment land.[238] Besides, a fundamental opposition to touching private property which had been guaranteed by the *sharī'a* and by the constitution may have played a role.[239] There was opposition too, to the Shāh's pro-Israeli policy, to all measures taken towards equal rights for women, as well as to the plan to send teachers educated by the state as an 'army of knowledge' (*sipāh-i dānish*) into the remotest villages in order to break up the education monopoly of the mullahs. The Shāh's increasing autocracy, growing corruption and the violence of the police, secret service and military all added to the traditional picture of royal tyranny (*ẓulm*). More and more frequently the clerics came into conflict with state authority, while the Shāh's attacks on the 'reactionary' clergy became more severe.

After the death of Āyatallāh Burūjirdī on 30th March 1961 the *'ulamā'* no longer had a generally recognised leader. Attempts by the Shāh to hand over succession in the *marja'iyyāt* to the Iraqi (and therefore less dangerous for Iranian internal policy) *marja'* Sayyid Muḥsin al-Ḥakīm in Najaf failed.[240] The majority of the mujtahids were certainly hostile, but for the time being they had in mind reform of the religious institutions rather than the overthrow of the régime.[241] After Burūjirdī's death a group of clerics and laymen discussed the possibilities of reform and the future organisation of the clergy in monthly reports of the Tehran Religious Association (*Anjuman-i Māhhāna-yi Dīnī*). Several of these reports appeared in 1961 under the title 'A study of the dignity of the *marja*ʿ and spirituality'.[242] The basis for most of the contributions, which were made by leading mujtahids and also by one pious layman, the engineer Mahdī Bāzārgān, was the Quranic verse charging all believers to 'order that which is good and forbid that which is objectionable' (*al-amr bi 'l-maʿrūf wa 'l-nahy ʿan al-munkar*). Rejection of all secular rule could be inferred from the interpretation that the community of believers was thereby called upon to rule itself. It is characteristic of the discussion of these reformers that they doubted the necessity to create a new 'most learned' *marjaʿ-i taqlīd*. In the contributions made by the mujtahids Murtażā Jazā'irī and Maḥmūd Ṭāliqānī prominence is given to the fact that recognition of a single highest *marja*ʿ is a relatively new phenomenon which was not known by the earlier Shia; at the same time, they questioned whether a single scholar could be the 'most learned' in all religious questions. The two mujtahids therefore urged the establishment of a validating committee (*shūrā-yi fatvā'ī*) in which the most distinguished mujtahids of the country – like the leadership committee of the Sunni Azhar University in Cairo – could discuss all questions which arise and reach decisions by a common *fatwā*. The *ijtihād*, until now exercised by every mujtahid separately and with individual responsibility, should be undertaken by the group and thus become stronger in its efficacy. One further concern of the reformers was modernisation of teaching material in the religious universities. The most important demand, however, was for the clergy's financial independence both from the state and from the goodwill of the believers. Income from their notarial role had been removed from the *ʿulamā'* by the statute of 1932; allowances from the endowments (*awqāf*) diminished or were frequently misapplied; moreover, the state sought to bring them under its control. The most important source of income thus remained the Quranic fifth (*khums*), taken voluntarily from the believers, of which half was administered by the clerics as the 'Imam's share' (*sahm-i imām*) and used for religious purposes. Every *marjaʿ-i taqlīd* had to have this money collected by assistants from among his followers, and deceit and embezzlement were common. Although Burūjirdī had tried to check this abuse by introducing lists of donations there could be no question of the regulated raising of this 'church tax'. In addition to that the reformers criticised the believers' preference for making payments to the conservative mujtahids who for their part were inclined to say what the masses wanted to hear in order to receive higher incomes.

'Organisation of the Imam's share' (*sāzmān dādan bi-sahm-i imām*) was thus one of the main demands of the reformers who wanted to make the clergy independent of the state and the faithful by the right of disposal over regular income from *awqāf* and *khums*. It is clear that the Shāh viewed such attempts to establish an independent Shiite 'church' with utter mistrust, and in March 1963 he put an end to the monthly meetings held by the Religious Association.[243]

Clerical opposition to the Shah's régime now began to become radical. A minority, whose spokesman was the as yet unknown Āyatallāh Khumaynī, a pupil of Hā'irī, even dared to demand the abolition of the monarchy. When the Shāh had his plans for a White Revolution blessed by a referendum in January 1963 clashes resulted on 22nd March, on the occasion of the commemoration of the death of the sixth Imam Ja'far al-Ṣādiq in the Fayziyya madrasa in Qumm between religious students (*ṭullāb*) and agents of the secret service SAVAK who had forced their way into the school. On 2nd June (10th Muḥarram) in a sermon Khumaynī urged resistance to the 'Yazīd of our time', and demonstrations against the 'tyrants' ensued. The following day Khumaynī and a further fourteen clerics were arrested in Qumm, Mashhad and Shīrāz. In the large towns in Iran news of the arrests led to disturbances, and on 5th June street fights took place in Tehran. The Shah gave orders for the soldiers to open fire, and a large number of people were killed. Khumaynī, who was freed for a short while, was arrested once again in November 1964 and deported. For more than a decade the Shāh was able to suppress all opposition, including that of the clerics, violently with the support of the army, the police and the secret service.

While the clergy once more relapsed into its normal quietism, there was a noteworthy attempt in lay intellectual circles to modernise Shiite tradition and make it more immediately relevant. The focus for these efforts was the Ḥusayniyya-yi Irshād (the Ḥusayniyya of Guidance) a meeting-place founded to honour al-Ḥusayn (see below p. 142) in Qulhak near Tehran. There Dr 'Alī Sharī'atī (1933–1977) soon came to predominate among the intellectuals occupied with lectures and publications. He was a religious scientist and sociologist with a doctorate from the Sorbonne, whose ideas not only took their bearings from the Islamic modernists Jamāl al-Dīn Afghānī (d. 1897), Muḥammad 'Abduh (d. 1905) and Muḥammad Iqbāl (d. 1938) but also from Karl Marx and Max Weber, Jean Paul Sartre, Herbert Marcuse and Frantz Fanon. Convinced that in a traditional Shiite society every attempt to free the people would fail if it did not respect Shiite values and symbols Sharī'atī sought to give the Imāmī picture of history a new progressive-revolutionary significance: the original Islam of

Muḥammad and ʿAlī thus appears as a model of a classless society and the Imams were commissioned to realise it; after the *ghayba* the role of leading the *umma* – that is the Imamate – falls to the intellectual enlightener (*rawshan-fikr*); the revolutionary leader recognised by the people takes the place of the Imam martyr; waiting (*intiẓār*) for the Hidden Imam becomes a revolutionary perspective, a prospect of the future classless *umma*. It is understandable that the Shiite clergy, whom Sharīʿatī attacked vigorously for their reactionary behaviour and rote learning, and basically declared to be superfluous, denounced him as a foreign agent. At the end of 1973 the Shāh closed down the Ḥusayniyya-yi Irshād, and Sharīʿatī left Iran in 1977 after a long period of detention and died shortly afterwards in England under obscure circumstances. His writings appealed greatly to the Iranian intelligentsia, especially to the students, but the Iranian revolution soon left his ideology behind, marked as it was all too strongly by western ideas.[244]

Bibliography

J. Greenfield, 'Die geistlichen Schariegerichte in Persien', *Zeitschr. f. vergl. Rechtswiss.* 48 (1934), 157-67. A.K.S. Lambton, 'A Reconsideration of the Position of the *marjaʿ al-taqlīd* and the Religious Institution', *SI* 20 (1964), 115-35. P. Avery, *Modern Iran*, London 1965. H. Algar, 'The Oppositional Role of the Ulama in Twentieth-Century Iran', in: N.R. Keddie (ed.), *Scholars, Saints and Sufis*, Berkeley/Los Angeles 1972, 231-55. E.A. Doroshenko, *Shiitskoe dukhovenstvo v sovremennem Irane (The Shiite Clergy in Present-Day Iran)*, Moscow 1975. S. Akhavi, *Religion and Politics in Contemporary Iran: Clergy-State Relations in the Pahlavi Period*, Albany 1980. E. Abrahamian, *Iran Between Two Revolutions*, Princeton 1982. Y. Richard, *Der verborgene Imam*, Berlin 1983. A. Kelidar, 'The Shii Imami Community and Politics in the Arab East', *MES* 19 (1983), 3-16 (about the Shiites of Iraq since 1920).

ISLAMIC REVOLUTION AND ISLAMIC REPUBLIC IN IRAN

An analysis of the multifarious economic, social and political causes of the Islamic Revolution in Iran cannot be undertaken in the present work, and for this reference should be made to the rapidly increasing specialist literature. It is well known that the Shiite clergy played a major role in the upheaval – even though they were not its only authors – and that after depriving all other opposition groups of their power they finally enforced their concept of a total theocratic state. Here the revolutionary events will be considered chiefly in the light of the historical development of the Twelver Shia, the culmination and logical conclusion of which they appear to be. Moreover, it will be seen that the establishment of the Islamic Republic was a revolutionary innovation even for the Shia themselves, an audacious step into untrodden virgin territory.

The driving force behind this development was the Āyatallāh Sayyid Rūḥallāh Mūsavī Hindī Khumaynī.[245] Born in 1902 in the small town of Khumayn (half way between Hamadān and Iṣfahān, 60 km south east of Arāk) he, like his closest acquaintances and pupils, came from a traditional small-town rural milieu and modest commercial background; and like almost all mujtahids of the radical wing he owed his education exclusively to the Shiite clergy's educational institutions which had been reformed since the 1920s but which were still run strictly along traditional lines. In Arāk in 1918 he attached himself to the Āyatallāh Hā'irī and followed him to Qumm in 1922 (see above p. 119). In 1936 he obtained the qualification (*ijāza*) of a mujtahid. In 1945 he put his views forward for the first time in a paper which critically disputed the ideas of the anti-clerical liberal Aḥmad Kasravī and – subsequently – the laicising policies of Reza Shāh; besides demanding control of the monarch by the mujtahids, the idea of abolishing the monarchy already appears.[246] During the unrest in Qumm in June 1963 he publicly opposed the Shāh for the first time (see above p. 123). After his deportation he lived in Turkish Bursa for a few years and then settled at the shrine of Najaf in October 1965, where his propaganda activities directed against the Shāh were tolerated by the Iraqi Baʿth government. Khumaynī's most important work, 'Islamic Government' (*Ḥukūmat-i islāmī*), appeared in Najaf. This is a treatise based on two lectures given on 21st January and 8th February 1970 which were noted down by his pupils and which expose the godlessness of every monarchy and already foreshadow the future theocratic state of the Islamic Republic.[247] Rapprochement between Iraq and Iran in 1975 – particularly on the Kurdish question, occasionally forced the Āyatallāh to exercise more restraint, and when he was deported from Iraq in October 1978 Iranian domestic change – clearly not without his powerful assistance – had already been set into motion.

The Revolution began in the summer of 1977 when leading opposition politicians of the National Front, including Shāhpūr Bakhtiyār, urged the Shāh to re-apply the 1906 constitution in its entirety. In November and December of the same year high prices, low salaries and lack of provisions caused the first wildcat strikes. When Khumaynī was vehemently attacked and derided in the Shāh-controlled press in January 1978 demonstrations took place in Qumm and then in other towns; the exile in Najaf became the martyr and the awaited saviour. Half-hearted concessions by the Shāh to the clergy – for example the reintroduction of the Islamic calendar which had been replaced by an 'Iranian' era – came too late. After bloody clashes between religious students (*ṭullāb*) and the police, numerous *'ulamā'* declared the Shāh's rule to be incompatible with Islamic law. When the militia fired on a mass demonstration on 8th September there were hundreds, perhaps thousands of dead, and after this 'Black Friday' the breach could no longer be patched up. The spiral of violence – strikes, closing down of the bazaar with subsequent mass demonstrations, bloody repression by the police and the army, ceremonies of mourning for the victims and renewed demonstrations, and, finally, the implementation of martial law – now turned even faster. From France, where he had gone after his deportation from Iraq on 6th October 1978, Khumaynī now called publicly for the abrogation of the monarchy and the establishment of an Islamic Republic, and participants in a demonstration immediately following the 'Āshūrā' processions on 12th December adopted this demand in a resolution.[248] In order at least to save the throne for the dynasty the Shāh dismissed the military government in office (from November 1978), commissioned the opposition politician Bakhtiyār to form a civilian government and on 16th January – evidently under American pressure – he left the country. Khumaynī flew to Tehran from Paris on 1st February, but did not recognise the government set up by the Shāh, and the engineer Mahdī Bāzārgān (see above p. 122) formed a provisional revolutionary government. When the army declared itself neutral after battles lasting several days, Bakhtiyār, who was now without any support, resigned and went into exile.

The opposition which had toppled the Shāh was an immensely broad-based and popular movement. It included communists and socialists, middle-class liberals and intellectuals, different religious splinter groups and the moderate as well as the radical wing of the Shiite clergy. Khumaynī and his supporters, however, succeeded in eliminating all the other opposition groups one after another, and gradually realised his concept of the Islamic Republic. The main reason for his success is surely to be found in the fact that he was the only person in a position to mobilise and direct large masses of people. His speeches and proclamations were circulated in the mosques by the country's 80,000 to 100,000 or so mullahs[249] with the aid of recorded cassettes and he was able to mobilise a following the like of which was not possessed either by the middle-class intellectuals or by the communist Tūdah party which counted for its support on the oilfield workers. Even Bāzārgān's revolutionary government, formed from middle-class technocrats, soon lost any real influence; local revolutionary committees, revolutionary guards and revolutionary courts exercised the real power and these, which often represented diverging interests, came increasingly under the control of the central revolutionary council dominated by Khumaynī's supporters. Two laymen (Banī Ṣadr and Quṭb-zādah) and eight mujtahids sat on this council, which included the highly esteemed and very popular Āyatallāh Ṭāliqānī, the later State President Khāmana'ī, the later Speaker of the Parliament, Rafsanjānī and – as the leading intellectual figure – Muḥammad Bihishtī, leader of the Islamic Republican Party (IRP) which owed its loyalty to Khumaynī.[250]

After the population had voted in favour of establishing an Islamic Republic in a referendum held on 30th and 31st March 1979 serious arguments ensued over its future form between Khumaynī's political supporters and those who wanted to maintain at least some traces of pluralism and democracy. At a congress in Tehran University the revolutionary council and the IRP demanded that the people's sovereignty be replaced by the absolute sovereignty of God, and that Khumaynī's concept of the 'government of the legal scholar' (*vilāyet-i faqīh*) be made the principle of the constitution. The liberal Āyatallāh Maḥmūd Ṭāliqānī (b. 1910), one of the authors of the memorandum of 1961 (see above p. 122) who considered constitutionalism, democracy and socialism to be thoroughly compatible with Islam and had contacts with the liberal and left-wing opposition, was unable to carry the revolutionary council with him and became almost totally silent in the last few months before his death (10th September 1979).[251] The Āyatallāh Kāẓim Sharī'at-Madārī (b. 1905 in Tabrīz), who favoured a constitutional monarchy controlled by the mujtahids and was Khumaynī's most prominent opponent, did not hold any post during the Revolution. The Muslim People's Party of Iran (MPRP),[252] which was inspired by him and had its roots in Sharī'at Madārī's home province of Āzarbayjān, was declared counter-revolutionary after the victory of the Khumaynī wing and at the end of 1979 was forced to dissolve itself. In 1980 Sharī'at-Madārī was placed under house arrest in Qumm.[253]

The political realisation of Khumaynī's ideas for a totally Islamic theocratic state took place with the help of the new constitution under the control of the lawyers which was to replace the (theoretically still valid) constitution of 1906, for whose reinstatement many opponents had fought and given their lives. The outline of the constitution which Khumaynī delivered to the head of government Bāzārgān, and which was published by the provisional government on 16th May 1979, had apparently already been worked out during Khumaynī's exile in Neauphle-le-Château near Paris;[254] in spite of objections and opposition it was passed in the form demanded by the Islamic Republican Party under Bihishtī's leadership. At the elections to the constitutive assembly on 3rd August 1979 the IRP won sixty of the seventy-three seats, and Bihishtī assumed the presidency. On 2nd and 3rd December the constitution was ratified by a referendum.

The 'constitutional law of the Islamic Republic of Iran' (*qānūn-i asāsī-yi Jumhūrī-yi Islāmī-yi Irān*) translated Khumaynī's concept of a purely Islamic government (*hukūmat-i islāmī*) into reality. Article 2 gives God exclusive authority (*ikhtiṣāṣ-i ḥākimīyat va tashrīʿ*), article 4 prescribes that 'all civil, criminal, financial, economic, administrative, cultural, military, political and all other statutes and regulations . . . (must) be in keeping with Islamic measures; . . . the Islamic legal scholars of the watch council (*shūrā-yi nigahbān*) will keep watch over this.' The latter comprises six religious jurists (*fuqahā'*) and six secular jurists (*ḥuqūqdān*) who are elected by parliament for six years (article 91). According to article 5, 'during the absence of the removed twelfth Imam – may God hasten his return! – government (*vilāyat-i amr*) and leadership of the community (*imāmat-i ummat*) in the Islamic Republic of Iran belongs to the rightful God-fearing . . . legal scholar (*faqīh*) who is recognised and acknowledged as the Islamic leader by the majority of the population.' Article 107 mentions Āyatallāh Khumaynī explicity by name in this capacity and attributes the title 'most talented' (*ʿalī qadr*) *marjaʿ-i taqlīd* to him. After his arrest in 1963 Khumaynī was declared *marjaʿ-i taqlīd* by several *marjaʿs* – including his later opponent Sharīʿat-Madārī – and was thus saved from prosecution and death. The plebiscite on the constitution now confirmed him in this status. If there is no leader generally recognised as the sole authority then 'a leadership committee of Islamic legal scholars would assume leadership' (article 5) made up of three to five people (article 107 ff.).

The connotations of the Arabic-Persian terms are lost in translation of the constitutional text. For a Shiite a formulation such as 'leadership of the community' (Pers. *imāmat-i ummat,* Arab. *imāmat al-umma*) inevitably awakens associations with the rule of the twelfth Imam. In fact, the Islamic Republic intends to realise its empire of God here and now – if only in Iran at first. The eschatological vision is realised at the present time. Khumaynī's authority, legitimised by the constitution, could be described as an anticipated plebiscitary de facto Imamate. The rule of the Mahdī is already being enforced by the will of the people, even before his actual return. A Shiite would certainly not concede that this return is actually superfluous. In the Islamic Republic the provisional arrangements with which the Imāmī Shia had experimented ever since the *ghayba* of the twelfth Imam are in fact replaced for the first time by a definitive, immediate theocracy. At the same time the *ʿulamā'*'s representative role, which had been developed over the course of several centuries, is consummated by direct political government authority. This is what is essentially revolutionary about Khumaynī's and Bihishtī's conception, and which met with bitter opposition from the conservative mujtahids precisely for that reason. The propaganda, seen to have been handled mainly by the mass of the lower-rank clergy, swept all objections away. During the presidential elections on 25th January 1980 Khumaynī's partisans suffered an unforeseen setback when they had to withdraw their candidate at the last minute because of his non-Iranian origins, thus allowing the moderate Banī Ṣadr to be elected unexpectedly. At the parliamentary (*majlis*) elections on 14th March and 9th May 1980, however, Bihishtī's IRP, together with the religious splinter groups which were allied to them, won a comfortable majority which allowed them to force upon the President the IRP man Raja'ī as Prime Minister. Out of the 245 members of Parliament there were 98 clerics and 51 bāzārīs, representatives of the traditional petty bourgeois and artisan class allied to the radical clerics. At this point the IRP 'clearly acquires the class character of the petty bourgeois of the bazaar, whose ideal of a liberal and protected economy it shares.'[255]

Further events – the outcome of taking hostages in the American Embassy, the overthrow of President Banī Ṣadr by Parliament on 21st June 1981, the course of the Iraq-Iran Gulf War (from 22nd September 1980) – do not need to be described in detail here. Opposition to the régime is only ever voiced abroad or given expression in assassination attempts, but even the bomb attack on the headquarters of the IRP on 28th June 1981 in which Bihishtī lost his life, and the bomb attack two days later which claimed as victims the new President Raja'ī and the Prime Minister Bā Hunar, were unable to shake the absolute autocracy of the IRP.

Although Khumaynī's death on 3rd June 1989 did not lead to any fundamental change in the 'mullacratic' system it did produce significant shifts in the internal balance of power. The previous State President Sayyid 'Alī Khāmini'ī (b. 1940 in Mashhad) whom the 'Council of Experts' (Art. 108 of the Constitution) had designated as Khumaynī's spiritual successor as early as 4th June had neither the charisma nor the spiritual authority of his predecessor. He was not even an Āyatallāh, but bore the more modest title of a *Ḥujjat al-Islām*. Real power devolved on the new State President 'Alī Akbar Hāshimī Rafsanjānī to whom a change in the Constitution prepared before the death of Khumaynī transferred the powers of Head of State (August 1989). Even though the office of President continues to be filled by a member of the clergy today his new power does denote a real shift away from the religious forces in favour of the political.

Primary sources in translation

Translations of the constitution of 1979, the writings and speeches of Khumaynī and other documents of the Revolution are available at the embassies of the Islamic Republic of Iran. The following academic translations exist: H. Algar, *Islam and Revolution. Writings and Declarations of Imam Khomeini*, Berkeley 1981. Imam Khomeini, *A Clarification of Questions. An Unabridged Translation of Resaleh Towzih al-Masael*, trans. J. Borujerdi, London 1984. I. Itscherenska/N. Hasan, Ajatollah Chomeini: Der islamische Staat, Berlin 1983. S. Tellenbach, Untersuchungen zur Verfassung der Islamischen Republik Iran vom 15. November 1979, Berlin 1985 (with a translation of the constitution).

Secondary sources

It is not possible even to approach giving a complete list of the boundless literature on the Islamic Revolution here; moreover, the list of the standard works named here will already be out of date by the time this volume is published. All new publications are continuously registered in *The Quarterly Index Islamicus* (London, quarterly) and in the *Abstracta Iranica* (Leiden, yearly). – M. M. J. Fischer, *Iran From Religious Dispute to Revolution*, Cambridge/Massachusetts 1980; 'Becoming Mollah: Reflections on Iranian Clerics in a Revolutionary Age', *Iranian Studies* 13 (1980), 83-117. S. A. Arjomand, 'The State and Khomeini's Islamic Order', *Iranian Studies* 13 (1980), 147-64; *From Nationalism to Revolutionary Islam*, London 1984. F. Steppat, 'Islamisch-fundamentalistische Kritik an der Staatskonzeption der islamischen Revolution in Iran', *Festschrift Spuler*, Leiden 1981, 443-52. N. R. Keddie, *Roots of Revolution. An Interpretative History of Modern Iran*, New Haven/London 1981 (with a contribution by Y. Richard); *Religion and Politics in Iran. Shi'ism From Quietism to Revolution*, New Haven/London 1983 (with several contributions by different authors); N. R. Keddie/E. Hooglund (eds), *The Iranian Revolution and the Islamic Republic*, Ann Arbor 1982. J. Calmard, 'Les olamâ, le pouvoir et la société en Iran: les discours ambigu de la hiérocratie', in: J.-P. Digard (ed.), *Le cuisinier et le philosophe, Hommage à M. Rodinson*, Paris 1982, 253-61. N. Calder, 'Accommodation and Revolution in Imami Shi'i Jurisprudence: Khumayni and the Classical Tradition', *MES* 18 (1982), 3-19. H. Algar, *The Roots of the Islamic Revolution*, London 1983. Sh. Mahdavi, 'Women and the Shii Ulama in Iran', *MES* 19 (1983), 17-27. Y. Richard, *Der verborgene Imam*, Berlin 1983. H. Bashiriyeh, *The State and Revolution in Iran 1962-1982*, London 1984. K.-H. Göbel, *Moderne schiitische Politik und Staatsidee. Nach Taufīq al-Fukaikī, Muḥammad Ǧawād Muġnīya, Rūḥullāh Ḫumainī*, Opladen 1984. Sh. Bakhash, *The Reign of the Ayatollahs. Iran and the Islamic Revolution*, London 1985. D. Hiro, *Iran under the Ayatollahs*, London 1985. R. Mottahedeh, *The Mantle of the Prophet. Religion and Politics in Iran*, London/New York 1985; G. Aneer, *Imām Rūḥullāh Khumainī, Shāh Muḥammad Rižā Pahlavī and the Religious Traditions of Iran*, Uppsala 1985. D. Gholamasad, *Iran – Die Entstehung der 'Islamischen Revolution'*, Hamburg 1985. A. Taheri, *Chomeini und die Islamische Revolution*, Hamburg 1985. F. Riyahi, *Ayatollah Khomeini*, Frankfurt a. Main 1986. R. W. Cottam, 'The Iranian Revolution', in: J. R. I. Cole/N. R. Keddie (eds.), *Shi'ism and Social Protest*, New Haven 1986, 55-87. M. Kramer (ed), *Shi'ism, Resistance and Revolution*, London 1987.

THE SHIA IN LEBANON

Until their involvement in the civil war in 1983 the Shiite minority in Lebanon had hardly been noticed by the general public. Their main area of settlement to the south of the Litānī river in the Tyre hinterland was the sphere of operation for the Palestine Liberation Organisation (PLO), and under the patronage of a few landowning families the Shiite farmers eked out a poor existence. It was only the destruction of the PLO in Lebanon after the Israeli invasion in 1982 that made the Shiites masters in their own land.

In Lebanon the Twelver Shia were called *metāwile* (sing. *metwālī*, French métouali). The dialect word is derived from the Classical Arabic *mutawallī*, 'supporter, devotee', a word with which the Shiites have from time immemorial described themselves as adherents of the Imams. In Jabal 'Āmil east of Tyre the Shiite proportion of the population is the highest at around 80%, and here are found the most important urban centres, Mays al-Jabal, Tibnīn and Tyre (Ṣūr). North of the Litānī, around Nabaṭiyya, the Shiites form 60% of the population. The second Shiite settlement area is the Biqā' plain with Baalbak (Ba'labak), Zahla and Hirmil with around 70% Shiites.[256]

The origin of the Shiite communities of Lebanon remains obscure. Some have sought to identify in the Metāwile descendants of the Qarmaṭīs[257] or of the Nizari Assassins.[258] In any case the Shiite faith is already attested in Jabal 'Āmil at the end of the 4th/10th century;[259] and it was probably brought there by the Arabian clan of the Banū 'Āmila (from the Judhām tribe) which colonised the mountainous country of Galilee and south Lebanon in the 3rd/9th century. In the 14th century Muḥammad ibn Makkī al-'Āmilī (executed in 786/1384) from Jizzīn east of Sidon (Ṣaydā) introduced the theories of the Ḥilla school into Lebanon (see above p. 67 ff and p. 75), and in the 16th century several scholars from Jabal 'Āmil worked in Ṣafavid Iran and played a considerable part in transforming it into a Shiite country (see above p. 87). Since then relations between the Lebanese and Iranian Shiites have been very close; the Lebanese Muḥammad al-Ḥurr al-'Āmilī (d. 1104/1692), who taught in Iranian Mashhad, composed a two-volume biographical lexicon of the scholars from Jabal 'Āmil.[260]

After the First World War the Lebanese Shiites successfully resisted integration into a Sunni-dominated Greater Syria. However, they played only a modest political role in Lebanon, which became independent in 1944, alongside the Maronite Christians and the Sunnis. According to the informal proportional system of the so-called national pact agreed upon in 1943 they provided 19 members of parliament (Christians 54; Sunnis 20; Druze 6). While the posts of

State President and Prime Minister were reserved for the Christians and the Sunnis, the Shiites had to be content with the post of parliamentary Speaker, and they always provided the Minister of Agriculture in the cabinet. At the last census held in 1932 155,000 Shiites were counted. Today their number amounts to something over 1 million according to various estimates; and with c. 30% of the population they are probably now the largest religious community in Lebanon (Maronites 25%; Sunnis 21%).[261]

The spiritual leader of the Lebanese Shiites until his death in 1957 was Sayyid ʿAbd al-Ḥusayn Sharaf al-Dīn who lived in Tyre and had studied in Najaf and Cairo. His successor in 1959 was an Iranian of Lebanese descent, Sayyid Mūsā al-Ṣadr (b. 1928), the son of a mujtahid from Qumm. 'Imam' Mūsā al-Ṣadr became the founder of the Shiite power base in southern Lebanon. By appealing directly to the masses of poor farmers he gained a following which emancipated itself from the patronage of the big landowners. On his initiative Parliament established a supreme National Shiite Council of which he became president in 1967, and which made it its business to represent the interests of all Shiites in Lebanon, but in particular to promote the socially and economically backward areas in the south and on the Biqāʿ plain. Mūsā al-Ṣadr's politico-military Shiite organisation *Amal* (hope), founded in 1975, was at first in no state to shake the position of power of the PLO in southern Lebanon, which was felt to be 'foreign'. On 31st August 1978 Mūsā al-Ṣadr disappeared without trace during a visit to Libya.

The Israeli invasion of Lebanon in June 1982 liberated *Amal* from their main rivals, the PLO. Since then their main objective has been to prevent renewed infiltration of PLO fighters into the Palestinian camps in southern Beirut and southern Lebanon. When on the Day of ʿĀshūrā (16th October) 1983 the mourning procession in remembrance of Karbalā' clashed with Israeli soldiers in Nabaṭiyya, the representative of the missing Imam Mūsā al-Ṣadr, Shaykh Muḥammad Mahdī Shams al-Dīn, issued a legal opinion (*fatwā*) which declared resistance to all foreign powers to be within the law. Financial and military support from the Islamic Republic of Iran fortified the position of the Shiites even more; around 1,000 Iranian Pāsdārān,[262] smuggled in from Syria, settled in Baalbek, which became the centre of the Shiite militia in the Biqāʿ plain. The erstwhile military *Amal* chief, the teacher Ḥusayn Mūsawī, founded a pro-Iranian 'Islamic *Amal*' there, and Iranian instructors trained the fighters of a new Khumaynī-orientated organisation named (after Quran 5,56) 'God's Party' (*Ḥizb Allāh*). Their spiritual authority is the Beiruti Shaykh Muḥammad Ḥusayn Faḍlallāh (b. 1934 in Najaf the son of a Lebanese mujtahid). The kamikaze-style bomb attacks since 1983 against foreign embassies and military installations, and the taking of European and American hostages, are the responsibility of this radical pro-Iranian wing. On the other hand, the leader of *Amal*, the lawyer and justice minister Nabīh Birrī, was anxious to put an end to all foreign influence on the Shiites of Lebanon. On 6th February 1984, with the help of the Druze, Birrī's *Amal* militia assumed power in the western Muslim part of Beirut. Since then the *Ḥizb Allāh* , which supports the PLO in its fight against Israel, has been gaining more and more ground in Beirut and southern Lebanon. For that reason, on 22nd February 1978, the Syrian President Ḥāfiẓ al-Asad caused Syrian troops to occupy western Beirut in order to forestall uncontrollable developments which might lead to a military confrontation with Israel.

Bibliography

H. Lammens, 'Les "Perses" du Liban et l'origine des Métoualis", *MUSJ* 14 (1929), 32-9. L. Massignon, Art. Mutawālī, EI¹ (suppl. vol.). J. Aucagne, *L'Imam Moussa Sadr et la communauté chiite, Travaux et jours* (Univ. St-Joseph, Beirut) 53 (1974), 31-51. M. Momen, *An Introduction to Shi'i Islam*, New Haven/London 1985, 264-8; map of southern Lebanon on page 271. A. Hourani, 'From Jabal 'Āmil to Persia', *BSOAS* 49 (1986), 133-40. F. Ajami, *The Vanished Imam. Musa al Sadr and the Shia of Lebanon*, London 1986. H. Cobban, 'The Growth of Shi'i Power in Lebanon and its Implications for the Future', in: J. R. I. Cole/N. R. Keddie (eds), *Shi'ism and Social Protest in Lebanon*, ibid, 156-78. M. Pohl-Schöberlein, *Die schiitische Gemeinschaft des Südlibanon (Ǧabal 'Āmil) innerhalb des libanesischen konfessionellen Systems*, Berlin 1986.

THE TWELVER SHIA IN THE GULF STATES

In Iraq, the land of origin of the Shia, the Shiites who make up around 55% of the 14 million inhabitants are still the largest religious group today (Sunnis 40%). The Shiites live predominantly in the rural regions of the southern provinces of Karbalā', Ḥilla, al-Dīwāniyya, al-Kūt, al-'Amāra and Muntafiq as well as in the slum suburb al-Thawra (now called Saddam's Town) near Baghdad. Important centres of Shiite learning are the shrines of the Imams in Najaf, Karbalā', al-Kāẓimiyya (previously al-Kāẓimayn) and Sāmarrā, which are visited by thousands of pilgrims and students from all over the world; a large proportion of the mullahs and āyatallāhs who live permanently on the 'thresholds' (*'atabāt*) are of Iranian or Lebanese descent. After the death in 1970 of the *marja' al-taqlīd* of Najaf, the Great Āyatallāh (*Āyatallāh al-'uẓmā*) Muḥsin al-Ḥakīm, his rank was transferred to the Iranian Abu 'l-Qāsim al-Khū'ī, who abstains in political matters. Apart from him, the Āyatallāh Sayyid Muḥammad Bāqir al-Ṣadr, born after 1930, became very influential beyond the borders of Iraq as the theoretician of a future Islamic economic order in an Islamic state (*Iqtiṣādunā*, 'Our Economy' 1960, Beirut [11]1979; *al-Bank al-lā-ribāwiyya*, 'The Bank without Usury' 1973). After the Revolution in Iran al-Ṣadr was sentenced to death for high treason by an Iraqi court on 8th April 1980 and executed. An Arab-Iraqi Shiite state is being fought for underground and from abroad by the organisation 'The Islamic Call' (*al-daʿwa al-islāmiyya*); competing with it is the Iran-orientated group the 'freedom fighters' (*al-mujāhidūn*). The secularist Arab-nationalist Baʿth regime (from 1968) has been seeking to suppress the influence of the Shiite clergy within the community, and takes action against any form of opposition with merciless severity. Early in 1980 President Ṣaddām Ḥusayn deported 20,000 Shiites predomin-antly of Iranian descent from Iraq, and in 1983 seven members of the renowned Āyatallāh family al-Ḥakīm were executed. From the beginning of the war with Iran in September 1980, however, the Baʿth régime, whose representatives are recruited exclusively from the Sunni minority, has been treating the Shiites with caution and has been trying to win them over with promotion of the holy places as well as with development projects in rural areas.

On the Arabian Peninsula the Shia have been strongly represented on the Gulf coast from time immemorial. For Saudi Arabia estimates fluctuate considerably between 100,000 and 440,000; a realistic figure would be around 350,000 (6%).[263] The Shiites live almost exclusively in the eastern province of al-Ḥasā (al-Aḥsā'); 95% of the inhabitants of the port of al-Qaṭīf and around half of all workers on the oilfields are Shiites. On 28th November 1979 the Muḥarram mourning processions – the first allowed by the Saudi Wahhābī state – developed into pro-test demonstrations against the Saudi régime, and bloody encounters ensued with the National Guard. Since then the Saudis have taken pains to counter the very active Iranian propaganda by special promotion of the underdeveloped Shiite region.

There are Shiite minorities in all the Gulf states: in Kuwait 271,000 (20%), in Qaṭar 50,000 (20%), in the United Arab Emirates 60,000 (7%), in ʿUmān 1,000 (0.1%). It is only in Baḥrayn, an old centre of the Shia (see above, p. 87), that Shiites form the majority of the population; however, estimates vary between 70 and 98%. In December 1981 a Shiite plot to overthrow the Sunni ruling house was discovered there.

Bibliography

(Anon.), 'Le programme des études chez les chiites et principalement chez ceux de Nedjef.' (Par un Mésopotamien), *RMM* 23 (1913), 268-79. F. Jamali, 'The

Theological Colleges of Najaf', *MW* 50 (1960), 15-22. 'A. F. Al-Nafisi, *Dawr al-shī'a fī taṭawwur al-'Irāq al-siyāsī al-ḥadīth*, Beirut 1973. A. Kelidar, 'The Shii Imami Community and Politics in the Arab East', *MES* 19 (1983), 3-16. Th. Koszinowski, 'Irak', in: W. Ende/U. Steinbach (eds), *Der Islam in der Gegenwart*, Munich 1984, 365-9. M. Momen, *An Introduction to Shi'i Islam*, Oxford 1985, 272-6. J. R. I. Cole/N. R. Keddie (eds), *Shi'ism and Social Protest*, New Haven 1986; in particular: R. K. Ramazani, *Shi'ism in the Persian Gulf*, 30-54; H. Batatu, *Shi'i Organisations in Iraq: al-Da'wah al-Islamiyah and al-Mujahidin*, 179-200; J. Goldberg, *The Shi'i Minority in Saudi Arabia*, 230-46.

THE DESCENDANTS OF THE QIZILBĀSH: SHIITE TURKS IN TURKEY, THE USSR AND AFGHANISTAN

Since their first brush with Islam in the 8th century the Turkic peoples of Central Asia, Iran and Anatolia have been predominantly Sunnis, generally of Ḥanafī observance, and the great Turkish dynastics of the Ghazanavids, Seljuqs or Ottomans have consistently appeared as the champions of the Sunna. The Turcoman tribes were an exception, having acquired an unorthodox form of Imāmī Shiism in their westward drift into northern Iran and eastern Anatolia; they formed the armies of the first Ṣafavids under the Turkish name *Qizilbāsh* (Red Heads) and from the 16th century were more or less subjected to orthodox Twelver Shiism (see above p. 80). Their descendants are the (Azeri-)Turkish-speaking Shiites of the northern Iranian province of Āzarbayjān and the Soviet Republic of Āzarbayjān as well as the Shiites in Turkey, the Alevis (from Arabic *'alawī:* Alids or 'Alī venerators) in central and eastern Anatolia, and also in the hinterland of the Aegean coast where the Ottoman authorities settled numerous tribes. The Alevis (who must not be confused with the 'Alawīs/Nuṣayrīs of the region of Tarsus and Adana; cf. below p. 159) also call themselves *Kizilbaşi*, and their Shiism remains unorthodox to the present day. The predominantly rural descendants of the erstwhile Qizilbāsh Turcomans practise the rites of the (urban) Bektashi dervish orders with whom they are organisationally allied, in particular by the 'ceremony of the union' (*ā'īn-i jam'*), a feast in which both men and women participate and newly-married couples are initiated. At this ceremony, the symbols of which refer to the sufferings of the Imams, music and the consumption of alchohol (wine or raki) play a central role. Since the Turkish government does not publish any figures the strength of the Shiite minority can only be estimated approximately.[264]

In Afghanistan *Qizilbāsh* denotes the sedentary and urban descendants of those Turcomans who immigrated into the west of the country during the Ṣafavid period. Today they constitute the orthodox Twelver Shiite element in the towns of Herāt and Qandahār, and in

Kābul where they have gone in large numbers as bodyguards from the end of the 18th century. A large proportion of the Hazares of central Afghanistan, a minority group of Mongol descent, are also superficially Shiite. The largest ethnic groups of Afghanistan, the Pashtūns, Tājīks (Iranians) and Özbeks (Turks) are, by contrast, Ḥanafī Sunnis; with c. 1.3 million people the Shiites only make up around 6%,[265] according to other estimates 10 to 15% of the population.[266]

Bibliography

I. Mélikoff, 'Notes sur les coutumes des Alevis: à propos de quelques fêtes d'Anatolie centrale', in *Festschrift P. N. Boratav*, Paris 1978, 273-80. A. Gökalp, 'Une minorité chîite en Anatolie: les Alevî', *AESC* 35 (1980), 748-63. M. Momen, *An Introduction to Shi'i Islam*, Oxford 1985, 269-72; 278 f. A. J. Dierl, *Geschichte und Lehre des anatolischen Alevismus-Bektasişmus*, Frankfurt a. Main 1985 (not to be recommended; compare the review by J. P. Laut, in: *ZDMG* 137 (1987), 432). D. B. Edwards, 'The Evolution of Shi'i Political Dissent in Afghanistan', in: J. R. I. Cole/N. R. Keddie (eds), *Shi'ism and Social Protest*, New Haven 1986, 201-29.

TWELVER SHIISM IN THE INDIAN SUB-CONTINENT

From the 14th century Twelver Shiism was introduced into India by dynasties whose erstwhile spheres of rule are still marked today by the three big Twelver Shia regions in India and Pakistan. Twelver Shiism had already gained a foothold in the Dekkan under the first Islamic state, the Bahmanī sultanate founded in 1347 by a mercenary leader, and in the 16th century it expanded into its five successor states, the Dekkan sultanates of Berar, Ahmadnagar, Bidar, Bijapur and Golkunda (the last with its capital Hyderabad founded in 1589), which were politically, culturally and religiously under the influence of the Iranian Ṣafavid empire. Even after the Dekkan sultanates had merged with the empire of the Sunni Mughals in the 17th century a strong Twelver Shiite minority survived in the region of Hyderabad and continues to do so up to the present day.

The stronghold of Indian Twelver Shiism is, however, the former territory of the principality of Awadh (Eng. Oudh) between the Ganges and the Himalayas with its capital at Lakhnaw (Lucknow, Uttar Pradesh) which was founded by a governor (*nawwāb*) of the Mughal Emperor in 1722 and recognised by the British as a sovereign kingdom from 1819 to 1856. At the end of the 18th century Sayyid Dildār 'Alī, a pupil of the Āyatallāh Bihbihānī from Karbalā' (see above p. 102) the first Indian mujtahid, founded the Uṣūlī school of Lucknow which henceforth maintained close relations with fellow-believers in Iraq. The Nawwāb Āṣaf al-Dawla (1774-1797) donated half a million rupees to build the Āṣafiyya (named after him) or Hindiyya canal, completed in 1793, which was designed to provide Najaf with water, and he and his successors generously endowed the shrines in Iraq and the scholars and pupils working there. Up to the present day the most significant madrasas of the Indian Twelver Shia are to be found in Lucknow.

The Shia were accepted in Kashmir under the princely house of the Chaks (1505-1586); Kashmir and the Punjab formed the third area with a strong Shiite minority on the sub-continent.

The number of Indian Twelver Shiites is difficult to assess because, on the one hand, many practise *taqiyya* in the Sunni environment and, on the other hand, the Muḥarram rites are even partly observed by the Sunnis. The numbers may be anything between 8 and 28 million.[267] In Pakistan the Shiites with 12 million form around 15% of the population;[268] they live mainly in the Punjab, in the region of Lahore and in Karachi, where numerous refugees from Oudh settled after the division of British India in 1947. The Twelver Shiites of Pakistan whose Muḥarram practices have been influenced by the Iranian ones[269] have had strong leanings towards Iran throughout their history, and the Āyatallāh Khumaynī was able to count on a strong following in Karachi.

At the end of the 19th century Shiism was spread from India and Zanzibar into all the countries of East Africa by traders from Gujarat. The 'Twelver' (*Ithnā-ʿashariyya*) communities in Kenya, Tanzania and Madagascar were founded at the beginning of this century by Indian Nizārī-Ismāʿīlīs (Khojas; see below, p. 190) who did not wish to give in to the centralising policy of the Agha Khan and therefore apostasised to the Imāmiyya; they brought Twelver Shiite scholars into the country from Iraq or from Lucknow and in 1945 united their local communities (*jamāʿat*) into an African confederation which has displayed great enterprise particularly in the area of school education and religious instruction.

Bibliography

1. India and Pakistan:
J. N. Hollister, *The Shi'a of India*, London 1953 (reprint 1979). R. B. Barnett, *North India Between Empires. Awadh, the Mughals and the British 1720-1801*, Berkeley/Los Angeles 1980. A. Schimmel, *Der Islam im indischen Subkontinent*, Darmstadt 1983. D. Khalid, 'Pakistan', in: W. Ende/ U. Steinbach (eds), *Der Islam in der Gegenwart*, Munich 1984, 281-92. M. Momen, *An Introduction to Shi'i Islam*, Oxford 1985, 276-8. J. R. I. Cole/N. R. Keddie (eds), *Shi'ism and Social Protest*, New Haven 1986, 15-20. J. R. I. Cole, '"Indian Money" and the Shi'i Shrine Cities of Iraq, 1786-1850', *MES* 22 (1986), 461-80; *Roots of North Indian Shi'ism in Iran and Iraq: Religion and State in Awadh, 1722-1859*, Berkeley/Los Angeles (1988). S. A. A. Rizvi, *A Socio-Intellectual History of the Isna 'Ashari Shi'is in India*, 2 volumes, Canberra 1986.

2 East Africa:
S. S. A. Rizvi/N. Q. King, 'Some East African Ithna-Asheri Jamaats (1840-1967)', *JRA* 5 (1973), 12-22; 'The Khoja Shia Ithna-asheriya Community in East Africa (1840-1967)', *MW* 64 (1974), 194-204. D. Houssen, 'Note sur la communauté des Khoja shiites de Tananarive', *Archipel* 17 (1979), 71-9.

CULTIC AND LEGAL PECULIARITES OF THE TWELVER SHIA

The Imāmī legal school (*madhhab*), also called the 'Jaʿfari' after the sixth Imam, does not differ from the Sunni legal schools or 'rites' much more than these latter do from one another. The differences in terms of cult are minimal; pilgrimage and fasting are practised according to the same ritual. A Shiite – not just Imāmī – peculiarity is the appendage to the call to prayer: 'Hasten to the best of deeds' (*ḥayya ʿalā khayr al-ʿamal*). The Shiites accuse the second Caliph ʿUmar of having arbitrarily changed this original formula. At the ritual ablutions before prayer the Shiites insist on washing their feet while the Sunnis declare symbolic washing of the shoes (*al-masḥ ʿalā' l-khuffayn*) to be permissible.

Alongside the Quran and the transmitted sayings of the Prophet the sayings of the Imams are an important legal source, and their decisions have normative power. In addition, for the Shiites the 'gate of independent legal ruling' (*bāb al-ijtihād*) which, according to Sunni interpretation, has been closed for ever since the establishment of the legal schools in the 9th century, still remains open for qualified legal scholars, the mujtahids (see above p. 68 f).

A well-known peculiarity of Imāmī law is temporary marriage by contract in exchange for a precisely fixed sum given to the woman. This temporary marriage, called in Arabic *mutʿa* (enjoyment), was apparently an old Arabian pagan institution which was still practised by the Prophet and some of his Companions but then abrogated. As in the case of the formula of the call to prayer, the Shiites here too reproach Caliph ʿUmar for wilfully having changed a practice approved by the Prophet, and refer to the Quranic verse 4,24: 'When you have had your enjoyment of them (in legitimate intercourse) then give them their reward as a duty'. Numerous sayings of the Imams who expressly approved of the 'marriage of pleasure' and thus regulate details connected with it are transmitted.[270] The Sunnis, Ismāʿīlīs and Zaydīs, on the other hand, reject *mutʿa* as scarcely concealed prostitution. Modern controversies over the permissibility of *mutʿa*, however, appear to be more or less theoretical; it is not practised by the Arab Shiites of Lebanon and Iraq and even in Iran its social significance appears to be very slight.

The Imāmīs do not accept the repudiation of a wife by pronouncing the three-fold divorce formula, a form of divorce which makes the resumption of marriage very difficult. Even the Sunni jurists morally disapproved of this form of divorce, which was probably very common, without actually prohibiting it. According to the Imāmī view even the descendants of female dependents are entitled to inheritance; if this had not been the case then Imams descended from Fāṭima would hardly have been regarded as heirs of the Prophet.

Bibliography

W. Heffening, Art. Mut'a, EI[1], 1936. D. M. Donaldson, 'Temporary Marriage in Iran', *MW* 26 (1936), 358-64. H. Löschner, *Die dogmatischen Grundlagen des šī'itischen Rechts*, Cologne 1971. F. Castro, *Materiali e ricerchi sul Nikāḥ al-Mut'a*, Rome 1974. I. K. A. Howard, 'Mut'a Marriage Reconsidered in the Context of Formal Procedures', *JSS* 20 (1975), 82-92. D. von Denffer, Mut'a – Ehe oder Prostitution? Beitrag zur Untersuchung einer Institution des ī'itischen Islam, *ZDMG* 128 (1978), 299-325. W. Madelung, 'Shi'i Attitudes toward Women as Reflected in Fiqh', in: A. L. S. Marsot (ed.), *Society and the Sexes in Medieval Islam*, Malibu 1979, 69-79. W. Ende, 'Ehe auf Zeit (*mut'a*) in der innerislamischen Diskussion der Gegenwart', *Wdl* 20 (1980), 1-43.

THE 'SIGHING OF THE AFFLICTED ONE' THE VISITATION OF GRAVES, FLAGELLATION PROCESSIONS AND PASSION PLAYS

'With their brows lying on the holy ground of the sacred graves, weeping incessantly, bearing the death of their lords upon their bodies' – thus R. Strothmann, alluding to 2. Corinthians 4, 10, characterised the Shiites: 'the Shī'a won over those souls who needed to weep away their own grief and that of the world in tears for Ḥusayn and the other martyrs.'[271] However, in the piety of simple believers the 'sighing of the afflicted one' (*nafas al-mahmūm*) has occasionally taken on forms which have been disapproved by canonical legal scholars or dismissed as inadmissible innovations.

For the Shiites all the Imams – with the exception of the twelfth – suffered a violent death as martyrs or witnesses (*shuhadā'*, sing. *shahīd*): slain, poisoned or died in prison. This suffering of the Imams, especially of al-Ḥusayn, his dependants and companions, almost becomes self-sacrifice. The 'sinless ones' voluntarily take upon themselves a portion of the punishment which is actually due to sinful people, their surrogate suffering saves mankind from the impact of God's justice in all its severity. In addition, self-sacrifice qualifies the martyr to assume a role of mediation (*waṣīla*) with God and to intercede (*shafā'a*) on behalf of the faithful. This belief in surrogate suffering comes so close to Christian conceptions that it has been possible to call Shiite Imamology 'Islamic Christology'.[272] Nevertheless, the differences should not be blurred. The notion of an existential sinfulness, an 'original sin' from which mankind has to be redeemed is alien to the Shia as it is to Islam in general; the passion of the Imams fits only the punishment incurred by the believer for individual wrong. M. Ayoub in *Redemptive Suffering in Islam* (1971) has studied this aspect of Shiite piety in detail.

Man can pay off his debt of gratitude to the Imams in one of two ways: by weeping at their graves or by being prepared to accept martyrdom himself. The common formula used as an address to the Imams in Shiite traditions, 'Could I but be your ransom! (*juʿiltu fidāka*)' expresses the wish of the believer to make the Imam's self-sacrifice unnecessary by suffering himself. 'Since the Lord of the future life takes pleasure in sorrow and since it serves to purify God's servants – behold! we therefore don mourning attire and find delight in letting tears flow. We say to the eyes: stream in uninterrupted weeping forever!'[273] Weeping at the grave of al-Ḥusayn is as old as the Shiites themselves; even the 'penitents' of the year 65/684 stopped at Karbalā' on their way to Syria to repent with blackened faces their moral complicity in al-Ḥusayn's downfall.[274]

Visiting (*ziyāra*) the graves of the four Imams at al-Baqīʿ cemetery in Medina, ʿAlī's rediscovered grave in Najaf, the shrines of al-Ḥusayn in Karbalā', of Mūsā al-Kāẓim and Muḥammad al-Jawād at the Sharīf cemetery to the north of Baghdad (al-Kāẓimayn), of ʿAlī al-Riḍā in Mashhad and of the last two Imams (al-ʿAskariyyayn) in Sāmarrā has been one of the meritorious deeds of the Shiites from time immemorial. Ever since the Būyid period, rulers and great men have built, embellished and maintained the mausolea, and the pious endowments (*awqāf*) of countless believers have added to the wealth of the shrines. The Būyids were also the first to be interred at the 'thresholds' (*ʿatabāt*), but transportation of the bodies (*naql al-janā'iz*) with its macabre caravans of the dead emitting smells of decay was condemned as an innovation by many Shiite legal scholars.[275]

Lamenting the Imams reaches its climax in Muḥarram, the month of the passion of al-Ḥusayn. During the first nine days the suffering of the Imam and his companions at the camp of Karbalā' is remembered, on the tenth (*ʿāshūrā'*) his death and on the thirteenth his interment. Forty days after his death (*yawm al-arbaʿīn:* the fortieth day) the customary Islamic commemorative ceremony takes place.

The ʿĀshūrā'[276] festival has been attested in Iraq from the Būyid period; requesting a sip of water – in remembrance of the thirst of al-Ḥusayn and his followers whose path to the Euphrates was obstructed – is mentioned by the sources as the oldest dramatic element of the ritual, from which the passion play developed very much later. It was not until 17th century Ṣafavid Iran that European travellers first observed the processions of flagellants going through the streets during the first ten days of Muḥarram;[277] it was then repeatedly reported that processions (*dasta*) from individual city quarters regularly came to blows in street fights. Since the 'gates of paradise stand open' during the first ten days of Muḥarram eternal bliss was in store for those who met their death at that time.

Today the processions of flagellants, which were forbidden by Reza Shāh in 1928, have once again become commonplace. During the first days of Muḥarram groups of flagellants are seen beating their breasts with fists or open hands (Pers. *sīna-zan:* breast beater) or scourging their backs with bundles of iron chains (*zanjīr-zan*). Not until the Day of 'Āshūrā' do the sword scourgers appear, shrouded in white death shirts and bloodily beating their brows with swords or daggers (*tīgh-zan, ghama-zan*). The processions of flagellants seem to have spread from Iran to Iraq and Pakistan and India; they were introduced into southern Lebanon – in particular into Nabaṭiyya – only at the end of the 19th century by Iranian immigrants. The processions have contributed further visual and dramatic elements to the later Passion Play. It was frequently customary to lead the saddled riderless horse of al-Ḥusayn in the procession, and in many places a rider even represented the Imam himself. The tableaux vivants carried on floats – such as Yazīd with the severed head of al-Husayn – have largely disappeared today; however, replicas of al-Ḥusayn's coffin or of the mausoleum of Karbalā' are borne along in the procession.[278] As with all popular Muḥarram customs, the processions of flagellants have occasionally been rejected by Shiite legal scholars, but in the present century they have found a prominent advocate in Mīrzā Ḥusayn Nā'īnī (d. 1936) the *marja' al-taqlīd* of Najaf.[279] Nevertheless, the mullahs themselves do not appear as scourgers. The 'Āshūrā' processions, in which thousands of excited believers participate, are traditionally occasions for political demonstrations and public rebellion against any form of 'tyranny'. The history of the passion of al-Ḥusayn can be constantly retold with up-to-date material, and since the Islamic Revolution in Iran 'all scenes have been Karbalā', all months Muḥarram and all days 'Āshūrā'.[280]

The origins of the 'Āshūrā' mourning rites are assumed to lie in pre-Islamic traditions. B. D. Eerdmans (1894) saw reminiscences of the ancient oriental cult of the slain Spring god Tammuz (Adonis) in some details of the Shiite Muḥarram customs. However, even if lamentation for the death of Tammuz seems in fact to have been practised in northern Mesopotamia well into the Islamic era,[281] the evidence adduced by Eerdmans is too weak to support his hypothesis. It is more likely that there are influences of the ancient Iranian custom of lamenting the death of the mythical hero Siyāwush as it continued to be celebrated in north-eastern Iran in the 4th/10th century; G. van Vloten (1892) was the first to indicate the relevant passage in Narshakhī's *The History of Bukhara*.[282]

The dramatic passion plays form a second cluster of Muḥarram customs, and these are performed in mosques and private houses, in public places or in specially constructed buildings. The usual Arabic and Persian term *taʿziya* means 'offering condolences' (the verbal noun from *ʿazzā*) and it originally embraced all the mourning rites in remembrance of Karbalāʾ. The dramatic portrayal of the events of the passion as a roleplay with spoken dialogue seems to have developed from the recitation of martyrologies (*maqātil,* sing. *maqtal*) and elegies (*marāthī,* sing. *marthiya*) on the death of the Imams, which is attested as early as the Būyid and Seljuq periods,[283] although texts are only available from the time of the Ṣafavids.[284] In Iran, the recitations of such poems, which are given throughout the year on Fridays and on all Shiite festival days in private houses, mosques and bazaars, are called *rawża-khwānī,* 'Rawza declamation', after the title of the model still used today, the 'Garden of the Martyrs' (*Rawżat al-shuhadāʾ*) by Kamāl al-Dīn Ḥusayn Wāʾiẓ Kāshifī (d. 910/1504).[285] Dramatic performances of the passion of Karbalāʾ are not attested for during the Ṣafavid period. The earliest testimony comes from William Francklin who witnessed in 1786 the performance of two plays in Shīrāz which – judging from his description – probably were if anything pantomimic in character and therefore similar to the silent tableaux vivants of the processions.[286] A real theatrical performance with dialogues is first reported by James Morier who watched 'The Martyrdom of al-Ḥusayn' in Tehran in 1811.[287]

The Shiite passion play (*taʿziya*) in Iran clearly came into being around the turn of the 19th century and experienced its full blossoming under the Qājār dynasty. The organisers were fraternities or clubs (*anjuman*) of the urban artisan class, and wandering semi-professional troops of actors reinforced by local laymen performed the generally anonymous plays handed down in written form in the courtyards of mosques and *imāmzādas* or even in the Ḥusayniyyas, club houses dedicated to the remembrance of al-Ḥusayn. Such Ḥusayniyyas dating back to Qājār times, richly decorated with graphic depictions of the drama at Karbalāʾ on glazed tiles, have been preserved in such places as Kirmānshāh or Shīrāz.[288] From the middle of the 19th century permanent circus-like theatrical buildings (*takya*) were constructed. In 1873 Nāṣir al-Dīn Shāh established the 'state takya'

(*takya-yi dawlat*) near to the palace in Tehran, where the court and foreign guests of the Shāh attended the *ta'ziya* performances.

Texts of *ta'ziya* plays have been edited and translated by Europeans from the mid-19th century (Chodzko 1852 and 1878; Gobineau 1865); L. Pelly (1879) translated into English thirty-seven of the fifty-two plays he collected, W. Litten(1929) edited fifteen plays in facsimile. The most important collection however is that of E. Cerulli who acquired no less than 1,055 plays – mainly in Persian and a few in Azeri-Turkish – during his time as Italian ambassador to Iran from 1950 to 1955. These texts which are now kept in the Vatican library[289] have stimulated a whole series of new studies on the origin and development of the *ta'ziya*.

Originally the *ta'ziya* performances were limited to the first ten days of the month of Muḥarram and took their themes solely from the events at Karbalā'. On the first days the fate of al-Ḥusayn's companions, wives, sisters and sons was the focus of attention: 'Abbās, one of al-Ḥusayn's half-brothers, has his hand chopped off while attempting to ladle out water; al-Ḥusayn's elder son 'Alī al-Akbar falls in battle; the baby 'Alī al-Aṣghar is pierced by arrows; the nephew al-Qāsim ibn al-Ḥasan, who is engaged to one of al-Ḥusayn's daughters meets a martyr's death before the wedding. The martyrdom of al-Ḥusayn was reserved for the Day of 'Āshūrā, and the bloody processions of the sword scourgers followed this. 'Alī's only surviving son, 'the one in the middle' (*al-Awsaṭ*), later the fourth Imam, and his mother, the Sasanian princess Shahrbānū, are the principal characters of the plays which deal with the imprisonment of the survivors, their deportation to Syria and their humiliation at the court of the Umayyad Caliph Yazīd in Damascus. Only gradually were the *ta'ziya* performances extended to celebratory occasions throughout the year, and their repertoire was extended by including Biblical, Quranic and old Iranian epic subject matter.

Imāmī scholars have frequently shown themselves to be reserved or negative towards *ta'ziya*, in particular since the subject matter was occasionally quite unorthodox, as shown by the play about the passion of the mystic al-Ḥallāj.[290] For quite different reasons the anticlerical reformer Reza Shāh wanted to put an end to the *ta'ziya* performances, thus striking at the heart of the religious tradition of the Shia in Iran. After Reza Shāh had forbidden the sword scourgers from participating in the processions in 1928 he went on to ban the *ta'ziya* processions in 1932, and finally, in 1935, he stopped the Muḥarram processions altogether. While the flagellant processions gradually began to take place again after his abdication in 1941 the *ta'ziya* did not recover from the forced interruption in its tradition and has almost totally died out in Iran today, although it has remained alive in Iraqi Kāẓimayn (al-Haidari 1975) and in Lebanese Nabaṭiyya (Maatouk 1974).

Bibliography

1. *Places of pilgrimage:*
A. Nöldeke, *Das Heiligtum al-Husains zu Kerbelâ*, Berlin 1909. G. Krotkoff, 'Kazimen – ein shi'itischer Wallfahrtsort', *Bustan* 9, number 3-4 (1968), 59-62. J. al-Khalīlī, *Mawsū'at al-'Atabāt*, 4 volumes, Baghdad 1969-72. M. Bazin, *Qom et sa région*, unpublished thesis Paris (Sorbonne) 1970; 'Qom, ville de pèlerinage et centre régional', *Revue géographique de l'Est* 1973, 1-2, 77-135. B. Scarcia Amoretti, 'Nascita di un emāmzāde' (1973), *OM* 54 (1974), 309-11. M. Streck, Art. Meshhed, EI[1]. E. Honigmann, Art. Karbalā'; M. Streck/A. A. Dixon, Art. Kāẓimayn; J. Calmard, Art. Ḳum; EI[2]. H. Algar, Art. 'Atabāt, EI[2] SUPPL.
2. *Muḥarram processions:*
G. van Vloten, 'Les drapeaux en usage à la fête de Huçeïn à Téhéran', *Internat. Archiv für Ethnographie* (Leiden) 5 (1892), 105-11. B. D. Eerdmans,'Der Ursprung der Ceremonien des Hosein-Festes', *ZA* 9 (1894), 280-307. I. Lassy, *The Muharram Mysteries among the Azerbaijan Turcs of Caucasia*, Helsingfors 1916. H. Massé, *Croyances et coutumes persanes*, Paris 1938, I, 120-40. E. Neubauer, 'Muḥarram-Bräuche im heutigen Persien', *Der Islam* 49 (1972), 249-72. E. H. Waugh, 'Muḥarram Rites: Community Death and Rebirth', in: F. E. Reynolds/E. H. Waugh (eds), *Religious Encounters with Death*, Philadelphia 1977, 200-13. W. Ende, 'The Flagellations of Muḥarram and the Shī'ite 'Ulamā'', *Der Islam* 55 (1978), 19-36. P. Heine, 'Ross ohne Reiter. Überlegungen zu den Ta'ziya-Feiern der Schiiten des Iraq, *ZMRW* 63 (1979), 25-33. H. G. Kippenberg, 'Jeder Tag 'Ashura, jedes Grab Kerbala. Zur Ritualisierung der Strassenkämpfe im Iran', in: K. Greussing/J.-H. Grevemeyer (eds), *Religion und Politik im Iran*, Frankfurt a. Main 1981, 217-56. J. Hjärpe, 'The Ta'ziya Ecstasy as Political Expression', in: N. G. Holm (ed.), *Religious Ecstasy*, Stockholm 1982, 167-77.
3. *Passion plays:*
a) Collections, Editions and Translations: A. Chodzko, Djungui Chehâdet. *Le cantique du martyre, ou Recueil des drames religieux que les Persans du rite cheia font annuellement représenter dans le mois de Moharrem*, Paris 1852; *Théâtre persan. Choix de Téaziés ou drames, traduits pour la première fois du persan*, Paris 1878. A. de Gobineau, 'Les noces de Kassim', in: *Les religions et philosophies dans l'Asie Centrale*, Paris 1865, 405-37. L. Pelly, *The Miracle Play of Hasan and Husain, Collected from Oral Tradition*, 2 volumes, London 1879. Ch. Virolleaud, *La Passion de l'Imam Hosseyn. Drame persan publié et traduit*, Paris 1927; *Le théâtre persan ou Le Drame de Kerbéla*, Paris 1950. W. Litten, *Das Drama in Persien*, Berlin/Leipzig 1929 (15 plays in facsimile). R. Henry de Generet, *Le Martyre d'Ali Akbar*, Lüttich/Paris 1946 (No. 18 in Chodzko's collection). E. Rossi/A. Bombaci, *Elenco di drammi religiosi persiani*, in: *Studi et testi No. 209*, Vatican 1961 (catalogue of Cerulli's collection). D. Monchi-Zadeh, *Ta'ziya. Das persische Passionsspiel. Mit teilweiser Übersetzung der von Litten gesammelten Stücke*, Stockholm 1967.
b) Studies: E. Bertel's, *Persidskij Teatr*. Leningrad 1924. A. Krymski, *Pers'kij Teatr*, Kiev 1925. R. Strothmann, Art. ta'ziya, EI[1] (1934). H. W. Duda, 'Das persische Passionsspiel', *ZMRW* 49 (1934), 97-114. J. Hytier, 'Vie et mort de la tragédie religieuse persane', *Les Cahiers du Sud* 1947, 246-70. E. Cerulli, 'Le théâtre persan et ses origines', *La nouvelle Clio* 7-9 (1955-1957), 181-8; 'Le

théâtre persan', in: *Le shīʿisme imâmite, Colloque de Strasbourg*, Paris 1970, 281-94. I. Mélikoff, 'Le drame de Kerbela dans la littérature épique turque', *REI* 34 (1966), 133-48. H. Müller, *Studien zum persischen Passionsspiel*, Freiburg i. Br. 1966. P. Mamnoun, *Taʿziya,. Schi'itisch-Persisches Passionsspiel*, Vienna 1967. H. Massé, 'Poèmes funèbres consacrés aux Imâms', in: *Le shīʿisme imâmite, Colloque de Strasbourg*, Paris 1970, 271-9. G. Thaiss, 'Religious Symbolism and Social Change: the Drama of Husain', in: N. R. Keddie (ed.), *Scholars, Saints and Sufis*, Berkeley 1972, 348-66. J. Calmard, 'Le mécénat des représentations de taʿziye', in: *Le monde iranien et l'Islam* 2 (1974), 73-126. F. Maatouk, *La représentation de la mort de l'Imam Hussein à Nabatieh (Liban-Sud)*, Beirut 1974. I. al-Haidari, *Zur Soziologie des schiitischen Chiliasmus. Ein Beitrag zur Erforschung des irakischen Passionsspiels*, Freiburg i. Br. 1975; 'Die Taʿziya, das schiitische Passionsspiel im Libanon', *ZDMG* Suppl. III/1 (1977), 430-7. Ch. Shackle, 'The Multani *marsiya*', *Der Islam* 55 (1978), 281-311. P. J. Chelkowski (ed.), *Taʿziyeh. Ritual and Drama in Iran*, New York 1979 (20 articles by different authors about the *taʿziya* in Anatolia, Lebanon, Iraq and India). W. O. Beeman, 'A Full Arena. The Development and Meaning of Popular Performance Traditions in Iran', in: M. E. Bonine/N. R. Keddie (eds), *Continuity and Change in Modern Iran*, Albany 1981, 285-305.

NOTES TO CHAPTER TWO

1 80/699 and 86/705 are also traditionally given as the year of his birth.
2 The graves of the Imams al-Ḥasan, ʿAlī Zayn al-ʿĀbidīn, Muḥammad al-Bāqir and Jaʿfar al-Ṣādiq in the al-Baqīʿ cemetery were destroyed by the Wahhābīs in 1806.
3 Nawbakhtī, *Firaq*, 27; Qummī, *Maqālāt*, 37, l. 1.
4 Shaykh al-Mufīd, *Kitāb al-Irshād*, 6.
5 Nawbakhtī, *Firaq*, 57ff. Qummī, *Maqālāt*, 79ff.
6 Qummī, *Maqālāt*, 87, § 164.
7 The year of birth is also traditionally given as 120/737 or 129/746.
8 W. Madelung, 'A Treatise of the Sharīf al-Murtaḍā on the Legality of Working for the Government', *BSOAS* 43 (1980), 18ff.
9 Compiled by V. Klemm, 'Die vier *sufarā'* des Zwölften Imam', *WdO* 15 (1984), 127; cf. W. Madelung, Art. al-Mahdī, EI[2].
10 Nawbakhtī, *Firaq*, 77 has Ramaḍān 233 (April/May 848). Shaykh al-Mufīd, *Irshād*, 505, on the other hand, has 243 (857).
11 Besides these frequently mentioned dates Ibn Khallikān gives 8th Jumāda I = 1st March, *Wafayāt al-aʿyān* (ed. I. ʿAbbās) II, 94, no. 169.
12 Nawbakhtī, *Firaq*, 84f.; Qummī, *Maqālāt*, 102ff.
13 Shaykh al-Mufīd, *Irshād*, 530ff.
14 Momen, *Introduction to Shiʿi Islam*, 161f.
15 In Nawbakhtī, *Firaq*, and Qummī, *Maqālāt* (both towards the end of the 9th century) there is not yet any talk of *safīrs*; writers of the 10th century such as Kulaynī (d. around 940) and Kashshī (d. around 950) know several *safīrs*, but do not yet acknowledge any proper institution.
16 The customary Shiite form of the name, al-Samarrī, is presumably a folk etymology called forth by the reminiscence of Sāmarrā, which should be correctly read as al-Sāmarrā'ī. We must no doubt assume a vocalisation of al-Simmarī, after a place Simmar near Kashkar between Wāsiṭ and Baṣra; Samʿānī, *Ansāb* VII, 137, and Suyūṭī, *Lubb al-lubāb, s.v.*
17 V. Klemm (1984).

18 For the portrayal of Shalmaghānī in orthodox Twelver Shiism see J. M. Hussain (1982), 126ff.
19 Ibn Bābūya al-Qummī, *Kamāl al-Dīn*, ed. Ghaffārī, 516; Ṭūsī, *Kitāb al-Ghayba*, ed. Ṭihrānī, 243. M. Momen, *Introduction to Shiʿi Islam*, 164. V. Klemm, *Die vier sufarāʾ*, 135.
20 Shaykh al-Mufīd, *Irshād*, 525.
21 Shaykh al-Mufīd, *Irshād*, 551.
22 Shaykh al-Mufīd, *Irshād*, 541ff.
23 The *Fihrist* of Ibn al-Nadīm, written in 377/988, and *Fihrist kutub al-Shīʿa* of Ṭūsī (d. 458/1066). Both writers were Shiites and wrote at Baghdad.
24 Naṣr b. Muzāhim, *Waqʿat Ṣiffīn*, ed. F. Kāshānī, Tehran 1884; ed. ʿA. M. Hārūn, Cairo 1365/1946.
25 Yaʿqūbī, *Taʾrīkh*, ed. Th. Houtsma, 2 vols, Leiden 1883.
26 Cf. Najāshī, *Rijāl*, 178. For the controversy about the attribution of *Kitāb Ithbāt al-waṣīya li ʾl-imām ʿAlī ibn Abī Ṭālib* cf. Ch. Pellat, 'Masʿūdī et l'imamisme, in: *Le shīʿisme imâmite, Colloque de Strasbourg*, Paris 1970, 69-90, and J. ʿA. Mashkūr in: *Sümer* 20 (1964), no. 1-2.
27 Nawbakhtī, *Firaq al-Shīʿa*, ed. H. Ritter, *Die Sekten der Schiʿa*, Istanbul 1931; French by M. J. Mashkur, 'An-Nawbakhtī, Les sectes īʿites', *RHR* 153-5 (1958-9); [2]Tehran 1980. Qummī, *Kitāb al-Maqālāt wa ʾl-Firaq*, ed. M. J. Mashkur, Tehran 1963.
28 A list of authors and titles is given in W. al-Qāḍī, 'The Development of the Term *Ghulāt* in Muslim Literature', in *Akten des VII. Kongresses für Arabistik und Islamwissenschaft*, Göttingen 1974 (1976), 316f.
29 Ed. ʿAlī Akbar al-Ghaffārī, Tehran 1381/1961; [2]1968-9. Eng. translation by Muh. Hasan Rizvi, I, Tehran 1978.
30 Today Shahr-e Sabz in Soviet Uzbekistan. *Rijāl al-Kashshī*, ed. Sayyid Aḥmad al-Ḥusaynī, Karbalāʾ, no date; ed. Ḥasan al-Muṣṭafawī, Mashhad 1348/1969 under the title *Ikhtiyār maʿrifat al-rijāl, al-maʿrūf bi-Rijāl al-Kashshī*.
31 *Ṣūrat al-arḍ* (ed. Kramers), 370.
32 Cf. J. Calmard, 'Le chiisme imamite en Iran à l'époque seldjoukide d'après le Kitāb al-Naqḍ', *Le Monde iranien et l'Islam* I, Geneva/Paris 1971, 54.
33 Published in Najaf 1378/1958.
34 Published in Tabrīz 1371/1951.
35 Authors and titles have been compiled by V. Klemm, *Die vier sufarāʾ*, 127f.
36 Lith. Tehran 1318/1900.
37 E. Kohlberg, 'From Imāmiyya to Ithna-Ashariyya', *BSOAS* 39 (1976), 524.
38 Also the abridged and slightly different title *Kamāl al-dīn wa-tamām al-niʿma*; ed. Āyatallāh Kamrahī, 2 vols, Tehran 1378/1959; ed. ʿAlī Akbar Ghaffārī, 2 vols., Tehran 1390/1970; printed in Najaf 1389/1970.
39 Eg. S. A. Arjomand, *The Shadow of God and the Hidden Imam*, Chicago 1984, 35ff.; cf. M. Momen, *Introduction to Shiʿi Islam*, 147ff.
40 E. Kohlberg, 'Some Imāmī-Shīʿī Views on Taqiyya', *JAOS* 95 (1975), 395-402.
41 Nawbakhtī, *Firaq*, 90, l. 6; Qummī, *Maqālāt*, 102, l. 8.
42 *Kāfī* I, 179; cf. Momen, 148.
43 D. Sourdel, 'L'imamisme vu par le Cheikh al-Mufīd', *REI* 40 (1972), 228; W. Madelung, Art. ʿIṣma, EI[2].
44 H. Busse (1969), 421. For the office of the *naqīb* see below p. 48.
45 At Karbalāʾ al-Ḥusayn's small group found access to the Euphrates and thus to drinking water blocked by government troops; the martyrdom of the third Imam began with thirst; see above p. 15.

46 Ibn al-Jawzī, *Muntaẓam* VII, 15, Ibn Taghrībirdī, *Nujūm* (Cairo edition) III, 334.

47 Ibn al-Jawzī, *Muntaẓam* VII, 16. The graves of the 'two Kāẓims' (*al-Kāẓimayn*), i.e. the seventh and ninth Imams, to the north of the city, also belonged to the 'graves of the Qurayshites'.

48 H. Busse, 425.

49 Mas'udı, *Les Prairies d'or*, ed./trans. Pavet de Courteille and Barbier de Meynard 1861-1908, IV, 289; revised edition by Ch. Pellat, Beirut 1966-1979, III, 93 (§ 1612). Mez, *Renaissance*, 67.

50 Ibn Ḥawqal, *Ṣūrat al-arḍ*, ed. Kramers, *BGA* II, 240.

51 On the expansion of the Sharīf families in Iran see C. E. Bosworth (1973), 194ff.; J. Calmard, 'Le Chiisme imamite en Iran', in: *Le Monde iranien et l'Islam* IV (1971), 63.

52 On the office of *naqīb* see E. Tyan, *Histoire de l'organisation judiciaire en pays d'Islam*, Paris 1938/1943; Leiden [2]1960, II, 329-41. In east Iranian Nīshāpūr the office of *naqīb* has remained within one Ḥasanid family since 395/1004; R. W. Bulliet, *The Patricians of Nīshāpūr*, Cambridge/Mass. 1972, 234ff.

53 H. Busse, 430.

54 Ed. A. Ṣaqr, Cairo 1946; ed. K. al-Muẓaffar, Najaf [2]1965.

55 Ibn al-Jawzī, *Muntaẓam* VII, 237.

56 Ed. Muḥ. Kāẓim al-Kutubī, Najaf 1381/1962; ed. Ḥusayn al-A'lamī, Beirut [3]1399/1979. For the Eng. translation by Howard see p. 58.

57 *Sharḥ 'aqā'id al-Ṣadūq*, also: *Taṣḥīḥ al-i'tiqādāt*, ed. 'Abbāsqulī Ṣ. Wajdī, Tabrīz 1371/1951 (together with *Awā'il al-maqālāt*).

58 In particular from al-Karājakī (d. 449/1057), *Kanz al-fawā'id*, Lith. Mashhad 1323/1905, 186-94.

59 Ed. 'Abbāsqulī S. Wajdī, Tabrīz 1371/1951; French translation by Sourdel (1972).

60 Ibn al-Jawzī, *Muntaẓam* VII, 255; Ibn al-Athīr, *Kāmil*, ed. Tornberg, (reprint Beirut) IX, 236. Veccia Vaglieri (1958), 40ff.

61 Ed. 'A.S. al-Ahl, Beirut [2]1963; with commentary by Ibn Abi 'l-Ḥadīd ed. M. A. Ibrāhīm, 20 vols, Cairo [2]1965-1967.

62 Ed. A. Q. Gurjī, 2 vols, Tehran 1348/1969-70.

63 Brunschvig (1970), 210; Arjomand (1984), 52f.

64 Printed in Najaf 1375/1956.

65 10 vols, Najaf 1380/1960.

66 *Rijāl al-Ṭūsī*, Muḥ. Ṣādiq Āl Baḥr al-'Ulūm, Najaf, no date; ed. M. K. al-Kutubī, Najaf 1381/1961.

67 Also under the title *Kitāb al-fuṣūl fi 'l-uṣūl*, in: *al-Jawāmi' al-fiqhiyya*, lith. Tehran 1276/1859; *'Uddat al-uṣūl*, lith. Tehran 1314/1896.

68 *Al-Fuṣūl al-'ashara*, published in Najaf 1370/1951.

69 *Risālat al-ghayba*, trans. Sachedina (1978), 117-24.

70 Nawbakhtī, *Firaq*, 57; Qummī, *Maqālāt*, 80. The meaning of the name is unclear.

71 *Kitāb al-ghayba*, ed. A. B. Ṭihrānī, Najaf 1385/1965.

72 A. A. Sachedina, *Islamic Messianism*, Albany 1981, 109ff.

73 Al-Ḥusayn ibn Aḥmad al-Būshanjī (end of 4th/10th century), *Kitāb 'Amal al-sulṭān*; Muḥ. b. Aḥmad ibn Dā'ūd al-Qummī (d. 378/988), *Risāla fī 'amal al-sulṭān*.

74 *Mas'ala fi 'l-'amal ma'a al-sulṭān*, ed./trans. Madelung, *BSOAS* 43 (1980), 22ff.

75 *'Kaffārat al-'amal ma'a al-sulṭān qaḍā ḥawā'ij al-ikhwān'*; al-Murtaḍā, *Mas'ala*, in: Madelung (1980), 25 and 29.
76 Trans. Chittik (1980), 68-82.
77 Momen, *Introduction*, 189.
78 Kulaynī, *Kāfī* VII, 411.
79 *Ikmāl al-dīn*, Najaf 1389/1970, Madelung (1982), 166.
80 Madelung (1980), note 25.
81 *Al-Nihāya fī mujarrad al-fiqh wa 'l-fatāwā*, printed in Tehran 1342/1963. Arjomand (1984), 51; cf. Momen, *Introduction*, 189.
82 Madelung (1980), note 25.
83 Madelung (1982), 166f.
84 Ed. Flügel, Leipzig 1871-1872 (reprint Beirut 1964); ed. R. Tajaddod, Tehran 1391/1971; Eng. translation by B. Dodge, *The Fihrist of al-Nadīm*, 2 vols, New York 1970. Ibn al-Nadīm's profession of Shiism can be recognised, for example, by his use of the terms *khaṣṣī* ('special one') for a Shiite and *'āmmī* ('commoner') for a Sunni.
85 Najāshī, *Kitāb al-rijāl*, lith. Bombay 1317/1899; printed in Tehran (Chāpkhāna-yi Muṣṭafavī), no date (vol. I).
86 Ed. Muḥ. Ṣādiq, Najaf [2]1380/1960.
87 *Siyāsetnāma*, ed. Ch. Schefer, Paris 1891, 139; English trans. by H. Darke, *The Book of Government or Rules for Kings*, London, 1978, 164-5; CHI V, 292.
88 Ed. Muḥaddith, Tehran 1331/1952. The underlying treatise of the renegades, entitled 'Some Shiite atrocities' (*Ba'd faḍā'iḥ al-rawāfiḍ*) has not been preserved, but is cited in detail by 'Abd al-Jalīl.
89 In the *Siyāsetnāma* of the vizier Niẓām al-Mulk a Shiite (Ismā'īlī) missionary is advised: 'Go to Rayy, Āba, Qumm, Kāshān and to the provinces of Ṭabaristān and Māzandarān: everyone is Rāfiḍi there and confesses Shiism'; ed. Schefer, 184; trans. Darke, 209; Calmard, *Le chiisme imamite en Iran à l'époque seldjoukide*, 52.
90 Calmard, 50 and 64.
91 Calmard, 62-4.
92 Calmard, 65.
93 Calmard, 62.
94 H. Halm, 'Die Anfänge der Madrasa', *ZDMG Suppl. III/1*, 438-48.
95 Subkī, *al-Ṭabaqāt al-kubrā* IV, 313.
96 Calmard, 60f.
97 Calmard, 61.
98 Calmard, 66.
99 Calmard, 66f.
100 The most important is *Majma' al-bayān fī tafsīr al-Qur'ān*, printed in Tehran, 5 vols, 1379/1959; also *Jāmi' al-jawāmi' fī tafsīr al-Qur'ān*, printed in Tehran, 5 vols, 1382-3/1962; printed in Cairo, 12 vols, from 1378/1958.
101 *Kitāb al-Iḥtijāj*, printed in Najaf 1386/1966.
102 *Ma'ālim al-'ulamā' fī fihrist kutub al-Shī'a wa-asmā' al-muṣannifīn minhum qadīman wa-ḥadīthan*, ed. 'A. Iqbāl, Tehran 1353/1934.
103 Ed. Ch. Schefer, *Chrestomathie persane*, Paris 1883, I, 131-71; ed. 'A. Iqbāl, Tehran 1335/1956 – Part V about the *ghulāt* ed. H. Raḍī, Tehran 1343sh./1963-64.
104 Cited from Yūsuf al-Muṭahhar al-Ḥillī, father of the well-known Shiite scholar (see p. 67), in the presence of Hülegü; Khvānsārī IV, 233, citing Ibn

al-Muṭahhar; Strothmann, 44f. Similarly Waṣṣāf, *Tajziya,* ed./trans. Hammer-Purgstall, *Geschichte Wassaf's*, Vienna 1856.
105 *Rawḍat al-jannāt* IV 66, 25ff., cited from Strothmann, 32.
106 Strothmann, 24.
107 Strothmann, 31.
108 Strothmann, 33f.
109 Only shortly beforehand the shrine of Kāẓimayn had been restored after a fire by the Abbasid Caliph (!) al-Ẓāhir (622-3/1225-6); Ibn al-Ṭiqṭaqā', ed. Ahlwardt, 379. For the destruction of Kāzimayn by the Mongols see Rashīd al-Dīn, *Jāmiʿ al-tawārīkh,* ed./trans. Quatremère, Paris 1836, 302.
110 Waṣṣāf, ed./trans. Hammer-Purgstall, I, 118; Spuler (1955), 243.
111 Literally 'corner'; meeting house for a derwish order.
112 Ibn Baṭṭūṭa, *Riḥla,* ed./trans. Defrémery and Sanguinetti, Paris 1853-8, II, 99f.
113 It was apparently the first town to possess a stone quadrant; Strothmann 27f. About the astronomer Ṭūsī's influence in Europe *ibid,* 11ff.
114 *Qawāʿid al-ʿaqā'id,* Tehran 1305/1888; *Tajrīd al-ʿaqā'id,* Tehran, no date; *Risāla fī 'l-imāma,* ed. Muḥ Taqī Dāneshpažuh, Tehran 1335/1956; Italian trans. by B. Scarcia Amoretti (1972).
115 Strothmann, 84.
116 Qāshānī, cited by Spuler (1955), 243f., note 12.
117 Ibn Baṭṭūṭa (Defrémery/Sanguinetti) II, 43f., 57-61.
118 Strothmann, 88ff.
119 Krawulsky, 297f.
120 G. Makdisi, 'Notes on Ḥilla and the Mazyadids in Medieval Islam', *JAOS* 74 (1954), 249-62.
121 Arjomand, *Shadow of God,* 54. For Idrīs al-Ḥillī see *GAL* G I, 406.
122 Occasionally the dates of his lifetime are given as being significantly later: 638-726/1240-1326; cf. *GAL* G I, 406.
123 *Sharā'iʿ al-islām:* printed in Tehran 1364/1944; ed. Muḥ. Jawād Mughniyya, 2 vols.. Beirut no date (c. 1963); ed. ʿAbd al-Ḥusayn Muḥ. ʿAlī (al-Baqqāl), vol. I, Cairo 1977. Russ. translation by Kazembeg, St. Petersburg 1862 (in addition *JA* 1865, 295); French translation by A. Querry (1871/1872). *Al-Nāfiʿ fī mukhtaṣar al-sharā'iʿ,* ed. Muh. Taqī al-Qummī, Cairo 1376/1957.
124 *Kashf al-murād fī sharḥ Tajrīd al-iʿtiqād,* printed in Qumm 1372/1952.
125 Recently efforts have also been made among Sunnis to reopen the door of *ijtihād* in order to give new impulses to paralysed Islam; see R. Peters, '*Idjtihād* and *Taqlīd* in 18th and 19th Century Islam', WdI 20 (1980), 131-45.
126 Cf. the overview given in H. Löschner, *Die dogmatischen Grundlagen des šīʿitischen Rechts,* Cologne 1971, 155ff.
127 Ed. ʿAbd al-Ḥusayn Muḥ. ʿAlī (al-Baqqāl), Najaf 1390/1970.
128 *Mabādi',* 240-52.
129 *Mabādi',* 241, l. 3: *li-anna 'l-ijtihād qad yukhṭi'u wa-qad yuṣību.*
130 Islamic Quranic studies make allowance for the phenomenon of earlier Quranic verses – therefore divine revelations – having been abrogated by later verses (*nāsikh:* abrogating; *mansūkh:* abrogated); for example, the direction of prayer which was initially towards Jerusalem was later focused on Mecca (Quran 2. 136-45). The resultant 'change of mind' (*badā'*) by God is a particular problem of Islamic theology.
131 *Mabādi',* 244.

132 *Mabādi'*, 247.
133 *Mabādi'*, 248.
134 R. Brunschvig, 'Les *uṣūl al-fiqh* imâmites à leur stade ancien', in: *Le shî'isme imâmite, Colloque de Strasbourg*, 206.
135 *Mabādi'*, 248.
136 V. Minorsky, 'Jihān-Shāh Qara-qoyunlu and his Poetry', *BSOAS* 16 (1954), 271-97.
137 H. R. Roemer (1976), 282f.
138 The terms for the Islamic mystic (*ṣūfī*) and for mysticism (*taṣawwuf*) are derived from the wool (*ṣūf*) of the cowl; the mystic ascetic is called *faqīr* 'pauper' in Arabic; this corresponds to the Persian *darvīsh* (dervish), 'beggar'.
139 Corbin's works have appeared mainly in the Eranos Jahrbücher (EJ) of the C. G. Jung Circle in Ascona; eg. 'L'Imâm caché et la rénovation de l'homme en théologie shî'ite', *EJ* 28 (1960), 47-108; 'Pour une morphologie de la spiritualité shî'ite', *EJ* 29 (1961), 57-107 and 'Le combat spirituel du Shî'ism', *EJ* 30 (1961), 83-125. Corbin's *Histoire de la philosophie islamique* I, Paris 1964, and *L'homme de lumière dans le soufisme iranien*, Paris 1971 are imbued with the same ideas; finally 'Imâmologie et philosophie', in: *Le shî'isme imâmite, Colloque de Strasbourg*, Paris 1970, 143-74.
140 S. H. Nasr, 'Le shî'isme et le soufisme. Leurs relations principielles et historiques', in: *Le shî'isme imâmite*, 215-33.
141 E. Meyer, 'Tendenzen der Schiaforschung: Corbins Auffassung von der Schia', *ZDMG* Suppl. III/1 (1977), 551-8.
142 H. Algar, 'Some Observations on Religion in Safavid Persia', *Iranian Studies* 7 (1974), 290.
143 *Awṣāf al-Ashrāf*, printed in Tehran 1306/1928.
144 In relation to this see the conversation between the historian Khvānsārī and Sayyid Muḥammad Bāqir Mūsavī Rashtī in Iṣfahān, cited by Strothmann, *Die Zwölfer-Schî'a*, 81f.
145 Henry Corbin in particular deserves praise for his editing of the work by Ḥaydar-i Āmulī: H. Corbin/O. Yahia, *La philosophe shi'ite. Sayyed Haydar Amoli (VIIIe/XIVe siècle)*, *Bibl. iranienne 16*, Paris/Tehran 1969 (Arabic ed. of *Jāmi' al-asrār* and *Risālat naqd al-nuqūd fī ma'rifat al-wujūd*); *Le Texte des Textes (Naṣṣ al-Nuṣūṣ)*. *Commentaire des 'Fosûs al-hikam' d'Ibn 'Arabī, Bibl. iran*, 22, Paris/Tehran 1975.
146 Smith (1970), 55f., citing Ḥāfiẓ-i Abrū.
147 Yāqūt, *Mu'jam al-buldān, s.v. Qāshān*, cites *Firaq al-Shī'a* by one Aḥmad ibn 'Alī ibn Bāba al-Qāshī (6th /12th century); the passage, however, does not relate – or at least not exclusively – to Qāshān/Kāshān, but rather to several Iranian towns: 'One of the peculiarities which I myself have seen in our country (or: in our towns, *fī bilādinā*) is that a few Alid landowners (*aṣḥāb al-tanāyāt*) adhere to this faith (i.e. of the expected Imam-Mahdī); every morning they expect the Qā'im to appear to them; moreover, they do not simply wait, but most of them mount their horses wearing swords and fully armed and thus come out of their villages in order to welcome their Imam; they then return home full of regret because nothing came of it. These are dreams of people who are not quite right in the head.' On *tānī'/tunnā'/tana'a:* F. Løkkegaard, *Islamic Taxation*, Copenhagen 1950 (reprint 1977), 170f.
148 Ibn Baṭṭūṭa (Defrémery/Sanguinetti) II, 98f. On the symbol of the riderless

horse: P. Heine, 'Ross ohne Reiter. Überlegungen zu den Taʿziya-Feiern der Schiiten des Iraq', *ZMRW* 63 (1979), 25-33; H. G. Kippenberg, 'Zu einem normativen Symbol Vorderasiens: das gesattelte Pferd, in: Kippenberg *et al. Visible Religion: Annuals for Religious Iconography* I, 1982, 76-97.

149 Krawulsky (1981), 296.

150 For the Twelver Shia of Lebanon see below p. 131 ff.

151 Printed in Najaf 1967.

152 R. Vasmer, Art. Māzandarān, EI[1].

153 I. Mélikoff, 'Le drame de Kerbela dans la littérature épique turque', *REI* 34 (1966), 133-48.

154 Cahen (1970), 118.

155 The meaning of the name which has not been conclusively established is probably related to the Arabic verb *shaʿshaʿa* 'to gleam, beam' and has presumably only been connected with the Arabic *mushaʿshaʿ* 'drunken, tipsy' by opponents.

156 Cf. B. Scarcia Amoretti in *CHI* VI, 629.

157 H. Halm, Art. Ahl-e Ḥaqq, *Encycl. Iran.*

158 Roemer (1985).

159 Khunjī, *Tārīkh-i ʿālam-ārā-yi Amīnī* (trans. Minorsky), 63; Mazzaoui (1972), 73.

160 H. R. Roemer, in: *CHI* VI, 197f., supposes that this Lāhījī is the same as a man with the same name who, like Nūrbakhsh and Muḥammad ibn Falāḥ, was a pupil of Aḥmad ibn Fahd al-Ḥillī.

161 Mélikoff (1975), 51f.

162 Minorsky (1940), no. 249, 10 and 12.

163 Mélikoff, 58.

164 Minorsky, no. 249, 1 and 14.

165 Mélikoff, 59.

166 Minorsky, no. 249, 5.

167 Minorsky, no. 204.

168 *CHI* VI, 214.

169 *Lā ilāha illā 'llāh, Muḥammad rasūl Allāh:* There is no god but God; Muhammad is the Messenger of God. *Lā ilāha illā 'llāh; Ismāʿīl valī Allāh:* There is no god but God; Ismāʿīl is the intimate friend of God.

170 Ch. Grey (trans.), *A Narrative of Italian Travels in Persia in the 15th and 16th Centuries, Hakluyt Society Ser. 49*, London 1873, 206.

171 Glassen (1970), 213.

172 In the middle of the 8th/14th century Ḥamdallāh Mustawfī knew of only the southern coast of the Caspian Sea (Gīlān, Māzandarān), Rayy and Varāmīn, Qumm and Kāshān, Sabzavār and Khūzistān as predominantly Shiite areas of Iran. According to a report by the Ottoman envoy Durrī Efendī in 1720 a third of the population of Iran was still Sunni; *CHI* VI, 618.

173 Cf. Glassen (1972).

174 Ḥasan-i Rūmlū, *Aḥsan al-tavārīkh,* trans. Seddon, Baroda 1934, 27. He probably meant *Sharāʾiʿ al-islām* by al-ʿAllāma al-Ḥillī.

175 Glassen (1970), 96.

176 Scarcia Amoretti, in: *CHI* VI, 639.

177 The shaykhs of the order in Ardabīl appear – in spite of their well-known Kurdish descent – to have felt themselves to be sayyids; the descent of Shaykh Ṣafī from the Prophet is said to have been 'discovered' during a

pilgrimage to Mecca. Shah Ismā'īl had apparently been convinced ever since his childhood that he was a true sayyid; see also H. R. Roemer, in: *CHI* VI, 198-200; idem, *Sheich Ṣafī von Ardabīl. Die Abstammung eines Ṣūfī-Meisters der Zeit zwischen Sa'dī und Ḥāfiẓ*, in: W. Eilers (ed.), *Festgabe deutscher Iranisten zur 2500-Jahrfeier Irans*, Stuttgart 1971, 106-16.

178 G. Hermann, 'Zur Entstehung des *ṣadr*-Amtes', *Festschrift Roemer*, Beirut 1979, 278-95.

179 Lambton (1956), 134f.

180 Karakī, *Risāla fī ṣalāt al-jum'a; GAL* S II, 575.

181 Karakī, *Risāla qāṭi'a al-lajāj fī taḥqīq ḥill al-kharāj*, printed in : *al-Riḍā'īyat wa 'l-kharājiyyat*, lith. Tehran 1313/1895. Cf. also Madelung (1981), 196.

182 Madelung, 197f.

183 For the persecution of the dervishes cf. especially Arjomand (1984), 112f.

184 The present-day structure of the Mashhad shrine dates mostly from 1045/1635 under Shāh Ṣafī; Nādir Shāh had the dome gilded in the 18th century.

185 His main work is the 'Medina Observations', *al-Fawā'id al-Madaniyya;* printed in Tehran in 1321/1904.

186 For Suhrawardī's *Ishrāq* cf. H. Corbin, *Histoire de la philosophie islamique* I, Paris 1964, 284ff.; R. Gramlich, *Die Gaben der Erkenntnisse des 'Umar as-Suhrawardī ('Awārif al-ma'ārif), übersetzt und eingeleitet*, Wiesbaden 1978.

187 Corbin (1956), 359ff., Arabic text with translation, 369-71.

188 *Al-Ḥikma al-muta'āliyya fi 'l-asfār al-arba'a al-'aqliyya*, printed in Tehran 1282/1865; analysed in M. Momen, *Introduction to Shi'i Islam*, 219, and *CHI* VI, 680ff. (S. H. Nasr).

189 Āshtiyānī is the editor of Mullā Ṣadrā's *al-Mabda' wa 'l-ma'ād* (Tehran 1976) and the *Anthologie des philosophes iraniens depuis le XVIIe siècle jusqu'à nos jours*, Tehran/Paris 1971 (Bibliothèque iranienne 18).

190 See above, p. 72 f.

191 Arjomand, *The Shadow of God*, 181.

192 E. G. Browne, *A Literary history of Persia* IV, 369; W. Madelung, 'Legality of the *kharaj*' (cf. p. 90), 201.

193 Chardin, *Voyage du chevalier Chardin en Perse*, ed. L. Langlès, Paris 1811, V, 205ff.: Des sentiments des Persans sur le droit du Gouvernement.

194 Chardin, 209f.

195 Chardin, 215f.

196 Chardin, 210.

197 Chardin, 217.

198 Kaempfer, *Am Hofe des Persischen Grosskönigs* (1684-1685). The first book of Amoenitates Exoticae in German; W. Hinz, Leipzig 1940 (reprinted in Tübingen 1977), 130f.

199 Various sources give Majlisī's date of death as 27th Ramaḍān 1110 (1699) or 1111 (1700); Pampus, 47.

200 Arjomand (1984), 154f.; quoting Sayyid 'Abd al-Ḥusayn Khātūnābādī, *Vaqāyi' al-sinīn va 'l-a'vām*, Tehran 1352/1973, 566.

201 B. Scarcia Amoretti, *CHI* VI, 648f., showed how this assimilation of the Shia to the Sunni legal schools was even noticeable in the polemic of the Sunni Ottomans and Uzbeks.

202 Algar (1969), 31, note 28.

203 B. Scarcia Amoretti, *CHI* VI, 653.

204 *Introduction to Shi'i Islam*, 185.

205 Algar (1969), 65.
206 Madelung (1982), 166; Momen, *Introduction*, 209.
207 Arjomand (1984), 140; 242.
208 Arjomand, 245f.
209 *Marja'* – in Classical Arabic actually *marji'* – is the noun of place of the verb *raja'a* 'to return', therefore: the place to which one returns, to which one goes or appeals, authority. *Taqlīd* is the verbal noun of *qallada* 'to entrust, authorise'. The two words stand in a genitive relationship (status constructus), therefore the instance of authorisation. The term is generally freely translated in the literature; Momen, *Introduction*, 175: 'reference point for imitation'; MacEoin, *Changes*, 160f.: 'source of imitation'.
210 *Jawāhir al-kalām*, ed. 'A. al-Qūchānī, 23 vols, Tehran 1392/1972.
211 Algar, 162f.; Cole, 40f. (with biographical digest); Momen, 311; S. Murata, Art. Anṣārī' Mortażā, Encycl. Iran; Cole, 42ff. gives an analysis of Anṣārī's Persian 'Path of Salvation' (*Sirāṭ al-najāt*) for laymen about the duty of *taqlīd*.
212 Algar, 210; MacEoin, 166.
213 For details see Sachedina (1980) and Calder (1982).
214 Calder, 43f.; cf. Sachedina, 286ff.
215 Madelung (1982), 166.
216 Algar, 61; Arjomand, 232.
217 Lambton (1970), 182f.; Kohlberg (1976), 97ff.; Arjomand, 62.
218 'Withdrawing the Veil'; the nickname *Kāshif al-Ghiṭā'*, 'he who withdraws the veil' relates to this title.
219 Lambton, 189.
220 Algar, 82-93.
221 Verbal noun of the Arabic *kaffara*; cf. *kāfir* , 'unbeliever'.
222 Arjomand, *The Shadow of God*, 230.
223 Kashfi, *Tuḥfat al-muluk*, Tehran 1857. Arjomand, 225ff.; Momen, *Introduction*, 194f.
224 A. J. de Gobineau, *Trois ans en Asie (1855-1858)*, Paris 1980, 386; Algar, 160.
225 Algar (1969), 24.
226 Algar, 102.
227 In Algar, 215 the Christian dates have been erroneously reversed; cf. E. G. Browne (1910), 54.
228 *Salṭanat vadī'i'īst ki bi-mawhabat-i ilāhī az ṭaraf-i millet bi-shakhṣ-i pādshāh mufavvaż shuda.*
229 The cossack brigade was set up in 1879 with Russian support as Nāṣir al-Dīn Shāh's bodyguard; its originally Russian and partially also British officers were gradually replaced by Iranians; after the First World War foreigners could no longer serve as officers in the unit. Riżā Khān came from Astarābād and was the son of a Persian officer.
230 For 'Abbās, the son of Umm al-Banīn, see Shaykh al-Mufīd, *Kitāb al-Irshād*, 345ff.
231 Cf. Akhavi (1980), 37, with the text of §16.
232 Akhavi, 46-53.
233 Akhavi, 41f.
234 A.-H. Ḥā'irī, Art. Ḥā'irī, EI² Suppl.
235 Akhavi, 63.
236 Akhavi, 76ff.; Momen, *Introduction* 253 and fig. 60.
237 Akhavi, 93.

238 Richard (1983), 61.
239 Akhavi, 92.
240 Algar (1972), 244; Akhavi, 100.
241 Akhavi, 101f.
242 *Baḥṣī dar-bāra-yi marja'iyyat va rūḥāniyyat,* Tehran 1383 */1341 sh* analysed by A. K. S. Lambton (1964).
243 Akhavi, 119-129.
244 A. Shari'ati, *On the Sociology of Islam. Lectures,* Eng. by H. Algar, Berkeley 1979; *Marxism and Other Western Fallacies. An Islamic Critic,* Eng. by R. Campbell, Berkeley 1980. M. Bayat-Philipp, 'Shi'ism in Contemporary Iranian Politics: The Case of Ali Shari'ati', in: E. Kedourie/ S. G. Haim (eds), *Towards a Modern Iran, Studies in Thought, Politics and Society,* London 1980, 155-68. Cf. also Akhavi, 143-58; Richard, 113-22; H. Algar, *The Roots of the Islamic Revolution,* London 1983, 71-98.
245 The title *Ayatallāh* (the wondrous sign of God) only became generally used for the highest ranking clergy in recent times, while the second rank of *mujtahids* have the title *Ḥujjat al-Islām* (Proof of Islam); J. Calmard, Art. Āyatullāh, EI[2], Suppl. The title *Sayyid* (Arabic master) distinguishes Khumaynī as a descendant of the Prophet; the first 'surname' *Mūsavī* shows descent from the seventh Imam Mūsā al-Kāẓim. *Rūḥallāh* (Arabic God's spirit) is the first name; the second 'surname' *Hindī* (Arabic *Hindī,* 'Indian') is said to indicate the family's earlier connections with Kashmir, perhaps coming from there; the actual last name *Khumaynī* refers to Khumayn, the birthplace of the Āyatallāh.
246 *Kashf al-Asrār* (Revelation of the Secrets), Tehran 1324sh; Richard (1983), 102f.
247 Printed first in Najaf ([3]1391/1971), reprinted after the Revolution several times in Tehran; translations by H. Algar (1981) and I. Itscherenska/N. Hasan (1983); cf. also T. Nagel, *Staat und Glaubensgemeinschaft im Islam* II, Zürich/Munich 1981, 310-20.
248 Translated in F. Riyahi (1986), 53-5.
249 For the estimates cf. Bashiriyeh (1984), 166, Taheri, 234 and Riyahi, 46. The number of 10,000 mullahs (for 20,000 mosques!) given by Akhavi (1980), 129, is clearly a printing error (for 100,000).
250 For details of the founding of the party and its programme see Richard, 134ff.
251 For details about him cf. Richard, 107ff.
252 Persian *Ḥizb-i Khalq-i Musalmānān-i-Īrān* , Party of the Muslim People of Iran.
253 For details about him cf. Richard, 105ff. and 128.
254 Ṣādiq Ṭabāṭabā'ī said this to the German journalist Scholl-Latour who flew in the same aircraft as Khumaynī to Tehran; P. Scholl-Latour, *Allah ist mit den Standhaften,* Stuttgart 1983, 93-7.
255 Richard, 139. On this judgement of the social causes of the Iranian Revolution all observers are in agreement; cf. Bashiriyeh, 84ff.
256 Momen (1985), 268; map of southern Lebanon p. 271. E. Wirth, *Syrien. Eine geographische Landeskunde,* Darmstadt 1971, map p. 172f. (Distribution of the religious communities in Syria and Lebanon).
257 M. von Oppenheim, *Vom Mittelmeer zum Persischen Golf* I, Berlin 1899, 132, note 2.
258 P. Casanova, *Revue d'Egypte* I, 443; Lammens (1929), 33.
259 Muqaddasi, *Aḥsan al-taqāsīm, BGA* III, 179, l. 18; cf. Ya'qūbī, *Buldān,*

BGA VII, 327, l. 2.
260 *Amal al-āmil fī tarājim 'ulamā' Jabal 'Āmil*, Baghdad 1385/1965.
261 D. McDowall, *Lebanon: A Conflict of Minorities*, London 1983, 9.
262 Persian: the 'guards' of the Islamic Revolution.
263 Goldberg, 230.
264 Momen, 272: 7.; Gökalp, 748: 10.
265 Momen, 278.
266 Edwards, 202.
267 Momen, 277.
268 Momen, 278.
269 Cf. Momen, fig. 45-50.
270 Collected and translated by Castro (1974).
271 R. Strothmann, *Die Zwölfer-Schī'a*, Leipzig 1926, 6.
272 M. Ayoub, *Redemptive Suffering*, 199.
273 Raḍī al-Dīn Ṭā'ūsī (d. 664/1266), *al-Malhūf 'alā qatlā 'l-ṭufūf*; as in Strothmann, *Die Zwölfer-Schī'a*, 146.
274 Tabari, *Annales* II, 546ff., after Abū Mikhnaf; cf. above p. 17.
275 W. Ende, 'Eine schiitische Kontroverse über *Naql al Čanā'iz*, *ZDMG* Suppl. IV, 1980, 217f.
276 The term *'Āshūrā'* – from the Hebrew *'āshōr* with the Aramaic determinative ending *-a* – originally denotes the twenty-four hour fast held on 10th Muḥarram following Jewish practice which Muḥammad replaced in the second year of the Hijra with the now customary Ramaḍān fast; Ph. Marçais, Art. 'Āshūrā', EI[2].
277 The first was Pietro della Valle in Iṣfahān on 8th January 1618; *Fameux voyages de Pietro della Valle gentilhomme romain*, Paris 1664, II, 178ff.
278 Illustrations in Momen, *Introduction*, fig. 43-50.
279 W. Ende (1978), 29.
280 'Alī Sharī'atī, *Shahādat*, Tehran 1350/1971 sh, 104; H. G. Kippenberg (1981), 245.
281 Under the year 456/1064 the Mosul chronicler Ibn al-Athīr mentions rites which recall lamentations for Tammuz, and reports that they were still very much alive at his time, in the year 600/1204; *Kāmil* (reprint Beirut) X, 41f.
282 *Tārīkh-i Bukhārā*, ed. Ch. Schefer, *Description topographique et historique de Boukhara*, Paris 1892, 15 and 21f.; trans. R. N. Frye, *The History of Bukhara*, Cambridge/Mass. 1954, 17 and 23; van Vloten (1892), 107f.; H. Müller (1966), 133f. and 190ff.; Monchi-Zadeh (1967), 8f.; Mamnoun (1967), 17f.
283 J. Calmard, 'Le chiisme imamite en Iran à l'époque seldjoukide d'après le *Kitāb al-Naqḍ*, *Le Monde iranien et l'Islam* IV (1971), 64f.
284 H. Massé (1970).
285 Printed in Tehran 1334sh/1956.
286 W. Francklin, *Observations made on a Tour from Bengal to Persia in the Years 1786-7*, London [2]1790 (reprint Tehran 1976), 246-50; Monchi-Zadeh (1967), 18, note 1; Mamnoun (1967), 25f.
287 J. Morier, *A Second Journey through Persia*, London 1818, 175-84.
288 Illustrations in Chelkowski (1979), 77ff. and Momen, *Introduction*, fig. 42.
289 Catalogued by Rossi/Bombaci (1961).
290 L. Massignon, 'Le Majlis de Mansûr-e Hallâj, de Shams-e Tabrêzi et du Mollâ de Roum', *REI* 23 (1955), 69-91.

III

The Extreme Shia

THE KUFAN 'EXTREMISTS' (*GHULĀT*)

Since its inception the Shia has included a trend which, although basing itself on the Imams, has been judged as heretical and attacked as 'exaggeration' or 'extremism' (*ghulūw*) by the orthodox Imāmiyya. In particular, the 'extremists' are said to have committed three acts of heresy: the claim that God takes up his abode in the bodies of the Imams (*ḥulūl*), the belief in metempsychosis (*tanāsukh*), and the spiritual interpretation of Islamic law which thereby loses its obligatoriness and no longer needs to be followed literally – that is to say, open antinomianism (*ibāḥa*). Though the last point has served as a pretext to accuse the *ghulāt* of all possible excesses and unnatural abominations there is certainly no doubt on the basis of surviving original testimonies that the accusations of opponents were fundamentally correct. The Imams are not human individuals for the *ghulāt*, but rather are only 'veils' in which the deity constantly reclothes himself; the miracle of transfiguration belongs to the standard repertoire of *ghulāt* tradition in which an Imam transforms himself into Muḥammad, Fāṭima, ʿAlī and the other Imams one after the other to the amazement of his disciples.[1] Notions of migration of the soul are attested repeatedly, but they have nothing to do with Indian Karma doctrines and rather resemble a kind of metempsychosis as it occasionally appears in the gnosticism of late antiquity. Among the *ghulāt* these ideas are usually bound up with decidedly pre-Islamic myths of a gnostic type about the origin and the redemption of the world. Frequently to be found, too, is the doctrine that Quranic commands are 'only men' who must be followed – i.e. pseudonyms for the Imams – Quranic prohibitions, on the other hand, are coded references to all false authorities which should be avoided; the antinomianism of the Syrian Nuṣayrīs (ʿAlawīs), for example, is obvious.

The *ghulūw* is – like the Shia itself – originally a purely Iraqi phenomenon. It can best be explained as an attempt to establish pre-Islamic gnostic traditions as the eternal truth of all revelations, and thus also as the secret inner sense of the latest, Quranic revelation. It is not possible to name a definite pre- or extra-Islamic source for these ideas, although a heretical Judaism coloured by gnosticism comes to mind. On the other hand, Manichaeism can be ruled out as a precursor because neither the cosmogonical-soteriological model nor the terminology of the *ghulāt* has unambiguously Manichaean characteristics.

In Shiite tradition the line of the 'extremists' begins with a certain ʿAbdallāh ibn Saba' who is said to have visited ʿAlī in Kūfa and to have worshipped him as God. ʿAlī, filled with indignation, thereupon sent him back to al-Madā'in (Seleucia-Ctesiphon) whence he seems to have come.[2] That the old Hellenistic-Sasanian metropolis of Mesopotamia played an important role in transmitting pre-Islamic traditions is testified by the fact that several well-known *ghulāt* came from there. Apparently starting from Ctesiphon/al-Madā'in the *ghulūw* appears in every place where the Shia took root, i.e. in Kūfa, Qumm and Baghdad. The bizarre mythology of the *ghulāt* accompanies the dogmatic development of the Shia like a shadow: first the *ghulūw* appears in Kaysanite guise,[3] then it is 'Jaʿfarised' and attaches itself to the Imams of the Ḥusaynid line who in turn constantly distance themselves from it.[4] It is striking that the chiefs and spokesmen of the *ghulāt* circle in Ctesiphon and Kūfa are almost exclusively *mawālī*, artisans, small traders and money-changers of non-Arabian origin. Their teachings had hardly any impact among the Arabian fighters of the garrison town of Kūfa.

The most important *ghālī* at the time of the sixth Imam Jaʿfar al-Ṣādiq appears to have been the Kufan cloth merchant Abu 'l-Khaṭṭāb who was killed in the Kūfa mosque by the security forces in the first years of the Abbasid Caliphate – sometime between 750 and 755 – together with some seventy of his followers. The earliest original text of *ghulāt* tradition, the 'Original Book' (*Umm al-kitāb*), comes from the circle of his disciples. This is an apocalypse in which the fifth Imam Muḥammad al-Bāqir reveals to a circle of initiated scholars the secrets of the cosmology and the redemption of human souls, represented as light imprisoned in bodies of flesh.[5] A similar apocalypse, the 'Book of Shadows' (*Kitāb al-aẓilla*) contains supposed revelations of the sixth Imam Jaʿfar al-Ṣādiq to his disciple al-Mufaḍḍal; the author of this document is presumably a Kufan *ghālī* called Muḥammad ibn Sinān (d. 220/835), a contemporary and supporter of the eighth Imam ʿAlī al-Riḍā.[6] This text also begins with a gnostic cosmogony which accounts for the earthly imprisonment of the souls in bodies; the doctrine of the phantom existence of the Imams is particularly clear in the re-interpretation of the events of Karbalā', where al-Ḥusayn did not suffer an actual martyr's death, but rather became 'veiled' and went into occultation.[7]

Apart from these two original texts, the Imāmī *rijāl* books (see above p. 43) occasionally transmit the teachings of the *ghulūw* under the names of notorious 'extremists'. The most detailed reports about the numerous groups and sub-groups of the *ghulāt*, however, are to be found in the heresiographical *firaq* works by Nawbakhtī and Qummī (see above p. 42). Both literary genres played a part in the fight against the 'extremists' whose doctrines were branded as heretical. The *ghulāt* defended themselves against this charge by reviling their opponents as 'curtailers' (*muqaṣṣira*) who withheld from the Imams recognition of their true divine status.

One of the most prominent *ghulāt* at the time of the tenth and eleventh Imams was the Baṣran Isḥāq al-Aḥmar, who worked in Baghdad and died there in 286/899. His opponent is known to be a certain Ibn Nuṣayr, who apparently enjoyed support in the court circles of the Baghdad Caliphate. The memory of a schism of the *ghulāt* community is associated with the names of these two heresiarchs; henceforth the Isḥāqīs and Nuṣayrīs attacked one another in their writings. The Isḥāqīs are attested in Baghdad and Ctesiphon/al-Madā'in; later we find them in the marshes on the lower Tigris between Baṣra and Wāsiṭ. The sect appears to have spread beyond Aleppo on the northern Syrian coast to al-Lādhiqiyya (Lattakieh) and Jabla (Djeble), from where they were expelled in the 7th/13th century by their Nuṣayrī rivals who have continued to live there up to the present day.

Primary sources in translation

P. Filippani-Ronconi, *Ummu'l-Kitāb* (Ital.), Naples 1966. H. Halm, *Die islamische Gnosis. Die extreme Schia und die Alawiten*, Zurich/Munich 1982. M. J. Mashkur, 'An-Nawbahtī. Les sectes î'ites', *RHR* 153 (1958), 68-78 and 176-214; 154 (1958), 67-95 and 146-172; 155 (1959), 63-78; Tehran ²1980.

Secondary sources

W. al-Qadi, 'The Development of the Term *Ghulāt* in Muslim Literature', *Akten des VII Kongresses für Arabistik und Islamwissenschaft*, Göttingen 1976, 295-319. H. Halm, '"Das Buch der Schatten". Die Mufaḍḍal-Tradition der Ġulāt und die Ursprünge des Nuṣairiertums', *Der Islam* 55 (1978), 219-66; 58 (1981), 15-86; *Die islamische Gnosis. Die extreme Schia und die Alawiten*, Zurich/Munich 1982. R. Freitag, *Seelenwanderung in der islamischen Häresie*, Berlin 1985 (Islamkundl. Unters. 110).

THE *GHULĀT*-SECTS OF TODAY: AHL-I ḤAQQ AND NUSAYRĪS ('ALAWĪS)

Descendants of the Kufan *ghulāt* have only survived to the present time in two mountainous areas of retreat, far from the centres of political power and from Sunni as well as Shiite orthodoxy. In the east the Ahl-i Ḥaqq (followers of the truth) are found in west Iranian

Lūristān and in the region of Kirmānshāh, and are described by their neighbours as *'Alī-ilāhī* ('Alī deifiers) even though 'Alī plays only a subordinate role in their religious ideas. Basically the religion of Ahl-i Ḥaqq is a superficially Islamicised polytheistic mythology of Indo-Iranian extraction. The Islamic veneer, however, is definitely extreme-Shiite, as shown by their beliefs about metempsychosis; here the influence of the nearby Iraqi lowlands is probably discernible. Several documents of the Ahl-i Ḥaqq have been edited by Muhammad Mokri since 1962 and translated into French.

The Nuṣayrī sects (see above p. 158), which probably originated in Baghdad, held their own on the mid-Euphrates ('Āna), in the Syrian coastal mountain range (Jabal Anṣāriyya, transmogrified from Jabal al-Nuṣayriyya) and in today's Turkish Cilician plain around Adana and Tarsus. The Nuṣayrīs trace their doctrines back to the revelations of the eleventh Imam al-Ḥasan al-'Askarī to his pupil Ibn Nuṣayr; the actual founder of the sect, however, seems to have been a certain al-Khaṣībī who, under the authority of the Būyids, initially worked in al-Karkh, the Shiite suburb of Baghdad, but then led a vagrant life and propagated his teachings in Mosul and Aleppo. He died in Aleppo in 346/957 or 358/969, and several of his writings and collections of poems (*dīwān*) have been passed down by the sect. His grandson and pupil al-Ṭabarānī moved in 423/1032 to the then Byzantine Laodikeia (al-Lādhiqiyya) on the north Syrian coast, and through his numerous writings he became the perfector of the Nuṣayrī religion. Al-Ṭabarānī and his pupils apparently converted the rural population of the Syrian coastal mountain range and the Cilician plain to Nuṣayrism.

Present-day Nuṣayrīs not only transmit the writings of their 'fathers' Khaṣībī and Ṭabarānī but also the Kufan 'Book of Shadows' (see above p. 157) and they appeal expressly to Kufan *ghulāts* such as Abu 'l-Khaṭṭāb. Their gnostic cosmogony which is closely related to that of the Iraqi apocalypses, their deification of 'Alī who sent Muḥammad as Prophet, their docetic re-interpretation of al-Ḥusayn's martyrdom, their doctrines on metempsychosis, and their spiritual interpretation (*ta'wīl*) of Quranic revelation and Islamic law conclusively demonstrate that the Nuṣayrīs are the only Islamic sect to preserve the unbroken tradition of the Kufan *ghulūw*.[8]

Because a considerable proportion of the soldiers and officers of the Syrian army are recruited from the farmers of Jabal Anṣāriyya, members of the sect have held the most important positions in the Syrian party and the state apparatus ever since the coup of the Nuṣayrī head of the air force, Ḥāfiẓ al-Asad, in 1970. Today they dominate in the country, though the sect with some 600,000 members only make up around 11% of the population.[9] Opposition criticism of al-Asad's regime likes to use anti-Nuṣayrī religious slogans in order to bring the head of state into disrepute as a non-Muslim and a heretic, while al-Asad tries to counter this by public participation at prayers in the mosque. In order to dispel talk of heresy the Nuṣayrīs have from the beginning of the present century called themselves "ʿAlawīs' (*ʿAlawiyyūn*), i.e. ʿAlī supporters or Shiites, and thus have attempted to get themselves recognised as a normal rite (*madhhab*) with equal rights within the Islamic community. This was the purpose behind the 'History of the ʿAlawīs' which was written in Ottoman Turkish by a Nuṣayrī from Adana, Amīn Ghālib al-Ṭawīl, who worked as a judge in the Syrian town of Tellkalakh during the French mandate; it was then published in Arabic in 1924.[10]

We owe our first acquaintance with the Nuṣayrī religion to the Arabian traveller Carsten Niebuhr, who crossed Jabal Anṣāriyya in 1766.[11] In 1864 a Nuṣayrī convert to Christianity, Sulayman Efendi from Adana, published an exposé in Beirut in which he gives an account of, among other things, the cosmogony, the initiation rites and a few liturgical texts.[12] The first European monograph was produced from these sources, the 'Histoire et religion des Noseirîs' (1900) by René Dussaud, which is still readable today even though it has been superseded in many details. Since 1946 the Hamburg orientalist Rudolph Strothmann has published and analysed a number of Nuṣayrī texts.

Primary sources in translation

1. *Ahl-i Ḥaqq:*

M. Mokri (ed./trans.), *La Grande Assemblée des Fidèles de Vérité au tribunal sur le mont Zagros en Iran (Dawra-y Dīwāna-Gawra)*, Paris 1977; *Šāh-Nāme-ye Ḥaqīqat, Le Livre des Rois de Vérité: Histoire traditionelle des Ahl-e Ḥaqq*, 2 volumes, Paris/Tehran 1966, 1971.

2. *Nuṣayrīs:*

J. Catafago, 'Die drei Messen der Nossairer', *ZDMG* 2 (1848), 388-94. PH. Wolff, 'Auszüge aus dem Katechismus der Nossairer', *ZDMG* 3 (1849), 302-9. E. E. Salisbury, Notice of *Kitāb al-Bākūra as-Sulaimānīja* ..., 'The Book of Sulaimân's First Ripe Fruit, Disclosing the Mysteries of the Nusairian Religion, by Sulaiman 'Effendi of 'Adhanah: with Copious Extracts', *JAOS* 8 (1866), 227-308. R. Dussaud, *Histoire et religion des Nosairîs*, Paris 1900 (with several liturgical texts). R. Strothmann, 'Die Nuṣairī nach Ms. arab. Berlin 4291', in: *Documenta Islamica Inedita, Festschrift R. Hartmann*, Berlin 1952, 173-87; 'Die Handschrift Kiel arab. 19', *Abh. d. Dt. Akad. d. Wiss. Berlin, Kl. f. Sprachen, Lit. u. Kunst, Jahrg. 1952*, no. 5, Berlin 1953, 24-45; 'Esoterische Sonderthemen bei den Nusairi', *ibid*, 1956, no. 4, Berlin 1958, H. Halm, *Die islamische Gnosis*. Zurich/Munich 1982, 305 ff. (several liturgical texts on initiation and the calendar of festivals).

Secondary sources

1. *Ahl-i Ḥaqq:*
V. Minorsky, 'Notes sur la secte des Ahlé-Haqq', *Revue du monde musulman* 40 (1920), 20-97; 45 (1921), 205-302. Art. Ahl-i Ḥaḳḳ, in EI[2]. H. Halm, Art. Ahl-e Ḥaqq, in *Encycl. Iran.*
2. *Nuṣayrīs:*
R. Dussaud, *Histoire et religion des Noseirîs*, Paris 1900. L. Massignon, 'Esquisse d'une bibliographie Nusayrie', *Mélanges R. Dussaud* II, 1939, 913-22. J. Weulersse, *Le Pays des Alaouites*, 2 volumes, Tours 1940. R. Strothmann, 'Die Nuṣairī im heutigen Syrien', *Nachr. d. Akad. d. Wiss. Göttingen, phil.-hist. Kl. No. 4* (1950), 29-64; 'Morganländlische Geheimsekten in abendländischer Forschung', *Abd. d. Dt. Akad. d. Wiss. Berlin, Kl. f. Sprachen, Lit. u. Kunst*, 1952, no. 5, Berlin 1953, 7-23. C. Cahen, 'Note sur les origines de la communauté syrienne des Nuṣayris', *REI* 38 (1970), 243-9. N. van Dam, *The Struggle for Power in Syria. Sectarianism, Regionalism and Tribalism in Politics, 1961-1980*, London [2]1980. H. Halm, *Die islamische Gnosis. Die extreme Schia und die 'Alawiten*, Zurich/Munich 1982. M. Moosa, *Extremist Shiites. The Ghulat Sects*, Syracuse, N.Y., 1987.

NOTES TO CHAPTER THREE

1 Halm (1982), 132ff.
2 M. G. S. Hodgson, Art. 'Abd Allāh b. Saba', EI[2]. Friedlaender's assumption that Ibn Saba' was a Yemeni Jew and that his teachings are connected to those of the Abyssinian Falashas is considered to be superseded today; I. Friedlaender, ''Abdallāh b. Saba', der Begründer der „ī'a, und sein jüdischer Ursprung', *ZA* 23 (1909), 296-327; 24 (1908), 1-46.
3 Halm (1982), 55ff. (Bayān ibn Sim'ān); 69ff. (Ibn Ḥarb).
4 *Ibid*, 84ff.
5 Ed. W. Ivanow, *Der Islam* 23 (1936), 1-132 (facsimile); see also the same author's, 'Notes sur l'Ummu'l-kitāb des Ismaéliens de l'Asie Centrale', *REI* 6 (1932), 419-81. Italian translation by P. Filippani-Ronconi (1966); German translation of the supposedly earliest part: Halm (1982), 113-98.
6 Ed. A. Tamer/I.-A. Khalifé, *Kitāb al-Haft wa 'l-Aẓillat*, Beirut 1960, [2]1969; ed. M. Ghālib, *Kitāb al-Haft al-Sharīf*, Beirut 1964.
7 Partial translation in Halm (1982), 246-74.
8 Halm (1982), 298ff.
9 E. Wirth, *Syrien. Eine geographische Landeskunde*, Darmstadt 1971, 452 (for the year 1964). For the distribution of the 'Alawīs, *ibid*, map pp. 172/173.
10 *Ta'rīkh al-'Alawiyyīn*, Lattakieh 1924; Beirut [3]1979.
11 Niebuhr, *Reisebeschreibung nach Arabien und den umliegenden Ländern*, Copenhagen 1774-78 (reprint Graz 1968), II, 439-44.
12 *al-Bākūra al-Sulaymāniyya fī Kashf asrār al-diyāna al-nuṣayriyya*, Beirut 1864; cf. also the partial translation by Salisbury (1866).

IV

The Ismāʿīliyya or Sevener Shia

DEFINITIONS BY THE MOVEMENT ITSELF AND BY OTHERS

The usual names for the second branch of the Shia are imprecise and misleading. The term 'Sevener Shia' (*Sabʿiyya* from the Arabic: *sabʿa:* seven) – by analogy with the 'Twelver Shia' – gives the impression that the group deals with a line of only seven Imams. While this was certainly the case for the initial period, and later for the old believers called Qarmathians, other groups continued the line of Imams; thus the present Agha Khan is considered by his followers to be the forty-ninth Imam.

The name *Ismāʿīliyya* refers to Ismāʿīl, the son of the Imam Jaʿfar al-Ṣādiq. Although he died before his father in 138/755 all Ismāʿīli groups recognise him to be the former's rightful successor and continue the line of Imams from him (instead of from his brother Mūsā al-Kāẓim). Ismāʿīl himself, however, plays no particular role in history or in the teaching system of the Ismāʿīlīs; neither is he, as is often maintained, the seventh Imam; instead he is the sixth because the Ismāʿīlīs adjudge a special role to ʿAlī and begin the line of Imams with al-Ḥasan. They regard Ismāʿīl's son Muḥammad as the seventh Imam with whom the line originally ended (cf. genealogical tree p. 32).

The Imāmī heresiographer al-Nawbakhtī mentions two Shiite groups, one of which awaited the return of the 'hidden' Ismāʿīl[1] while the other recognised his son Muḥammad as Imam; the second of these groups would appear to be the predecessor of the 'Ismāʿīlīs' who were to begin their mission a century later, but the connection between this group and the Ismāʿīlīs remains obscure.[2]

The earliest term the Ismāʿīlīs used to describe their faith in their writings is 'religion of truth' (*dīn al-ḥaqq*) or 'knowledge of truth' (*ʿilm al-ḥaqq*); its proclamation is the 'call to truth' (*daʿwat al-ḥaqq*), their supporters are the 'supporters of truth' (*aṣḥāb* or *ahl al-ḥaqq*). The imprecise foreign term 'Ismāʿīlīs', however, is accepted and used today by those themselves who profess this faith. Other foreign terms such as Bāṭinites, Qarmathians or Assassins are discussed below in the appropriate context.

THE PROBLEM OF DESCENT OF THE ISMĀ'ĪLĪ IMAMS

Like the Imāmī Shia in their infancy the Ismā'īlīs also experienced several crises of authority and repeatedly vacillated between recognising a present corporeal Imam and the notion of an absent 'hidden' Imam. The notion of the *ghayba* was clearly the original doctrine. The seventh Imam Muḥammad ibn Ismā'īl was expected to return, and he would herald a new era as Mahdī and Qā'im. When the Fāṭimid family came to the fore, claiming to be the Imams, their claim of descent from Ja'far was disputed from the very beginning, and led to vehement controversies which have continued in scholarly literature to the present day.

The 'call to truth' (*da'wat al-ḥaqq*) was heard for the first time around the middle of the 3rd/9th century. In Khūzistān, the (now Iranian) area along the river Kārūn at the northern end of the Gulf, the first proclaimer of the new doctrine was a man called 'Abdallāh who was also called 'Abdallāh the Elder (*al-Akbar*) by later Ismā'īlī tradition.[3] The identity and descent of this forefather of both the later Egyptian dynasty of Fāṭimid Caliphs and of the Agha Khans, and who was apparently also the founder of the Ismā'īlī doctrinal system, are obscure. For the Ismā'īlīs themselves he is an 'Alid and descendant of Ja'far al-Ṣādiq; for their opponents he is a cheat of dubious extraction with a falsified family tree.

As early as the beginning of the 4th/10th century the rumour was being spread that 'Abdallāh was the son of a heretic and an impostor called Maymūn al-Qaddāḥ, and that he had fabricated an infamous nihilistic pseudo-religion in order to destroy Islam from the inside. This version, which opponents of the Egyptian Fāṭimids put into circulation,[4] survived tenaciously and was still being taken seriously by European academics in the 19th century. S. de Sacy describes (1838) the founder of the sect as 'a man whose aim was to propagate materialism, atheism and immorality', and even in 1862 M. J. de Goeje calls his plans 'truly satanic'.[5] Not until the real Ismā'īlī texts became known was it seen just how erroneous such suspicions were. In 1874 S. Guyard published several 'Fragments relatifs à la doctrine des Ismaelis', and in 1898 P. Casanova was able to establish in his 'Notice sur un manuscript de la secte des Assassins' that 'the Assassins had been badly slandered when they were accused of atheism and debauchery by their opponents'.[6] Guyard considered the founder of the Ismā'īliyya to be a philosopher who had attempted to fuse Islamic with Greek thought,[7] and it was only very much later that it was realised that the adoption of Neoplatonic speculation – such as Guyard found in the texts he had published – represented a later stage of development in Ismā'īlī doctrine.

Even after the exposure of the *black legend* academic research was only reluctantly able to detach itself from the supposed forefather Maymūn al-Qaddāḥ and the 'Qaddāḥids'. In 1940, in an attempt to harmonise the contradictory information of very late sources, B. Lewis constructed two parallel lines of Imams: a true ʿAlid line which had kept itself hidden, and a trustee line, advanced as mere camouflage, behind which the true Imams had hidden themselves. The descendants of Maymūn al-Qaddāḥ were such 'camouflage' Imams and the true ʿAlid line became prominent again with the second Fāṭimid Caliph al-Qā'im.[8] Lewis's theory may be regarded as superseded today, since soon after the appearance of his work, W. Ivanow completely demolished the Qaddāḥid legend. In 'The Alleged Founder of Ismailism' (Bombay 1946) he demonstrated that Maymūn and his son ʿAbdallāh had nothing to do with the Ismāʿīliyya; the two Ismāʿīlī transmitters of traditions lived in Mecca in the first half of the 2nd/8th century and were supporters of the Imams Muḥammad al-Bāqir and Jaʿfar al-Ṣādiq (see above p. 32), and ʿAbdallāh ibn Maymūn has clearly been falsely identified with ʿAbdallāh al-Akbar, some 100 years later, the founder of the Ismāʿīliyya.[9] However, this does not clarify the latter's real identity. His supposed ʿAlid extraction remained dubious, especially since the Fāṭimids initially claimed that their forefather was the son of Jaʿfar al-Ṣādiq's eldest son, ʿAbdallāh al-Afṭaḥ (see above p. 32) who, moreover, according to both Sunni and Shiite sources, died with no male descendants, while the later official genealogy of the Egyptian Fāṭimids makes ʿAbdallāh al-Akbar a son of Muḥammad ibn Ismāʿīl. Recently, A. Hamdani and F. de Blois (1982) have attempted to rescue the ʿAlid descent of the Fāṭimids with the help of a complicated reconstruction by declaring both genealogies to be true – the one through ʿAbdallāh ibn Jaʿfar al-Ṣādiq and the one through Muḥammad ibn Ismāʿīl ibn Jaʿfar al-Ṣādiq – as the respective paternal and maternal lines, but this attempt is not very convincing.

Doubts concerning the ʿAlid extraction of the Ismāʿīlīs need to be taken seriously. Contemporaries of the Fāṭimids were unanimous in disputing their descent from Jaʿfar al-Ṣādiq; the genealogy of the House of the Prophet and the institution of the ʿAlid *naqīb* whose duty it was to guard the ʿAlid genealogical tree (see above p. 49 f) were so firmly established at that time that it would hardly have been possible to make a true ʿAlid out to be an imposter. Moreover, while true ʿAlids who emerged as pretenders to the throne or as Mahdīs certainly had their claims to power denied often enough, the authenticity of their genealogy had never been denied. The Damascene Sharīf Akhū Muhsin Muhammad ibn ʿAlī, a male descendant of Muḥammad ibn

Ismā'īl, wrote a document around 374/985, later much cited, in which he denied any relationship between the Fāṭimids and his house.[10]

If the changing 'Alid genealogical trees of the Fāṭimids are taken as blatant propaganda for legitimacy on the one hand and the Qaddāḥid legend as a polemic invention on the part of the Fāṭimids' opponents on the other, then only two respectable (but nevertheless incompatible) versions remain, which can be traced back to Iraqi writers of the early 4th/10th century. According to al-Ṣūlī (d. 336/946) 'Abdallāh was the son of a heretic called Sālim who was executed under the Abbasid Caliph al-Mahdī (158-169/775-785) and who, in turn, was the descendant of a non-Arab client (*mawlā*) Sindān al-Bāhilī. This forefather is said to have been head of the police troops in Kūfa under the Caliph Mu'āwiya and his governor Ziyād (after 661).[11] This genealogy would therefore lead to the circle of the *ghulāt* from Kūfa recruited predominantly from the *mawālī*. According to the Kufan Ibn Niẓām (writing before 345/956) 'Abdallāh emerged in Baṣra, not as the descendant of 'Alī ibn Abī Ṭālib, but rather of his brother 'Aqīl ibn Abī Ṭālib, and was also recognised as such by the clients of this clan.[12] If this genealogy is correct then the Fāṭimids would at least be members of the House of the Prophet even though they would not be 'Alids.

Primary sources in translation

The Qaddāḥid legend can be found in the version according to Ibn Rizām by Ibn al-Nadīm, *Fihrist*, trans. B. Dodge, *The Fihrist of al-Nadīm*, New York 1970, I, 462-7, and according to Ibn Rizām/Akhū Muḥsin/Nuwayrī, *Nihāyat al-'arab*, by S. de Sacy, *Exposé de la religion des Druzes*, Paris 1838 (reprint Paris/ Amsterdam 1964), Vol.I, LXXIII ff. and CLXV ff.

Secondary sources

B. Lewis, *The Origins of Ismā'īlism*, Cambridge 1940 (reprint New York 1975). W. Ivanow, *The Alleged Founder of Ismailism*, Bombay 1946. H. F. Hamdani, *On the Genealogy of Fatimid Caliphs*, Cairo 1958. W. Madelung, 'Das Imamat in der frühen ismailitischen Lehre', *Der Islam* 37 (1961), 43-135. A. Hamdani/F. de Blois, 'A Re-Examination of al-Mahdī's Letter to the Yemenites on the Genealogy of the Fatimid Caliphs,' *JRAS* 2 (1982), 173-207. H. Halm, 'Les Fatimides à Salamya'. 1. A propos des généalogies des Fatimides', REI 54 (1986), 133 ff; *Das Reich des Mahdi*, Munich 1991.

THE BEGINNINGS OF THE ISMĀ'ĪLĪ MISSION (DA'WA)

According to several independent sources,[13] 'Abdallāh 'the Elder', the supposed founder of Ismā'īlī doctrine, first delivered his message in his home town of 'Askar Mukram in Khūzistān, a small town on the Dujayl (Kārūn) between Tustar (Shushtar) and al-Ahwāz.[14] He sent out 'callers' or 'propagandists' (*du'āt*, sing. *dā'ī*) who recruited followers for the awaited Mahdī, but the hostile behaviour of the inhabitants of 'Askar Mukram forced him to leave the town; both his houses were destroyed. He went to Baṣra where he was received by clients of the clan of 'Aqīl ibn Abī Ṭālib (see above p. 165). Forced once again to flee because of his teachings, he finally settled in the small rural Syrian town of Salamya (Greek: Salamiás, today Salamiyya) 35 km south east of Ḥamah, which was just being recolonised at that time by a prince of the House of the Abbasids.[15] He and his descendants continued to live there as respected traders under their (real?) 'Aqīlid family name. Another branch of the family apparently lived in north Iranian Ṭaliqān in Daylam south of the Caspian Sea (not far from the later Alamūt, see below p. 185).

The first community was actually founded under 'Abdallāh himself in the villages east of Kūfa. A propagandist called al-Ḥusayn al-Ahwāzī won over a cattle breeder and driver called Ḥamdān Qarmaṭ[16] and his brother-in-law 'Abdān, and the latter organised and led the rapidly growing Iraqi community. Qarmaṭ's conversion – his name was to stick to the Iraqi Ismā'īlīs – dates from the year 261/875 or 264/878.[17] During the years 269-271/882-884 the governor of Kūfa imposed a poll tax on members of the sect and the money went into his own pocket. Rivals calumniated him in Baghdad and thus revealed for the first time that in the rural area around Kūfa the 'Qarmaṭians' had founded a non-Islamic religion (*dīn ghayr al-islām*) and had decided to fight Muḥammad's community with the sword.[18] In fact, in order to prepare for the awaited appearance of the Mahdī, 'Abdān collected supplies and weapons and put them in a circular walled enclosure built in 279/982 at the (now unidentifiable) village of Mahtamābād near Kūfa.[19] This 'place of migration' (*dār al-hijra*) was, like Medina after the Hijra of the Prophet Muḥammad, to be the nucleus for a fundamentally revived Islamic community. 'Abdān organised the Ismā'īlī communities in the outlying villages and raised certain taxes including the fifth (*khums*) reserved for the Imam (Quran 8,41; cf. above p. 106) which was reserved for the awaited Mahdī.

Ismā'īlī propaganda (*da'wa*) was aimed in particular at the Imāmī Shiites who had been shaken by the death of their eleventh Imam al-Ḥasan al-'Askarī in 260/874 (see above p. 35). The head of the sect, 'Abdallāh, is said to have instructed the first propagandist sent to Iran, Khalaf, as follows: 'Go to Rayy, for there, in Rayy, Āba, Qumm, Qāshān and in the provinces of Ṭabaristān and Māzandarān there are many Shiites who will hear your message'; Khalaf thereupon settled in the village of Kulayn, south of Rayy – home of the Imāmī collector of traditions, al-Kulaynī (see above p. 42).[20] Rayy became the centre of the

Ismā'īlī mission in the mountain region of Daylam south of the Caspian Sea.

The first head of the Ismā'īliyya, 'Abdallāh al-Akbar, died at some unknown time in the Syrian district of Salamya, and in the 11th century the Fāṭimid Caliphs erected a large dome for him there as a cenotaph which continues to be venerated today as his burial place by the Ismā'īlī Syrians.[21] 'Abdallāh was succeeded by his son Aḥmad, about whom nothing more is known, and then by his grandson Muḥammad Abu 'l-Shalaghlagh. This third Great Master sent two propagandists to the Yemen in the year 267/881. The one, the Iraqi Ibn Ḥawshab, says in his autobiography (of which only fragments have come down to us) that he had been a disappointed Imāmī, confused and cast into doubt by the alleged *ghayba* of the twelfth Imam. His companion, 'Alī ibn al-Faḍl, was a young Yemeni Shiite who had visited Karbalā', after making the pilgrimage to Mecca, in order to weep at al-Ḥusayn's grave, and there he was addressed by an Ismā'īlī propagandist.[22] These biographical details once more show that the Ismā'īlī *da'wa* owed a good deal of its success at the end of the 3rd/9th century to the uncertainty and confusion within the Imāmī community after the death of the eleventh Imam. After staying in Aden for two years, where he earned his living as a cotton trader, Ibn Ḥawshab founded an Ismā'īlī cell in the Yemeni highlands. He created the *dār al-hijra* from a ruined castle in the Miswar massif (west of Ṣan'ā') and here in 270/883 he publicly summoned a following for the awaited Mahdī. His companion 'Alī ibn al-Faḍl settled in the Sarw Yāfi' mountain (Jabal Yāfi'ī) north of Aden and proselytised among the neighbouring tribes, calling them to Holy War against the ruler of the country, the Prince of Laḥj; and he too built a fortified *dār al-hijra*. In the year 270/883 Ibn Ḥawshab's nephew al-Haytham set out by ship from Aden to Sind (Pakistan) to spread the *da'wa* there.

Starting from Iraq 'Abdān spread the word among the Bedouin tribes west of the Euphrates, the Asad, Ṭayyi' and Tamīm, and several clans of the Kalb tribe in Palmyra were won over to the cause of the awaited Mahdī. The dā'ī Abū Sa'īd al-Jannābī, a furrier, settled in al-Qaṭīf on the east Gulf coast as a flour trader; his first supporters were small artisans and traders, camel traders and butchers, and also Bedouins of the Kilāb tribe from the hinterland. With their support he then subjugated al-Aḥsā' (present-day Hufūf) and the Hajar oasis, making al-Aḥsā' his *dār al-hijra*; and he then subjugated the whole oasis region, and eventually, in 286/899, even the port town of al-Qaṭīf.

The most successful cell of the Ismā'īlī *da'wa* came into being in present-day Algeria. The dā'ī Abū 'Abdallāh al-Shī'ī, an Iraqi who had worked for several years in Yemen, was sent to Mecca by Ibn Ḥawshab to propagate the cause of the future Mahdī during the pilgrimage season. There he met Kutāma Berbers who seem already to have made a fleeting acquaintance with the Shiite faith in their native country, the Lesser Kabylia (north-west of Constantine). Abū ʿAbdallāh al-Shīʿī followed them home to their country, then converted a few clans and founded a *dār al-hijra* on the Īkjān mountain near the small town of Mīla.[23] Gradually all Kutāma tribes were won over to the *daʿwa* and were organised, cared for and taxed in a similar way to ʿAbdān's Iraqi community.[24] In the year 281/902 military expansion began with the occupation of Mīla and in a few years led to the conquest of the whole of north-east Algeria and Tunisia. In Spring 296/909 the successful dāʿī made his entry into Kairouan and began stamping coins with the title of the still unnamed Mahdī whose imminent appearance was promised.

In a mere twenty-five years, from c. 875 to 900, the Ismāʿīlī *daʿwa* had formed a network of cells and communities which spanned the whole Islamic world from North Africa to Pakistan, from the Caspian Sea to the Yemen. The *daʿwa* was directed by the leaders in Syrian Salamya through messages and letters. Because their declared aim was to overthrow the Abbasid Caliphate in Baghdad they had to proceed conspiratorially. In the towns the dāʿīs camouflaged themselves as merchants and traders, and they went around openly only in remote tribal areas out of reach of the state's power, such as the Yemeni highlands, the Syrian-Arabian desert or Kabylia. The adepts were sworn in in the name of the awaited Mahdī and were under obligation to remain silent; the name of the Mahdī was known only to a few initiates. Several early sources agree that the earliest *daʿwa* related to the return of Muḥammad ibn Ismāʿīl ibn Jaʿfar al-Ṣādiq[25] who died about 800. This was even conceded by the Fāṭimids, but they claimed that this early doctrine resulted from a misunderstanding.[26] After the schism of 286/899 the old faithful 'Qarmaṭians' kept to the original doctrine and the Mahdī figure of Muḥammad ibn Ismāʿīl (see below p. 171).

Several treatises have survived from the time of the underground propaganda which give us insights into the earliest doctrine.[27] According to these, divine revelation has fallen upon the prophets one after the other since the time of creation; they are called 'speakers' or 'spokesmen' (*nāṭiq*) because they each proclaimed a religion of law for their communities: Adam, Noah, Abraham, Moses, Jesus and Muḥammad. The 'speakers', however, only presented the outer (*ẓāhir*) form of religion with its rituals and its legal prescriptions, but did not reveal its inner (*bāṭin*) sense. For this purpose each of them had a 'deputy' (*waṣī*) who knew the secret meaning of all rites and regulations and only revealed them to a small circle of initiates.[28] Those who knew the secret doctrine of the six prophets were Seth (or Abel), Shem, Isaac, Aaron, Simon Peter (*Shim'ūn al-Ṣafā*) and 'Alī. In each cycle (*dawr*) a succession of seven Imams followed the 'speaker' and his 'deputy', the last of whom would be the next 'spokesman'; different lists with the names of earlier cycles have come down, and they are generally characters from the Old or the New Testament.[29] In the last cycle the *nāṭiq* Muḥammad and the *waṣī* 'Alī are succeeded by the Imams al-Ḥasan, al-Ḥusayn, 'Alī Zayn al-'Ābidīn, Muḥammad al-Bāqir, Ja'far al-Ṣādiq and Ismā'īl; the seventh Imam, Muḥammad ibn Ismā'īl, did not die but went into occultation instead, and will appear once more as the Mahdī-Qā'im.[30] He will not, however, produce any new religion of law but will instead declare all the old ones obsolete, including those of Islam. The 'repeal of the laws' (*raf' al-sharā'i'*)[31] will make room for the paradisaical original religion without cult or laws which was practised by Adam and the angels in Paradise before the Fall: the 'original religion of Adam' (*dīn Adam al-awwal*) consists only in praise of the Creator and His recognition as the Only God (*tawḥīd*).[32]

The system of prophetic cycles was bound up with a strong gnostic-tinged cosmology and soteriology, the outlines of which can only be reconstructed with difficulty, because this older form of the doctrine was overlaid with Neoplatonic ideas from an early stage (see below, p. 178).[33] Only a single treatise about the origin of the cosmos – written by the Egyptian dā'ī Abū 'Īsā al-Murshid – has been preserved; according to this, the higher, non-material world of heaven was created by God's first creature Kūnī, a female hypostasis of the word of creation *kun* (be, become); subsequently Kūnī, who considers herself to be God, rebels against her creator, and the result is the formation of the lower material world.[34] Such gnostic notions are certainly of extra-Islamic origin, but no definite model can be established; the names, terms and concepts tend to bring to mind an unorthodox Judaeo-gnostic milieu in Mesopotamia. The Ismā'īlī system is, however, genuinely Islamic; probably the first head of the sect, 'Abdallāh the Elder, was its creator.

The Ismā'īlī Imam and Mahdī doctrine claimed to be the actual hidden inner sense (*bāṭin*) of Quranic revelation: all details of the secret doctrine are to be found encoded in the Quran and need only to be decoded. The method of reading this secret sense from the text of the Quran and from the prescriptions of law – for example, prayer, fasting, pilgrimage – is called 'interpretation' (*ta'wīl*, the verbal noun from *awwala*). This striving for the true meaning of Quranic revelation which remains hidden from the majority of Muslims has given the Ismā'īlīs the name 'Bāṭinīs' (*Bāṭiniyya*). An early example of

Bāṭini Quranic exegesis is given in the 'Book of Guidance' (*Kitāb al-rushd wa 'l-hidāya*) translated by W. Ivanow and attributed to the Yemeni dāʿī Ibn Ḥawshab.

Primary sources in translation

1. *Reports of the earliest daʿwa:*
Ibn Rizām by Ibn al-Nadīm, *Fihrist*, trans. B. Dodge, *The Fihrist of al-Nadīm*, New York 1970, I, 462 ff. Ibn Rizām by Akhū Muḥsin/al-Nuwayrī, trans. S. de Sacey, *Exposé de la religion des Druzes*, Paris 1838 (reprint Paris/Amsterdam 1964), Vol. I, CLXVI ff. Niẓām al-Mulk, *Siyāsatnāma*, English trans. by H. Darke, 208ff. Aḥmad ibn Ibrāhīm al-Naysābūrī, *Istitār al-imām*, trans. W. Ivanow, *Ismaili Tradition Concerning the Rise of the Fatimids*, London/Calcutta/Bombay 1942, 157-83.
2. *Early Ismāʿīlī treatises*:
Al-Ḥusayn ibn Faraḥ ibn Ḥawshab (?), *Kitāb al-rushd wa'l-hidāya*, trans. W. Ivanow, *Studies in Early Persian Ismailism*, Bombay 1955, 29-59 (The Book of Righteousness and True Guidance). Likewise the book ascribed to Ibn Ḥawshab: *Kitāb al-ʿālim wal-ghulām*, trans. W. Ivanow, ibid, 61-86 (The Book of the Teacher and the Pupil; paraphrase with partial translation). The untitled cosmogonic treatise by Abū 'Isā al-Murshid is edited with paraphrases and partial translation in S. M. Stern, *Studies in Early Ismāʿīlism*, Jerusalem/Leiden 1983, 3-29.

Secondary sources

W. Ivanow, *A Guide to Ismaili Literature*, London 1933; 'The Organisation of the Fatimid Propaganda', *JBBRAS* 15 (1939), 1-35; *Ismaili Tradition Concerning the Rise of the Fatimids*, London/Calcutta/Bombay 1942,; *Brief Survey of the Evolution of Ismailism*, Leiden 1952; *Studies in Early Persian Ismailism*, Bombay 1955; *Ismaili Literature: A Bibliographical Survey*, Tehran 1963. A. H. Hamdani, *The Beginnings of the Ismāʿīlī Daʿwa in Northern India*, Cairo 1956. S. M. Stern, 'The Early Ismāʿīlī Missionaries in North-West Persia and in Khurasān and Transoxania', *BSOAS* 23 (1960), 56-90 (reprinted in Stern, *Studies in Early Ismāʿīlism*, Jerusalem/Leiden 1983, 189 ff.); The Earliest Cosmological Doctrines of Ismāʿīlism', in: *Studies in Early Ismāʿīlism*, 3-29. W. Madelung, 'Das Imamat in der frühen ismailitischen Lehre', *Der Islam* 37 (1961), 43-135; Art. Ismāʿīliyya, EI²; 'The Account of the Ismāʿīlis in *Firaq al-shīʿa*', in: Stern, *Studies in Early Ismāʿīlism*, 47-55. F. Dachraoui, 'Les commencements de la prédication ismāʿīlienne en Ifrīqiya', *SI* 20 (1964), 89-102. H. Halm, *Kosmologie und Heilslehre der früher Ismāʿīliyya*, Wiesbaden, 1978; 'Methoden und formen der frühesten ismailitischen *daʿwa*', *Festschrift B. Spuler*, Leiden 1981, 123-36; 'Die *Sīrat Ibn Ḥausab*. Die ismailitische *daʿwa* im Jemen und die Fatimiden', *WdO* 12 (1981), 107-35; 'Les Fatimides à Salamya', REI 54 (1986), 133 ff; *Das Reich des Mahdi*, Munich 1991.

THE SCHISM OF 899: FĀṬIMIDS AND QARMATHIANS

In the year 286/899 tensions emerged within the Ismāʿīlī *daʿwa* which led to a permanent schism.[35] The third Great Master of the Ismāʿīlīs, Muḥammad Abu 'l-Shalaghlagh, died leaving no male heirs; he had designated his nephew as his successor and gave him his daughter in marriage.[36] For the first time this nephew now advanced the claim no longer simply to be he who pronounced and prepared the way for the awaited Mahdī, but actually to be the Mahdī himself. Until now the Great Master of the sect in Salamya was only regarded as the representative or 'guarantor' (*ḥujja*. literally: argument, proof) of the awaited Mahdī.[37] The fourth Master, however, who was called either ʿAlī or Saʿīd – he was later the first Fāṭimid Caliph al-Mahdī[38] announced his claim to the dāʿīs who were working in the remote mission areas. The director of the Iraqi communities, ʿAbdān, thereupon himself appeared in Salamya and challenged the Master. He replied that the *daʿwa* as it had existed up to the present in the name of the Mahdī Muḥammad ibn Ismāʿīl was wrong; he himself was the only true Imam.

With this innovation the Ismāʿīliyya turned away from the *ghayba* model to recognise living Imams. However, the change in doctrine continued to meet with rejection; leading dāʿīs – ʿAbdān in Iraq, al-Jannābī in eastern Arabia, ʿAlī ibn al-Faḍl in South Yemen – together with their communities deserted the 'impostor' in Salamya, while the other Yemeni dāʿī Ibn Ḥawshab, and Abū ʿAbdallah al-Shīʿī who was working with the Kutāma Berbers, changed over to the new line. The *daʿwa* split in two; henceforth the 'Imams' in Salamya – the Fāṭimids – and their adherents were opposed by the apostates in Iraq and eastern Arabia who continued to wait for the Mahdī Muḥammad ibn Ismāʿīl.

The old faithful who had apostacised from Salamya continued to be called 'Qarmaṭians' in Iraq and on the coast of the Gulf. After ʿAbdān was murdered by a dāʿī loyal to the Fāṭimids, the Iraqi communities came under the leadership of ʿAbdān's brother. In Mosul two Qarmathian dāʿīs, the brothers Banū Ḥammād, wrote books which they attributed to ʿAbdān, and several titles have been handed down to us.[39] In 313/925 the Baghdadi police found white clay seals on arrested Qarmathians with the slogan: 'Muḥammad ibn Ismāʿīl, the Imam, the Mahdī, the One near to God'.[40]

The Qarmathian community of Abū Saʿīd al-Jannābī (d. 300/913) in east Arabian al-Aḥsā' (Hufūf) developed under his son Abū Ṭāhir into a local principality whose power was rooted in the Bedouin tribes of the north Arabian peninsula. For years these Qarmathians from Baḥrayn[41] attacked caravans of pilgrims on their way to Mecca or Medina from Iraq or extorted protection money from them; in 317/930 they even forced their way into Mecca during the pilgrimage ceremonies, broke the Black Stone from the Kaʿba and carried it off to al-Aḥsā', and it was not until 339/951 that the Caliph of Baghdad was able to procure the return of the stone by means of negotiation. In 318/930 the Baḥraynī

Qarmathians conquered ʿUmān, and in 319/931 they even occupied Kūfa for more than three weeks. In the same year the dāʿī Abū Ṭāhir presented a young Persian prisoner-of-war to his community as the awaited Mahdī, handed over authority to him and declared all previous religions to be invalid: The true religion, 'the religion of our father Adam', the 'original religion of Adam' – i.e. the original paradisaical religion without laws – had now been revealed, and 'the talk of Moses, Jesus and Muḥammad' had shown itself to be lies and deception.[42] The latent antinomianism of the Ismāʿīliyya becomes evident here for the first time. The dāʿī, however, had the young man removed soon afterwards, no doubt because it was obvious that he was not the true Mahdī.

After establishing their authority in Egypt the Fāṭimid Caliphs attempted to persuade the Baḥrayni Qarmathians to recognise them as Imams; a letter of 362/973 from the Fāṭimid al-Muʿizz to the leader of the Qarmathians, al-Ḥasan al-Aʿṣam, has been handed down in its entirety.[43] But all attempts of this nature failed, and the schism was never again healed. The dāʿīs from the house of al-Jannābī ruled as a local dynasty over the oasis region of al-Aḥsā' until the 14th century. Soon after their extinction the Qarmathian faith seems also to have disappeared, and the population of the Gulf coast turned towards Imāmī Twelver Shiism.

Primary sources in translation

Ibn Rizām's report of the schism (according to Nuwayrī): S. de Sacy, *Exposé de la religion des Druzes*, I, CXCIII ff. Sources on the young man being made Mahdī in Baḥrayn: M. J. de Goeje, *Mémoire sur les Carmathes du Bahraïn et les Fatimides*, Leiden 1862, ²1886, 129 ff.

Secondary sources

M. J. de Goeje, *Mémoire sur les Carmathes* . . . (see above; largely superseded); 'La fin de l'empire des Carmathes du Bahraïn', *JA* 5 (1895), 5-30. W. Madelung, 'Fatimiden und Baḥrainqarmaṭen', *Der Islam* 34 (1959), 34-88; 'Das Imamat in der frühen ismailitischen Lehre', *Der Islam* 37 (1961), 43-135; Art. Ḳarmaṭī, EI². S. M. Stern, 'Ismāʿīlis and Qarmaṭians, *L'élaboration de l'Islam*, Paris 1961, 99-108; reprinted in Stern, *Studies in Early Ismāʿīlism*, Jerusalem/Leiden 1983, 289-98. J. Salt, 'The Military Exploits of the Qarmaṭians', *Abr-Nahrain* 17 (1976-7), 43-51. H. Halm, *Das Reich des Mahdi*, Munich 1991.

THE IMAMATE OF THE FĀṬIMIDS (899-1171)

After the fourth head of the Ismāʿīlīs had put forward his claim to be the awaited Imam and Mahdī in 286/899 the Ismāʿīlī communities which recognised him began to hope for an early political revolution and a fundamental revival of Islam. The Yemeni highlands west of

Ṣan'ā' were already under the control of the dā'ī Ibn Ḥawshab (see above p. 167); in the year 289/902 the Ismā'īlīs also went on the offensive in North Africa and Syria. In present-day Algeria the dā'ī 'Abdallāh al-Shī'ī (see above p. 167), supported by the Kutāma tribes, began the conquest of North Africa from Mount Īkjān by occupying the town of Mila; in Syria the da'ı Yaḥya ibn Zakariyya', the 'man on the female camel' (*ṣāḥib al-nāqa*), led the Bedouin tribes of Palmyra against Damascus. The attack on Syria does not appear to have been ordered by the Mahdī in Salamya, but rather to have been undertaken by the overzealous dā'ī on his own initiative; in any case the Mahdī secretly left Salamya with his son and fled to Ramla in Palestine, where he awaited the outcome of events. The Ismā'īlīs did not succeed in conquering Damascus; after the dā'ī fell he was replaced by his brother al-Ḥusayn ibn Zakāriyya, the 'man with the birthmark' (*ṣāḥib al-shāma*). In the summer of 290/903 he established a short-lived Mahdī state in the central Syrian towns of Baalbak, Ḥimṣ, Salamya, Ḥamah, Ma'arrat al-Nu'mān and Afāmiya, and minted coins and held prayers in the name of the Mahdī. In vain he charged the Mahdī in letters to come forth at last, but the Mahdī did not leave his hiding place. In November 903 the dā'ī's troops were routed at Ḥamāh by the Iraqi government troops, and in Salamya the disappointed dā'ī, who now doubted the authenticity of the Mahdī, killed his house servants and fled. He was seized at the Euphrates and brought to Baghdad where he revealed the identity of the Mahdī on the rack; warrants to search for the Mahdī were thereupon taken out in the whole of the empire. The Mahdī had gone from Palestine to Egypt and vacillated between going to Yemen or North Africa; disguised as a merchant he joined a caravan to the Maghrib and settled in the oasis town of Sijilmāsa (present day Rissānī on the eastern side of the High Atlas). In the following years he maintained correspondence with the *dār al-hijra* on Mount Īkjān, whose military expansion he apparently directed himself. When the dā'ī Abū 'Abdallāh al-Shī'ī conquered Kairouan in 296/March 909 the Mahdī state was proclaimed there – as it had been six years previously in Syria. On 6th January 910 (297) 'Abdallāh[44] al-Mahdī, as he called himself, occupied the town and assumed the title of Caliph.

The rival Ismā'īlī Caliphate was to last until 567/1171. The dynasty of the Ismā'īlī Imam-Caliph is known by the name 'Fāṭimid' because of their claimed descent from Fātima and 'Alī, but it is still not clear whether they ever used this name themselves; in their documents the Fāṭimids generally describe themselves as 'the dynasty of truth' (*dawlat al-ḥaqq*; cf. above p. 162).

The establishment of an Imām dynasty meant renouncing the

immediate fulfilment of the eschatological expectations fed by the *daʿwa* which were associated with the appearance of the Mahdī. The fact that ʿAbdallāh al-Mahdī was unable to bring about the wonders expected of him led to a mood of annoyance among his supporters which went as far as open rebellion, and several dāʿīs who demanded from the Mahdī signs as proof of his mission – including Abū ʿAbdallāh al-Shīʿī, the actual founder of the Fāṭimid state – were removed. The Imam-Caliph now directed the eschatological expectations to his son who was designated successor to the throne under the name Abu 'l-Qāsim Muḥammad ibn ʿAbdallāh. He thus bore the full name of the Prophet – a characteristic feature of the Mahdī – and on his accession to the throne in 322/934 he followed the example of the Baghdad Caliphs and assumed a Mahdī title as his regnal name: al-Qā'im bi-amr Allāh, 'the one who takes up the cause of God'. After eliminating the religious opposition the dynasty was firmly in the saddle. Various ʿAlid genealogical trees were used to bolster their legitimacy.[45]

The Fāṭimids ruled over North Africa for four generations, first in the palace town al-Mahdiyya built by al-Mahdī in 300-305/912-917 on the Tunisian coast, then in al-Manṣūriyya near Kairouan. The new ideological orientation of the *daʿwa* was the work of the jurist and chief judge al-Nuʿmān ibn Muḥammad al-Tamīmī (d. 363/974) who founded the Ismāʿīlī legal school with his legal compendium 'The Pillars of Islam' (*Daʿā'im al-Islām*), and at the same time revealed the secret sense (*bāṭin*) of the legal and cultic prescriptions in several *ta'wīl* works (see above p. 169).[46] The Fāṭimids did not allow any antinomian experiments whatsoever; the *qiyāma*, the era of Qā'im – whose identity remained hidden – was shifted into the distant future; a whole series of future Imams was envisaged, although speculations about the date of the beginning of the *qiyāma* did not cease.[47] Until then, however, observance of Islamic law was obligatory even for the Ismāʿīlīs; the Fāṭimid Caliphs distinguished themselves as builders of mosques – including the Azhar in Cairo – and as generous patrons of the places of pilgrimage in Mecca and Medina.

In the year 358/969 the Fāṭimid general Jawhar occupied the Nile Delta and succeeded in gaining recognition for the Fāṭimid Imam al-Muʿizz (341-365/953-975) as Caliph in negotiations with the Muslim notables of Fusṭāṭ (Old Cairo). In a contract the Egyptian Sunnis were guaranteed freedom of belief and maintenance of their cultural differences, although in fact the agreement was not afterwards observed in all its points.[48] In 362/973 al-Muʿizz moved into the new *dār al-hijra* founded by Jawhar which was initially called al-Manṣūriyya and then had the name 'the Victorious' (*al-Qāhira*, Cairo). Palestine and southern Syria soon came under Fāṭimid control; and even the sharīfs of Mecca recognised the Ismā'īlī Caliph of Cairo who thus became patron of the places of pilgrimage.

Under the pressure of public opinion and opposing political propaganda, especially from the Baghdadī Caliphs, the Fāṭimids were forced to legitimise themselves by revealing their descent. Fāṭimid genealogy received its final official form either under al-Mu'izz or his successor al-'Azīz (365-386/975-996). According to this the forefather of the dynasty and founder of the doctrine 'Abdallāh the Elder (see above p. 163) was a son of Muḥammad ibn Ismā'īl; he was then succeeded in an uninterrupted father-son line by the 'Hidden Imams' of Salamya: Aḥmad, al-Ḥusayn and 'Abdallāh al-Mahdī. Al-Mahdī's predecessor and uncle, Muḥammad Abu 'l-Shalaghlagh (see above p. 167) was eliminated from the Imam line.[49] The claimed descent of Muḥammad ibn Ismā'īl, however, met with general disbelief; in Damascus shortly after 373/983 the Sharīf Akhū Muḥsin, a genuine descendant of Muḥammad ibn Ismā'īl, wrote a pamphlet which sought to expose the Fāṭimids as frauds.[50] In the year 402/1011 on the Caliph's orders renowned scholars, jurists and genealogists published a formal legal opinion in Baghdad which disputed the Alid descent of the Fāṭimids. Signatories included the *naqīb* of the Alids, the Sharīf al-Raḍī (compiler of *Nahj al-balāgha*) and his brother, the Sharīf al-Murtaḍā (see above p. 53).[51]

As the new *dār al-hijra,* Cairo under the Fāṭimids became the centre of the Ismā'īlī *da'wa*. The Fāṭimids did not force their Sunni subjects to adopt the Ismā'īlī faith, but numerous conversions did take place as a result of intensive propaganda. A senior dā'ī (*dā'ī 'l-du'āt*) was now leading the inner as well as the external mission; he frequently acted as the chief judge (*qāḍī 'l-quḍāt*) at the same time and was thus equally responsible for *ẓāhir* and *bāṭin*. In the Cairo palace he held public teaching sessions every Thursday, the 'meetings of wisdom' (*majālis al-ḥikma*) in which the adepts (*mustajīb*) – men and women separated – were initiated into the Ismā'īlī secret doctrine after making their vows (*mīthāq*). Several collections of such lectures, which had to be authorised by the Imam-Caliph (the lecture manuscript was initialled by him) have been preserved.[52] In every provincial capital a dā'ī worked beside the judge (*qāḍī*) who 'was entrusted with rightly-guided propaganda' (*mutawallī al-da'wa al-hādiya*); Ramla, Ascalon and Acre in Palestine, Tyre on the Lebanese coast, Damascus and the mountain region of Jabal al-Summāq north of Ma'arrat al-Nu'mān in Syria are mentioned in a list from the year 385/995.[53]

Beyond the boundaries of the Fāṭimid empire the *da'wa* continued to work by conspiratorial means for the overthrow of the Baghdadi

Caliphate. Cairo sought to coordinate the work of the disguised dāʿīs in the remote mission areas (*jazāʾir* sing. *jazīra:* island). The notion that these 'dioceses' actually added up to twelve in number is utopian, and in fact only a possible six can be accounted for. In Iraq, the heartland of the Baghdadi Caliphate itself, Baṣra and Mosul were centres of Ismāʿīlī propaganda; the dāʿī al-Kirmānī, head of this 'diocese', came to Cairo around 400/1010 (see below p. 180). The Fāṭimids enjoyed short-lived success there when a rebellious Turkish general al-Basāsīrī seized the capital Baghdad and ruled in the name of the Fāṭimids for more than a year – from December 1058 until January 1060.

The centre of the *daʿwa* in north-west Iran was, as always, Rayy from where the communities in the mountainous country of Daylam south of the Caspian Sea were directed. Fārs and Kirmān in south-west Iran appear to have formed an 'island' on their own; the dāʿī al-Mu'ayyad, who came to the court in Cairo in 439/1048 and left behind an interesting document justifying his conspiratorial activity, operated in Shīrāz.[54] Eastern Iran (Khurasān) formed a further *jazīra* with the neighbouring Afghan and Central Asian regions; the dāʿī Nāṣir-i Khusraw, who lived in his home town of Balkh,[55] made the pilgrimage in 437/1045 via Aleppo and Jerusalem to Mecca and subsequently spent some three years in Cairo before returning home via Mecca, Yemen, al-Qaṭīf and Baṣra. His account of the journey and his comprehensive theological writings are two of the most important landmarks of Ismāʿīlī literature in the 11th century.

The *daʿwa* in Yemen, almost as old as the Ismāʿīliyya itself, enjoyed its greatest success when the dāʿī ʿAlī ibn Muḥammad founded the dynasty of the Ṣulayḥids and brought Ṣanʿāʾ and Aden under his control. The Ṣulayḥids ruled Yemen as vassals of the Fāṭimids until 532/1138; the letters exchanged between the Fāṭimid al-Mustanṣir (427-487/1036-1094) and the Ṣulayḥids,[56] which are still extant, show that the latter were also responsible for the *daʿwa* in ʿUmān and India. In Sind (present-day Pakistan) the dāʿī Jalam ibn Shaybān had seized the town of Multān before 347/958 and destroyed the colossal statue of the god Aditya. Sind remained in Ismāʿīlī hands until the conquest of Multān by the Sunni Sultan Maḥmūd of Ghazna in 401/1010.

The political success of the Fāṭimids even impressed the 'Qarmaṭī' Ismāʿīlī communities which had once refused to recognise ʿAbdallāh al-Mahdī as Imam. It seems that by now many at least conceded a leading role in the *daʿwa* to the Fāṭimids, without recognising them as Alid Imams; they were considered to be no more than 'deputies' (*khulafāʾ*, sing. *khalīfa,* caliph) of the Mahdī Qāʾim Muḥammad ibn

Ismā'īl whose return continued, as ever, to be awaited. Other communities had recourse to an explanation which seems to have quickly spread; according to this the first Fāṭimid 'Abdallāh al-Mahdī and his three predecessors in Salamya were definitely not Alids (but rather Qaddāḥids); with the second Fāṭimid Caliph al-Qā'im, however, the true line of the Alid Imams had once more seized the reins of power. This Imāmī doctrine, which was firmly rejected by the Fāṭimids themselves, was clearly widespread in Iran[57] and was taken up again by the Druze (see below p. 181); in 1940 B. Lewis based his – now no longer tenable – hypotheses on this doctrine.[58]

Primary sources in translation

Al-Mahdī's flight from Salamya to the Maghrib is described from his own experience by his slave and later chamberlain Ja'far al-Ḥājib; Engl. trans. by W. Ivanow, Ismaili Tradition Concerning the Rise of the Fatimids, London/Calcutta/Bombay 1942, 184-223; French by M. Canard, 'L'autobiographie d'un chambellan du Mahdi Obeidallah le Fatimide', Hesperis 39 (1952), 279-392 (reprinted in Canard, Miscellanea Orientalia, London 1973). An official portrayal of the early history of the Fatimid Caliphate is Istitār al-imām by Naysābūrī written under al-'Azīz, Engl. by W. Ivanow, Ismā'īlī Tradition 157-83; extracts from Iftitāḥ al-da'wa by Qāḍī al-Nu'mān, ibid, 224-31. The account of Nāṣîr-i Khusraw's journeys: French by C. Schefer, Sefer Nameh: Relation du voyage de Nassiri Khosrau, Paris 1881; Engl. by W. M. Thackston, Nāṣer-e Khosraw's Book of Travels, New York 1986. Abu 'l Fawāris Aḥmad ibn Ya'qūb (dā'ī at the time of al-Ḥākim), al-Risāla fi 'l-imāma, ed./trans. S. N. Makarem, The Political Doctrine of the Ismā'īlīs (The Imamate), New York 1973.

Secondary sources

1. *The history of the Fāṭimid empire.*

G. Wiet, 'Les Fatimides', in: G. Hanotaux (ed.), Histoire de la nation égyptienne IV, Paris 1937, 179-308. M. Canard, Art. Fāṭimids, EI². H. Halm, 'Die Fatimiden', in: U. Haarmann (ed.), Geschichte der arabischen Welt, Munich 1987, 166-216. F. Dachraoui, Le califat fatimide au Maghreb, 296-362/909-973. Histoire politique et institutions, Tunis 1981. T. Bianquis, Damas et la Syrie sous la domination fatimide 359-468 H/969-1076, Vol. I, Damascus 1986.

2. *The Fāṭimid da'wa:*

H. F. Hamdani, 'The History of the Ismā'īlī Da'wat and its Literature During the Last Phase of the Fatimid Empire, JRAS (1932), 126-36; 'The Letters of Al-Mustanṣir bi'llah, BSOAS 7 (1933-5), 307-24; Al-Ṣulayḥiyyūn wa 'l-ḥaraka al-fāṭimiyya fi 'l-Yaman, Cairo 1955. W. Ivanow, 'The Organisation of the Fatimid Propaganda', JBBRAS 15 (1939), 1-35. S. M. Stern, 'Ismā'īlī Propaganda and Fatimid Rule in Sind', IC 23 (1949), 298-307 (reprinted in Stern, Studies in Early Ismā'īlism, Jerusalem/Leiden 1983, 177 ff.); Cairo as the Center of the Ismā'īlī Movement, Le millénaire du Caire: mélanges, 1972 (Studies in Early

Ismāʿīlism, 234 ff.). A. Hamdani, The Sīra of the Dāʿī al-Muʾayyad fī l-Dīn ash-Shīrāzī, unpub. thesis. London 1950; The Beginnings of the Ismāʿīlī Daʿwa in Northern India, Cairo 1956; 'Evolution of the Organisational Structure of the Fāṭimī Daʿwah. The Yemeni and Persian Contribution', in: Arabian Studies 3 (1976), 85-114. I. K. Poonawala, Biobibliography of Ismāʿīlī Literature, Malibu 1977, Ch. I, 31-132. H. Halm, 'Die Söhne Zikrawaihs und das erste fatimidische Kalifat (290/903), WdO 10 (1979), 30-53; 'Der Treuhänder Gottes. Die Edikte des Kalifen al-Ḥākim, Der Islam 63 (1986), 11-72; *Das Reich des Mahdi*, Munich 1991; T. Nagel, Staat und Glaubensgemeinschaft im Islam, Zurich/ Munich 1981, I, 223-47.

THE PERSIAN SCHOOL: THE ADOPTION OF NEOPLATONISM

The most important change experienced by the Ismāʿīlī *daʿwa* in the Fāṭimid period was the transformation of the gnostic myths about the origin of the world and redemption (see above p. 169) into a system shaped by Neoplatonic concepts.

From the end of the 8th century, partly at the suggestion of the Abbasid Caliphs in Baghdad, philosophical and natural science texts were translated from Greek through Syriac-Aramaic into Arabic. The adoption of the works of Plato and Aristotle, and the Neoplatonists Plotinus (d. 270) and Proclus (d. 485), brought an independent Arabic-Islamic school of philosophy into being which eagerly absorbed ancient philosophy and sought to harmonise it with Quranic revelation and Islamic law.[59] The first exponent of this school was the Kufan al-Kindī (d. after 256/870); his two most important successors al-Fārābī (d. 339/950) and Ibn Sīnā (Avicenna, d. 428/1037) came from the border area dividing north-east Iran and Central Asia. There apparently even Ismāʿīlī theology was first clad in a cloak of Neoplatonic terms.

The founder of the neoplatonising 'Persian School' was the dāʿī Muḥammad al-Nasafī,[60] who began his activities in Nīshāpūr and later in Bukhara reputedly converted the Sāmānid Amīr Naṣr ibn Aḥmad and several of his courtiers to the Ismāʿīliyya, but was executed in 332/ 943 by the latter's son and successor Nūḥ.[61] Citations from his main work *al-Maḥṣūl* (the produce, the result) are preserved in later Ismāʿīlī documents.

Nasafī's theology and cosmology can be reconstructed in terms of their characteristic features:[62] God is neither Thing nor Not-Thing; His being goes beyond all linguistic concepts and is beyond all knowledge. By means of His creative word He creates (*abdaʾa*) from nothing the original creature (*al-mubdaʿ al-awwal*), the Intellect (*al-*

'aql), which – eternal and perfect – rests in itself and through thought grasps all Being in itself. In it the (universal) Soul (*nafs*), whose essence, unlike that of the Intellect, is movement in time, comes into being (*tawallada*); it is imperfect because its constant movement is symptomatic of its striving for perfect knowledge which it will one day obtain with the help of the Intellect. Its movement produces matter (*hayūlā*, from Greek. *hýle*), while the repose of the Intellect gives rise to form (*ṣūra*); thus the material world is formed. The individual human soul is a part (*juz'*) of the Universal Soul and likewise strives restlessly for perfection and peace, which it ultimately finds in knowledge in the universal intellect.

Nasafī's new teaching led to a literary controversy within the *da'wa* to which we owe the preservation of fragments of his lost book in the form of quotations. His contemporary, Abū Ḥātim al-Rāzī, the dā'ī of Rayy, criticised it in a few points in a work entitled 'The correction' (*al-Iṣlāḥ*).[63]; by contrast it was defended by Abū Ya'qūb al-Sijistānī (d. around 390/1000), who seems to have been Nasafī's pupil and Rāzī's successor in Rayy, in his book 'The support' (*al-Nuṣra*).

Sijistānī's prolific output – from almost twenty titles about a dozen are still in existence[64] – develops the Neoplatonic-Ismā'īlī doctrine for the first time in its full breadth. His main work is the 'Book of the keys' (*Kitab al-maqālīd*) which was analysed by P. E. Walker; his 'Book of the sources' (*Kitāb al-yanābī'*), partially translated into French by H. Corbin, is a concise portrayal of the essential parts of his theology and appears to have been intended for a wider audience. With Sijistani the position of the Universal Soul in the higher intelligible world is ambiguous, as it is already in Plotinus: it has 'two sides', one turned upwards towards the Intellect, and one directed downwards towards matter. As it does not resist the temptation to yield to pressure to become enmeshed in the material world and to' forget' (*nasiya*) its origins, so it must be remembered and set free by the Intellect. As a part of the Universal Soul the human soul thus has a share in its downward movement and in its reascent, but it is not possible for it to return by its own strength. It is the knowledge (*'ilm*) alone which the Intellect has at its disposal that enables it to do this. The inspired prophets, and their heirs the Imams, are messengers of the Intellect, and initiation into Ismā'īlī doctrine is precisely the act of knowledge which reminds the soul of its origin and makes its return possible. Knowledge is redemption. While it is only available for a few initiates now, at the time of the *qiyāma*, the era of the awaited Qā'im (Mahdī) it will become universally apparent. This is paradise renewed.

The fusing of Ismāʿīliyya and Neoplatonism took place outside the Fāṭimids' sphere of influence and without their involvement. The three authors mentioned above, operating in Iran, obviously did not recognise the Fāṭimids either as Alids or as Imams and at best conceded them the role of deputies (*khulafā'* see above, p. 176) of the awaited Mahdī Qā'im Muḥammad ibn Ismāʿīl. All three were therefore 'Qarmaṭīs'.[65] As long as the Fāṭimids had their court in Tunisia Neoplatonism did not find a way into the literature of their *daʿwa*, and even after their move to Cairo (362/973) the old gnostic mythology remained predominant, as is demonstrated by the cosmogonical treatise written by Abū ʿĪsā al-Murshid for the Caliph al-Muʿizz (see above p. 169). It was not until the beginning of the 11th century that the Fāṭimid *daʿwa* received the ideas of Neoplatonist theology, but not in the form developed by Nasafī and Sijistānī. Not long before the year 390/1000 the dāʿī of Iraq, Ḥamīd al-Dīn al-Kirmānī (d. after 411/1020) came to the Fāṭimid court in Cairo. In his essay 'The Garden' (*al-Riyāḍ*) he attempted to settle the controversy of the three elder writers of the Persian school.[66] His own Neoplatonic system, described in the comprehensive theological summa 'The Repose of the intellect' (*Rāḥat al-ʿaql*),[67] differs markedly from the theology of Nasafī and Sijistānī who are much closer to Plotinus. According to Kirmānī, from the first intellect a second emanates (*inbaʿatha*) called 'soul', and from this a third, and so on, up to the tenth. The intellects of the third to the ninth level move the seven planetary spheres, while the lowest, the Functionary Intellect (*al-ʿaql al-faʿʿāl*, intellectus agens) rules as a demiurge over the sublunar material world it has created.[68] To the ten intellects correspond ten degrees of earthly *daʿwa:* to the speaker-prophet (*nāṭiq*) corresponds the first intellect, to the *waṣī* the second, to the Imam the third, and so on, down to the lowest grade of the simple dāʿī who influences the soul of the believer he has converted, and brings him along the path to truth; as the early world only communicates with the first intellect via the ten levels of the intelligible world so the adept only has access to the true sense of the revelation proclaimed by the *nāṭiq* via the degrees of the *daʿwa* hierarchy.

In the 11th century Kirmānī's theology became the official form of the Fāṭimid *daʿwa.* His doctrine regarding the ten intellects is found in the writings of leading dāʿīs such as al-Mu'ayyad (d. 470/1077) and Nāṣir-i Khusraw (d. around 481/1088). Further developed in the 12th century by the Ṭayyibīs of Yemen (see below p. 193) and transmitted to India, it characterises the theology of the Ismāʿīlīs up to the present day.[69]

Primary sources in translation

Sijistānī, *Kitāb al-yanābī'*, French by H. Corbin, *Le Livre des Sources*, in: *Trilogie Ismaelienne*, Tehran/Paris 1961, *Bibl. Iran.* Vol. 9 (28 out of 40 extracts; the choice is not felicitous). Nāṣir-i Khusraw, *Rawshanā'ī-nāma* (*The Book of Enlightenment*), German by H. Ethé, *ZDMG* 33 (1879), 645-65 and 34 (1880), 428-64, 617-42; *Sa'ādat-nāma*, French by E. Fagnan, 'Le Livre de la félicité', *ZDMG* 34 (1880), 643-74; Engl. by G. M. Wickens, *IQ* 2 (1955), 117-32; 206-21; *Gushāyish va rahāyish*, Ital. by P. Filippani-Ronconi, *Il libro dello scioglimento e della liberazione*, Naples 1959.

Secondary sources

W. Ivanow, Nasir-i Khusraw and Ismailism, Leiden/Bombay 1948; *Brief Survey of the Evolution of Ismailism*, Leiden 1952; 'An Early controversy in Ismailism', in: *Studies in Early Persian Ismailism*, Bombay [2]1955, 87-122. S. Pines, 'La longue recension de la Théologie d'Aristote dans ses rapports avec la doctrine ismaélienne', *REI* 22 (1954), 7-20. A. E. Bertéls, *Nasir-i Hosrov i Ismailism*, Moscow 1959. S. M. Stern, 'Ibn Hasday's Neoplatonist', *Oriens* 13-14 (1961), 58-120. S. M. Makarem, *The Doctrine of the Ismailis*, Beirut 1972. P. E. Walker, *Abū Ya'qūb al-Sijistānī and the Development of Ismaili Neoplatonism*, unpubl. thesis, Chicago 1974; substantial parts of this dissertation have been published as articles: 'An Ismā'īlī Answer to the Problem of Worshipping the Unknowable, Neoplatonic God', *AJAS* 2 (1974), 7-21; 'The Ismaili Vocabulary of Creation', *SI* 40 (1974), 75-85; 'Cosmic Hierarchies in Early Ismā'īlī Thought: The View of Abū Ya'qūb al-Sijistānī', *MW* 66 (1976), 14-28. H. Corbin, 'Naṣir-i Khusrau and Iranian Isma'ilism', *CHI* IV (1975), 520-42. I. K. Poonawala, 'Al-Sijistānī and His Kitāb al-Maqālīd', *Festschrift N. Berkes*, Leiden 1976, 274-83. A. M. Heinen, 'The Notion of ta'wīl in Abū Ya'qūb al-Sijistānī's Book of the Sources (*Kitāb al-Yanābī'*)', *Hamdard Islamicus* 2 II (1979), 35-45. Y. Marquet, 'La pensée d'Abū Ya'qūb as-Sijistānī à travers l' "Iṯbāt an-Nubuwwāt" et la "Tuḥfat al-Mustajībīn"', *SI* 54 (1981), 95-128. T. Nagel, *Staat und Glaubensgemeinschaft im Islam*, Zurich/Munich 1981, 247-64.

THE DRUZES

Not the least of the reasons for the astounding successes of the Ismā'īlī *da'wa* was undoubtedly the tempting prospect that the soon to be expected return of the Mahdī-Qā'im would bring back the original lawless and paradisaical religion. But it was not long before the delay in the messianic arrival caused problems for the Qarmaṭīs; thus the dā'ī Abū Ḥātim al-Rāzī from Rayy had been obliged to flee when the date predicted by him for the return of the Mahdī passed uneventfully, and in Baḥrayn in 319/931 a Mahdī had even been presented and the law declared to be annulled (see above p. 172). By establishing an Imam dynasty in the Fāṭimid *da'wa* the return of the Mahdī-Qā'im was pushed into the distant future, but even then latent antinomianism remained virulent and at the beginning of the 11th century broke out in a full-scale antinomian movement.

The earliest evidence is the 'Admonishing missive' (*al-Risāla al-wā'iẓa*) by the dāʿī al-Kirmānī of 408/November 1017.[70] In this, Kirmānī, who had probably already spent several years in Cairo, rebuked another dāʿī, Ḥasan ibn Ḥaydara al-Akhram, whose unorthodox teachings disturbed him; al-Akhram had maintained that the era of the Qā'im (*qiyāma*) had begun, that the Caliph al-Ḥākim was God and that Islamic revelation and its Ismāʿīlī interpretation were mere superstitions. Al-Akhram, who came from Central Asian Farghāna, enjoyed the favour of the Caliph, but he was assassinated during a ride with al-Ḥākim's followers.

His successor was Ḥamza al-Labbād (the feltmaker), a Persian dāʿī from Zūzan in eastern Iran and the real founder of Druzism. His letters, which have been preserved amongst the holy canon of Druze documents, begin in Ṣafar 408/June-July 1017; he also taught of the divinity not only of al-Ḥākim but also of the earlier Fāṭimid Caliphs from al-Qā'im onwards,[71] as well as the abrogation of Quranic revelation (*tanzīl*) and its Ismāʿīlī interpretation (*ta'wīl*). In place of both of these came the simple confession of God's oneness (*tawḥīd*) which made all cultic acts superfluous. Ḥamza's supporters were even accused of polluting thc mosqucs with faeces and urinating on copies of the Quran. Ḥamza, who called himself the 'leader of the adepts' (*hādī al-mustajībīn*), spent most of his time in a mosque in front of the town gate Bāb al-Naṣr in the north of Cairo where the Caliph al-Ḥākim visited him on his rides in order to hold conversations with him. Ḥamza sent an emissary to urge the officers and courtiers to recognise the divinity of al-Ḥākim, and made the adepts take an oath to the new teachings. One of Ḥamza's subordinates, a young Turk from Bukhara named Anūshtekīn, also called al-Darzī (Pers. the tailor), who bore the title 'supporter of the leader' (*sanad al-hādī*) became so active a missionary in Cairo that followers of the new doctrine were named Darzīs (*al-Darziyya*) or Druzes (*Durūz*, pl. of *Darzī*) after him.

The Caliph al-Ḥākim appears at least to have tolerated the activities of the extremist dāʿīs. Whether he himself inclined to their doctrine is uncertain, but in not one of his countless surviving edicts does he lay claim to his own divinity. A bitter opponent of the Darzīs was the Ismāʿīlī supreme dāʿī Qut Tegin (Arabised: Khuttakīn), whom Darzī had vainly attempted to convert; and several clashes ensued between the Ismāʿīlīs and the Darzīs. The unrest culminated when (probably in the year 408/1017-18) several supporters of Darzī delivered a letter to the Chief Qāḍī, who was holding court in the ʿAmr mosque of Fusṭāṭ (Old Cairo), which, instead of beginning with the usual formula 'In the name of God, the Merciful, the Compassionate' opened with the words 'In the name of God, al-Ḥākim, the merciful, the compassionate'. The Chief Qāḍī rejected the letter with indignation and the angry crowd fell upon the messengers and killed three of them. In the town there were riots against supporters of the new doctrine; Darzī fled to the Caliph's palace and al-Ḥākim was only able to calm the Ismā'īlīs by assuring them that he had had him executed.[72] The mob thereupon besieged Ḥamza's home outside the town gate and set it on fire, but the dā'ī was able to escape along with his twelve companions. The unrest induced Ḥamza – perhaps at al-Ḥākim's behest – to suspend his *da'wa* temporarily in the year 409/1018, and even afterwards it was probably no longer openly pursued. In his writings Ḥamza criticises Darzī's excess of zeal and disobedience.

In his letters, all of which stem from the years 408-11/1017-1020, Ḥamza developed 'Druze' theology, a bizarre conglomeration of old Ismā'īlī, Neoplatonic and extreme Shiite conceptions and terms. D. W. Bryer (p. 240) claims that Ḥamza threw the whole Ismā'īlī system into the air 'like a juggler', caught it again and put it back together just as he wanted.[73] The basic prevailing idea, however, is constantly recognisable: the creator God (*al-Bār*), who had withdrawn from the sight of man after Adam's fall, reincarnated himself in the Fāṭimid Caliphs starting with al-Qā'im through to al-Ḥākim; the era of concealment (*satr*) is followed by one of revealment (*kashf*) in which all religions – even Islam and Ismā'īliyya – become irrelevant.

By sending delegations of individual dā'īs Ḥamza attempted to cover the whole of Egypt and Syria with a net of Druze communities – a *da'wa* within the *da'wa*. The collection of his letters constitutes the first two volumes of the Druze canon.[74] The disappearance of the Caliph al-Ḥākim, who probably fell victim to a palace conspiracy during one of his rides out at night (in 411/February 1021), strengthened the Druzes even more in their belief: the creator God had once again withdrawn from ungrateful mankind. In treatise no. 35 of the Druze canon, the 'missive of occultation' (*Risālat al-ghayba*), and other texts, God's renewed concealment is interpreted as a trial (*imtiḥān*) for the believers.[75]

After al-Ḥākim's disappearance Ḥamza fell silent and his 'vizier' Bahā' al-Dīn al-Muqtanā took over direction of the Druze *da'wa*, which now had to operate underground, since the Caliph al-Ẓāhir, al-Ḥākim's successor, forbade dissemination of the new doctrine in two edicts and persecuted its followers. Bahā' al-Dīn operated from Alexandria; his letters, which form volumes III-IV of the Druze canon, were directed to communities in Cairo and Upper Egypt, in Wādī Taym Allāh at the foot of Hermon in southern Lebanon, in the mountainous country of Jabal al-Summāq in northern Syria, and also to Ismā'īlī cells outside the Fātimid empire in Iraq and Iran, Ḥijāz,

Yemen, Baḥrayn and India. Internal conflicts, however, threatened Bahā' al-Dīn's authority; in 425/1034 he officially suspended the *da'wa* but letters written by him continue to be attested up to 434/1043.

In Egypt Druzism soon succumbed to persecution by the Fāṭimids and disappeared entirely. It managed to survive only in southern and central Lebanon and in Ḥawrān in southern Syria. There, even today, the writings of Ḥamza and Bahā' al-Dīn are only accessible to a minority of initiated scholars, the 'intelligent' (*'uqqāl*, sing. *'āqil*), who study the writings every Thursday in secluded cells (*khalawāt* sing. *khalwa*) in the mountains – clearly a reminiscence of the Fāṭimid Thursday teaching sessions (*majālis al-ḥikma*). By contrast, the majority of the 'ignorant' (*juhhāl*) do not know the secrets of their own religion. Under such circumstances the Druze doctrine could not continue to develop, and for centuries the Druze of Lebanon have therefore been a group of people rather than a real religious community.[76] Only in recent times have Druze intellectuals attempted to make the basic ideas of their religion known to their fellow-believers and to make them attractive in a modern form.[77] Manuscripts of the Druze canon had already reached Europe at the end of the 18th century, but the full text has still not been published up to the present day; only individual treatises have been edited. S. De Sacy's pioneering 'Exposé de la religion des Druzes' (1838) is based on an analysis of the canon and academic research of the Druze religion begins with this work.

Primary sources in translation

S. de Sacy, *Chrestomathie arabe*, Paris 1826, II, 191-278 (French trans. of eight texts from the Druze canon). E. von Döbeln, 'Ein traktat aus den schriften der Drusen', *MO* 3 (1909), 89-126 (ed. and trans. of treatise 14). Numerous historical sources are translated in de Sacy, *Exposé*, and Bryer, *Origins*.

Secondary sources

S. de Sacy, *Exposé de la religion des Druzes*, 2 vols. Paris 1838 (reprint Amsterdam 1964). H. Guys, *Théogonie des Druzes*, Paris 1863; *La nation druze, son histoire, sa religion, ses moeurs et son état politique ...*, Paris 1863 (reprint Amsterdam 1979). P. K. Hitti, *The Origins of the Druze People and Religion, with Extracts from their Sacred Writings*, New York 1928 (reprint New York 1966; Hitti's hypothesis of the Persian origins of the Druzes is regarded as superseded today). H. Wehr, 'Zu den Schriften Hamza's im Drusenkanon', *ZDMG* 96 (1942), 187-207. M. G. S. Hodgson, 'Al-Darazī and Ḥamza on the Origin of the Druze Religion', *JAOS* 82 (1962), 5-20; Art. Al-Darazī, Durūz, EI². W. Madelung, Art. Ḥamza b. 'Alī, EI². D. W. Bryer, 'The Origins of the Druze Religion', *Der Islam* 52 (1975), 47-84; 239-62; 53 (1976), 5-27. J. van Ess, 'Chiliastische Erwartungen und die Versuchung der Göttlichkeit. Der Kalif al-Ḥākim', *Abh. d. Heidelberger Akad. d. Wiss., phil.-hist. Kl.*, 1977.

N. M. Abu-Izzeddin, *The Druzes. A New Study of their History, Faith and Society*, Leiden 1984. H. Halm, 'Der Treuhänder Gottes. Die Edikte des Kalifen al-Ḥākim', *Der Islam* 63 (1986), 11-72.

THE NIZĀRĪS: 'ASSASSINS' AND KHOJAS

When the Fāṭimid Caliph al-Mustanṣir died in 487/1094 the question of his succession split the Ismā'īlī communities. The Caliph had designated his son Nizār as the future Imam, but the vizier and army chief al-Afḍal ibn Badr al-Jamālī, who really controlled Egyptian politics, set up another prince, his son-in-law al-Musta'lī, on the throne. Nizār fled to Alexandria where his armed rebellion was defeated and he himself arrested and executed.

This violent intervention in the Imam succession resulted in the defection of the Iranian *da'wa* . Its leadership was taken over by a man who, until then, had been loyal to the Fāṭimids and had worked successfully as a missionary and agitator within the Seljuq empire. Born in Qumm the son of a Twelver Shiite Kufan, Ḥasan-i Ṣabbāḥ had come to Rayy with his father in his youth and was won over by the Ismā'īlī dā'īs. Ordained as a dā'ī in 464/1072, he worked in Iṣfahān and Āzarbayjān and travelled to Cairo in 470/1078; after his return in 474/1081 he conducted missionary activity in Iṣfahān, Kirmān, Yazd and Khūzistān and then devoted himself to the *da'wa* in Daylam south of the Caspian Sea. In 483/1090 he succeeded in capturing Alamūt castle on the upper course of the Shāh-Rūd in the eastern Elburz mountain range and remained there for the rest of his life; he died in 518/1124. Alamūt became the cente of a small dā'ī principality which embraced the villages near the meadows watered by the Rūdbār and a few surrounding castles, including Lanbassar (Lammassar). In 484/1091 Ḥasan-i Ṣabbāḥ sent a dā'ī into the small oasis towns of Quhistān in the east of the central Iranian salt desert – Qāyin, Zūzan, Tūn, Ṭabas Masīnān – where the *da'wa* had probably already had a foothold for some time (Ḥamza, the founder of the Druze came from Zūzan), and stirred up open rebellion against the Baghdad Caliphs and the Seljuq sultan. In 485/1092 Sultan Malikshāh failed in his attempt to quell the two rebellious Ismā'īlī centres by armed force; the siege of Alamūt remained unsuccessful, and an expedition against Quhistān was cut short by the death of the sultan (November 1092).

Shortly before, in 485/October 1092, one of Ḥasan-i Ṣabbāḥ's emissaries managed to murder the Seljuq vizier Niẓām al-Mulk; dressed as a Sufi, the assassin approached the minister's sedan and stabbed him. This attack was the first in a whole series of attempted assassinations which was intended to sweep leading politicians and religious dignitaries out of the way and weaken the Seljuq regime;

Ḥasan-i Ṣabbāḥ was responsible for some fifty acts of terrorism. The Assassins, who moved around in groups of between two and ten men, called themselves the 'ones prepared to sacrifice themselves' (Arabic: *fidā'iyyūn*, Pers.: *fidāiyān*, sing. *fidā'ī/fidāī*) because they usually met their deaths in these operations. The origin of the name *ḥashīshī* – from which the French *assassin* is derived – which the fidā'īs were called in Syria, is unclear. The word actually means 'ḥashīsh consumer' but was presumably used only in the sense of 'madman, irresponsible person'.[78] There is no evidence that the murders were committed under the influence of drugs; neither is this claimed by Marco Polo in his fairytale report in which the 'old man of the mountains' is said to have pampered his murder accomplices in an artificial paradisaical garden.[79]

Two years after the murder of the vizier Niẓām al-Mulk, the Fāṭimid al-Mustanṣir died in Cairo and his son Nizār was killed. Thereupon the Persian *da'wa* refused to recognise al-Musta'lī's successor as Imam and made itself independent from Cairo. Whether the 'Nizāris' considered the Imam Nizār to be in occultation and awaited his return is not clear; it was only claimed later that a grandson of Nizār – whose sons had been killed along with him – had been saved and brought from Egypt to Alamūt where he remained in hiding. In any case, for the time being, the Nizārī *da'wa* once more reverted to the notion of occultation (*ghayba*) and propagated the idea of a hidden anonymous Imam. Under the guidance of Ḥasan-i Ṣabbāḥ the 'new mission' (*al-da'wa al-jadīda*) enjoyed further successes in Iran; on the south-east edge of the Elburz mountains the Ismā'īlīs gained the castle of Girdkūh which threatened the important road from Rayy to eastern Iran, and near the Seljuq capital Iṣfahān they occupied the castles of Shāhdiz and Khalinjān; even in the mountainous country of Arrajān north-east of the Gulf bases were established. The Seljuq princes, who were tied up in relentless wars of succession to the throne, generally left the Ismā'īlīs in peace; a few even made use of the fidā'īs to clear opponents out of the way while others, by paying money to Alamūt, bought themselves protection from attacks. Even the Seljuq court and the army, in particular the units of Daylamite mercenaries – were infiltrated by Ismā'īlīs.

From about 1100 Persian dā'īs from Alamūt attempted to introduce the *da'wa* from Aleppo into the mountain villages of the northern Syrian Jabal al-Summāq. The castles of Shayzar and Afāmiya on the Orontes were their main targets and the small town of Sarmīn was one of their centres. From 1126 to 1129, and with the agreement of the Seljuq amīrs of Damascus, Persian dā'īs occupied the castle al-Marqab near Bāniyās on the Syrian coast, and threatened the neighbouring Crusader states. In 515/1121 the Egyptian vizier al-Afḍal, who had been dethroned by the Imam Nizār, was murdered and in 524/1130 the Fāṭimid Caliph al-Āmir fell victim to an attack by Nizārī fidā'īs.

When Ḥasan-i Ṣabbāḥ died in 518/1124 he was succeeded as head of the *daʿwa* by the lord of the neighbouring castle of Lammassar, the Daylamite Buzurg-Ummīd, whom he had designated himself and who in turn before his death in 532/1138 appointed his son Muḥammad to be his successor. He thus founded a dāʿī dynasty which now ruled over the small Ismāʿīlī state of Alamūt in the high valley of Rūdbār and the castles in Syria and east Iranian Quhistān which were under his suzerainty for more than a century (the castles at Iṣfahān and in Arrajān had already been conquered by the Seljuqs shortly after 1100). The assassination attempts continued, the most prominent victims being the Baghdadi Caliphs al-Mustarshid (1135) and al-Rāshid (1138) and the Seljuq Sultan Dā'ūd (1148), next came several viziers and governors and especially a succession of qāḍīs from the big towns who had opposed the Ismāʿīlīs with formal legal opinions and sermons. It became usual for prominent people to wear breastplates under their clothing.

The Nizārī Ismāʿīliyya gained new impetus under Buzurg-Ummīd's grandson Ḥasan II (557-561/1162-1166). In the third year of his reign he declared that the *qiyāma*, the era of the Qā'im, had begun and that Islamic law, which had until then been scrupulously observed, was annulled at the bidding of the Hidden Imam; after a sermon in the courtyard of Alamūt castle to an assembled crowd which turned its back to Mecca, the dāʿī invited the audience to a feast in the middle of Ramaḍān (17th Ramaḍān 559/8th August 1164). The communities in Quhistān and Syria followed suit; Islamic worship was forbidden on pain of punishment.

In 561/January 1166 Ḥasan II was stabbed at Lammassar by a supporter of the old doctrine. His son Muḥammad II (561-601/1166-1210) now claimed for the first time that he and his father were true descendants of the Fāṭimid Nizār and thus were themselves Imams. The *ghayba* model was thus once more cast aside. At the same time the rank of the now re-apparent Imam acquired a new importance: the *imām qā'im*, i.e. the Imam who brings in the *qiyāma* and abrogates the law (and in principle every Imam may do this) replaced an apocalyptic Mahdī-Qā'im. But in the reign of the very next Imam, Jalāl al-Dīn Ḥasan III, the Imam put an end to the episode of *qiyāma*, re-introduced the *sharīʿa* and made contact with the Sunni Abbasid Caliph of Baghdad whose political power and religious authority were increasing considerably after the death of the last Seljuq sultan

(590/1194). Ḥasan III had mosques built in the villages of Rūdbār and publicly burnt his predecessors' writings.

Under his son 'Alā' al-Dīn Muḥammad III (618-653/1221-1255) – Marco Polo's *Aloadino* – the antinomian trend again gained the upper hand. The re-introduction of the *sharī'a* was interpreted as a transitional period of concealment (*satr*) for the sake of dissimulation (*taqiyya*). At this time the mathematician and astronomer Naṣīr al-Dīn Ṭūsī (b. 597/1201) was studying in the well-stocked library of Alamūt (see above p. 63 ff). The scholar played a not insignificant role in the capitulation of Khūrshāh, the last Imam of Alamūt, in 654/ December 1256 to the Mongol Khan Hülegü when the latter was preparing to conquer the whole of Iran. The castles of Alamūt and Maymūndiz were demolished; only Lammassar and Girdkūh held out for a while. The Imam was brought to the court of the great Khan Kubilai in Mongolia and killed on his way home; his family is said to have been killed previously in Qazvīn. Hülegü's vizier, the historian 'Aṭā Malik-i Juvaynī had the opportunity to look over the contents of the Alamūt library and make use of them for his historical work before he destroyed the lot.[80]

In Syria the Nizārī dā'īs – without exception Persians sent from Alamūt – had acquired or conquered several castles between 1130 and 1140: al-Qadmūs, al-Kahf, Kharība, Ruṣāfa, al-Khawābī, al-Qulay'a, al-Manīqa, al-'Ullayqa, Abū Qubays and Maṣyāf, which were all in the mountain region of the southern Jabal Bahrā' (present-day Jabal Anṣāriyya) between Bāniyās on the Mediterranean coast and the Orontes depression of Ḥamāh.[81] In this hardly accessible mountain region the 'Assassins' established a small territorial state similar to that of Alamūt and pursued a clever see-saw policy in the border area between the Crusader states of the coast and the Seljuq (later Zengid) amīrates of Aleppo and Damascus; assassinations of prominent Crusaders, eg. Count Raymond II of Tripoli (1130), did not prevent occasional alliances with the Franks against the Sunni amīrs.

The most famous prince of the Syrian Assassin state is Rāshīd al-Dīn Sinān, the Crusaders' 'old man from the mountains' (*vetulus de montanis*) . According to his autobiography, which still exists in fragments, he came to Alamūt from Baṣra in his early years and was educated there. In 557/1162 Imam Ḥasan II sent him to Syria where he proclaimed the beginning of the *qiyāma* and the abrogation of the law in 559/1164. His most dangerous opponent was Sultan Ṣalāḥ al-Dīn (Saladin) who overthrew the Fāṭimid dynasty in Cairo in 567/1171 and extended his rule to Syria. Saladin, who twice only just managed to escape the attacks of the fidā'īs, devastated the north Syrian centres of the Nizārīs in Jabal al-Summāq, Ma'arrat Maṣrīn and Sarmīn on his march to Aleppo; in 572/1176 he occupied Maṣyāf castle but had to withdraw again and recognise the independence of the *da'wa* principality. Rāshid al-Dīn Sinān also appears to have made himself largely independent of Alamūt, and to have gone his own way in doctrine; surviving documents give him a quasi-divine status. The last spectacular success of the Old Man of the Mountains was the murder of the king of Jerusalem, Conrad of Montferrat, in Tyre in 1192, supposedly at the instigation of the English King Richard the Lion-heart, but according to other sources on Saladin's orders. Rashīd al-Dīn Sinān died between 588-590/1192-1194. Under his successors, who were again installed from Alamūt, the principality of the Assassins was for some time obliged to pay tribute to the orders of St. John and the Knights Templars; after the fall of Alamūt in 654/1256 it came under the sovereignty of the Egyptian Mamlūk sultan Baybars who conquered all the Assassins' castles in the years 670-672/1271-1273.

In the 14th century contact between the Syrian and Persian Nizārī communities was broken off because each was annexed to different branches of the Imāmī family which in turn descended from the Imams of Alamūt. The Syrian Nizārīs held their ground, as a tolerated sect burdened with a special tax in the Ottoman empire, in the 'castles of mission' (*qilā' al-da'wa*) around al-Qadmūs and al-Kahf as well as in Maṣyāf, while the communities in Jabal al-Summāq went under. As Imams they recognised the successors of one Muḥammad Shāh, who was able temporarily to occupy Alamūt in 776/1374 with the help of the Daylamite Nizārīs. His descendants later lived in Sulṭāniyya in Āzarbayjān; in 928/1522, however, the Imam Shāh Ṭāhir Ḥusaynī was forced by the Ṣafavid Shāh to leave Iran and go into exile in Ahmadnagar in the Indian Deccan (east of Bombay) for being a trouble-maker. In 1796 the Syrian Nizārīs lost contact with the last known Imam of this line, Muḥammad Bāqir; when their messengers had searched in vain for the latter's descendants in India in 1887 the larger part of the Syrian communities attached itself to the Āghā Khan (see below). A minority in Maṣyāf and in the mountain region around al-Qadmūs adhere to the old vanished Imam line, while the Āghā Khāns are recognised as Imams in al-Khawābī and in the villages around Salamya which were resettled by the Ismā'īlīs in the mid-19th century.[82] In 1964 the number of Ismā'īlīs in Syria was 56,000, 1% of the total population.[83] They have a rich literature which goes back to the time of the Fāṭimids[84], and which, thanks to numerous editions by their scholars 'Ārif Tāmir and Muṣṭafā Ghālib, has been accessible to research for several decades.

In Iran the Nizārī communities around Alamūt have disappeared since the 16th century under pressure from the Ṣafavids. Small communities have survived in Khurāsān and Badakhshān, Quhistān (Qāyin, Bīrjand), Kirmān and Yazd. The other Imam line can be traced from the end of the 15th century in the village of Anjudān near Maḥallāt (100 km south west of Qumm). It is said to be descended from the Great Masters in Alamūt, and is the so-called Qāsim-Shāhī line to which today's Āghā Khān belongs. As notables, big landowners and governors they have played a political role in Kirmān from the 18th century, especially under the Qājār dynasty; the Imam Ḥasan ʿAlī Shāh Maḥallatī was distinguished by Fatḥ ʿAlī Shāh with the title *Āghā Khān* (Turk: prince) which his descendants have borne ever since. After a failed rebellion attempt in Kirmān the first Āghā Khān had to flee to Afghanistan in 1842 and finally settled in Bombay in 1845.

The communities of the Nizārī-Ismāʿīlīs in north-west India, the Khojas (from Pers. *khwāja:* master)[85] developed when the Hindu trader caste of the Lohanas was converted to Islam. Even today the Khojas are almost exclusively traders. Their centres lie in the Punjab (Ucch, Multan, Rawalpindi), in Sind on the lower Indus and in Indian Gujarat (Kutch and Kathiawar with the towns Nawanagar, Junagarh, Patan, Ahmadabad). There are Nizārī communities too in the Pakistani north-west border province (Chitral) and on the upper Indus in the Karakorum region (Hunza, Gilgit) as well as in the western Tarim basin in Chinese Sin-Kiang (Yārkand, Kāshghar). Today Indian Khojas live as traders in almost all the countries of East and South Africa as well as in Ceylon and Burma.

The Khojas venerate several dāʿīs who came from Iran in the 14th and 15th centuries and conducted missionary activity in the Indus area and in Gujarat. The most important is Pīr Ṣadr al-Dīn (15th century) whose shrine is near Ucch. He made broad concessions to the religious ideas of the Hindus. In his main work, the *Das Avatar,* the Imams are portrayed as reincarnations of the god Vishnu, and the belief is widespread that he who does not recognise the True Imam is condemned to reincarnation. The Indian and Pakistani Nizārīs have practically no tradition of medieval Ismāʿīlī literature, although the non-Ismāʿīlī *Umm al-kitāb* (see above p. 157) is disseminated among the communities of the Pamir-Karakorum region. The literature of the Indian Khojas consists almost exclusively of pious legends in Indian languages heavily mixed with Hindu and Tantric ideas.[86] Little importance is ascribed to Islamic ritual such as the pilgrimage or fasting in Ramaḍān; community houses (*jamāʿat-khāna*) replace the mosques, and prayer rituals have little to do with the Islamic *salāt.*

It is not known when the Khojas began to recognise the Imams of the Qāsim-Shāhī line as their leaders. After the first Āghā Khān had moved to India he had to establish his authority before the High Court in Bombay; a ruling by the Judge Sir Joseph Arnould in 1866 upheld his status as Imam of the Khojas and his right to dispose of community assets freely (the Āghā Khān case). In a second court case in 1905 the third Āghā Khān had this right confirmed (the Haji Bibi case); thereupon a proportion of the Indian and East African Khoja communities apostasised to the Twelver Shia (see above p. 137). The Āghā Khān III, Sulṭān Muḥammad Shāh, born in Karachi in 1877 and enthroned in Bombay in 1885 as the 48th Imam, used the considerable resources of endowments, taxes and gifts granted to him – on the occasion of his 60th and 70th jubilee he was given his weight in diamonds and platinum – to strengthen his authority in the Indian and East African communities (*jamā'at*) and to found social institutions such as meeting houses, schools and hospitals. In this the Imam, who had gained social prominence in Europe, pursued a progressive modernist policy; as early as 1937 he set about organising cooperatives and founding insurance companies in Africa, and in numerous decrees (*firmān*) he urged his supporters to innovate and invest, to mobilise socially and to gain higher education. He placed particular emphasis on school education and the vocational training of girls who, among the Khojas, did not wear the veil. Āghā Khān III was also diplomatically and politically active; during the Abyssinian conflict of 1935 he represented Persia at the League of Nations in Geneva, and he is regarded as one of the founding fathers of the Muslim state of Pakistan. After his death at Versoix near Geneva he was buried in a mausoleum at Aswan in Egypt, in 'the land of his fathers' (the Fāṭimids), as is emphasised in the epitaph. He was succeeded by his grandson Karīm Āghā Khān IV who was born in Geneva in 1936 (his father, Prince 'Alī Khān, was killed in a car accident). He is continuing the policies of his grandfather; the London Institute of Ismā'īlī Studies founded by him in 1977 endeavours to collect all available Ismā'īlī literature and, in collaboration with European and American scholars, to make it accessible to research.

The number of Imāmī Khojas amounts to about 20 million,[87] of whom some 2 million are in Pakistan where numerous Khojas settled after being expelled from Uganda in 1972. Karachi has superseded Bombay as the most important community on the sub-continent; the Āghā Khān is a Pakistani citizen but spends most of his time in Paris.

Primary sources in translation

1. *Alamūt:*

Ḥasan-i Ṣabbāḥ, *al-Fuṣūl al-arba'a*, Engl. by M. G. S. Hodgson, *The Order of the Assassins* (see below), 325-28. 'Aṭa Malik-i Juvaynī, *Tārīkh-i Jāhān-gushā*,

Engl. by J. A. Boyle, *The History of the World-Conqueror*, Manchester 1958, II, 666-725; French by C. Defrémery, 'Essai sur l'histoire des Ismaéliens ou Batiniens de la Perse, plus connus sous le nom d'Assassins', *JA* 8 (1856), 353-87; 15 (1860), 130-210.
2. *Syria:*
Al-qaṣīda al-shāfiya, Engl. by S. N. Makarem, Beirut 1966. B. Lewis, 'Kamāl al-Dīn's Biography of Rašīd al-Dīn Sinān', *Arabica* 13 (1966), 225-67. *Manāqib Rāshid al-Dīn Sinān*, French by S. Guyard, 'Un grand maître des Assassins', *JA* 9 (1877), 387-450. Untitled treatise by Rāshid al-Dīn Sinān: S. Guyard, *Fragments relatifs à la doctrine des Ismaélis*, Paris 1874, 275-7.

Secondary sources

1. *Alamūt:*
F. Stark, *The Valleys of the Assassins*, London 1936. W. Ivanow, 'An Ismā'īlī Poem in Praise of Fidawis, *JBBRAS* 14 (1938), 63-72; Alamut and Lamasar, Tehran 1960. M. G. S. Hodgson, *The Order of Assassins. The Struggle of the Early Nizârî Ismâ'îlîs Against the Islamic World*, The Hague 1955; Art. Alamūt, Ḥasan-i Ṣabbāḥ, EI²; 'The Ismā'īli State', *CHI* V, 422-82. B. Lewis, *The Assassins. A Radical Sect in Islam*, London 1967. P. Willey, *The Castles of the Assassins*, London 1963. P. Filippani-Ronconi, *Ismaeliti ed 'Assassini'*, Milan 1973.
2. *Syria:*
D. Lebey de Batilly, *Traité de l'origine des anciens Assassins porte-couteaux*, Lyon 1603. S. Guyard, 'Un grand-maître des Assassins au temps de Saladin', *JA* 9 (1877), 324-489. M. van Berchem, 'Epigraphie des Assassins de Syrie', *JA* 9 (1897), 453-501. D. Schaffner, *Relations of the Order of Assassins with the Crusaders During the Twelfth Century*, unpubl. diss. Chicago 1939. C. E. Nowell, 'The Old Man of the Mountain', *Speculum* 22 (1947), 497-519. N. N. Lewis, 'The Ismailis of Syria Today', *JRCAS* 39 (1952), 69-77. B. Lewis, 'The Sources for the History of the Syrian Assassins', *Speculum* 27 (1952), 475-89; 'Saladin and the Assassins', *BSOAS* 15 (1953), 239-45; 'The Ismā'īlites and the Assassins', in: K. M. Setton (ed.), *A History of the Crusades* I, Philadelphia 1955, 99-132; *The Assassins. A Radical Sect in Islam*, London 1967; Art., Ḥashīshiyya, EI². N. A. Mirza, *The Syrian Ismā'īlīs at the Time of the Crusades*, diss. Durham 1963. I. K. Poonawala, *Biobibliography of Ismā'īlī Literature*, Malibu 1977, 287-97. W. Madelung, Art., Ismā'īliyya, EI².
3. *India and East Africa:*
S. Mujtaba Ali, *The Origins of the Khojas and Their Religious Life Today*, Bonn 1936. W. Ivanow, 'The Sect of Imām-Shāh in Gujarat', *JBBRAS* 12 (1936), 19-70; 'A Forgotten Branch of the Ismā'īlīs', *JRAS* (1938), 57-79; 'Tombs of Some Persian Ismā'īlī Imāms', *JBBRAS* 14 (1938), 49-62; 'Satpanth', in: *Collectanea* I, Leiden 1948, 1-54. J. N. Hollister, *The Shi'a of India*, London 1953 (reprint 1979). Aga Khan, *The Memoirs of Aga Khan. World Enough and Time*, New York 1954; H. S. Morris, 'The Divine Kingship of the Aga Khan: A Study of Theocracy in East Africa', 'Southwestern Journal of Anthropology' 14 (1958), 457-72. – *The Constitution of the Shia Imāmi Ismailis in Africa*, Nairobi 1962. Karim Aga Khan, *Speeches*, 2 vols, Mombasa 1963/4. S. C. Misra, *Muslim Communities in Gujarat*, New York/Bombay/London 1964, 54-65. J. N. D. Anderson, 'The Isma'ili Khojas of East Africa. A New Constitution and Personal Law for the Community', *MES* 1 (1964), 21-39. Z. Noorally, The First Agha Khan and the British 1838-1868, unpubl. diss. London 1964. S. T. Lokhandwalla, 'Islamic Law and Ismaili Communities (Khojas and Bohras)',

IESHR 4 (1967), 155-76. E. Kjellberg, *The Ismailis in Tanzania*, Dar es Salaam 1967. H. S. Morris, *The Indians in Uganda*, Chicago/London 1968. A. K. Adatia/N. Q. King, 'Some East African *Firmans* of H.H. Aga Khan III.', *JRA* 2 (1969), 179-91. H. Algar, 'The Revolt of Āgha Khān Maḥallātī and the Transference of the Ismā'īlī Imāmate to India', *SI* 29 (1969), 55-81. W. Fischauer, *The Aga Khans*, London 1970. I. K. Poonawala, *Biobibliography* (see above), 298-311. A. Nanji, 'Modernization and Changes in the Nizari Ismaili Community in East Africa – A Perspective', *JRA* 6 (1974), 123-39; *The Nizārī Ismā'īlī Tradition in the Indo-Pakistan Subcontinent*, Delmar, N.Y. 1978. P. B. Clarke, *The Ismaili Khojas: A Sociological Study of an Islamic Sect*, unpubl. M.Ph. thesis, London 1974 (King's College); 'The Ismailis: A Study of a Community', *The British Journal of Sociology* 27 (1976), 484-94; 'The Ismaili Sect in London: Religious Institutions and Social Change', *Religion* 8 (1978), 68-84. A. Z. Khan 'Isma'ilism in Multan and Sind', *JPHS* 23 (1975), 36-57. G. Khakee, 'The Das Avatara of Pir Shams as a Linguistic and Literary Evidence of the Early Development of Ismailism in Sind', *Sind Quarterly* 8 (1980), 44-7.

MUSTA'LĪ TAYYIBĪS AND BOHORAS

The Fāṭimid Caliph al-Musta'lī, who was enthroned in Cairo in 487/1094 instead of his brother Nizār, and his son and successor al-Āmir, were not only recognised as Imams in Egypt and Syria but also in Yemen and India. However, when al-Āmir fell victim to an attack by Nizārī fidā'īs in 524/1130 a further schism took place in the Ismā'īlī *da'wa*. Al-Āmir had left an eight-month-old son behind called al-Ṭayyib who had been designated successor to the throne immediately after his birth, in the confusion surrounding the succession, however, his rights were passed over, and nothing is known about the child's further fate. In 526/February 1132 a cousin of the murdered al-Āmir, 'Abd al-Majīd, ascended the throne under the name al-Ḥāfiẓ; the last Fāṭimid Caliphs (until 567/1171) were descended from him. The Imamate of this collateral line was promoted by the official Fāṭimid *da'wa* in Egypt and Syria, but in Yemen the last Fāṭimids were only recognised by the princes of Aden and a few rulers of Ṣan'ā'. The Ṣulayḥid queen al-Sayyida 'Arwa in Dhū Jibla (south-west of Ibb) used the opportunity to shake off Cairene sovereignty; she supported the dā'ī of Yemen, Dhu'ayb ibn Mūsā, who adhered to the Imamate of the vanished child al-Ṭayyib. The Ṭayyibī propagandists won the predominant section of the Yemeni communities over to their cause and even after the end of the Ṣulayḥid dynasty (532/1138) the Yemeni and the Indian *da'wa*, which had since time immemorial been dependent on it, remained Ṭayyibī. As with the Nizārīs, the *ghayba* model also prevailed in the case of the Ṭayyibīs: the True Imam al-Ṭayyib is simply in occultation, and leadership of the community has been taken over for the period of his absence by the 'Absolute' or 'Universal' dā'ī (*al-dā'ī al-muṭlaq*) as his representative. After the death of Dhu'ayb ibn Mūsā in 546/1151 this office fell to Ibrāhīm al-

Ḥāmidī who handed it down to his son Ḥātim.

Ibrāhīm al-Ḥāmidī, who worked among the non-Ismāʿīlī princes of the Yām clan until his death in Ṣanʿā' in 557/1162, was the founder of the Ṭayyibī doctrine; in his principal work, the 'Boy's treasure' (*kanz al-walad*),[88] he develops al-Kirmānī's ideas. A gnostic cosmic drama of rebellion, fall and redemption – created from as yet unknown sources – is grafted on to the Kirmānī system of the ten intellects (see above p. 180). The Third Intellect disputes its rank with the Second and is thrown down as punishment; as the Tenth Intellect it now creates, as a demiurge (*mudabbir*) the material world from the shadow cast by its hubris. At the same time, as the spiritual Adam (*Ādam al-rūḥānī*) it is the celestial prototype of earthly human beings whose redemption takes place on the model of its salvation: purified by knowledge and remorse the Tenth Intellect rises again to its original position beside the Creator.

One further essential innovation of Ibrāhīm al-Ḥāmidī was the acceptance of the 'Epistles of the Sincere Brethren' (*Rasā'il ikhwān al-ṣafā'*), a Neoplatonic, philosophico-scientific encyclopaedia consisting of fifty-two treatises which were put together in Baṣra in the 4th/10th century by Arab intellectuals.[89] After the first discoveries of the original Ismāʿīlī texts by S. Guyard (1874) and P. Casanova (1898) European research initially assumed that the 'Epistles' represented the original doctrine of the Ismāʿīliyya. Investigations by W. Ivanow and S. M. Stern, however, refuted this claim; Stern, who identified the authors of the 'Epistles',[90] demonstrated that the Yemeni Ṭayyibīs of the 12th century were the first to hear and respond to the Baṣran encyclopaedia; the *Kanz al-walad* by Ibrāhīm al-Ḥāmidī is the earliest Ismāʿīlī text which cites the 'Epistles' a number of times. However, a few researchers such as Y. Marquet and A. Hamdani continue to assert the original Ismāʿīlī character of the encyclopaedia.[91] The Ṭayyibīs consider the second Hidden Imam from Salamya, Aḥmad ibn ʿAbdallāh (see above p. 167), to be the author of the 'Epistles'.[92]

While the Ṭayyibī communities soon disappeared in Egypt and Syria[93] they have survived up to the present day in Yemen and India. In Yemen the office of dāʿī muṭlaq was kept in the Ḥāmidī family until 605/1209, and was then transferred to a tribe of Umayyad descent, the Banu 'l-Walīd al-Anf al-Qurashī, who held it until 946/1539. The dāʿīs, to whom we owe a whole series of works on Ismāʿīlī doctrine and history[94], lived in Ṣanʿā' at first, and then from the 14th century in Dhū Marmar castle in the Ḥarāz massif (east of al-Ḥudayda on the Red Sea). For the most part the tribes in this area professed Ismāʿīliyya. When the Zaydī Imams from Ṣaʿda and Ṣanʿā' extended their power southward in the 15th century (see below, p. 208) the Ṭayyibī communities were severely persecuted; in 829/1426 the dā'ī muṭlaq 'Alī ibn 'Abdallāh had to leave Dhū Marmar castle and seek refuge in the mountains. His nephew and successor Idrīs 'Imād al-Dīn (1392-1468), who succeeeded his uncle as the 19th dā'ī in 832/1428, was the last significant head of the Yemeni Ṭayyibīs, a man who distinguished himself equally as a politician, a warrior and a writer. He is the author of a history of the Imams (including the Egyptian Fāṭimids) in several volumes.[95] Idrīs successfully defended the Ḥarāz massif against the Zaydīs, but at the same time he prepared to transfer the dā'ī office to India.[96]

Until this time the Yemeni dā'ī muṭlaq had also been the leading authority for the Ṭayyibīs in north-west India. The Fāṭimid *da'wa* was supposedly taken to India by a Yemeni dā'ī called 'Abdallāh who is said to have gone ashore in Cambay (Khambhat) in Gujarat in 460/1067; in Cambay, too, the grave of a Ṭayyibī dā'ī, Muḥammad 'Alī (d. 532/1137) is venerated.[97] By conducting missionary activity among the Hindus the *da'wa* spread around the Gulf of Cambay among the urban artisans and traders. Up to modern times the main centres are Sidhpur, Patan and Ahmadabad to the north, and Surat and Bombay to the south of Cambay. The communities were connected by sea with the centre in Yemen, and Indian Ismā'īlīs went to Yemen to study the secrets of the doctrine with masters close to the dā'ī muṭlaq. Thus an Indian Ḥasan ibn Nūḥ al-Hindī (al-Bharuchī) distinguished himself as a learned author under the two successors of the dā'ī Idrīs 'Imād al Dīn;[98] one of his pupils, Yūsuf ibn Sulaymān from Sidhpur, was nominated 24th dā'ī muṭlaq in 946/1539 and was the first Indian to hold this position. At this time he was already living in his home town of Sidhpur again, but in 1544 he returned to Yemen which had meanwhile been conquered by the Sunni Ottomans, and he died there in 974/1567. His successor, the 25th dā'ī muṭlaq, finally settled in India where on the whole the Ṭayyibī community were able to live their own undisturbed life under the rule of the Mughal emperor. However, a schism which split the community after the death of the 26th dā'ī muṭlaq in 999/1591 brought unrest: the Indians appointed Dā'ūd ibn Quṭbshāh Burhān al-Dīn as dā'ī while in Yemen Sulaymān al-Hindī, a nephew of the first Indian dā'ī, claimed to have been designated successor by the late dā'ī muṭlaq. The graves of the two rivals in Ahmadabad are venerated up to the present day by their respective supporters.

The Yemeni *da'wa* remained predominantly 'Sulaymānī'. Since 1640 the title of dā'ī muṭlaq in Yemen has remained within the Makramī family who were originally from Najrān (in today's Saudi Arabia, near the Yemeni border). They regained a foothold in the Ḥarāz mountains in 1763 and successfully defended this old Ismā'īlī region against the Zaydī Imams of Ṣanʿāʾ. It was not until 1872 that the Ottoman general Aḥmad Mukhtār Pāshā brought an end to the independence of the Ismāʿīlīs by capturing al-ʿAttāra castle. The present Sulaymānī dāʿī muṭlaq, al-Sharafī al-Ḥusayn ibn al-Ḥasan al-Makramī (from 1976) is believed to be living in Saudi Arabia. There are Sulaymānī communities in Najrān and Ḥarāz; and in India a small and rapidly diminishing minority exists in Bombay and Hyderabad (Dekkan); Baroda (east of Cambay) is the seat of the representative (*manṣūb*) of the Yemeni dāʿī.[99]

At the time of the schism of 1591 the vast majority of the Indian communities recognised the Indian Dāʾūd ibn Quṭbshāh as the 27th dāʿī muṭlaq; he died in 1021/1612 in his residence at Ahmadabad in Gujarat. Since the end of the 18th century the dāʿīs, who were recruited from the knightly warrior caste of the Rajputs, have resided in Jamnagar (Nawanagar) on the Gulf of Kutch. In 1785 Surat became the official residence of the dāʿī muṭlaq (who was also called *Sayyidnā* or *Mullajī Ṣāḥib*). The Ismāʿīlī seminary founded in 1809 by the 43rd dāʿī Ṣayf al-Dīn in Surat, the *Dars-i Sayfī* (also *Jāmiʿa Sayfiyya:* Sayfi University) is the most important centre of Ismāʿīlī learning in India up to the present day.[100]

The Indian Ṭayyibī (or Mustaʿlī) Ismāʿīlīs call their creed the 'rightly-guided call' (*daʿwat-i hādiya*); and they also use the name Bohras or Bohoras, 'tradesmen' (from Gujarati: *vohōrvū:* to trade). By this name they are generally known in India. Their number is estimated at a good half million in India, and of these more than half live in Gujarat. The largest community is that of Bombay (Maharashtra) with some 60,000 people; from the 1920s Bombay has also been the permanent seat of the Dāʾūdī dāʿī muṭlaq and his central administration. In addition there are significant communities in Burhanpur, Indore and Ujjayn (Madhya Pradesh), in Udaypur (Rajasthan) and in the Pakistani city of Karachi (25,000). The Yemeni Dāʾūdī community is estimated at around 2,500[101] (as opposed to 100,000 Sulaymānīs).[102] Since the 19th century Indian Dāʾūdī Bohoras from Zanzibar have settled in all the ports on the East African coast and in Uganda; in 1967 their number was about 15,000.[103]

The office of dāʿī muṭlaq is handed on by the dāʿī himself by means of 'clear designation' (*naṣṣ-i jalī*) to a suitable, i.e. pious and learned, successor. In practice the circle of possible candidates is limited to the closest relatives of the dāʿī. The present dāʿī dynasty (Ibn Shaykh Jīwanjī) has held the office from 1817 with only one interruption. The 51st dāʿī muṭlaq, Ṭāhir Sayf al-Dīn (1915-1965) endeavoured to extend his official authority to absolute power in all secular and spiritual concerns of the Bohora communities. For this he used the enormous funds made up of donations and endowments, and more importantly canonical taxes (*zakāt, ṣadaqat al-fiṭr, khums*) and additional taxes and dues raised by his agents (*'āmil*) in all the communities in India and East Africa. He punished opponents with excommunication (*salām banḍh:* refusal to greet, i.e. being excluded from kissing the hand of the dā'ī) which, for those affected, meant not only exclusion from all mosques and sanctuaries and the refusal of all religious ceremonies such as weddings and funerals, but also total social and commercial isolation (Arabic *barā'at:* turning away). Refractory communities were disciplined by a form of interdict – suspension of all religious ceremonies by the dā'ī's representatives. As early as the 1920s a liberal opposition built up against the autocracy of the dā'ī muṭlaq, and in two spectacular court cases the 'reformists' attempted to force the dā'ī to give annual accounts of the amount and use of income from the endowments (Chanḍa Bhā'ī Gulla case, Bombay 1917-1922) and to limit his right to pronounce excommunication to cases of theological deviation (Burhanpur Durgah case, Burhanpur 1931, London 1947). In 1949 the Parliament of Bombay removed the dā'ī's right to excommunicate (Prevention of Excommunications Act), but he contested the law in 1958, appealing to articles 25 and 26 of the Indian constitution according to which every religious community has the right to profess its own beliefs and to settle its own affairs. In 1961 the Bombay Supreme Court quashed the statute as unconstitutional, almost certainly because of the good relations between the dā'ī and the Congress Party which he supported with donations and by activating a considerable voting potential during the elections. The dā'ī's success aggravated the dispute between the reformists and the dā'ī's strong, traditionally-minded following; the conflict even continues under the present 52nd dā'ī muṭlaq, Muḥammad Burhān al-Dīn (from 1965), and splits numerous communities and families. The spokesmen for the reformists – a minority of generally rich entrepreneurs and intellectuals who can cope with the social and economic consequences of excommunication (Noman L. Contractor, Aṣghar 'Alī Engineer, Ismā'īl Attarwala) – are leading the battle against the supremacy of the dā'ī and his conservative supporters, mostly small traders of the Indian and East African towns, by press campaigns, committees of inquiry and publications.[104] Their main aims, the revival of the Prevention of Excommunications Act and prohibition of the *barā'at,* have not yet been achieved.

The dā'ī muṭlaq is the sole representative of the Hidden Imam, an (unknown) descendant of the Imam al-Ṭayyib who disappeared in 1130. In this capacity the dā'ī lays claim to all the Imam's prerogatives and is 'quasi infallible' (*kal-ma'ṣūm*). Every concern of any Bohora requires his consent (*raza* from the Arabic *riḍā*). He is the highest authority in all questions relating to doctrine, and the Dars-i Sayfī seminary in Surat is managed by his brother Yūsuf Najm al-Dīn. Initiation into the interpretation of the inner sense (*bāṭin*) of *sharīʿa* regulations through study of the esoteric literature is reserved for pupils at the seminary and requires the dāʿī's approval.

Despite the strongly gnostic hue of the Ṭayyibī 'truths' (*ḥaqā'iq*), the obligatory character of the *sharīʿa* has never been seriously questioned by antinomian experiments. The Dā'ūdī Bohoras are Shiite Muslims for whom the five 'pillars' of Islam (confession of faith, prayer, pilgrimage, fasting during Ramaḍān and the payment of alms tax) apply without restriction. Two further 'pillars' are added: devotion (*walāya*) to the Hidden Imam and his representative, and a strict commitment to purity (*ṭahāra*) which demands a full bath before certain festivals and the wearing of special white clothing at prayer. But there is no Friday sermon (*khuṭba*) because this is reserved exclusively for the Hidden Imam, and hence there is no pulpit (*minbar*) in the mosque. A prayer that the Imam will soon return replaces the *khuṭba*. Apart from the general Islamic festivals the Bohoras also celebrate the designation of ʿAlī as Imam at Ghadīr Khumm (18th Dhū 'l-Ḥijja); on this occasion fifteen-year-old boys and girls make the vow (Arabic *mīthāq*, Pers. *mīsāq*) of obedience to the Imam and the dāʿī; older members of the community are able to renew the oath.[105] Al-Ḥusayn's martyrdom at Karbalā' is commemorated by fasting on the Day of ʿĀshūrā (10th Muḥarram) and by meetings (*majālis*) in which the passion story of the martyr is recited, while weeping listeners beat their breasts with their hands. Processions of flagellants are unknown.

The fact that the latent antinomianism of all Ismāʿīlī groups, including the Ṭayyibī Bohoras, has not quite disappeared is shown by the example of a numerically insignificant sect, the Mahdibaghs (c. 1,000 in Bombay and Nagpur), whose founder ʿAbd al-Ḥusayn claimed in 1906 to be the *ḥujja* of the Hidden Imam with whom he alleged to be in communication and on whose orders he announced the beginning of a new age of revelation (*dawr-i kashf*) and thus the abrogation of Islamic law (*sharīʿa*).[106]

The Indian Bohoras have preserved the heritage of Fāṭimid literature almost in its entirety. Most of the surviving early Ismāʿīlī, Fāṭimid and Ṭayyibī literature comes from the libraries of the Bohoras, whose holdings were first investigated by the Russian orientalist Vladimir Ivanow who found his way to India after the October Revolution. Ivanow's 'Guide to Ismaili Literature' written in Bombay and printed in London in 1933 became the basis of the research which now began into the history of the Ismā'īliyya. Ismā'īlī scholars from India have made a significant contribution to making Ismā'īlī literature accessible, and to investigating it. The legal compendium by the Fāṭimid Qāḍī al-Nu'mān (d. 363/974 in Cairo), the 'Pillars of Islam' (*Da'ā'im al-islām*), which is still binding for the Bohoras, has been edited and commented upon by the lawyer Asaf A. A. Fyzee (*Fayżī*), one of the Sulaymānī minority;[107] and in 1957 Fyzee bequeathed his large collection of manuscripts to the University of Bombay.[108] Among the Dā'ūdīs the dā'ī muṭlaq jealously protects his prerogative to watch over the secret knowledge, and his consent (*raza*) is required to study the holy books. Opposition reformers are however striving for the abolition of this discipline attaching to secret knowledge, in particular the scholarly Yemeni Hamdānī family from Surat. Fayżallāh al-Hamdānī (1877-1969), who was excommunicated along with the whole of his family for opposing the absolute claim of the dā'ī muṭlaq in the Bombay High Court was the first Dā'ūdī to make his important library accessible to the public and to researchers.[109] His son Ḥusayn (ibn) F.(ayżallāh) al-Hamdānī and his grandson Prof. 'Abbās (ibn) Ḥ.(usayn) al-Hamdānī (University of Wisconsin, Milwaukee) have gained international standing as editors and researchers; Ismail K. Poonawala (University of California, Los Angeles) catalogued the entire known literature of all the Ismā'īlī groups in his 1977 *Biobibliography of Ismā'īlī Literature*. Recently even the family of the dā'ī has shown a rather more liberal attitude towards questions of publication; one of the dā'ī's brothers, Ḥamīd al-Dīn, is a distinguished publisher of Ismā'īlī works.

Primary sources in translation

D. B. M. K. Jhaveri, 'A Legendary History of the Bohoras', *JBBRAS* 9 (1933), 37-52 (translation of the Arabic *al-Tarjama al-ẓāhira li-firqat burhat al-Bahira*). Sayyidnā al-Ḥusayn ibn 'Alī ibn Muḥammad ibn al-Walīd (8th dā'ī muṭlaq, d. 667/1268), *Risālat al-mabda' wa 'l-ma'ād*, French by H. Corbin, 'Cosmogonie et eschatologie', in: Corbin, *Trilogie ismailienne*, Tehran/Paris 1961, 131-200.

Secondary sources

P. Casanova, 'Les derniers Fâṭimides', *MIFAO* 6 (1897), 415-45. H. F. al-Hamdani, 'The Life and Times of Queen Saiyidah Arwā the Sulaiḥid of the Yemen', *JRCAS* 18 (1931), 505-17; 'The History of the Ismā'īlī da'wat and its Literature During the Last Phase of the Fāṭimid Empire', *JRAS* (1932), 126-36; 'Rasā'il Ikhwān aṣ-Ṣafā in the Literature of the Ismā'īlī Ṭaiyibī Da'wat', *Der Islam* 20 (1932), 281-300; 'A Compendium of Ismā'īlī Esoterics', *IC* 11 (1937), 210-20 (about the *Zahr al-ma'ānī* by Idrīs 'Imād al-Dīn); *al-Ṣulayḥiyyūn*, Cairo 1955. W. Ivanow, *A Guide to Ismaili Literature*, London 1933. A. A. A. Fyzee, 'A Chronological List of the Imams and Da'is of the Musta'lian Ismailis', *JBBRAS* 10 (1934), 8-16; 'Three Sulaymani Dā'īs: 1936-1939', *JBBRAS* 16 (1940),

101-4; Art. Bohorās, EI[2]. B. Lewis, 'An Ismaili Interpretation of the Fall of Adam', *BSOAS* 9 (1937-39), 691-704 (about the *Idāḥ wa 'l-bayān* by the 8th dā'ī muṭlaq al-Ḥusayn ibn 'Alī, d. 667/1268). A. O. Habibullah, *A Brief Biographical Sketch of His Holiness Sardar Doctor Sayedna Taher, Saifudin Saheb, Dai al-Mutlaq of Dawoodi Bohras*, Bombay 1947. S. M. Stern, 'The Succession to the Fatimid Imam al-Āmir, the Claims of the Later Fatimids to the Imamate and the Rise of Ṭayyibī Ismailism', *Oriens* 4 (1951), 193-255. J. N. Hollister, 'The Shi'a of India', London 1953 (reprint 1973). S. T. Lokhandwalla, 'The Bohras, a Muslim Community of Gujarat', *SI* 3 (1955), 117-35; 'Islamic Law and Ismaili Communities (Khojas and Bohras)', *IESHR* 4 (1967), 155-76. A. Hamdani, *The Beginnings of the Ismā'īlī Da'wa in Northern India*, Cairo 1956; 'The dā'ī Ḥātim ibn Ibrāhīm al-Ḥāmidī (d. 596A.H./1199 A.D.) and his Book *Tuḥfat al-qulūb*', *Oriens* 23-24 (1974-75), 258-300; 'An Early Fatimid Source on the Time and Authorship of the *Rasā'il Iḥwān al-Ṣafā*'', *Arabica* 26 (1979), 62-75. S. C. Misra, *Muslim Communities in Gujarat*, Bombay/London 1964, 15-53 (The Bohra Community and their Da'is in Gujarat). H. A. Ladak, *The Fatimid Caliphate and the Ismaili Da'wa from the Appointment of al-Musta'lī to the Suppression of the Dynasty*, unpubl. Ph.D. thesis London (SOAS) 1971. H. Amiji, 'The Bohras of East Africa', *Journal of Religion in Africa* 7 (1975), 27-61. I. K. Poonawala, *Biobibliography of Ismā'īlī Literature*, Malibu 1977, 133-250. A. A. Engineer, *The Bohras*, Sahibabad 1980. W. Madelung, Art. al-Ḥāmidī, Ismā'īliyya, EI[2]. A. K. Irvine, Art. Ḥarāz, EI[2].

NOTES TO CHAPTER FOUR

1 *Firaq al-Shī'a*, 57f.: the 'pure' or 'true' Ismā'īlīs (*al-Ismā'īliyya al-khāliṣa*); they seem to have soon disappeared.
2 Nawbakhtī, *Firaq*, 58 and 61, calls this group 'Mubārakīs', allegedly after their spokesman, one of Ismā'īl's freed men; however, according to Ismā'īlī sources *al-Mubārak* (the blessed) was the name of Ismā'īl himself.
3 Naysābūrī, *Istitār al-Imām*, ed. Ivanow, 95; trans. Ivanow, *Ismaili Tradition Concerning the Rise of the Fatimids*, London/Calcutta 1942, 162.
4 This version probably goes back to anti-Fāṭimid Qarmaṭī circles and is first found in the Kufan Ibn Rizām (who wrote before 345/956) from whom Ibn al-Nadīm adopted it (*Fihrist*, ed. Tajaddud 238f.). It was widely disseminated at the time of the first Fāṭimid Caliphs by the Damascene Sharīf Akhū Muḥsin who used it (after 372/983) polemically against the Fāṭimids; extensive fragments are found in such Egyptian writers as Nuwayrī, Ibn al-Dawādārī and Maqrīzī.
5 S. de Sacy, *Exposé de la religion des Druzes* I, LXXI; M.J. de Goeje, *Mémoire sur les Carmathes du Bahraïn et les Fatimides*, 2.
6 *Notice*, 159.
7 *Fragments*, 185.
8 Lewis (1940), 72; cf. also the review by W. Ivanow, *JBBRAS* 16 (1940), 107-10.
9 The cause of the confusion appeared to lie in the fact that the Ismā'īlīs were for a time called 'Maymūnīs'; *al-Maymūn* (the Blissful One) was the name given to the Imam Muḥammad ibn Ismā'īl whom the 'Maymūnīs' awaited as Mahdī; H. Halm, *Kosmologie und Heilslehre der frühen Ismā'īlīya*, Wiesbaden 1978, 9f.
10 See note 4 above.
11 'Arīb al-Qurṭubī, Ṭabarî Continuatus, ed. de Goeje, 52.

12 *Fihrist*, ed. Tajaddud, 238, l. 16f. and l. 25; Akhū Muḥsin in Ibn al-Dawādārī, *Chronicle* VI, ed. al-Munajjid, 19 l. 5ff. and 65.
13 The earliest sources for the activities of 'Abdallāh are based on Iraqi informants: al-Ṣūlī (d. 336/946) in 'Arīb, 53, cites an 'expert on Shia history' called 'Alī ibn Sirāj al-Miṣrī (or al-Baṣrī?); the report by the Kufan Ibn Rizām al-Ṭā'ī (writing before 345/956), which was used by Ibn al-Nadīm and Akhū Muḥsin, is based on the statements of a doctor who had worked under the Ismā'īlīs; in 294/907 Ṭabarī, *Ann.* III, 2124ff., took statements from captured Ismā'īlīs in Baghdad. By contrast, the *Istitār al-imām* by Naysābūrī (before 386/996), which emerged in Fāṭimid Egypt, appears to preserve the Fāṭimid family tradition.
14 Ruins of Band-i Qīr on the Āb-i Gargar; Streck/Lockhart, art. 'Askar Mukram, EI².
15 Naysābūrī, *Istitār*, 94f.; cf. Ibn Rizām by Ibn al-Nadīm, *Fihrist*, ed. Tajaddud, 238, l. 18, and Akhū Muḥsin in Ibn al-Dawādārī, VI, 19.
16 W. Madelung, Art. Ḥamdān Ḳarmaṭ, EI².
17 Ibn al-Nadīm, *Fihrist*, 238, l. 7 from the foot of the page; Akhū Muḥsin in Ibn al-Dawādārī 64, l. 6f.
18 Ṭabarī, *Ann.* III, 2127.
19 Akhū Muḥsin in Ibn al-Dawādārī, VI, 52. The village has been narrowed down to a position in the district (*ṭassūj*) of al-Furāt on the eastern bank of the Kufan branch of the Euphrates.
20 Niẓām al-Mulk, *Siyāsat-nāma*, ed. Schefer, Paris 1891, 184f. ; Stern (1960), 56-60.
21 H. Halm, 'Les Fatimides à Salamya, 3., Maqām al-Imām. Le sanctuaire fatimide à Salamya', REI 54 (1986), 144 ff.
22 Halm (1981), 109f.
23 Ancient Mileve or Mileu, north west of Constantine. On the situation of Īkjan see M. Forstner, *Das Wegenetz des Zentralen Maghreb in islamischer Zeit*, Wiesbaden 1979, 58-61.
24 The most detailed source is the 'Opening of the da'wa' (*Iftitāḥ al-da'wa*) by Qāḍī al-Nu'mān, ed. W. al-Qāḍī, Beirut 1970; ed. F. al-Dashrāwī, Tunis 1975.
25 Nawbakhtī, *Firaq*, 61: 'Muḥammad ibn Ismā'īl, the Imām, Qā'im and Mahdī'; Ibn Rizām/Akhū Muḥsin (Ibn al-Dawādārī, VI, 51): 'this bad proselytising took place initially, as they alleged, in the name of Muḥammad ibn Ismā'īl ibn Ja'far'; ibid, 52, l. 4f.: 'the propaganda took place in the name of Muḥammad ibn Ismā'īl; he was alive (they claimed) and had not died; at the end of time he would appear as the Mahdī of the community.'
26 Akhū Muḥsin/Ibn al-Dawādārī, VI, 65f.; letter from the Fāṭimid Caliph al-Mahdī to the Yemeni community, in: H. F. Hamdani, *On the Genealogy of Fatimid Caliphs*, Cairo 1958.
27 Apart from the 'Book of rightful guidance' (*Kitāb al-rushd wa 'l-hidāya*), attributed to the Yemeni dā'ī Ibn Ḥawshab (see Bibliography), in particular the 'Book of Disclosure' (*Kitāb al-kashf*) attributed to his son; this is a collection of six very old treatises; ed. R. Strothmann, London 1952; ed. M. Ghālib, Beirut 1984.
28 In later sources the *waṣī* is also called *asās* (foundation).
29 Halm (1978), 32ff.
30 Also Nawbakhtī, *Firaq*, 61.
31 Nawbakhtī, *Firaq*, 62, talks about the abrogation of Muḥammad's law

(*naskh sharī'at Muḥammad*) and declares: 'They say that God is giving Adam's Paradise to Muḥammad ibn Ismā'īl, which means, according to their view, that all forbidden things and everything that God has created in the world are allowed.' On the repeal of the religions of law (*raf' al-shara'i'*) see also Sijistānī, *Ithbāt al-nubuwwāt,* ed. 'A. Tāmir, Beirut 1966, 180.

32 W. Madelung, 'Fatimiden und Bahrainqarmaten', *Der Islam* 34 (1959), 76.

33 Halm (1978).

34 Cf. S. M. Stern, 'The Earliest Cosmological Doctrines of Ismā'īlism', in: Stern (1983), 3-29.

35 The main source is Ibn Rizām in Akhū Muḥsin/Ibn al-Dawādārī, VI, 65-8; also Ibn Ḥawqal, *Ṣūrat al-arḍ,* 295; trans. Kramers/Wiet, *Configuration de la terre,* Paris 1964, II, 289f.

36 This flaw in the succession of the Fāṭimid Imamate has been attested by unsuspecting early sources: in the first place by al-Mahdī's own statements in a letter to the Yemenis (H. F. Hamdani, *Genealogy,* Arabic text 11, l. 6), then by the anonymously written *Sīrat al-Mahdī* (Idrīs 'Imād al-Dīn, *'Uyūn al-Akhbār,* ed. M. Ghālib, Beirut 1975, V, 89). The later official Fāṭimid doctrine removed this flaw by denying the Imamate of al-Mahdī's uncle and declaring al-Mahdī's father al-Ḥusayn ibn Aḥmad 'Abdallāh to be Imam in his place; Madelung (1961), 100.

37 Ibn Rizām in Akhū Muḥsin/Ibn al-Dawādārī, VI, 67, l. 4 and 69, l. 9; Madelung (1961), 61ff.

38 Al-Mahdī calls himself ''Alī ibn al-Ḥusayn ibn Aḥmad ibn 'Abdallāh' in his letter to the Yemenis (H. F. Hamdani, *Origins,* Arabic text 11 last item.); *Sa'īd* (the Happy One), he says, is only a pseudonym; see p. 174.

39 Poonawala, *Biobibliography of Ismā'īlī Literature,* 31ff. and 45. The Neoplatonic treatise 'The Tree of Certainty' (*Shajarat al-yaqīn*) also goes under the name of 'Abdān, ed. 'A. Tāmir, Beirut 1982.

40 Ibn al-Jawzī, *Muntaẓam,* VI, 195, also see 313.

41 The name al-Baḥrayn is not limited in medieval Arabic sources to the island called by that name today but is used for the entire coast of the Gulf.

42 Madelung (1959), 75ff.

43 De Sacy, *Exposé* I, CCXXVIII ff.; Madelung (1959), 85-8.

44 In non-Fāṭimid sources generally 'Ubaydallāh; hence the dynasty is also called Banū 'Ubayd.

45 Halm, 'Les Fatimides à Salamya, 1. A propos des généalogies des Fatimides', REI 54 (1986), 133 ff.

46 *Da'ā'im al-islām,* ed. A. A. A. Fyzee, 2 vols, Cairo 1951/61; ²1963/69. *Asās al-ta'wīl,* ed. 'A. Tāmir, Beirut 1960. *Ta'wīl al-Da'ā'im,* ed. M. H. al-A'ẓamī, Cairo 1968-72. W. Madelung, 'The Sources of Ismā'īlī Law, *JNES* 35 (1976), 29-40. A. A. A. Fyzee, *Compendium of Fatimid Law,* Simla 1969.

47 Halm, 'Zur Datierung des isma'ilitischen "Buches der Zwischenzeiten"', *WdO* 8 (1975), 97ff.

48 Jawhar's guarantee of security (*amān*) is quoted verbatim in Maqrīzī, *Itti'āẓ al-ḥunafā',* I, ed. al-Shayyāl, Cairo 1968, 103-6.

49 For the first time in Naysābūrī, *Istitār,* 95f.; trans. Ivanow, *Rise,* 162f.

50 For Akhū Muḥsin's document see also note 4.

51 Ibn al-Jawzī, *Muntaẓam,* VII, 255f., under the year 402 A.H.; Ibn al-Athīr, *Kāmil,* under the year 402A.H..

52 Only *Majālis al-Mustanṣiriyya* by the Supreme dā'ī al-Malījī dating from 451/1059 has been printed, ed. M. K. Ḥusayn, Cairo, no year given; over 700 lectures by the dā'ī al-Mu'ayyad have been preserved in numerous

manuscripts; the first three hundred have been published: *al-Majālis al-Mu'ayyadiyya,* ed. M. Ghālib, 3 vols, Beirut 1974-84.

53 Stern, 'Cairo as the Center, ...', quoting 'Abd al-Jabbār.

54 *Sīrat al-Mu'ayyad,* ed. M. K. Ḥusayn, Cairo 1949; V. Klemm, *Die Mission des fāṭimidisehen Agenten al-Mu'ayyad fī ad-dīn in Šīrāz,* Frankfurt a.M. 1989.

55 Ancient Baktra; ruins to the west of Mazār i Sharīf in north-west Afghanistan.

56 H. F. al-Ḥamdānī (1933-1935).

57 S. M. Stern, 'Heterodox Ismā'īlism at the Time of al-Mu'izz', *BSOAS* 17 (1955), 10-33 (*Studies in Early Ismā'īlism,* 257ff.); W. Madelung, *Imamat,* 73ff.

58 B. Lewis, *The Origins of Ismā'īlism,* Cambridge 1940.

59 Plotinus's *Enneads* IV-Vi were translated into Arabic from Aramaic in 840 and were considered to be 'Aristotle's Theology' by the Arabs. An Arabic paraphrase existed of Proclus' 'Elements of Theology' under the title 'Explanation of the pure Good' (*Kitāb al-īḍāḥ fi 'l-khayr al-maḥḍ,* Latin, *Liber de causis*). R. Walzer, Art. Aflūṭīnūs, EI[2]; C. Endress, *Proclus Arabus,* Beirut 1973.

60 From Najaf or Nakhshab; ruins at present-day Karshi in Uzbekistan.

61 Poonawala, *Biobibliography,* 40ff.

62 Walker, *Development,* Ch. V.

63 Walker, *Development,* Ch. VI.

64 Poonawala, 82ff.; Walker, *Development,* 199-217.

65 Madelung, *Imamat,* 101ff.; Walker, *Development,* 100.

66 Ed. 'A. Tāmir, Beirut 1960.

67 Ed. M. K. Ḥusayn/M. M. Ḥilmī, Cairo 1952; ed. M. Ghālib, Beirut 1967.

68 The concept of the Aristotelian Working Intellect (*nous poiētikós*) working as a demiurge was communicated to the Arabs by translations of the works of the Aristotelian commentator, Alexander of Aphrodisias (c. 200); G. Strohmaier, Art. al-Iskandar al-Afrūdīsī, EI[2]. The seven intellects of the planetary spheres are perhaps an addition by Aramaic translators. The series of ten intellects is first found in al-Fārābī, then in Avicenna and, at the same time, in al-Kirmānī.

69 Concise portrayal in Makarem (1972).

70 Ed. M. K. Ḥusain, *Bulletin of the Fac. of Arts, Univ. of Egypt* 14 (1952), 1-29.

71 The first Fāṭimid al-Mahdī is not counted; cf. de Sacy. *Exposé,* I, 74-7. The Druze dā'īs therefore follow a doctrine common among the Qarmaṭīs of Iran and India.

72 Later sources maintain that al-Ḥākim let al-Darzī escape into Lebanon; his grave is still today presumed by the Druze to be in Nabī Shīt near Kfayr in Lebanese Wādī 'l-Taym, west of the Hermon.

73 Bryer (1975), 239-62 and (1976), 5-27 gives a systematic presentation of Ḥamza's doctrines.

74 Unpubl. ed. by Bryer in the Bodleian Library, Oxford.

75 De Sacy, *Exposé,* I, 207ff.

76 For the distribution of the Druze see E. Wirth, *Syrien,* Darmstadt 1971, map on p. 172-3; *TAVO* map A VIII 7 'Lebanon. Religionen' (K.-P. Hartmann).

77 A. al-Najjār, *Madhhab al-Muwaḥḥidīn, al-Durūz,* Cairo 1965. S. N. Makārim, *Aḍwā' 'alā maslak al-tawḥīd,* Beirut 1966; *The Druze Faith,* Delmar, N.Y., 1974. Cf. also W. Schmucker, *Krise und Erneuerung im libanesischen Drusentum,* Bonn 1979.

78 The more likely form *ḥashshāsh*, 'habitual hashish consumer', is not attested; cf. de Sacy, 'Mémoire sur la dynastie des Assassins et sur l'origine de leur nom', *Mémoires de l'Institut Royal* 4 (1818), 1-85; B. Lewis, Art. Ḥashīshiyya, EI².
79 Marco Polo, *Il Milione*, English trans. *The Travels*. The supposed drug taking is mentioned for the first time in the 12th century by Arnold of Lübeck, *Chronicon Slavorum* IV, 16.
80 For sources on the history of Alamūt see Lewis (1967), 145ff.
81 *TAVO* map B VIII 8 (I), 'Die Kreuzfahrerstaaten bis zum Ende des 12. Jahrhunderts' (P. Thorau); also P. Thorau, 'Die Burgen der Assassinen in Syrien und ihre Einnahme durch Sultan Baibars', in: *WdO* 18 (1987), 132-58.
82 'Ā. Tāmir, Furū' al-shajara al-ismā'īliyya al-imāmiyya,' *al-Mashriq* 51 (1957), 581-612. On the recolonisation of Salamiyya see N. N. Lewis (1952).
83 E. Wirth, *Syrien. Eine geograph. Landeskunde*, Darmstadt 1971, 452; for a map on the spread of the religious communities of Syria and Lebanon, *ibid*, 172/3.
84 Poonawala, *Biobibliography*, 287ff.
85 For the origin of the name see W. Ivanow, *A Guide to Ismaili Literature*, London 1933, 6f., note 3.
86 For this *Sat Panth* (Right Path) literature see W. Ivanow, *Satpanth*; Poonawala, 298-311.
87 Clarke (1978), 68.
88 Ed. M. Ghālib, *Die ismailitische Theologie des Ibrāhīm ibn al-Ḥusain al-Ḥāmidī*, Wiesbaden 1971.
89 First printed in Bombay 1888; reprint Cairo 1928; printed in Beirut, 4 vols, 1957. An analysis of the fifty-two treatises is given in A. Bausani, *L'Enciclopedia dei Fratelli della Purità*, Naples 1978.
90 S. M. Stern, 'The Authorship of the Epistles of the Ikhwān as-Ṣafā'', *IC* 20 (1946), 367-72.
91 Y. Marquet, Art. Ikhwān al-Ṣafā', EI²; *La philosophie des Ikhwān aṣ-Ṣafā': de Dieu à l'homme*, Algiers 1975. A. Hamdani (1979).
92 Idrīs 'Imād al-Dīn, *'Uyūn al-Akhbār*, IV, ed. M. Ghālib, Beirut 1973, 367ff.
93 The *Āmiriyya* was still attested in Galilee around Ṣafad in 723/1324; W. Madelung, Art. Ismā'īliyya, EI².
94 Poonawala, *Biobibliography*, 133ff.
95 Idrīs 'Imād al-Dīn, *'Uyūn al-Akhbār*; of the seven parts only IV to VI have been edited by M. Ghālib, Beirut 1974, 1975, 1978.
96 Poonawala, 169.
97 Jhaveri (1933), 39ff.; Engineer (1980), 100-8.
98 Poonawala, 178ff.
99 Ivanow (1933), 10, estimates the number of Indian Sulaymānīs to be 500 at the most. On the present-day *manṣūb* in Baroda, Mawlānā Muḥammad Shākir, see Engineer, 118.
100 Poonawala, 211; Engineer, 133.
101 All figures from Engineer, 144f.
102 M. El-Azzazi, *Die Entwicklung der Arabischen Republik Jemen*, Tübingen/Basel 1978, 46.
103 According to the internal census of the Central Council of the Dawoodi Bohra Jamats of East Africa; Amiji 1975), 27. Amiji estimates the total Bohra population of the world to be some half a million which is less than the number from Engineer, 144f., who specifies 560,000 in India and 75,000 outside India – of whom 30,000 are in Pakistan.

104 For this see the dossier published under the title 'The Syedna and His Flock, Documentation on the Dawoodi Bohras' in *New Quest* 7 (Jan./Feb. 1978), 45-70, with an article by N. L. Contractor. A. A. Engineer (1980) gives a detailed portrayal of the history of the reform movement; cf. his lecture 'Islam and Humanism' in: *New Quest* 7 (Jan./Feb. 1978), 19-27.

105 The Ṭayyibī *mīthāq* which alone binds the believers to the Hidden Imam goes back to the 3rd dā'ī muṭlaq Ḥātim ibn Ibrāhīm; *Tuḥfat al-qulūb* (trans. Engineer, 157f.). By contrast, the oath demanded by the Dā'ūdī dā'ī muṭlaq of all believers today has been geared to unconditional obedience to the dā'ī; Engineer, 158f.; the text of the oath formula is in *New Quest* 7 (Jan./Feb. 1978), 61-3.

106 On the Mahdibaghs or Mahdibaghwallas see Lokhandwalla (1955), 122; Engineer, 138f.

107 *Da'ā'im al-islām*, ed. Fyzee, Cairo 1952/1961; A. A. A. Fyzee, *Compendium of Fatimid Law*, Simla 1969.

108 M. Goriawala, *A Descriptive Catalogue of the Fyzee Collection of Ismaili Manuscripts*, Bombay 1965.

109 Poonawala, 238f.

V
The Zaydiyya

The legal tradition of the Zaydīs goes back to Zayd ibn ʿAlī, the grandson of al-Ḥusayn (and half-brother of the fifth Imam of the Twelvers, Muḥammad al-Bāqir) who was killed in 122/740 during a failed revolt against the Umayyad Caliph al-Hishām in Kūfa (see above, p. 20 f). The *juristic* works ascribed to Zayd are, however, not authentic;[1] they are products of the tradition of the Zaydī school which was developed in the second half of the 2nd/8th century in Kūfa. Among the earliest Zaydī trends noted by the Arab heresiographers the rigorous Jārūdīs are worth particular mention, being the only ones to consider ʿAlī the designated rightful successor of the Prophet (while the Butrites recognised Abū Bakr and ʿUmar as Caliphs). They expected that the True Imam would fight for his rights with the sword against usurpers.[2]

The earliest Kufan tradition of the Zaydiyya is reflected in the works of the Kufan al-Murādī (Muḥammad ibn Nuṣayr) who was still alive in 252/866; he is the most important collector of Zaydī legal traditions in the 3rd/9th century.[3] His contemporary, the Ḥasanid al-Qāsim ibn Ibrāhīm (d. 246/860),[4] a Medinan who taught in al-Rass near Medina, occupies a special place compared with the general Kufan tradition. His quite independent teachings pave the way for the later change of Zaydī theology to the rationalism of the Muʿtazilites.[5]

As may be expected, it is mainly the Imamate doctrine which distinguishes the Zaydīs from other Shiite trends. ʿAlī's right to the Imamate is undisputed; it is based on his early confession of Islam and his pre-eminence as the best (*al-afḍal*) of the Muslims. After him his sons al-Ḥasan and al-Ḥusayn are called to the Imamate by God's will through designation (*naṣṣ*). After them, however, the claim to the Imamate is handed down not through any particular line – as with the Imāmīs or the Ismāʿīlīs – but rather through the whole House of the Alids. All members of the Prophet's family are eligible for the Imamate. The two most important pieces of evidence for this are the Quranic verse 33, 33: 'Allah's wish is but to remove uncleanness far from you, O Folk of the Household, and cleanse you with a thorough cleaning', and a saying by the Prophet Muḥammad who promises to leave his community two treasures which guarantee right guidance: 'God's Book and my lineage, the Family of the House'. In principle every Alid thus has a claim to the Imamate; the true Imam is he who actually establishes himself sword in hand. The 'emergence' (*khurūj*) – the term could also be rendered as 'armed rebellion' – makes the Imam eligible. The Ḥusaynids venerated by the Twelvers as Imams are disqualified by their inactivity (*qu'ūd:* abstention/sitting). Even the Imāmī practice of *taqiyya,* the act of concealing one's Shiite convictions, is rejected.

'With a pinch of salt it might be said that the fundamental difference between the two main Shiite branches, the different Imāmī denominations and the Zaydīs, can be formulated as: the first tend in their constitutional theory towards determinism and faithfully accept as Imam whomsoever God gives them. The Zaydīs are synergists and, irrespective of the recognition of God, seek to cooperate as His agents in the fate of the nations.'[6]

The Zaydīs, therefore, acknowledge no Hidden Imam and no return of the Mahdī;[7] the Imam is neither infallible (*ma'ṣūm*) nor does he work miracles; children not of age are excluded from the Imamate.

Zaydī ideas were put into effect in the formation of two states in the 3rd/9th century, in Ṭabaristān, south of the Caspian Sea, and in Yemen. Both Imamates came into being through the 'emergence' of Ḥasanid pretenders.

The northern Zaydī state in Ṭabaristān was founded by a certain al Ḥasan ibn Zayd who set himself at the head of Daylamite supporters in 250/864 in Kalār, Shālūs (now Chālūs) and Sāriya (Sārī). He made Amul his residence after defeating the Abbasid governor, and subjugated Gurgān in the east, Gīlān in the west and the mountain region of Daylam in the south – the Elburz. His supporters even controlled the towns of Rayy and Qazvīn on occasion. After his death in 270/884 he was succeeded by his brother Muḥammad who was killed in 287/900 fighting the Baghdadi governors. The two brothers do not appear to have laid claim to the Imamate themselves but seem to have been satisfied with the title 'He who summons to the Truth' (*al-dā'ī ilā 'l-ḥaqq*). Fourteen years later an Alid pretender – this time a Ḥusaynid – was again able to set himself up as the prince of Ṭabaristān. After defeating the troops of the Sāmānid governor of Bukhara al-Ḥasan ibn 'Alī al-Uṭrūsh, called al-Nāṣir li 'l-Ḥaqq (He who conquers for the Truth) marched into Āmul. Al-Uṭrūsh, who founded his own school within the Zaydiyya (the Nāṣiriyya of the northern state) with his own theologico-juristic writings, successfully proselytised among the still pre-dominantly non-Islamic farmers and shepherds in the mountain region of Daylam. On his deathbed in 304/917 he is said to have designated his vizier, al-Ḥasan ibn al-Qāsim, a Ḥasanid, as his successor in place of one of his three sons; the latter, called the 'small dā'ī' (*al-dā'ī al-ṣaghīr*), fell in 316/928 in battle against the Sāmānids of

Bukhara, and thus the Zaydī state of Ṭabaristān met its end. In 359/964, however, in Hawsam in Gīlān (south west of the Caspian Sea) the Ḥasanid Abū ʿAbdallāh Muḥammad ibn al-Ḥasan from Baghdad, under the name al-Mahdī li-dīn Allāh, once more founded a Zaydī Imamate which continued under changing Ḥasanid dynasties into the 12th century.[8]

The southern Zaydī state lasted until our own time, and the Yemeni Imamate was not swept away until the Revolution of 1962. Its founder, Yaḥyā ibn al-Ḥusayn, was a grandson of the Zaydī scholar al-Qāsim ibn Ibrāhīm (see above p. 206) and bore the name al-Rassī after his family residence – al-Rass near Medina. After Yaḥyā had vainly attempted to gain a foothold in Ṭabaristān, quarrelling north Yemeni tribes called him in 280/893 to the country as a mediator and eventually the Khawlān tribe in Ṣaʿda recognised him as Imam under the name al-Hādī ilā 'l-Ḥaqq (He who leads the Way to the Truth). In protracted wars he extended his power to Najrān (in 284/897) and Ṣanʿāʾ (288/901). In his juristic writings al-Hādī continued the doctrine of his grandfather al-Qāsim, and the Zaydī legal school in Yemen is called the Qāsimiyya-Hadawiyya after these two authorities. In contrast to his grandfather, however, al-Hādī adopted the rationalist theology of the Baghdadi Muʿtazilites for the first time.[9]

After al-Hādī's death in 298/911 two of his sons succeeded him as Imam.[10] His grandson Yaḥyā transmitted the Medinan-Yemeni legal tradition to Daylam where it competed with the native Nāṣirī school from then on.[11] 'In the Caspian Imams of the 4th/10th century the influence of the theology of the Muʿtazilite School on the Zaydīs reached its apex.'[12]

In the 4th/10th century the Yemeni Imamate was weakened by troubles over the succession and was pushed back to the north by the Ismāʿīlī Ṣulayḥids, partisans of the Egyptian Fāṭimids (see above p. 176), who conquered Ṣanʿāʾ and Ṣaʿda. It was not until the beginning of the 12th century that descendants of the Imam al-Hādī once more began to extend their rule southwards from Najrān and Ṣaʿda; the Imam Aḥmad al-Mutawakkil (533-566/1138-1170) was the new founder of the Zaydī Imamate.[13] While the Caspian and Yemeni Imamates had gone their own separate political and theologico-juristic ways a rapprochement now took place with a reversal in the direction of influence: the literature of the north now received recognition in Yemen and particularly through Qāḍī Shams al-Dīn Jaʿfar (d. 573/1177) who had studied in Kūfa and Rayy.[14] The Yemeni Imams were now even recognised by the Caspian Zaydī communities who no longer had any political leadership. The northern communities soon lost any real significance; they shrank under pressure from the Ismāʿīlīs of

Alamūt (see above p. 185) and in the Ṣafavid period in the 16th century they were incorporated – like the Nizārī Ismā'īlīs – into the Twelver Shia.[15]

By contrast, the Yemeni Imamate prevailed even after the occupation of South Yemen by the Egyptian Ayyūbids (569-626/1174-1229). When the first Rasūlid Sultan of Zabīd, 'Umar (626-647/1229-1250), conquered Ta'īzz and Ṣan'ā', the Zaydī Imams once more withdrew to Ṣa'da for a century and a half. After the establishment of the Sunni Ṭāhirid dynasty of Laḥj and Aden, Ṣan'ā' was fought over at length between this dynasty and the Zaydī Imamate. In 933/1517 an army of the Egyptian Mamlūk sultan occupied Yemen, and the Imam had to retreat to Thulā. In the same year, however, Egypt was occupied by the Ottomans who were now extending their rule to the Red Sea coast. For a long time the Imam Sharaf al-Dīn successfully defended his rule against the Ottomans, but he was eventually defeated in 1539 and deported to Istanbul where he died in prison, and Yemen became an Ottoman province (*eyālet*). In 1595, al-Qāsim al-Manṣūr, a descendant of al-Hādī, emerged as Imam and declared war against the Ottomans; his son and successor Muḥammad al-Mu'ayyad (from 1620) led the fighting against the Turkish occupying force to a successful conclusion. In 1635 the last Ottoman governor left Yemen and Ṣan'ā' once again became the capital of an independent Zaydī Imamate for more than two centuries. In April 1872 the town was occupied by the Turks for the second time; Yemen was once more made into an Ottoman province (*vilāyet*) and the Imam was divested of all sovereign rights. The Imam Ḥamīd al-Dīn al-Manṣūr (1890-1904), who resided in Ṣa'da and in the castle of al-Ahnūm, attempted, in battle against the Turks and in negotiations with the Sublime Porte, at least to have his status recognised as the religious head of the Zaydīs. His son Yaḥyā al-Mutawakkil (1904-1948) was already *de facto* independent during the First World War; with the support of the Ḥāsid and Bakīl tribes he was able to march into Ṣan'ā' in November 1918. After his murder by a court côterie in 1948 his son Sayf al-Islām Aḥmad re-conquered Ṣan'ā' with the help of the loyal northern tribes and assumed the title of king. Aḥmad's Imamate (from 1948 to 1962) was frequently threatened by attempted coups from a modernist opposition, but it was his son Muḥammad al-Badr al-Manṣūr billāh who was overthrown by republican officers on 26th September 1962 after a reign which lasted only a week. After escaping to Saudi Arabia, with the help of the northern and eastern tribes al-Badr vainly attempted to win back his throne during the civil war from 1962-70. Since his death in English exile the Imamate has been vacant: according to Zaydī Imamate doctrine a quite permissible situation for which there are many precedents. The 'emergence' (*khurūj*) of a new Imam is theoretically possible. At present the Zaydīs, who with 4 million members make up about half the population of the former Yemen Arab Republic, (North Yeman)[16] are without a religious leader.

Bibliography

R. Strothmann, 'Die Literatur der Zaiditen', *Der Islam* 1 (1910), 354-67; 2 (1911), 49-78; *Das Staatsrecht der Zaiditen*, Strassburg 1912; *Kultus der Zaiditen*, Strassburg 1912; 'Das Problem der literarischen Persönlichkeit Zaid b. 'Alīs', *Der Islam* 13 (1923), 1-52. E. Griffini, *Corpus iuris di Zaid b. 'Alī*, Milan 1919. C. van Arendonk, *De Opkomst van het Zaidietische Imamaat in Yemen*, Leiden 1919 (*Les débuts de l'imāmat zaidite au Yemen*, Leiden 1960). A. Jeffery, 'The Qur'an Readings of Zaid b. 'Alī', *RSO* 16 (1936), 249-89. R. B. Serjeant, 'A Zaidi Manual of Ḥisbah of the 3rd Century (H)', *RSO* 28 (1953), 1-34; 'The Zaydīs', in: A. J. Arberry (ed.), *Religion in the Middle East II*, Cambridge 1969, 285-301. A. K. Kazi, 'Notes on the Development of Zaidi Law'. *Abr Nahrain* 2 (1960-61), 36-40. W. Madelung, *Der Imam al-Qāsim b. Ibrāhīm und die Glaubenslehre der Zaiditen*, Berlin 1965; *Streitschrift des Zaiditenimams Aḥmad an-Nāṣir wider die ibaditische Prädestinationslehre*, Wiesbaden 1985; 'Zu einigen Werken des Imams Abū Ṭālib an-Nāṭiq bi l-Ḥaqq', *Der Islam* 63 (1986), 5-10; *Arabic Texts Concerning the History of the Zaydi Imams of Ṭabaristān, Daylamān and Gīlān*, Beirut 1987. M. S. Khan, 'The Early History of Zaydī Shīʿism in Daylamān and Gīlān, *ZDMG* 125 (1975), 301-14. E. Kohlberg, 'Some Zaydi Views on the Companions of the Prophet', *BSOAS* 39 (1976), 91-8. E. Renaud, 'Eléments de bibliographie sur le Zaydisme', *IBLA* 43, no. 146 (1980), 309-21. B. Abrahamov, *The Theological Epistles of al-Ḳāsim ibn Ibrāhīm*, unpubl. Ph.D. thesis, Tel Aviv 1981; 'Al-Kasim ibn Ibrahim's Argument from Design', *Oriens* 29-30 (1986), 259-84; 'Al-Ḳāsim ibn Ibrāhīm's Theory of the Imamate', *Arabica* 34 (1987), 80-105; *Al-Ḳāsim ibn Ibrāhīm On the Proof of God's Existence. Kitāb al-Dalīl al-Kabīr*, Leyden 1990.

NOTES TO CHAPTER FIVE

1 Strothmann (1923); Madelung (1965), 53-61.
2 Madelung (1965), 44ff.: 'Die Dogmatik der frühen Zaidiya'.
3 Madelung (1965), 82ff.
4 Al-Qāsim b. Ibrāhīm b. Ismāʿīl b. Ibrāhīm b. al-Ḥasan b. al-Ḥasan b. 'Alī b. Abī Ṭālib.
5 Madelung (1965), 86-152.
6 Strothmann, *Staatsrecht*, 46.
7 Only the ephemeral sect of the Ḥusaynīs distributed mainly in western Yemen awaited the return of the Imam al-Ḥusayn al-Mahdī li-dīn Allāh (401-404/1010-1013); the sect was still in existence in the 15th century; Madelung (1965), 198-201.
8 Madelung (1965), 175-85.
9 Ibid., 163-8.
10 Strothmann, *Staatsrecht*, 59f.; Madelung (1965), 169ff.
11 Madelung (1965), 172-4.
12 Madelung (1965), 185.
13 Ibid., 210ff.
14 Ibid., 212-16.

15 On the situation of the Caspian communities from the 12th to the 16th century see Madelung (1965), 207-9 and 217f.
16 M. El-Azzazi, *Die Entwicklung der Arabischen Republik Jemen*, Tübingen/Basel 1978, 36. Now the two parts of Yemen are united as the Yemen Republic.

Index